THE PEOPLE'S ALMANAC®

Presents

The Book of Lists:

THE '90S EDITION

THE PEOPLE'S ALMANAC®

Presents

THE BOOK OF Lists

THE '90s EDITION

DAVID WALLECHINSKY AND AMY WALLACE

LITTLE, BROWN AND COMPANY

Boston • New York • Toronto • London

First Edition

Photo credits appear on pages 469–70.

Library of Congress Cataloging-in-Publication Data
  The People's almanac presents the book of lists / by David Wallechinsky and Amy Wallace. — The '90s ed.
      p.   cm.
    Includes index.
    ISBN 0-316-92079-7
    1. Encyclopedias and dictionaries.   I. Wallechinsky, David.
    II. Wallace, Amy.   III. Title: Book of lists.
AG106.P487   1993
031 — dc20   93-17197

10 9 8 7 6 5 4 3 2 1

MV-NY

Published simultaneously in Canada by Little, Brown & Company (Canada) Limited

PRINTED IN THE UNITED STATES OF AMERICA

This book is dedicated to the memory of
our father, Irving Wallace, who was
1 OF A KIND

EXECUTIVE EDITOR: Vicki Baker

RESEARCHERS: Danny Biederman
                      Lee Clayton
                      Cass Coty
                      Carol Dunlap
                      Jamie Keller
                      Carol Orsag Madigan
                      David Mick
                      Jean Soloner
                      Torene Svitil
                      Anita Taylor

EDITORIAL ASSISTANTS: Annette Brown
                      Cheryl Mick
                      Tammy Tucker

PHOTO EDITORS: Danny Biederman
                      Cass Coty
                      Jean Soloner

CONTENTS

2   MOVIES AND TV

3   THE ARTS

5 ANIMALS

7 FAMILY AND RELATIONSHIPS

8 CRIME

9 POLITICS AND WORLD AFFAIRS

10 AMERICA

11   TRAVEL

12 | LITERATURE

13 WORDS

15 SPORTS

ACKNOWLEDGMENTS

With special thanks to: Sylvia Wallace, Sue and Jeremy Beadle, Paul Sieveking, Ed Steinbrecher, Bill Mallon, Russell Johanson, David Sachs, Ed Victor, and Vicente Camera. And for providing moral support, Flora and Aaron Wallechinsky and, for wanting to know the sweetest vegetables, Elijah Wallechinsky.

INTRODUCTION

When we compiled the first *Book of Lists,* back in 1977, we had no idea that it would become a best-seller. We thought we were just having fun. Since that time we have collected more than seventy books of lists published by people other than ourselves and we have heard of many more. These have included nine books of lists about movies, four rock-and-roll books of lists, three Jewish books of lists, two Bible books of lists, and six general-sports books of lists, not to mention individual books of sports lists dealing exclusively with golf, tennis, baseball, soccer, rugby, and cricket. There are also specialized books of lists about food, sex, money, chess, women, London, Canada, Texas, Michigan, country music, classical music, and the Beatles.

Although we are pleased to have popularized a genre that so many people enjoy, we do not pretend to have been its founders. That honor goes to the Reverend Nathaniel Wanley, author of *Wonders of the Little World,* a book of lists first published in 1678. We didn't know about the Reverend Wanley when we wrote our own *Book of Lists,* but a glance through his table of contents shows striking similarities: "Of such People and Nations as have been scourged and afflicted by small and contemptible things," "Of such as having been extremely Wild, and Prodigal, or Debauched in their Youth, have afterwards proved excellent Persons," "Of such as have been seized with an extraordinary joy, and what hath followed thereupon."

Fans of our previous works—*The Book of Lists, The Book of Lists 2,* and *The Book of Lists 3*—might wonder how this volume differs from its predecessors. First of all, most of the lists are completely new in both subject and content. Some headings that have proved popular in earlier volumes, such as "Stupid Thieves" and "Strange Deaths," have been included again, but with all-new entries. In some cases, such as "Martina Navratilova's 8 Best Women Tennis Players of All Time" and "Arthur Schlesinger's 20 Best American Political Movies," we have asked experts and celebrities to update lists that they first prepared for us ten or fifteen years ago. The only material actually repeated from previous volumes of *The Book of Lists* are some entries from ranked lists such as "10 Highest-Rated Episodes of TV Series" and "The 40 Highest-Grossing Films of All Time (Adjusted for Inflation)."

We owe much of the inspiration for this volume to our father, Irving Wallace, who always hoped we would compile another edition. Whenever possible, we have concentrated on lists that cause readers to laugh out loud, gasp, shake their heads in wonder, or call out, "Wait until you hear this!" To quote Mark Twain's introduction to *The Adventures of Huckleberry Finn:* "Persons attempting to find a motive in this narrative will be prosecuted; persons attempting to find a moral in it will be banished; persons attempting to find a plot in it will be shot."

Presents

The Book of Lists:

THE '90S EDITION

1 PEOPLE

Ages of *16* People
Had They Lived Until 1994

1. John Belushi (1949–1982)	45
2. Janis Joplin (1943–1970)	51
3. Jimi Hendrix (1942–1970)	52
4. Otis Redding (1941–1967)	53
5. John Lennon (1940–1980)	54

Jimi Hendrix, the wise godfather
of psychedelic rock . . .   . . . or Las Vegas Jimi.

11 Men Who Cried in Public

1. JEFF BLATNICK, wrestler

   In July 1982 Blatnick was diagnosed as suffering from Hodgkin's disease, a form of cancer. His spleen and appendix were removed and he received radiation therapy. Two years later he won an Olympic gold medal in Greco-Roman wrestling. After his final match, which he dedicated to his deceased brother, Blatnick fell to his knees and burst into tears for the first time since his brother died seven years earlier.

2. DAVID, warrior king

   When David and his troops returned to the city of Ziklag, after being sent home by the princes of the Philistines, they discovered that the Amalekites had invaded the city and taken captive all of the women and children, including David's two wives. David and his followers immediately "lifted up their voices and wept until they had no more power to weep."

3. LOU GEHRIG, baseball player

   One of the most dramatic moments in baseball history took place in Yankee Stadium in New York on July 4, 1939. Lou Gehrig, a humble and popular star, had been diagnosed as having amyotrophic lateral sclerosis, a terminal disease. Between the games of a Fourth of July doubleheader, Gehrig appeared at home plate and delivered an emotional farewell speech. After telling the crowd "I'm the luckiest man on the face of the earth," he stepped away from the plate for the last time and wiped the tears from his eyes. Twenty-three months later he died, at the age of thirty-eight.

4. JESUS CHRIST, religious leader

After Lazarus died, Jesus led his disciples to visit Lazarus's sisters, Mary and Martha. When the friends of Lazarus agreed to show Jesus the cave where Lazarus's body was laid, Jesus wept.

5. BILL CLINTON, U.S. president

On the morning of his inauguration, President Clinton and his family attended services at Washington's Metropolitan African Methodist Episcopal church. As the choir sang hymns, tears rolled down Clinton's cheeks.

6. DEXTER MANLEY, football player

The flamboyant defensive end for the Washington Redskins testified in 1989 before the U.S. Senate Subcommittee on Education about his experience growing up with a learning disability. "I felt I was normal," he said, with tears in his eyes, "but I was told I was dumb and stupid." Two years later Manley cried in public again, this time during a press conference after he failed a drug test that forced his retirement from football.

7. EDMUND MUSKIE, U.S. senator

Muskie was the leading contender for the 1972 Democratic Party presidential nomination. However, his campaign was derailed when, angered by a vicious attack on his wife by New Hampshire newspaper editor William Loeb, he began weeping during a speech. It was later revealed that the newspaper attack was part of a "dirty tricks" campaign orchestrated by Richard Nixon's reelection committee.

8. RICHARD NIXON, U.S. president

During a 1977 television interview, Nixon told David Frost, "I never cry — except in public." Nixon's most famous public weep occurred in 1952 after he made his notorious "Checkers speech" and Dwight Eisenhower decided to allow him to remain on the Republican ticket as the vice-presidential candidate. Watching this performance, Nixon's college drama coach, Albert Upton, who had taught the future politician how to cry, remarked, "Here goes my actor."

9. MIKE SCHMIDT, baseball player

At a press conference to announce his retirement in 1989, Schmidt tried to read a prepared statement, but broke down and cried when he said, "Some eighteen years ago, I left Dayton, Ohio, with two very bad knees and a dream to become a major-league baseball player. I thank God the dream came true."

Jimmy Swaggart weeping as he confesses *some* of his sins.

10. JIMMY SWAGGART, evangelist

On February 21, 1988, Swaggart, tears streaming down his face, confessed before a crowd of 6,000 and on television to having committed "a sin," later revealed to be the hiring of prostitutes.

11. PATRICK SWAYZE, actor

Swayze was in the middle of a 1988 televised interview with Barbara Walters when he expressed regret that his father had not lived to see him become a star. Suddenly Swayze burst into tears. "It's like a water faucet when I talk about him," he later explained, "because I have so many things I wanted to say to him."

118 Sets of Celebrities with Shared Birthdays

CAPRICORN (December 22–January 20)

December 25, 1946	Jimmy Buffett (singer) and Larry Csonka (football player)
December 31, 1948	Tim Matheson (actor) and Donna Summer (singer)

January 3, 1897	Marion Davies (actress) and Pola Negri (actress)
January 3, 1945	Stephen Stills (singer/songwriter) and Victoria Principal (actress)
January 5, 1932	Umberto Eco (author) and Raisa Gorbachev (professor/First Lady of USSR)
January 8, 1942	Yvette Mimieux (actress) and Stephen Hawking (physicist)
January 10, 1949	George Foreman (boxer) and Linda Lovelace (porn actress)
January 17, 1931	James Earl Jones (actor), L. Douglas Wilder (governor of Virginia), and Don Zimmer (baseball player/manager)
January 19, 1943	Janis Joplin (singer) and Princess Margaret (member of British royal family)

AQUARIUS (January 21–February 19)

January 21, 1963	Hakeem Aboul Olajuwon (basketball player) and Detlef Schrempf (basketball player)
January 26, 1918	Philip José Farmer (author) and Nicolae Ceausescu (Romanian dictator)
January 29, 1960	Greg Louganis (diver) and Steve Sax (baseball player)
January 30, 1937	Vanessa Redgrave (actress) and Boris Spassky (chess player)
January 31, 1923	Carol Channing (actress) and Norman Mailer (author)
January 31, 1941	Placido Domingo (opera singer) and Richard Gephardt (U.S. congressman)
February 1, 1937	Don Everly (musician) and Garrett Morris (comedian)
February 6, 1931	Rip Torn (actor) and Mamie Van Doren (actress)
February 11, 1921	Eva Gabor (actress) and Lloyd Bentsen (U.S. Treasury secretary)
February 11, 1935	Manuel Noriega (Panamanian dictator) and Gene Vincent (singer)
February 13, 1944	Stockard Channing (actress), Peter Tork (singer/actor), and Sal Bando (baseball player)
February 15, 1905	Ayn Rand (author) and Harold Arlen (composer/musician)

February 15, 1951	Melissa Manchester (singer) and Jane Seymour (actress)
February 16, 1959	John McEnroe (tennis player) and Kelly Tripucka (basketball player)
February 18, 1927	George Kennedy (actor) and John Warner (U.S. senator)

PISCES (February 20–March 20)

February 20, 1924	Bobby Unser (auto racer) and Gloria Vanderbilt (fashion designer)
February 21, 1927	Erma Bombeck (columnist) and Hubert de Givenchy (fashion designer)
February 22, 1918	Charles Finley (baseball team owner) and Robert Wadlow (tallest person in history)
February 25, 1943	George Harrison (musician) and Sally Jessy Raphael (talk-show host)
March 1, 1927	Robert Bork (U.S. Court of Appeals circuit judge) and Harry Belafonte (singer)
March 2, 1931	Mikhail Gorbachev (Soviet political leader) and Tom Wolfe (author)
March 3, 1962	Jackie Joyner-Kersee (heptathlon athlete) and Herschel Walker (football player)
March 6, 1937	Ivan Boesky (banker) and Valentina Jereshkova-Nikolaeva (cosmonaut)
March 15, 1935	Judd Hirsch (actor) and Jimmy Swaggart (TV evangelist)

ARIES (March 21–April 19)

March 22, 1930	Pat Robertson (TV evangelist) and Stephen Sondheim (composer)
March 26, 1950	Teddy Pendergrass (singer) and Martin Short (actor)
March 29, 1943	Eric Idle (comic actor) and John Major (prime minister of Great Britain)
March 31, 1935	Herb Alpert (musician) and Richard Chamberlain (actor)
March 31, 1948	Albert Gore (U. S. vice-president) and Rhea Perlman (actress)
April 3, 1924	Marlon Brando (actor) and Doris Day (actress/singer)
April 4, 1922	Elmer Bernstein (composer) and William Manchester (author)

| April 6, 1937 | Merle Haggard (singer/songwriter) and Billy Dee Williams (actor) |
| April 7, 1939 | Francis Ford Coppola (director) and David Frost (entertainer) |

TAURUS (April 20–May 20)

April 23, 1942	Sandra Dee (actress) and Phil Esposito (hockey player)
April 26, 1938	Nino Benvenuti (boxer) and Duane Eddy (guitarist)
May 8, 1926	David Attenborough (author/naturalist) and Don Rickles (comedian)
May 8, 1940	Peter Benchley (author) and Rick Nelson (singer)
May 12, 1929	Burt Bacharach (composer) and Samuel Daniel Nujoma (president of Namibia)
May 12, 1936	Tom Snyder (talk-show host) and Frank Stella (artist)
May 16, 1955	Olga Korbut (gymnast) and Debra Winger (actress)

GEMINI (May 21–June 21)

May 22, 1938	Richard Benjamin (actor) and Susan Strasberg (actress)
May 23, 1910	Artie Shaw (bandleader) and Scatman Crothers (actor)
May 26, 1966	Helena Bonham-Carter (actress) and Zola Budd (distance runner)
May 28, 1944	Rudolph Giuliani (attorney) and Gladys Knight (singer)
June 5, 1898	Madame Chiang Kai-shek (political activist/author) and Federico Garcia Lorca (poet/playwright)
June 8, 1944	Don Grady (actor) and Boz Scaggs (singer/musician)
June 9, 1916	Robert McNamara (U.S. secretary of defense, president of World Bank) and Les Paul (musician/inventor)
June 11, 1910	Jacques-Yves Cousteau (marine naturalist) and Carmine Coppola (composer)
June 11, 1939	Jackie Stewart (auto racer) and Gene Wilder (actor)

Carl Lewis . . . and Princess Diana: both born on July 1, 1961.

June 15, 1943	Malcolm McDowell (actor) and Xaviera Hollander (author/prostitute)
June 17, 1917	John Hersey (author) and Dean Martin (singer/actor)
June 18, 1942	Roger Ebert (film critic) and Paul McCartney (singer/songwriter)
June 18, 1952	Carol Kane (actress) and Isabella Rossellini (model/actress)
June 21, 1921	Judy Holliday (actress) and Jane Russell (actress)

CANCER (June 22–July 21)

June 22, 1949	Meryl Streep (actress) and Lindsay Wagner (actress)
June 29, 1936	Elizabeth Hanford Dole (U.S. secretary of labor) and Harmon Killebrew (baseball player)
July 1, 1925	Farley Granger (actor) and Los Angeles (city)
July 1, 1961	Princess Diana (Princess of Wales) and Carl Lewis (track star)
July 5, 1951	Richard "Goose" Gossage (baseball player) and Huey Lewis (singer)
July 6, 1925	Merv Griffin (TV personality) and Bill Haley (singer)

July 6, 1935	Candy Barr (stripper) and the Dalai Lama (religious leader)
July 6, 1937	Ned Beatty (actor) and Vladimir Ashkenazy (pianist)
July 17, 1935	Diahann Carroll (actress/singer) and Donald Sutherland (actor)
July 19, 1941	Natalya Bessmertnova (Bolshoi prima ballerina) and Vikki Carr (singer)

LEO (July 22–August 21)

July 22, 1947	Albert Brooks (comedian), Danny Glover (actor), and Don Henley (musician)
July 23, 1936	Don Drysdale (baseball player/sportscaster) and Anthony Kennedy (U.S. Supreme Court justice)
July 26, 1922	Blake Edwards (producer) and Jason Robards (actor)
July 29, 1956	Patty Scialfa (singer) and Michael Spinks (boxer)
August 1, 1942	Jerry Garcia (singer/musician) and Giancarlo Giannini (actor)
August 3, 1905	Dolores Del Rio (actress) and Maggie Kuhn (founder of the Gray Panthers)
August 6, 1881	Louella Parsons (gossip columnist) and Sir Alexander Fleming (discoverer of penicillin)
August 10, 1928	Jimmy Dean (singer) and Eddie Fisher (singer)
August 16, 1930	Robert Culp (actor) and Frank Gifford (sportscaster)
August 18, 1922	Shelley Winters (actress) and Alain Robbe-Grillet (author/filmmaker)

VIRGO (August 22–September 22)

August 31, 1945	Van Morrison (singer) and Itzhak Perlman (violinist)
September 5, 1946	Loudon Wainwright III (singer), Freddie Mercury (singer), and Buddy Miles (musician)
September 8, 1922	Sid Caesar (comedian) and Lyndon Larouche, Jr. (political activist)
September 11, 1917	Ferdinand Marcos (Philippine dictator) and Jessica Mitford (author)

Margaret Thatcher . . . and Lenny Bruce: astrological twins.

September 15, 1946	Tommy Lee Jones (actor) and Oliver Stone (director)
September 16, 1925	Charlie Byrd (musician) and B. B. King (singer)
September 18, 1933	Robert Blake (actor) and Jimmy Rodgers (singer)

LIBRA (September 23–October 22)

October 1, 1924	Jimmy Carter (U.S. president) and William Rehnquist (chief justice of the U.S. Supreme Court)
October 4, 1941	Jackie Collins (author) and Anne Rice (author)
October 5, 1936	Václav Havel (playwright/president of Czech Republic) and Adrian Smith (basketball player)
October 12, 1935	Joan Rivers (comedienne) and Luciano Pavarotti (opera singer)
October 13, 1925	Margaret Thatcher (prime minister of Great Britain) and Lenny Bruce (comedian)
October 18, 1926	Chuck Berry (singer/musician) and Klaus Kinski (actor)
October 21, 1940	Pelé (soccer player), Manfred Mann (musician), Frances Fitzgerald (journalist), and Geoffrey Boycott (cricket player)

SCORPIO (October 23–November 21)

October 23, 1931	Jim Bunning (baseball player/U.S. congressman) and Diana Dors (actress)
October 30, 1632	Jan Vermeer (artist) and Sir Christopher Wren (architect)
October 31, 1931	Michael Collins (astronaut) and Dan Rather (newscaster)
October 31, 1950	John Candy (actor) and Jane Pauley (TV personality)
November 5, 1905	Joel McCrea (actor) and Mantovani (composer)
November 5, 1941	Art Garfunkel (singer) and Elke Sommer (actress)
November 17, 1944	Danny DeVito (actor), Lauren Hutton (model/actress), and Tom Seaver (baseball player)
November 20, 1956	Bo Derek (actress) and Mark Gastineau (football player)

SAGITTARIUS (November 22–December 21)

November 22, 1869	André Gide (author) and John Nance Garner (U.S. vice-president)
November 26, 1912	Eugene Ionesco (dramatist) and Eric Sevareid (broadcast journalist)
November 26, 1938	Rich Little (impressionist) and Tina Turner (singer)
November 28, 1949	Alexander Gudonov (ballet dancer) and Paul Shaffer (orchestra leader)
November 29, 1932	Jacques Réné Chirac (French political leader) and Diane Ladd (actress)
December 1, 1935	Woody Allen (actor/director) and Lou Rawls (singer)
December 3, 1930	Jean-Luc Godard (director) and Andy Williams (singer)
December 5, 1935	Little Richard (musician) and Calvin Trillin (author)
December 7, 1947	Gregg Allman (musician) and Johnny Bench (baseball player)
December 11, 1931	Bhagwan Shri Rajneesh (guru) and Rita Moreno (actress)
December 11, 1944	Teri Garr (actress) and Brenda Lee (singer)

| December 13, 1910 | Van Heflin (actor), Kenneth Patchen (poet), and Lillian Roth (singer) |
| December 21, 1918 | Donald Regan (banker/Ronald Reagan's chief of staff) and Kurt Waldheim (U.N. secretary general/president of Austria) |

NOTE: For more celebrities with shared birthdays, see *The Book of Lists #1*, pp. 17–22.

10 Celebrities Who Have Seen UFOs

1. MUHAMMAD ALI

   Ali claims to have seen UFOs on seven different occasions. On December 1, 1971, at 5:15 A.M., the Champ was jogging in Central Park, accompanied by his manager and several reporters. He spotted a bright light glowing in the sky, which moved until it was positioned directly above him. It looked, he said, "like a huge electric light bulb."

2. JIMMY CARTER

   Carter is the only U.S. president known to have reported seeing a UFO. He was attending a meeting of the Lions Club in Leary, Georgia, on January 6, 1969, and was waiting outdoors with ten other members for the meeting to begin. At about 7:30 P.M., all the men saw a sharply outlined light in the sky. Carter said it appeared "bluish at first — then reddish — but not solid. . . . It appeared as bright as the moon." Computer systems analyst Robert Sheaffer believes that Carter's sighting was a misidentification of the planet Venus.

3. SIR ERIC GAIRY

   The former prime minister of Grenada claims to have seen a UFO in 1975. He was leaving a late-night function and saw the object at about 2:00 A.M. He believes that other people live in other parts of the universe who are "more evolved scientifically and spiritually than we are."

4. GLENN FORD

   Ford had long been a confirmed skeptic about UFOs — he tracked them on radar during World War II and believed they were weather balloons or other ordinary objects. He changed his mind in 1974, when he saw a strange object in the sky over the Pacific Ocean while staying at his beach house in southern California. It was shaped like two discs "pressed inward toward each other," which hovered for eleven minutes, then shot off at a 90° angle.

5. JACKIE GLEASON

Gleason claimed to have seen two UFOs — one in 1965, seen while he was looking out of a hotel window in London; the other near his Florida home, seen while he was out walking his dog. He believed that mankind was being studied by beings from other planets.

6. DICK GREGORY

In 1967, while at a party at Big Sur, California, the activist and his friends saw three lights in the sky (one red, two green) that performed maneuvers for forty minutes. Gregory took pictures of the objects.

7. ORSON BEAN

In September 1968 Bean and his wife were driving near Patchogue, Long Island, when they spotted a UFO. They thought they were seeing a bright star, until the "star" shot forward at an estimated 5,000 miles an hour, then rose and disappeared. The incident changed the Beans' life and inspired them to sell their house and move to Australia.

8. CLYDE W. TOMBAUGH

The American astronomer who discovered the planet Pluto believes he may have twice sighted UFOs. The first time, he saw a geometrically arranged group of rectangles of light moving over the sky of New Mexico. He was doubtful that he had actually seen a UFO, though he admitted, "I was so unprepared for such a strange sight that I was really petrified with astonishment." He reported it to the FBI, requesting that it not be made public. When the story leaked out, he was deluged with crank letters, and has said little about his second sighting.

9. MEL TORMÉ

Tormé was walking his dog in New York City in August 1963 at 2:00 A.M. when he saw an odd light in the sky. For five minutes it performed figure eights and loops. Tormé, who has a pilot's license, was astonished, because he had never seen such maneuvers at such high speeds.

10. WILLIAM SHATNER

Appropriately enough, the star of *Star Trek* claims to have had his life saved by a UFO. He and four friends were on a motorcycle trip in the Mojave Desert when he stopped to drink some water. His companions had gone ahead when he discovered, to his dismay, that his bike wouldn't start. He had used up his supply of water, and eventually collapsed in the extreme heat. At that moment, a shiny, sleek craft passed over him, and he had an intuition that he should walk in a certain direction. This trek led him to a gas station and safety. He believes that he had received telepathic messages from the UFO.

23 Prominent People Who Died of AIDS

1. Peter Allen (1944–1992), entertainer/songwriter
2. Arthur Ashe (1943–1993), tennis player
3. Amanda Blake (1929–1989), actress
4. Bruce Chatwin (1940–1989), British travel writer
5. Roy Cohn (1927–1986), attorney
6. Brad Davis (1949–1991), actor
7. Denholm Elliott (1922–1992), actor
8. Perry Ellis (1940–1986), fashion designer
9. Michel Foucault (1926–1984), French philosopher
10. Halston (1932–1990), fashion designer
11. Keith Haring (1958–1990), pop artist
12. John C. Holmes (1945?–1988), porn star
13. Rock Hudson (1925–1985), actor
14. Larry Kert (1930–1991), actor/singer
15. Liberace (1919–1987), entertainer/pianist
16. Robert Mapplethorpe (1946–1989), photographer
17. Freddie Mercury (1946–1991), singer/songwriter
18. Ondrej Nepala (1951-1989), 1972 Olympic figure-skating champion
19. Rudolf Nureyev (1938–1993), ballet dancer
20. Anthony Perkins (1932–1992), actor
21. Robert Reed (1932–1992), actor
22. Tony Richardson (1928–1991), director
23. Max Robinson (1939–1988), anchorman

8 Actresses Who Won Beauty Contests

1. LAUREN BACALL

   In 1942 the eighteen-year-old future film star was a model with the Walter Thornton Modeling Agency in New York City. As a publicity stunt, Thornton held a Miss Greenwich Village 1942 contest, with himself as judge. His first choice to win turned out to be from New Jersey, so he gave the title to his second choice, Betty Bacall, who lived with her mother on Bank Street.

2. CLAUDIA CARDINALE

Cardinale and her parents were Italian citizens living in Tunis, Tunisia. In 1957 she entered a contest for the Most Beautiful Italian Girl in Tunis, which was sponsored by the Italian embassy. Cardinale won and was awarded a trip to Venice during the Venice Film Festival. The nineteen-year-old was immediately besieged by producers with movie offers. She refused them all for six months, but then gave in. Within two years she was receiving starring parts.

3. SYLVIA KRISTEL

Born and raised in Holland, Kristel became a model at seventeen. She entered the Miss TV Europe contest and won, an honor which led to appearances in three Dutch films. Within two years, she gained the starring role in the popular erotic film *Emmanuelle: The Joys of a Woman.*

4. SOPHIA LOREN

When she was fourteen years old, Loren, then known as Sofia Scicolone, transformed from an awkward, funny-looking girl into a beautiful, shapely young woman. Her mother, quick to take advantage, entered Loren in the Queen of the Sea beauty contest sponsored by Naples's *Il Mattino* newspaper, even though she didn't meet the minimum age of fifteen. Loren had no dress for the evening gown competition, so her grandmother made one for her out of the living room drapes. Then she needed a pair of white shoes, but all she had was one black pair; Loren's mother painted them white and prayed against rain. Loren didn't win the contest, but she was chosen one of the Queen's twelve princesses. Her prize was a train ticket to Rome, several rolls of wallpaper, a tablecloth with matching napkins, and thirty-five dollars. At the age of sixteen she was voted Miss Elegance at the Queen of the Adriatic Sirens contest. The next year, in 1957, Loren attended the Miss Rome beauty contest. One of the judges, a film producer named Carlo Ponti, picked her out of the audience and asked her to enter. She did, and won second place. She also married Ponti.

5. MICHELLE PFEIFFER

Tired of working as a checkout clerk in a grocery store, Pfeiffer entered a beauty contest and was crowned Miss Orange County, California, of 1976. This led to minor roles in such films as *Charlie Chan and the Curse of the Dragon Queen.*

Debbie Reynolds as Miss Burbank, 1948.

6. DEBBIE REYNOLDS

In 1948, when she was sixteen years old, Reynolds and a friend entered the Miss Burbank contest because everyone who entered received a silk scarf, a blouse, and a free lunch. She caused a sensation with her humorous imitation of Betty Hutton performing "I'm a Square in the Social Circle." She won the contest and the next day Warner Brothers Studios offered her a screen test.

7. CYBILL SHEPHERD

When Shepherd was sixteen, a cousin entered her in a Miss Teenage Memphis contest. She won and began modeling for a department store. A New York modeling agent saw her and persuaded her to enter CBS-TV's 1968 Model of the Year pageant. A victory in that contest earned her a modeling job in New York, the cover of *Seventeen* magazine, and an invitation to Elvis Presley's Christmas party.

8. RAQUEL WELCH

Welch was so skinny when she was young that the other girls in gym class called her Bird Legs. When she filled out, at age fourteen, she began entering and winning beauty contests. The first was Miss Photogenic at a photographers' convention. Then came Miss La Jolla, the Fairest of the Fair, Miss Contour, and Maid of California at the state fair. Tiring of beauty contests, Welch took a job as a host on a San Diego morning TV show before moving on to modeling and acting.

Madame Tussaud's . . .

At the end of each year since 1970, Madame Tussaud's Waxworks Museum in London has handed visitors a questionnaire that asked them a variety of questions, including which persons, past or present, they hated and feared the most; which they thought most heroic; and which they thought most beautiful.

. . . Most Hated and Feared

THE 1992 POLL
1. Saddam Hussein
2. Adolf Hitler
3. Margaret Thatcher
4. Muammar el-Qaddafi
5. Jack the Ripper

THE 1987 POLL
1. Adolf Hitler
2. Ronald Reagan
3. Muammar el-Qaddafi
4. Ayatollah Khomeini
5. Margaret Thatcher

THE 1982 POLL
1. Adolf Hitler
2. Margaret Thatcher

3. Ronald Reagan
4. Dracula
4. Yorkshire Ripper

THE 1977 POLL
1. Idi Amin
2. Adolf Hitler
3. Dracula
4. Dr. Hawley Harvey Crippen
4. Denis Healey

THE 1972 POLL
1. Richard Nixon
2. Idi Amin
3. Mao Tse-tung
4. Adolf Hitler
5. Satan

. . . Most Heroic

THE 1992 POLL
1. Superman
2. Marilyn Monroe
3. Arnold Schwarzenegger
4. Winston Churchill
5. Sylvester Stallone

THE 1987 POLL
1. James Dean
2. Batman
2. Indiana Jones
2. Elvis Presley

2. Sylvester Stallone

THE 1982 POLL
1. Superman
2. Douglas Bader
3. James Bond
4. Winston Churchill
4. Joan of Arc

THE 1977 POLL
1. Elvis Presley
2. Winston Churchill
2. Horatio Nelson

4. John F. Kennedy
4. Florence Nightingale

THE 1972 POLL

1. Joan of Arc

2. Abraham Lincoln
3. Horatio Nelson
3. John F. Kennedy
5. Winston Churchill

. . . Most Beautiful

THE 1992 POLL

1. Cindy Crawford
2. Cher
3. Joan Collins
4. Princess Diana
5. Jerry Hall

THE 1987 POLL

1. Joan Collins
1. Princess Diana
3. Marilyn Monroe
4. Madonna
5. Jane Seymour

THE 1982 POLL

1. Princess Diana
2. Sophia Loren

3. Marilyn Monroe
4. Victoria Principal
5. Bo Derek

THE 1977 POLL

1. Brigitte Bardot
2. Sophia Loren
3. Twiggy
4. Marilyn Monroe
5. Farrah Fawcett

THE 1972 POLL

1. Raquel Welch
2. Sophia Loren
2. Elizabeth Taylor
4. Brigitte Bardot
5. Jackie Kennedy

Top 15 Celebrity Q Scores

The Q score is determined by taking the number of people who said the celebrity was one of their favorites and dividing it by the familiarity percentage (percentage of people who recognized the celebrity).

Name	Q Score (%)	Familiarity (%)
1. Bill Cosby	48	91
1. James Stewart	48	69
3. Clint Eastwood	47	91
4. Steven Spielberg	46	77
5. Robin Williams	45	80
6. Whoopi Goldberg	44	84
6. Billy Crystal	44	83
8. Mel Gibson	43	84

9. Damon Wayans	42	43
10. Tim Allen	41	65
11. Estelle Getty	40	81
11. James Kiberd	40	21
13. Steve Martin	39	83
13. Jaleel White	39	61
13. Will Smith	39	51

Bottom 9 Celebrity Q Scores

Name (Least Popular First)	Q Score (%)	Familiarity (%)
1. Mike Adamle	3	36
2. Rebecca Chase	5	32
2. Kathleen Quinlan	5	29
4. Robin Givens	6	66
4. Linda McCartney	6	39
4. John Sununu (as CNN host)	6	33
7. Drew Barrymore	7	66
7. Roger Ebert	7	55
7. Dustin Berkovitz	7	25

NOTE: This 1992 survey was conducted by Marketing Evaluations, Inc., of Port Washington, New York, using a national sample of 1,800 individuals, males and females, ages six and up. Total number of celebrities on the list was 1,495.

Encyclopaedia Britannica's 15 Most Asked About Historical Figures

Encyclopaedia Britannica's Instant Research Service, located in Chicago, Illinois, fields more than 170,000 questions from the public each year. Here are the most asked about figures and the subjects about them most often queried in 1992.

1. JOHN F. KENNEDY (1917–1963), U.S. president

The assassination of John F. Kennedy and the Warren Report; achievements of the Kennedy administration; John F. Kennedy and the Cuban Missile Crisis.

2. WILLIAM SHAKESPEARE (1564–1616), English dramatist and poet

The Shakespeare controversy; Shakespeare's philosophy of life; the psychology of Shakespeare; Shakespeare and religion; Shakespearean comedy; Shakespearean tragedy; the universal appeal of Shakespeare's language; numerous reports on individual works, particularly *King Lear*, *Macbeth*, and *Hamlet*.

3. SIGMUND FREUD (1856–1939), Austrian founder of psychoanalysis

The position of Freud in the field of psychoanalysis; Freud's theory of child development; Freud's dream theory; Freud's views on women.

4. ERNEST HEMINGWAY (1894–1961), U.S. novelist, journalist

Biography; autobiographical background in Hemingway's works; Hemingway's style of writing; the use of violence and death in the writings of Hemingway; reports on individual works.

5. MARTIN LUTHER KING, JR. (1929–1968), U.S. civil rights leader, clergyman

Biography; Martin Luther King's theory of nonviolence; Martin Luther King's march from Selma to Montgomery.

6. ROBERT FROST (1874–1963), U.S. poet

Biography; humor and irony in the poetry of Robert Frost; metaphor in the poems of Robert Frost; the symbolism in "Stopping by Woods on a Snowy Evening."

7. EDGAR ALLAN POE (1809–1849), U.S. poet, short-story writer

Biography; Poe's style of writing; Poe and the use of the supernatural in his prose; Poe and the development of the detective story; reports on individual works.

8. MARK TWAIN (1835–1910), U.S. humorist

The life of Samuel Clemens and the humor of Mark Twain; Twain's importance as a novelist; Twain's satire; *Huckleberry Finn*.

9. CHARLES DICKENS (1812–1870), English novelist

Dickens as a social reformer; Dickens's language and style; reports on individual works, especially *Great Expectations* and *A Tale of Two Cities*.

10. EMILY DICKINSON (1830–1886), U.S. poet

Biography; the poetry of Emily Dickinson; the influence of Emily Dickinson on modern poetry.

11. JOHN STEINBECK (1902–1968), U.S. writer, novelist

    Steinbeck's contributions to American literature; Steinbeck as a socialist writer; short stories of John Steinbeck; reports on individual works.

12. LEONARDO DA VINCI (1452–1519), Florentine painter, sculptor, engineer

    Leonardo da Vinci as engineer, inventor, scientist.

13. AL CAPONE (1899–1947), U.S. gangster

    Biography; Al Capone and Chicago.

14. JOHN LOCKE (1632–1704), English philosopher

    Contributions of Locke to philosophical thought; Locke and the philosophical background of the constitution.

15. HERMAN MELVILLE (1819–1891), U.S. novelist

    Reports of various kinds on *Moby-Dick,* particularly the symbolism of the whale.

Kitty Kelley's *10* Historical Figures She Would Like to Have Written About

Biographer Kitty Kelley, formerly of the *Washington Post,* has probed the life of Jacqueline Onassis in *Jackie Oh!* and Elizabeth Taylor in *Elizabeth Taylor: The Last Star.* She created a sensation in 1986 with her highly controversial unauthorized biography of Frank Sinatra, *His Way.* Her next book, *Nancy Reagan: The Unauthorized Biography,* became a number-one best-seller, selling more than 1 million copies. She is currently trying to pierce the veil of secrecy surrounding the British monarchy.

1. Attila the Hun
2. Ivan the Terrible
3. Catherine the Great
4. Jack the Ripper
5. Billy the Kid
6. Eric the Red
7. William the Conqueror
8. Richard the Lion-Hearted
9. Vlad the Impaler
10. Zorba the Greek
    —Exclusive for
    The Book of Lists

Left: Brenda Joyce, better known as "Jane" in Tarzan. Right: Betty Page, the "Queen of Kink."

Richard Lamparski's
9 People He Couldn't Find

Richard Lamparski is best known for his ten-volume series of books, *Whatever Became of . . . ?*, which traces the lives of formerly famous personalities. Lamparski has hosted a radio show based on the series, and has worked as an executive in the motion picture and television industry. Despite his expertise, the whereabouts of certain personalities remain a mystery.

1. JOAN BARRY

    In 1945, when she was about twenty-five years old, the aspiring actress won a paternity suit against Charlie Chaplin. Her (or their) child, Carol Ann, was born in 1943.

2. JIMMY BOYD

    When he was twelve, his recording of "I Saw Mommy Kissing Santa Claus" sold 2-million-plus records within sixty days of its release in 1952. He sang with Bing Crosby in the movie *High Time* in 1960 and was married briefly to Yvonne "Bat Girl" Craig.

3. BRENDA JOYCE

    Film actress known mainly for her role as Jane in Tarzan movies.

4.–5. MISS VICKI AND TULIP

    The former wife of Tiny Tim and their daughter.

6. JOHNNY NASH

   An Arthur Godfrey discovery who had the hit recording "I Can See Clearly Now."

7. BETTY PAGE

   The undisputed "Queen of Kink" developed her (still) large following by displaying her skills as a bondage model and dominatrix and by modeling fetish gear in fifties underground publications.

8. PICCOLA PUPA

   A young Italian songstress popular for a time in the fifties. Danny Thomas, who was credited as her discoverer, was queried shortly before his death and said he had not heard from her in many years.

9. KOOL DIP SING

   The Asian vocalist who appeared frequently on the *Ed Sullivan Show* during the sixties.

   — Exclusive for *The Book of Lists*

If *18* Famous Men Were Known by Their Mothers' Maiden Names

1. Charlton Charlton
   (*Heston*)
2. Buster Cutler
   (*Keaton*)
3. Bill Dwire
   (*Clinton*)
4. Paul Fetzer
   (*Newman*)
5. Frank Garaventi
   (*Sinatra*)
6. Johnny Hook
   (*Carson*)
7. Orson Ives
   (*Welles*)
8. Arnold Jedrny
   (*Schwarzenegger*)
9. Sylvester Labofish
   (*Stallone*)
10. Anthony Oaxaca
    (*Quinn*)

11. Michael Scruse
    (*Jackson*)
12. Mick Scutts
    (*Jagger*)
13. Mike Smith
    (*Tyson*)
14. Rip Spacek
    (*Torn*)
15. Perry Travaglini
    (*Como*)
16. Martin Luther Williams
    (*King*)
17. Bruce Zirilli
    (*Springsteen*)
18. Zuchowski
    (*Liberace*)

NOTE: For more men listed by their mothers' maiden names, see *The Book of Lists #2*, pp. 4–5.

9 Celebrities Who Did Use Their Mothers' Names

1. **LAUREN BACALL**

   After Natalie Perske divorced her husband, William, she adopted the Romanian form of her maiden name — Bacal. Her daughter, Betty Joan Perske, also used Bacal, but added a second *l* and acquired *Lauren* in Hollywood.

2. **MEL BROOKS**

   Melvin Kaminsky was born in the kitchen of his parents' Brooklyn flat. His stage name is an adaptation of his mother's maiden name, Brookman.

3. **TOM EWELL**

   At birth, he was given his mother's maiden name, Yewell, as a first name. When he became an actor, he dropped the *Y* and used part of his real last name, Tompkins, as his first name.

4. **ANTHONY "TONY" FRANCIOSA**

   Jean and Anthony Papaleo separated when their son, Tony, was a year old. After that, Tony was given his mother's maiden name, Franciosa, as a surname.

5. **RITA HAYWORTH**

   Born Margarita Carmen Cansino, she shortened her first name and borrowed her mother's maiden name, Haworth, and added a *y*.

6. **DIANE KEATON**

   It happens that the real surname of the star of *Annie Hall* is Hall. But Keaton adopted her mother's maiden name to avoid being mistaken for another actress named Diane Hall.

7. **SHIRLEY MACLAINE**

   MacLaine and Warren Beatty started life as the Beaty siblings. He added an extra *t* and she improvised on her mother's maiden name, Maclean.

8. **SIMONE SIGNORET**

   Born Simone Kaminker, Signoret took her mother's maiden name when she went into acting.

9. **CLAUS VON BULOW**

   Claus Cecil Borberg, on whom the movie *Reversal of Fortune* was based, took his mother's maiden name, Bulow, after his parents were divorced. He added the aristocratic-sounding "von" later.

7 Famous People Who Changed Their Birthdays

> *"The secret of staying young is
> to live honestly, eat slowly, and
> lie about your age."*
> — Lucille Ball

1. LILLIAN GISH (October 14, 1893–February 27, 1993), actress

   Gish claimed to be sixteen when she made her movie debut in *The Musketeers of Pig Alley* (1912). She was really three years older. Her true year of birth was not discovered until 1984, when the American Film Institute located her birth certificate.

2. GENE HACKMAN (January 30, 1931–   ), actor

   As a sixteen-year-old high school student in Danville, Illinois, Hackman "suddenly got the itch to get out." He decided to join the Marine Corps, but needed parental consent. When his parents refused, Hackman lied about his age and was accepted. Three months later he was stationed in China.

3. ANN MILLER (April 12, 1923–   ), tap dancer and actress

   When she was eleven years old, Miller claimed to be eighteen in order to get a job as a dancer at the Black Cat Club in San Francisco. Three years later she again gave her age as eighteen so that she could sign a contract with RKO Studios. From then on her birthdate was given in most sources as 1919.

4. BERT PARKS (December 30, 1914–February 2, 1992), entertainer and host of Miss America beauty pageant

   In 1933 Parks lied about his age in order to get an audition with CBS-TV as a staff announcer. At eighteen, he became the youngest network announcer in the United States.

5. NANCY REAGAN (July 6, 1921–   ), actress and First Lady

   Although her year of birth is usually given as 1923, the high school and college records of the wife of U.S. president Ronald Reagan list 1921 instead.

6. LEE REMICK (December 14, 1935–July 2, 1991), actress

   At the age of sixteen, Remick claimed to be eighteen and landed a summer job as a dancer and then an actress at the Music Circus Tent in Hyannis, Massachusetts. One month after her seventeenth birthday she made her Broadway debut in the Reginald Denham comedy *Be Your Age*.

7. ETHEL WATERS (October 31, 1900–September 1, 1977), singer

When she was sixteen, Waters got a job performing at the Lincoln Theatre in Baltimore. She added four years to her age to appear more mature. This new birthday became so accepted that when she died, most obituaries gave her age as eighty instead of seventy-six.

NOTE: For more famous people who changed their birthdays, see *The Book of Lists #2*, pp. 3–4.

Name Droppers: **27** People Better Known by Their Middle Names

1. Maria Aquino, president of the Philippines (Corazon)
2. Daniel Armstrong, jazz musician (Louis)
3. Ernst Bergman, director (Ingmar)
4. Janet Caldwell, novelist (Taylor)
5. Sidney Chayevsky, playwright ("Paddy")
6. Charles Cummings, actor (Robert)
7. Ruth Davis, actress (Bette)
8. Courken Deukmejian, Jr., governor of California (George)
9. Dorothy Dunaway, actress (Faye)
10. Victoria Eggar, actress (Samantha)
11. Paul Goebbels, German Nazi (Joseph)
12. Samuel Hammett, novelist (Dashiell)
13. Richard Hess, German Nazi (Rudolf)
14. Mary Highsmith, novelist (Patricia)
15. Mary Hutton, actress/model (Lauren)
16. Delorez Griffith Joyner, track and field athlete/Olympian (Florence)
17. James McCartney, singer/songwriter (Paul)
18. Harold Moon, football player (Warren)
19. Helen Potter, illustrator/author (Beatrix)
20. James Quayle, U.S. vice-president (Dan)
21. Wesley Rickey, baseball executive (Branch)
22. Johann Strindberg, Swedish playwright (August)
23. Marie Warwick, singer (Dionne)
24. Samuel Wilder, film writer (Billy)
25. Howard Williams, singer (Andy)
26. James Wilson, British politician (Harold)
27. Marie Winger, actress (Debra)

NOTE: For more people better known by their middle names, see *The Book of Lists #3*, pp. 1–2.

14 Famous People Who Dropped Their Last Names

1. Eddie Albert (Edward Albert Heimberger)
2. Busby Berkeley (William Berkeley Enos)
3. Ray Charles (Ray Charles Robinson)
4. Vince Edwards (Vincent Edward Zoino)
5. José Ferrer (José Vicente Ferrer Otero y Cintrón)
6. Anna Karina (Hanne Karin Blarke Beyer)
7. Joe Louis (Joseph Louis Barrow)
8. Bela Lugosi (Bela Lugosi Blasko)
9. Katherine Mansfield (Kathleen Mansfield Beauchamp)
10. Carmen Miranda (Maria de Carmo Miranda de Cunha)
11. George Montgomery (George Montgomery Letz)
12. Annie Oakley (Phoebe Anne Oakley Moses)
13. Roger Vadim (Roger Vadim Plemiannkov)
14. Rudolph Valentino (Rudolpho Guglielmi di Valentina d'Antonguolla)

10 Famous People and Their Hobbies

1. YASIR ARAFAT (1929–   ), Palestinian political leader

   Cartoons. Arafat is addicted to watching television cartoons such as *Looney Toons.* He says it is "the best possible form of relaxation for people who live under a stress."

2. ROSEY GRIER (1932–   ), entertainer, former athlete

   Needlepoint. In his book *Rosey Grier's Needlepoint for Men,* he writes, "I had a weekly card game going for a couple of years, and the guys teased the hell out of me about my 'dainty' little hobby. Would you believe that my weekly night with the guys has turned into us spending half our time playing cards and the other half needlepointing?"

3. LILLIAN HELLMAN (1905–1984), U.S. writer

   Fishing. Hellman loved to fish, a sport she enjoyed with her lover Dashiell Hammett. According to another lover, Pete Smith, "She used me for that [fishing] more than for sex." Hellman always spent her birthday fishing by herself.

4. CLARE BOOTH LUCE (1913–1987), U.S. writer and diplomat

   Jigsaw puzzles. After dinner, Luce and her husband Henry adjourned to a jigsaw puzzle, completing two or three difficult

Rosey Grier puts the finishing touches on a piece of needlepoint.

puzzles a week. Luce had them specially designed for her at $100 apiece (in 1949 dollars), and each puzzle contained a piece in the shape of Clare's logo, *CBL*.

5. J. EDGAR HOOVER (1895–1972), FBI director

The races. Hoover and his longtime companion, Clyde Tolson, often centered their vacations on the racetrack. A favorite spot was the Del Mar Racetrack in California, where they put up at the Hotel Del Charro, also known as the "KKK West." Hoover said he found racing "a wholesome diversion" from "a grueling week of work at the FBI," and believed that a racetrack was "a help to the community," keeping people away from more dubious entertainment.

6. SIGMUND FREUD (1856–1939), Austrian psychoanalyst

Mushroom collecting. Freud and his children collected mushrooms on their frequent hiking holidays. According to his son, when Freud found a good one he threw his hat over it, blew a whistle to summon his family, then removed the hat to show off his prize. He also instituted a competition for the best and second-best mushroom. According to a family friend, Freud always won the money for both prizes.

7. CLARENCE DARROW (1857–1938), U.S. attorney

Crossword puzzles. Darrow did crossword puzzles every chance he got: in trains, hotel lobbies, and crossing the street. Chicago policemen led him by the arm through traffic while Darrow, without looking up from the newspaper, would ask them for a six-letter word beginning with *ts* meaning a South African dipterous fly. Once he tried to hide a puzzle from H. G. Wells by stuffing it behind a chair cushion. When Darrow made an ashamed confession, Wells exclaimed, "Don't be foolish. I work two of them every day of my life."

8. RICHARD NIXON (1913–   ), U.S. president

   Poker. Nixon first learned to play poker as a teenager working in a carnival. Later, in the navy, he played a quiet game but rarely lost. Occasionally, he took chances. Recalled a fellow player, "I once saw him bluff a lieutenant commander out of fifteen hundred dollars with a pair of deuces."

9.–10. HENRY FONDA (1905–1982), U.S. actor, and JAMES STEWART (1908–   ), U.S. actor

   Model airplanes and kites. When Fonda and Stewart roomed together at a hotel in New York they became obsessed with making model airplanes. They wouldn't allow the maids into their rooms (which were ankle-deep in balsa wood shavings) for fear of damaging the work in progress. They also had a kite-building period. Once they built a ten-foot kite that nearly blew away with Fonda, but he was rescued by Stewart.

Original Names of
48 Celebrated People

Familiar Name	Birth Name
1. Anouk Aimee	Françoise Sorya
2. June Allyson	Ella Gaisman
3. Julie Andrews	Julia Wells
4. Adam Ant	Steward Goddard
5. Bea Arthur	Bernice Frankel
6. Anne Bancroft	Anna Maria Louisa Italiano
7. Brigitte Bardot	Camille Javal
8. Pat Benatar	Patricia Andrejewski
9. Chuck Berry	Charles Edward Anderson
10. David Bowie	David Robert Jones
11. Albert Brooks	Albert Einstein
12. Mel Brooks	Melvin Kaminsky
13. Ellen Burstyn	Edna Rae Gillooly
14. Nicholas Cage	Nicholas Coppola
15. Diahann Carroll	Carol Diahann Johnson
16. Cyd Charisse	Tula Ellice Finkles
17. John Denver	Henry John Deutchendorf
18. Bo Derek	Cathleen Collins
19. Angie Dickinson	Angeline Brown

Henry John Deutchendorf.

20.	Erté	Romain DeTiroff
21.	Hammer	Stanley Kirk Burrell
22.	Hedda Hopper	Elda Furry
23.	Robert Joffrey	Abdullah Jaffa Anver Beykhan
24.	Michael Keaton	Michael Douglas
25.	Evel Knievel	Robert Craig
26.	Patti LaBelle	Patricia Louise Holte
27.	Ann Landers	Ester Pauline Friedman
28.	John le Carré	David John Moore Cornwell
29.	Huey Lewis	Hugh Anthony Cregg III
30.	Karl Malden	Mladen Sulilovich
31.	Toni Morrison	Chloe Anthony Wofford
32.	Juice Newton	Judy Cohen
33.	Mike Nichols	Michael Igor Peschkowsky
34.	Ross Perot	Henry Ray Perot
35.	Iggy Pop	James Jewel Osterburg
36.	Anne Rice	Howard Allen O'Brien*
37.	Axl Rose	William Bailey
38.	Susan St. James	Susie Jane Miller
39.	Susan Sarandon	Susan Tomaling
40.	Eric Satie	Alfred Leslie
41.	Jane Seymour	Joyce Frankenberg
42.	Charlie Sheen	Carlos Estevez
43.	Martin Sheen	Ramon Estevez
44.	Sting	Gordon Sumner
45.	Donna Summer	LaDonna Andrea Gaines
46.	Conway Twitty	Harold Jenkins
47.	Abigail Van Buren	Pauline Ester Friedman
48.	Stevie Wonder	Steveland Morris Hardaway

* Her parents had wanted a boy

Ramon and Carlos Estevez in *Wall Street*.

NOTE: For more original names of celebrated people, see *The People's Almanac #1*, pp. 1232–34, and *The People's Almanac #2*, pp. 1110–12.

24 Real Names That Sound Like Stage Names

1. Ursula Andress
2. Tallulah Bankhead
3. Humphrey Bogart
4. Marlon Brando
5. Primo Carnera
6. Olivia de Havilland
7. Clint Eastwood
8. Marianne Faithfull
9. Errol Flynn
10. Clark Gable
11. Hermione Gingold
12. Dustin Hoffman
13. Kris Kristofferson
14. Swoosie Kurtz
15. Gina Lollobrigida
16. Mercedes McCambridge
17. Dolly Parton
18. Elvis Presley
19. Cesar Romero
20. Franchot Tone
21. Rita Tushingham
22. Rudy Vallee
23. Gore Vidal
24. King Vidor

6 Fake "De"s

1. HONORÉ DE BALZAC

The great French novelist was the son of a civil servant named Balzac. He added the aristocratic "de" to his name and passed it on to his son.

2. PIERRE-AUGUSTIN CARON DE BEAUMARCHAIS

The author of *The Barber of Seville,* the most popular comedy of the eighteenth century, Caron was the son of a watchmaker. He married a widow and took over her first husband's position in court, as well as his property. One of those properties was in Beaumarchais, which name he then appended to his own.

3. FABRE D'EGLANTINE

Born Philippe Fabre, he was a popular playwright and politician who is credited with creating the names of the months and days that were used in the French Revolutionary calendar. Accused of "moderacy," he was guillotined on April 5, 1794.

4. DANIEL DEFOE

Born Daniel Foe, he had already adopted his "de" before he wrote his most famous novels, *Robinson Crusoe* and *Moll Flanders.*

5. ANDRÉ DE TOTH

Born Andreas Toth in Hungary, he transformed into a "de," moved to Hollywood, and became a successful director of violent Westerns and action dramas. He also directed the 3-D classic *House of Wax* (1953).

6. DAME NINETTE DE VALOIS

Born Edris Stannus and married to Arthur Connell, she is known as a dancer, a choreographer, and the founder of what became the Royal Ballet.

25 Achievers
After the Age of 80

1. At 99, DAVID EUGENE RAY of Franklin, Tennessee, started to learn to read.
2. At 99, MIECZYSLAW HORSZOWSKI, the classical pianist, recorded a new album.
3.–4. At 99, twin sisters KIN NARITA and GIN KANIE recorded a hit CD single in Japan and starred in a television commercial.
5. At 98, ceramist BEATRICE WOOD exhibited her latest work.
6. At 97, MARTIN MILLER of Indiana was working full-time as a lobbyist for senior citizens.
7. At 96, KATHRINE ROBINSON EVERETT was practicing law in North Carolina.

Japanese twins Kin Narita and Gin Kanie recorded a hit CD at the age of 99.

8. At 95, choreographer MARTHA GRAHAM prepared her dance troupe for their latest performance.

9. At 94, comedian GEORGE BURNS performed at Proctor's Theater in Schenectady, New York — sixty-three years after he first played there.

10. At 93, actress DAME JUDITH ANDERSON gave a one-hour benefit performance.

11. At 92, PAUL SPANGLER completed his fourteenth marathon. At 91, he swam 1,500 meters in 52 minutes, 41.53 seconds to set a world record for the over-90 age group.

12. At 91, HULDA CROOKS climbed Mt. Whitney, the highest mountain in the continental United States.

13. At 91, ARMAND HAMMER actively headed Occidental Petroleum.

14. At 88, DORIS EATON TRAVIS graduated from the University of Oklahoma with a degree in history.

15. At 87, MARY BAKER EDDY founded the *Christian Science Monitor*.

16. At 87, mystery writer PHYLLIS WHITNEY published her seventy-first book, *The Singing Stones*.

17. At 86, KATHERINE PELTON swam the 200-meter butterfly in 3 minutes, 1.14 seconds, a time that was almost 22 seconds faster than the *men's* world record for the 85-to-89 age group.

18. At 84, ED BENHAM ran a marathon in 4 hours, 17 minutes, 51 seconds.

19. At 84, AMOS ALONZO STAGG coached the College of the Pacific football team.

20. At 83, baby doctor BENJAMIN SPOCK was arrested at Cape Canaveral, Florida, for demonstrating on behalf of world peace.

21. At 83, in 1993, SIDNEY YATES of Chicago began his fifteenth term in the U.S. Congress.
22. At 82, LESLIE MARCHAND published the final volume of his twelve-volume *Byron's Letters and Journals.*
23. At 81, JACOB BLITZSTEIN of Los Angeles graduated from high school.
24. At 81, daredevil MARY VICTOR BRUCE flew a loop-the-loop after thirty-seven years out of the cockpit.
25. At 81, leftist journalist I. F. STONE published *The Trial of Socrates,* which became a best-seller.

NOTE: For more achievers after the age of 80, see *The Book of Lists #1*, pp. 3–4.

15 Well-Known Women Who Have Had Abortions

The women listed here have all gone public with their stories.

1. Anne Archer, actress
2. Bess Armstrong, actress
3. Judy Belushi, comedy writer/artist
4. Polly Bergen, actress/comedienne
5. Jill Clayburgh, actress
6. Joan Collins, actress
7. Barbara Corday, television executive
8. Linda Ellerbee, broadcast journalist
9. Ava Gardner, actress
10. Whoopi Goldberg, comedienne
11. Margot Kidder, actress
12. Rita Moreno, actress/singer
13. Kathy Najimy, actress/comedienne
14. Sinéad O'Connor, singer/songwriter
15. Nora Sayre, film critic/author

NOTE: For more well-known women who have had abortions, see *The Book of Lists #2*, p. 326.

Best and Worst Autograph Givers

The Autograph Collector's Magazine (P.O. Box 55328, Stockton, CA 95205) took a poll of collectors to learn whom they regarded as the best — or most cooperative — stars and the worst — or least cooperative — when it came to giving their autographs.

The Best Givers

Women	Men
1. Nancy Reagan	1. Ronald Reagan
2. Kelly LeBrock	2. Warren Beatty
3. Martha Raye	3. Michael Jackson
4. Cher	4. Steven Seagal
5. Sally Kirkland	

The Worst Givers

Women	Men
1. Barbra Streisand	1. Frank Sinatra
2. Julia Roberts	2. Bruce Willis
3. Demi Moore	3. John Denver
4. Madonna	4. Sam Shepard
5. Mary McDonnell	5. Jason Patric

17 High School Dropouts

1. Richard Avedon, photographer
2. Ellen Burstyn, actress
3. George Carey, archbishop of Canterbury
4. John Chancellor, news correspondent
5. Amadeo Peter Giannini, founder of the Bank of America
6. Cary Grant, actor
7. Peter Jennings, ABC newscaster
8. Billy Joel, singer/songwriter
9. John Major, British prime minister
10. Herman Melville, author
11. James Naismith, inventor of basketball
12. Wayne Newton, singer
13. Arnold Schönberg, composer
14. Edward Steichen, photographer
15. Tracey Ullman, actress
16. Leon Uris, author
17. Lawrence Welk, bandleader

NOTE: For more high school dropouts, see *The Book of Lists #1*, p. 276.

7 Famous People Expelled from School

1. RICHARD PRYOR (1940–   ), comedian

    Pryor was expelled from a Catholic grammar school in Peoria, Illinois, when the nuns discovered that his grandmother ran a string of brothels. At sixteen, he was expelled from Central High School for punching a science teacher named Mr. Think.

2. GUSTAVE FLAUBERT (1821–1880), author

    The eighteen-year-old Flaubert was first in his philosophy class at the College Royal. Nevertheless, he led a revolt against a substitute teacher, and when the noisy students were ordered to copy a thousand lines of poetry as punishment, Flaubert organized a petition in protest. The headmaster was unmoved, and Flaubert and two other boys were expelled.

3. TINA BROWN (1953–   ), magazine editor

    Formerly editor-in-chief of *Vanity Fair* and currently editor-in-chief of the *New Yorker,* Brown was expelled from three boarding schools by the time she was sixteen. "I got other girls to run away," she recalled, "and I organized protests because we weren't allowed to change our underpants." At one school the headmistress found her diary, "and opened it where I had described her bosom as an unidentified flying object."

4. JEAN-CLAUDE KILLY (1943–   ), ski champion

    Killy began skiing at the age of three, and by the time he was a teenager he often cut school to attend ski competitions. "Once you start racing in France," he said, "your schooling is finished." He was expelled at fifteen because of chronic truancy.

5. DIANA NYAD (1949–   ), swimming champion

    Nyad went through what she called a "late adolescence" in college, and was "a real basket case." She attended Emory University in Atlanta, where she undertook such pranks as parachuting from a fourth-floor dormitory window. During her sophomore year she was asked to leave. "It was kind of scary being kicked out of college," she recalled. "I began to wonder if maybe there really wasn't something wrong with me."

6. JACKIE COLLINS (1941–   ), novelist

    At sixteen, Collins was expelled from Francis Holland School in England for (among other crimes) truancy, smoking behind a tree during lacrosse, selling readings from her diary of naughty limericks, and waving at the neighborhood flasher. Says Collins, "I was a *bad* girl." She has since sent her own daughters to the same school.

7. ROGER DALTREY (1944–   ), musician

Daltrey was expelled from Acton County Grammar School in England. "I was an evil little so-and-so," he remembers, "I didn't fit in." The headmaster who expelled him commented, "When you have five hundred boys in uniform, and one in a teddy boy outfit, no wonder he didn't fit in."

NOTE: For more famous people who were expelled from school, see *The Book of Lists #2,* pp. 272–75.

The **40** Highest-Grossing Films of All Time (Adjusted for Inflation)

Title/Year	Adjusted Gross (1992)	Actual Gross
1. *Gone With the Wind* (1939)	$805,856,000	$ 79,375,077
2. *Snow White and the Seven Dwarfs* (1937)	606,525,700	61,752,000
3. *Star Wars* (1977)	450,912,400	193,777,000
4. *The Sound of Music* (1965)	357,428,400	79,800,000
5. *Jaws* (1975)	339,419,500	129,549,325
6. *E.T. The Extra-Terrestrial* (1982)	334,567,000	228,618,939
7. *101 Dalmatians* (1961)	323,583,600	68,648,000
8. *The Godfather* (1972)	290,804,100	86,275,000
9. *The Exorcist* (1973)	282,409,000	89,000,000
10. *The Jungle Book* (1967)	257,478,000	60,964,000
11. *The Sting* (1973)	248,177,200	78,212,000
12. *The Empire Strikes Back* (1980)	242,244,400	141,672,000
13. *Return of the Jedi* (1983)	239,139,400	169,193,000
14. *Grease* (1978)	208,252,700	96,300,000
15. *Close Encounters of the Third Kind* (1977)	192,556,400	82,750,000
16. *Ghostbusters* (1984)	182,228,700	132,720,000
17. *Raiders of the Lost Ark* (1981)	179,295,500	115,598,000
18. *Superman* (1978)	179,058,400	82,800,000
19. *Love Story* (1970)	176,854,400	48,700,000
20. *American Graffiti* (1973)	174,930,100	55,128,475
21. *Saturday Night Fever* (1977)	172,428,200	74,100,000

Title/Year	Adjusted Gross (1992)	Actual Gross
22. *Batman* (1989)	170,318,400	150,500,000
23. *One Flew Over the Cuckoo's Nest* (1975)	157,029,000	59,934,701
24. *National Lampoon's Animal House* (1978)	153,164,100	70,826,000
25. *Indiana Jones and the Temple of Doom* (1984)	149,660,400	109,000,000
26. *Home Alone* (1990)	148,631,000	140,099,000
27. *Beverly Hills Cop* (1984)	148,287,300	108,000,000
28. *Rocky* (1976)	140,265,300	56,624,972
29. *The Towering Inferno* (1974)	139,651,000	48,838,000
30. *Tootsie* (1982)	138,893,600	94,910,000
31. *Back to the Future* (1985)	138,114,500	105,496,267
32. *Smokey and the Bandit* (1977)	137,174,500	58,949,938
33. *Blazing Saddles* (1974)	136,682,900	47,800,000
34. *Indiana Jones and the Last Crusade* (1989)	130,709,400	115,500,000
35. *Terminator 2* (1991)	115,875,000	112,500,000
36. *Every Which Way but Loose* (1978)	112,235,900	51,900,000
37. *Jaws II* (1978)	112,235,900	51,900,000
38. *Gremlins* (1984)	109,156,000	79,500,000
39. *Star Trek* (1979)	108,641,600	56,000,000
40. *Heaven Can Wait* (1978)	106,829,500	49,400,000

10 Biggest Money-Losing Films (1980–1991)

Title/Year	Estimated Budget ($ millions)	Estimated Film Rentals ($ millions)	Estimated Loss ($ millions)
1. *Hudson Hawk* (1991)	60	8.0	52.0
2. *The Adventures of Baron Münchhausen* (1989)	52	3.9	48.1
3. *Ishtar* (1987)	55	7.7	47.3
4. *Havana* (1990)	50	5.0	45.0

The producers of *Hudson Hawk* try to pin the blame for its failure on the film's star, Bruce Willis.

5. *Inchon* (1982)	46	1.9	44.1
6. *Billy Bathgate* (1991)	50	7.0	43.0
7. *Cotton Club* (1984)	51	12.9	38.1
8. *Santa Claus* (1985)	50	13.0	37.0
9. *For the Boys* (1991)	45	9.0	36.0
10. *Heaven's Gate* (1981)	36	1.5	34.5

25 Greatest Films of All Time

In 1987 eighty film critics, writers, and directors from twenty-two countries voted for their ten favorite films. First choice on each list was awarded 10 points; tenth choice, 1 point. When a film expert chose to list his or her favorites in unranked order, each film was awarded 5½ points. Here are the twenty-five top-ranked films and their directors:

1. *Citizen Kane*/Orson Welles (U.S., 1940)
2. *The Rules of the Game*/Jean Renoir (France, 1939)
3. *Battleship Potemkin*/Sergei Eisenstein (USSR, 1925)
4. *8½*/Federico Fellini (Italy, 1963)
5. *Singin' in the Rain*/Gene Kelly and Stanley Donen (U.S., 1952)

6. *Modern Times*/Charles Chaplin (U.S., 1935)
7. *Wild Strawberries*/Ingmar Bergman (Sweden, 1957)
8. *The Gold Rush*/Charles Chaplin (U.S., 1925)
9. *Casablanca*/Michael Curtiz (U.S., 1942)
10. *Rashomon*/Akira Kurosawa (Japan, 1950)
11. *The Bicycle Thief*/Vittorio De Sica (Italy, 1948)
12. *City Lights*/Charles Chaplin (U.S., 1931)
13. *Children of Paradise*/Marcel Carné (France, 1945)
14. *Sunrise*/F. W. Murnau (U.S., 1927)
15. *The Earrings of Madame De ...* (a.k.a. *Diamond Earrings*)/ Max Ophüls (France/Italy, 1953)
16. *Grand Illusion*/Jean Renoir (France, 1937)
17. *The Searchers*/John Ford (U.S., 1956)
18. *2001: A Space Odyssey*/Stanley Kubrick (Great Britain, 1968)
19. *Some Like It Hot*/Billy Wilder (U.S., 1959)
20. *Ivan the Terrible, Parts I & II*/Sergei Eisenstein (USSR, 1941–1945)
21. *Jules and Jim*/François Truffaut (France, 1961)
22. *Stagecoach*/John Ford (U.S., 1939)
23. *Vertigo*/Alfred Hitchcock (U.S., 1958)
24. *The Seven Samurai*/Akira Kurosawa (Japan, 1954)
25. *Tokyo Story*/Yasujiro Ozu (Japan, 1953)

SOURCE: From JOHN KOBAL PRESENTS THE TOP 100 MOVIES by John Kobal. Copyright 1988 by John Kobal and The Kobal Collection. Used by permission of New American Library, a division of Penguin Books USA Inc.

Federico Fellini's
10 All-Time-Favorite Films

Born in Rimini, Italy, in 1920, Fellini began his film career as a screenwriter, co-authoring the scripts for *Open City* (1945) and *Paisan* (1946). Among the many classic films he has directed are four Academy Award winners — *La Strada* (1954), *The Nights of Cabiria* (1957), *8½* (1963), and *Amarcord* (1974) — as well as *La Dolce Vita* (1959), *Juliet of the Spirits* (1965), and *Satyricon* (1969).

1. Several Charles Chaplin pictures, in order by year: *The Circus* (1928), *City Lights* (1931), *Monsieur Verdoux* (1947)
2. *Stagecoach* (1939), by John Ford
3. A Marx Brothers picture or a Stan Laurel/Oliver Hardy picture
4. *Rashomon* (1950), by Akira Kurosawa
5. *Le Charme Discret de la Bourgeoisie* (*The Discreet Charm of the Bourgeoisie*) (1972), by Luis Buñuel
6. *2001: A Space Odyssey* (1968), by Stanley Kubrick

7. *Paisan* (1946), by Roberto Rossellini
8. *The Birds* (1963), by Alfred Hitchcock
9. *Smultronstallet* (*Wild Strawberries*) (1957), by Ingmar Bergman
10. *8½*, by Federico Fellini

— Exclusive for *The Book of Lists*

John Waters's
10 Favorite Overlooked Movies

John Waters, who hails from Baltimore, created such cult hits as *Pink Flamingos* (1972) and *Polyester* (1981). In 1988 he achieved a measure of "respectability" with the PG-rated *Hairspray*.

1. *Tremors* (Ron Underwood). Giant worms under the earth attack Kevin Bacon — it's great and somehow not cheesy.
2. *Rope* (Alfred Hitchcock). Leopold and Loeb, sort of.
3. *Moon in the Gutter* (Jean-Jacques Beineix). Beyond overlooked — *hated* by the public. My favorite lunatic art film.
4. *Story of Women* (Claude Chabrol). Isabelle Huppert as the real-life abortionist who was guillotined in Vichy, France.
5. *Tucker* (Francis Ford Coppola). Biography of the crackpot inventor of the "car of the future."
6. *Patty Hearst* (Paul Schrader). The best legal defense she ever had.
7. *The Naked Kiss* (Sam Fuller). A lurid melodrama where a prostitute who teaches crippled children falls in love with the town's

Finn Carter as Rhonda, being attacked by giant worms who emerge from under the earth in *Tremors* (1990).

most outstanding citizen and discovers that he is a child molester.

8. *The Wansee Conference* (Heinz Schirk). Horrifying re-creation of the actual suburban Berlin meeting of Nazi leaders where "the Final Solution" was planned.

9. *Of Unknown Origin* (George Pan Cosmatos). The best rat horror movie ever made.

10. *American Hot Wax* (Floyd Mutrux). The definitive version of the Alan Freed story.

— Exclusive for *The Book of Lists*

Pedro Almodóvar's
10 Best Films of All Time

The most celebrated and controversial Spanish director since Luis Buñuel, Almodóvar didn't begin making feature-length films until after the death of dictator Francisco Franco. Among Almodóvar's most noted works are *Women on the Verge of a Nervous Breakdown*, *Tie Me Up! Tie Me Down!*, and *High Heels*.

1. *Viaggio in Italia* (*Journey to Italy*) (Roberto Rossellini)
2. *Leave Her to Heaven* (John M. Stahl)
3. *Opening Night* (John Cassavetes)
4. *The Apartment* (Billy Wilder)
5. *To Be or Not to Be* (Ernst Lubitsch)
6. *El* (Luis Buñuel)
7. *La Règle de Jeu* (*Rules of the Game*) (Jean Renoir)
8. *The Quiet Man* (John Ford)
9. *Out of the Past* (Jacques Tourneur)
10. *North by Northwest* (Alfred Hitchcock)

— Exclusive for *The Book of Lists*

Gus Van Sant's *10*
Favorite Films of All Time

The movies of independent filmmaker Gus Van Sant focus on characters who are on the fringes of society, and on nonmainstream themes like the drug subculture, male prostitution, and homosexuality. The unorthodox writer and director has garnered critical acclaim for his low-budget movies *Drugstore Cowboy* and *My Own Private Idaho*.

1. *Sunrise* (F. W. Murnau)
2. *A Clockwork Orange* (Stanley Kubrick)
3. *Citizen Kane* (Orson Welles)
4. *Thoroughly Modern Millie* (George Roy Hill)
5. *The Birds* (Alfred Hitchcock)
6. *Luna* (Bernardo Bertolucci)
7. Andy Warhol's *Frankenstein* (Paul Morrisey)
8. *Juliet of the Spirits* (Federico Fellini)
9. *Superstar* (Todd Haynes)
10. *Star Wars* (George Lucas)

— Exclusive for *The Book of Lists*

Stephen King's
6 Scariest Scenes Ever
Captured on Film

The author of such best-selling novels of terror as *Carrie*, *Salem's Lot*, *Night Shift*, *The Stand*, *The Shining*, *The Dead Zone*, and *Fire Starter*, Stephen King is the modern master of the macabre. His style is highly visual, revealing an early and strong influence by movies. Although he has probably instilled more fear in the hearts of readers than any other contemporary writer, he, too, has experienced chilling moments in the darkness of the theater.

1. *Wait Until Dark* (Terence Young). The moment near the conclusion, when [Alan] Arkin jumps out at Audrey Hepburn, is a real scare.

Alan Arkin and Audrey Hepburn in *Wait Until Dark* (1967).

2. *Carrie* (Brian De Palma). The dream sequence at the end, when Sissy Spacek thrusts her hand out of the ground and grabs Amy Irving. I knew it was coming and I still felt as if I'd swallowed a snowcone whole.

3. *I Bury the Living* (Albert Band). In this almost-forgotten movie, there is a chilling sequence when [Richard] Boone begins to maniacally remove the black pins in the filled graveyard plots and to replace them with white pins.

4. *The Texas Chainsaw Massacre* (Tobe Hooper). The moment when the corpse seems to leap out of the freezer like a hideous jack-in-the-box.

5. *Night of the Living Dead* (George Romero). The scene where the little girl stabs her mother to death with a garden trowel in the cellar. . . . "Mother, please, I can do it myself."

6. *Psycho* (Alfred Hitchcock). The shower scene, of course.

SOURCE: Gabe Essoe, *The Book of Movie Lists* (Westport: Arlington House, 1981).

Oliver Stone's
12 Best Political Films

(*In No Particular Order*)

Writer-director-producer Oliver Stone's film credits include *Salvador* (1985), *Platoon* (1986), *Wall Street* (1987), *Talk Radio* (1988), *Born on the Fourth of July* (1989), *The Doors* (1991), and *JFK* (1991). He also wrote the screenplays for *Midnight Express* (1978), *Conan the Barbarian* (1982), *Scarface* (1983), and *The Year of the Dragon* (1985). His latest project is *Heaven and Earth*, the story of a Vietnamese woman and her struggles during the French and American wars.

1. *Mr. Smith Goes to Washington* (1939). Idealism intersects reality.

2. *Z* (1969). The first conspiracy film that unfolds like a thriller.

3. *Fail Safe* (1964). Intense Cold War dystopia done in stark television style.

4. *Dr. Strangelove, Or: How I Learned to Stop Worrying and Love the Bomb* (1964). Adds humor to the Cold War cocktail of dread.

5. *Seven Days in May* (1964). The coup d'état that actually occurred and is still unacknowledged — President John Kennedy himself said this would happen if he had another Bay of Pigs.

6. *The Manchurian Candidate* (1962). Brilliant Cold War paranoia from Richard Condon and, as time has confirmed, it is true.

7. *Battleship Potemkin* (1925). First successful intersection of film and politics to create change.

8. *Viva Zapata!* (1952). My model for *Salvador* — revolutionary as hero, classic finale.

9. *Citizen Kane* (1941). Revolutionary as antihero undone by politics.
10. *The Battle of Algiers* (1965). Classic mix of documentary and drama, rigorous discipline in its perception of "objectivity."

STONE NOTES: And two more with apologies: 11.–12. *JFK* and *Salvador*. Because I never thought either could get made, much less appreciated by a large audience.

— Exclusive for *The Book of Lists*

Arthur Schlesinger's
20 Best American Political Movies

Writer, educator, and historian, Schlesinger served as special assistant to Presidents John F. Kennedy and Lyndon Johnson. Two of his books — *The Age of Jackson* and *A Thousand Days: John F. Kennedy in the White House* — have won the Pulitzer Prize. He is a frequent contributor to major magazines and journals, as well as a film critic, reviewing movies with political themes.

Movies sending political messages:
1. *Modern Times* (Charles Chaplin, 1935)
2. *Nashville* (Robert Altman, 1975)
3. *The Great Dictator* (Charles Chaplin, 1940)
4. *The Informer* (John Ford, 1935)
5. *All Quiet on the Western Front* (Lewis Milestone, 1930)

Charlie Chaplin in *Modern Times* (1935).

6. *The Grapes of Wrath* (John Ford, 1940)
7. *Ninotchka* (Ernst Lubitsch, 1939)
8. *Casablanca* (Michael Curtiz, 1942)
9. *Dr. Strangelove* (Stanley Kubrick, 1964)
10. *Network* (Sidney Lumet, 1976)

Movies about politics:
1. *The Front Page* (Lewis Milestone, 1931)
2. *The Best Man* (Franklin Schaffner, 1964)
3. *All the President's Men* (Alan J. Pakula, 1976)
4. *A Face in the Crowd* (Elia Kazan, 1957)
5. *All the King's Men* (Robert Rossen, 1949)
6. *Wilson* (Henry King, 1944)
7. *State of the Union* (Frank Capra, 1948)
8. *The Great McGinty* (Preston Sturges, 1940)
9. *The Candidate* (Michael Ritchie, 1972)
10. *Meet John Doe* (Frank Capra, 1941)

— Exclusive for *The Book of Lists*

Tom Wiener's
20 Films for Insomniacs

Tom Wiener has been writing about movies for over twenty years. He is a former senior editor of *American Film* magazine. His articles and reviews have appeared in *American Film*, the *Washington Post*, *Library Journal*, *Metropolitan Home*, and other publications. He is the author of *The Book of Video Lists* (Andrews and McMeel).

WIENER NOTES: The first list contains truly boring, worthless films. These are personal choices, films I found sheer torture to sit through and would never recommend to anyone but an insomniac.

The second list contains what I'd call "slow movers," films by respected directors whose pace may be so glacial as to put a viewer to sleep. On the other hand, if you stay awake, you may be rewarded with a provocative experience. It's better than trying to count sheep.

Truly boring, worthless films:
1. *The Appaloosa* (98 minutes)
2. *The Blood of Others* (176 minutes)
3. *Endless Love* (115 minutes)
4. *Executive Action* (91 minutes)
5. *The Island* (1980)* (114 minutes)
6. *Quintet* (110 minutes)
7. *The Shooting* (82 minutes)
8. *True Stories* (111 minutes)

* *There is a 1962 Japanese film with the same title.*

Marlon Brando and John Saxon in *The Appaloosa:* "a truly boring, worthless film."

9. *Welcome to L.A.* (106 minutes)
10. *Where the Buffalo Roam* (96 minutes)

Slow movers:
1. *Barry Lyndon* (Stanley Kubrick; 183 minutes)
2. *Interiors* (Woody Allen; 93 minutes)
3. *L'Avventura* (Michelangelo Antonioni; 145 minutes)
4. *My Dinner with André* (Louis Malle; 110 minutes)
5. *My Night at Maud's* (Eric Rohmer; 105 minutes)
6. *Paris, Texas* (Wim Wenders; 150 minutes)
7. *The Passion of Joan of Arc* (Carl Dreyer; 114 minutes)
8. *Persona* (Ingmar Bergman; 81 minutes)
9. *Stranger Than Paradise* (Jim Jarmusch; 90 minutes)
10. *Tokyo Story* (Yasujiro Ozu, 134 minutes)

— Exclusive for *The Book of Lists*

Harry Dean Stanton in *Paris, Texas:* "a slow mover" by Wim Wenders.

Patrick Robertson's
10 Favorite Movie Oddities

Robertson's initial choice of ten favorite movie oddities appeared in *The Book of Lists #3*. Several thousand movies later, the author of *The Book of Firsts* and the continuously updated *Guinness Movie Facts and Feats* presents a new selection of offbeat happenings from Hollywood and beyond.

1. HOLLYWOOD HYPE

   Publicity stunts started early in the history of movies. Kalem's 1911 Irish melodrama *The Colleen Bawn* was one of the first pictures to be made overseas in the authentic location, and the producers knew their audience. They had several tons of earth shipped from Killarney to New York and made up into four-foot-square sods for distribution to theaters exhibiting the film. For the price of a ticket, Irish immigrants could once again savor the pleasure of standing on Ireland's soil. Twenty years later, publicity was about creating headlines. Publicist Pete Smith was inspired with the idea of getting Sam Goldwyn to say that there were only thirteen real actors in Hollywood and then to name them. Goldwyn liked the stunt except for the fact that it would mean he would be on speaking terms with only thirteen actors. He found the solution himself, naming twelve and leaving Hollywood to guess the name of the thirteenth.

2. KISS-KISS

   It took a while for kissing to be reckoned acceptable — the very first screen smooch in 1896, between May Irwin and John Rice in *The Widow Jones*, was pilloried in the press as "absolutely disgusting." It took a lot longer in the Far East. Thirty years later the first Asian screen kiss was bestowed on brave pioneer Mamie Lee in the 1926 Chinese production *Two Women in the House*. In Japan, where kissing was considered "unclean, immodest, indecorous, ungraceful, and likely to spread disease" — at least by Tokyo's prefect of police — some 800,000 feet of film were cut from American movies that same year, according to *Photoplay* magazine. Even today Singapore has special rules about "suggestive prolonged kissing" — it is not allowed in Malayan-language movies, but permitted in others.

3. INTRODUCING . . .

   RKO tried a unique experiment in 1944 with a film called *Days of Glory*, in which all nineteen featured players were making

their screen debut. One of the nineteen went on to stardom —
Gregory Peck.

4. WATCH MY LIPS . . .

Lauren Bacall sings in *To Have and Have Not* (U.S., 1944), or
rather she is seen to sing, because her voice needed to be
dubbed. The problem was that since she had such a deep
speaking voice, no female singer could be found who could
match it convincingly. The solution lay in choosing a male
singer and the voice heard emanating from Lauren Bacall's
lips is actually that of Andy Williams!

In *Singin' in the Rain* (U.S., 1952) Jean Hagen plays a spoiled
silent-screen star whose voice is too déclassé for talkies. The
producers secretly have her lines dubbed by a well-spoken ingenue, Debbie Reynolds. In reality Miss Reynolds's speech was
not considered classy enough and so the voice heard on the
soundtrack of the film-within-a-film is not hers at all. It is Jean
Hagen's own normal speaking voice.

5. LADIES SECOND

The oft-reiterated complaint that there are not enough good
parts for female stars is borne out by the figures. Of all the
Hollywood pictures released in 1990, only 18 percent had the
leading lady given the top billing. Backtrack seventy years and
what do we find? In 1920 no less than 57 percent of Hollywood
movies billed the female star above the leading man. Is the
motion picture business the only major area of human activity in the western world in which the woman's role has actually declined during the course of the twentieth century?

6. OLDEST EVER

Only one centenarian has ever played a speaking role on
screen. She was Jeanne Louise Calment, born in Arles, France,
on February 21, 1875; she played herself in the 1990 Canadian
movie *Vincent and Me* at the age of 114. The heroine of this
charming fantasy is a thirteen-year-old girl called Jo (Nina
Petronzio) who travels back through time to Arles to meet
moody genius Vincent van Gogh with the idea of trying to make
him smile. On her return she meets Mme. Calment, who used
to serve in her father's shop, where van Gogh bought his canvas, and was to become the last surviving person to have
known him. Jo says that van Gogh was kind to her. "Well, good
for you," replies Mme. Calment, "because he was always rude
to me!"

7. TEENAGE DRAG QUEENS — JAPANESE STYLE

There have been movies with all-male casts and other movies
with all-female casts. But the only one in which all the leading

roles were played by members of the opposite sex was the 1989 Japanese rites-of-passage picture *Summer Vacation 1999*. A story of teenage homosexual love at a regimented boys' boarding school in Japan, the movie had all the young males played by fourteen-year-old girls. Their voices were dubbed by boys of the same age.

8. BREAKING THE BARRIER

Sixties icon Marianne Faithfull was the first to breach the ultimate language barrier in pix when she uttered the dreaded F-word in Michael Winner's 1968 production *I'll Never Forget Whatshisname*. But the film with the doubtful distinction of overusing the most overused four-letter word the most times is Brian De Palma's 1984 *Scarface*, starring Al Pacino and wide-eyed ingenue Michelle Pfeiffer, in which it is spoken 206 times — an average of once every twenty-nine seconds.

9. OH MY GAHD . . . !

Some perverse people go to the movies just to spot the mistakes, though it is rare to find more than one in a movie. That's why Steven Spielberg's *Indiana Jones and the Last Crusade* (U.S., 1989) is cherished by blunder buffs. Set in 1938, the film has Indy crossing the Atlantic by airliner a year before the first transatlantic passenger service began, and starting back by airship a year after the transatlantic airship services ceased. In the airport lounge in Berlin two passengers are reading identical copies of the same German newspaper — fine, except that the papers are dated 1918, twenty years earlier. But the classic how-come-no-one-noticed-that-before-release humdinger of a howler is an intertitle reading "The Republic of Hatay," fol-

Marianne Faithfull in *I'll Never Forget Whatshisname* (1968) — the first to utter the F-word on film.

lowed immediately by a scene in which the ruler of the "republic" is addressed as "Your Royal Highness."

10. **THE REAL THING AT LAST**

By way of contrast, some things can be right even if they look wrong. Watching the rushes of his Humphrey Bogart gangster movie *Marked Woman* (U.S., 1937), producer Hal Wallis objected to the presence of an insignificant and puny-looking extra among the gangland tough guys. He asked director Lloyd Bacon why he had used an actor who looked so unlike a mobster. The mild little man was not an actor, Bacon explained. He was a member of the Lucky Luciano gang who had been cast to add realism.

NOTE: For more of Patrick Robertson's favorite movie oddities, see *The Book of Lists #3*, pp. 196–98.

15 Actors and Actresses Most Often Nominated for an Academy Award

(capital letters indicate an Oscar winner)

1. KATHARINE HEPBURN (12)

MORNING GLORY, 1933; *Alice Adams*, 1935; *The Philadelphia Story*, 1940; *Woman of the Year*, 1932; *The African Queen*, 1951; *Summertime*, 1955; *The Rainmaker*, 1956; *Suddenly Last Summer*, 1959; *Long Day's Journey into Night*, 1962; *GUESS WHO'S*

Katharine Hepburn as Ethel Thayer in *On Golden Pond* (1981).

COMING TO DINNER?, 1967; *THE LION IN WINTER*, 1968; *ON GOLDEN POND*, 1981.

2. BETTE DAVIS (10)

DANGEROUS, 1935; *JEZEBEL*, 1938; *Dark Victory*, 1939; *The Letter*, 1940; *The Little Foxes*, 1941; *Now, Voyager*, 1942; *Mr. Skeffington*, 1944; *All About Eve*, 1950; *The Star*, 1952; *Whatever Happened to Baby Jane?*, 1962.

3. JACK NICHOLSON (10)

Easy Rider (best supporting actor), 1969; *Five Easy Pieces*, 1970; *The Last Detail*, 1973; *Chinatown*, 1974; *ONE FLEW OVER THE CUCKOO'S NEST*, 1975; *Reds* (best supporting actor), 1981; *TERMS OF ENDEARMENT* (best supporting actor), 1983; *Prizzi's Honor*, 1985; *Ironweed*, 1987; *A Few Good Men* (best supporting actor), 1992.

4. LAURENCE OLIVIER (10)

Wuthering Heights, 1931; *Rebecca*, 1940; *Henry V*, 1946; *HAMLET*, 1948; *Richard III*, 1956; *The Entertainer*, 1960; *Othello*, 1965; *Sleuth*, 1972; *Marathon Man*, 1976; *The Boys from Brazil*, 1978.

5. MERYL STREEP (9)

The Deer Hunter (best supporting actress), 1978; *KRAMER VS. KRAMER* (best supporting actress), 1979; *The French Lieutenant's Woman*, 1981; *SOPHIE'S CHOICE*, 1982; *Silkwood*, 1983;

Laurence Olivier as Hamlet, the fourth of his 10 Academy Award–nominated performances.

Out of Africa (best supporting actress), 1985; *Ironweed*, 1987; *A Cry in the Dark*, 1988; *Postcards from the Edge*, 1991.

6. SPENCER TRACY (9)

San Francisco, 1936; *CAPTAINS COURAGEOUS*, 1937; *BOYS' TOWN*, 1938; *Father of the Bride*, 1950; *Bad Day at Black Rock*, 1955; *The Old Man and the Sea*, 1958; *Inherit the Wind*, 1960; *Judgment at Nuremberg*, 1961; *Guess Who's Coming to Dinner?*, 1967.

7. MARLON BRANDO (8)

A Streetcar Named Desire, 1951; *Viva Zapata*, 1952; *Julius Caesar*, 1953; *ON THE WATERFRONT*, 1954; *Sayonara*, 1957; *THE GODFATHER*, 1972; *Last Tango in Paris*, 1973; *A Dry White Season* (best supporting actor), 1989.

8. JACK LEMMON (8)

MR. ROBERTS (best supporting actor), 1955; *The Apartment*, 1960; *Days of Wine and Roses*, 1962; *Some Like It Hot*, 1969; *SAVE THE TIGER*, 1973; *The China Syndrome*, 1979; *Tribute*, 1980; *Missing*, 1982.

9. GERALDINE PAGE (8)

Hondo (best supporting actress), 1953; *Summer and Smoke*, 1961; *Sweet Bird of Youth*, 1962; *You're a Big Boy Now* (best supporting actress), 1966; *Pete 'n' Tillie*, 1972; *The Pope of Greenwich Village* (best supporting actress); *Interiors*, 1978; *THE TRIP TO BOUNTIFUL*, 1985.

10. INGRID BERGMAN (7)

For Whom the Bell Tolls, 1943; *GASLIGHT*, 1944; *The Bells of St. Mary's*, 1945; *Joan of Arc*, 1938; *ANASTASIA*, 1956; *MURDER ON THE ORIENT EXPRESS* (best supporting actress), 1974; *Autumn Sonata*, 1978.

11. RICHARD BURTON (7)

My Cousin Rachel (best supporting actor), 1952; *The Robe*, 1953; *Becket*, 1964; *The Spy Who Came In from the Cold*, 1965; *Who's Afraid of Virginia Woolf?*, 1966; *Anne of the Thousand Days*, 1969; *Equus*, 1977.

12. JANE FONDA (7)

They Shoot Horses, Don't They?, 1969; *KLUTE*, 1971; *Julia*, 1977; *COMING HOME*, 1978; *The China Syndrome*, 1979; *On Golden Pond* (best supporting actress), 1981; *The Morning After*, 1986.

13. GREER GARSON (7)

Goodbye Mr. Chips, 1939; *Blossoms in the Dust*, 1941; *MRS. MINIVER*, 1942; *Madame Curie*, 1943; *Mrs. Parkington*, 1944; *The Valley of Decision*, 1945; *Sunrise at Campobello*, 1960.

14. PAUL NEWMAN (7)

Cat on a Hot Tin Roof, 1958; *The Hustler*, 1961; *Hud*, 1962; *Cool Hand Luke*, 1967; *Absence of Malice*, 1981; *The Verdict*, 1982; *THE COLOR OF MONEY*, 1986.

15. PETER O'TOOLE (7)

Lawrence of Arabia, 1962; *Becket*, 1964; *The Lion in Winter*, 1968; *Goodbye Mr. Chips*, 1969; *The Ruling Class*, 1972; *The Stunt Man*, 1980; *My Favorite Year*, 1982.

SOURCE: Academy of Motion Picture Arts and Sciences.

14 Actors and Actresses Who Never Won an Oscar

1. Richard Burton (nominated 7 times but never won)
2. Peter O'Toole (nominated 7 times but never won)
3. Deborah Kerr (nominated 6 times but never won)
4. Thelma Ritter (nominated 6 times but never won)
5. Agnes Moorhead (nominated 5 times but never won)
6. Greta Garbo (nominated 4 times but never won)
7. Barbara Stanwyck (nominated 4 times but never won)
8. Kirk Douglas (nominated 3 times but never won)
9. Susan Sarandon (nominated 3 times but never won)
10. Morgan Freeman (nominated 2 times but never won)
11. Cary Grant (nominated 2 times but never won)

Greta Garbo in *Ninotchka* (1948).

12. John Barrymore (never nominated)
13. Peter Lorre (never nominated)
14. Pat O'Brien (never nominated)

NOTE: This list does not include special awards.

10 Actors and Actresses
Who Fell in Love on the Set

1. VIVIEN LEIGH AND LAURENCE OLIVIER

Cast as lovers in *Fire over England* (1937), Leigh and Olivier had little difficulty playing the parts convincingly. They were both married when they became powerfully infatuated with each other. Leigh was the opposite of Olivier's cool, calm wife, and he was a contrast to her intelligent but rather dry and un-romantic husband. The affair was ill-timed: Olivier's wife was about to give birth, and she guessed what was going on. At the christening party for his newborn son, Olivier stepped outside with Leigh and returned with lipstick on his cheek. On the set they were known as "the lovers." This was all too true for Oliv-ier, who complained to another actor that he was exhausted. "It's not the stunts," he groaned. "It's Vivien. It's every day, two, three times. She's bloody wearing me out." He also felt guilty, "a really wormlike adulterer, slipping in between another man's sheets." Eventually the two passionate actors divorced their respective spouses and married in 1940. Twenty years later they divorced, and Olivier married his third wife, actress Joan Plowright.

2. RONALD REAGAN AND JANE WYMAN

Jane Wyman had a hard time getting going with Ronnie, as he was known on the set of *Brother Rat*. Even before they were cast as lovers she had noticed him around the studio and sug-gested, "Let's have cocktails at my place." He innocently re-plied, "What for?" Wyman didn't realize how straitlaced Ronnie was — although she was divorcing her husband, she was still officially married. When they finally began dating, they discovered they had little in common. She liked night-clubbing; he jabbered away about sports. Wyman loathed ath-letics, but she took up golf, tennis, and ice-skating to be near Ronnie. "She's a good scout," Reagan told his mother after one date.

Reagan lived near his parents and visited them every day. Jane found his devotedness and general goodness intimidating. It wasn't until the sequel to *Brother Rat* — *Brother Rat and a Baby* — that they began to date seriously. While their courtship was romantic, the proposal, Wyman recalled, "was about as unromantic as anything that ever happened. We were about to be called for a take. Ronnie simply turned to me as if the idea were brand-new and had just hit him and said, 'Jane, why don't we get married?'" They were wed in 1940 and divorced in 1948.

3. KATHARINE HEPBURN AND SPENCER TRACY

Having seen Tracy's work, Hepburn got him to act opposite her in MGM's *Woman of the Year*, in which they would play feuding columnists who fall in love. The first time they met she said, "I'm afraid I'm a little tall for you, Mr. Tracy." Their producer, Joseph Mankiewicz, turned to Hepburn and said, "Don't worry, Kate, he'll soon cut you down to size."

After a few days of sparring on the set — at first Tracy referred to his co-star as "Shorty" or "that woman" — an attraction began to develop between them. Tracy was married and, although he lived apart from his wife, was a Catholic who wouldn't consider divorce. As the pair fell in love, their relationship was treated with unusual respect by the gossip columnists and was rarely referred to in print. One of the great Hollywood love affairs, their romance lasted twenty-five years, until Tracy's death in 1967 of a heart attack.

Explaining the phenomenal success of their screen chemistry, Hepburn said, "Certainly the ideal American man is Spencer. Sports-loving, a man's man . . . And I think I represent a woman. I needle him, I irritate him, and I try to get around him, yet if he put a big paw out, he could squash me. I think this is the sort of romantic ideal picture of the male and female in the United States."

4. LIZ TAYLOR AND RICHARD BURTON

The furor that attended the Burton-Taylor affair during the making of *Cleopatra* (1962) in Rome was as bombastic as the film they were starring in. Newspapers all over the world carried photos of the courting couple. Taylor was married at the time to Eddie Fisher, her fourth husband; Burton was also married.

In her memoirs, Taylor recalled their first conversation on the set. After the usual small talk, "he sort of sidled over to me and said, 'Has anybody ever told you that you're a very pretty girl?' And I said to myself, Oy gevaldt, here's the great lover, the great wit, the great intellectual of Wales, and he comes out with a line like that." Chemistry prevailed, however, and soon there was electricity on-screen and off between the two stars. There were breakups and reconciliations, stormy fights and passionate clinches, public denials and private declarations, Liz's drug overdose and Richard's brief affair with a model. "Le Scandale," as Burton called it, grew so public that Liz was denounced by the Vatican and accused of "erotic vagrancy." Liz wondered, "Could I sue the Vatican?" During one love scene, director Joseph Mankiewicz yelled, "Cut! I feel as though I'm intruding."

Burton and Taylor married for the first time in 1964, divorced, remarried, and finally redivorced in 1976. Taylor said of *Cleopatra*, "It was like a disease. An illness one had a very difficult time recuperating from."

5. HUMPHREY BOGART AND LAUREN "BETTY" BACALL

When Bacall was cast opposite Bogart in *To Have and Have Not* (1944), she was disappointed. She was nineteen, and it was her first movie role. She said, "I had visions of playing opposite Charles Boyer and Tyrone Power.... But when Hawks said it was to be Bogart, I thought, 'How awful to be in a picture with that mug; that illiterate.... He won't be able to think or talk about anything.'" Bacall soon learned that she was confusing Bogey with the characters he played. She was so nervous the first day of shooting that her hands were shaking; Bogart was kind and amusing and teased her through it. Soon they were falling in love. He was twenty-five years her senior, and unhappily married. Though the affair became serious, Bogart was reluctant to leave his wife. His friend Peter Lorre told him, "It's better to have five good years than none at all." Meanwhile, the

Bacall and Bogart in *To Have and Have Not* (1944).

courtship grew intensely romantic. In honor of Bacall's famous line in the movie, "If you want me, just whistle," Bogart gave Betty a small gold whistle. "Bogey," she said, "is the kind of fellow who sends you flowers." They were married in 1945 — he cried profusely at the wedding — and had twelve happy years until Bogart's death from cancer in 1957.

13 Movie Stars Who Turned Down Great Roles

1. GARY COOPER AS RHETT BUTLER

Cooper turned down the male lead in *Gone With the Wind* (1939). When he heard that the studio finally had its leading man, Cooper said, "I'm just glad it'll be Clark Gable who's falling flat on his face, and not Gary Cooper."

2.–3. ROBERT REDFORD OR WARREN BEATTY AS MICHAEL CORLEONE

These two stars both turned down the part of Corleone in *The Godfather* (1972). The role finally went to Al Pacino, over the initial objections of the producer, Robert Evans. Even after he

"Gosh, my dear, I just don't give a darn!" *Gone With the Wind* Cooper.

got the part, Pacino told the press he never felt wanted on the set, saying, "I would feel them all thinking, 'Who *is* this guy? *He's* playing Michael?' "

4. SYLVESTER STALLONE AS ALEX FOLEY

Stallone was originally cast in *Beverly Hills Cop* (1985) and rewrote his part, calling for more action scenes. Paramount balked at the expense, and Stallone quit. The part went to Eddie Murphy.

5.–6. ALEC GUINNESS OR ANTHONY HOPKINS AS GANDHI

Director Richard Attenborough searched long and hard for his leading man and wanted Guinness for the role. He received a warm letter of refusal, in which Guinness wrote, "My dear Dickie, I honestly believe that you can do better than me . . . because I am too old, too gray-eyed, too heavy and just plain too old." Anthony Hopkins also turned down the role, which finally went to Ben Kingsley. *Gandhi* was released in 1982, and Kingsley won an Oscar for his performance.

7.–8. DUSTIN HOFFMAN AS RICK DECKARD AND TOM SELLECK AS INDIANA JONES

Hoffman was originally slated to star in *Blade Runner* (1982), but when he pulled out of the project, the part went to Harrison Ford, who gave a virtuoso performance. Another Ford part — that of Indiana Jones in *Raiders of the Lost Ark* (1981) — was to have gone to Tom Selleck, but he was committed to his TV series, *Magnum P.I.* Hoffman, incidentally, got *his* break when Robert Redford turned down the lead in *The Graduate* (1967).

9. NORMA SHEARER AS MRS. MINIVER

Because the title role in *Mrs. Miniver* (1942) involved playing the mother of a grown son, Shearer turned it down. Greer Garson took the part and won an Oscar for her performance.

10. ELVIS PRESLEY AS JOHN NORMAN HOWARD

Barbra Streisand wanted Presley to play her down-and-out husband in the third version of *A Star Is Born* (1976). He allegedly rejected the part because it called for him to portray a has-been rock star, and because he didn't want to be bossed around by Streisand. The part went to Kris Kristofferson.

11. MARLON BRANDO AS T. E. LAWRENCE

Peter O'Toole, then a relatively unknown actor, was given the chance to play the title role in *Lawrence of Arabia* (1962) after Brando turned it down. O'Toole received an Oscar nomination for his performance.

Boris Karloff was forty-four — and had been an actor in movies for twelve years — when he finally became a star in *Frankenstein* (1931). Lugosi declined the role because it had no lines other than grunts and groans. John Carradine also turned down the part, saying he hadn't studied acting for so long to wind up playing monsters. Lugosi later changed his mind, and took the starring part in *Frankenstein Meets the Wolf Man* (1943).

15 Most Violent Movies (1987–1991)

The National Committee on Television Violence monitors television series and movies and calculates the number of acts of violence based on a weighted scale. For example, an angry push or shove counts as only ⅓ of an act of violence, whereas a murder, attempted murder, rape, or suicide counts as 1⅔ acts of violence.

	Acts of Violence per Hour
1. *Bloodfist* (Concorde, 1989)	183
2. *Delta Force II* (MGM/United Artists, 1990)	182
3. *Rambo III* (Tri-Star, 1988)	169
4. *Marked for Death* (Fox, 1990)	151
5. *Robocop 2* (Orion, 1990)	147
6. *Cyborg* (Cannon, 1989)	146
6. *The Running Man* (Tri-Star, 1987)	146
8. *Robin Hood: Prince of Thieves* (Warner Bros., 1991)	139
9. *Masters of the Universe* (Cannon, 1987)	137
10. *Above the Law* (Warner Bros., 1988)	134
10. *Fatal Beauty* (MGM/United Artists, 1987)	134
12. *Teenage Mutant Ninja Turtles* (New Line, 1990)	133
13. *Double Impact* (Columbia, 1991)	132
13. *Out for Justice* (Warner Bros., 1991)	132
15. *The Horror Show* (MGM, 1989)	129

8 Improbable
Movie Parents

1. Cary Grant played the son of Jessie Royce Landis in *North by Northwest* (1959). At the time, he was 55 and she was 54.
2. Angela Lansbury was 37 when she played the mother of 34-year-old Laurence Harvey in *The Manchurian Candidate* (1962).
3. Blair Brown was 39 and Mark Harmon was 36 when they played mother and son in *Stealing Home* (1988).
4. Lainie Kazan, 45, played the mother of Bette Midler, 42, in *Beaches* (1988).
5. Sean Connery, 58, played the father of Dustin Hoffman, 51, in *Family Business* (1989).
6. In *The Graduate* (1967), 25-year-old Katharine Ross played the daughter of Anne Bancroft, who was 36.
7. In *Indiana Jones and the Last Crusade* (1989), Sean Connery, 58, played the father of Harrison Ford, 46.
8. Anne Ramsey, 58, played the mother of Nick Nolte, 46, in *Weeds* (1987).

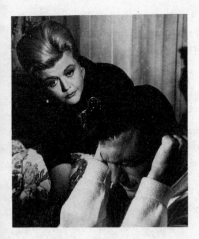

In *The Manchurian Candidate* (1962), 37-year-old Angela Lansbury played the mother of 34-year-old Laurence Harvey.

11 Nonperformers
Who Acted in Movies

It is common practice for celebrities to play themselves in films. But here are eleven noted personalities who actually attempted fictional roles.

1. **MUHAMMAD ALI**

   Played the role of Gideon Jackson, the first black senator, in *Freedom Road*, a 1979 made-for-TV movie.

2. **PATRICIA NIXON**

   The future First Lady of the United States had walk-on parts in *Becky Sharp* (1936) and *Small-Town Girl* (1937).

3. **ERNEST HEMINGWAY**

   The Nobel Prize–winning author had a bit part in *The Old Man and the Sea* (1958), based on his own novella.

4. **DIONNE QUINTUPLETS**

   The much-exploited quintet appeared in the final scenes of *Country Doctor* (1936), as well as two other features and two short subjects.

5. **JULIAN BOND**

   The 1977 feature *Greased Lightning*, which was filmed in Georgia, included a brief appearance by civil rights leader Julian Bond, as well as Maynard Jackson, who was then mayor of Atlanta.

6. **LEON TROTSKY**

   Three years before he joined Lenin and the Bolsheviks in creating the first Communist state, Trotsky played the part of a nihilist in the 1914 Hollywood spy drama *My Official Wife*.

7. **JERZY KOSINSKI**

   The internationally acclaimed author gave a convincing portrayal of a Bolshevik hard-liner in *Reds* (1981).

Hemingway at the helm, during the filming of *The Old Man and the Sea*.

8. KAREEM ABDUL-JABBAR

Fought with Bruce Lee in the kung fu film *The Game of Death* (1979). Also played a pilot in *Airplane* (1980).

9. PABLO PICASSO

Appeared in a crowd scene in Jean Cocteau's *The Testament of Orpheus* (1962). Also appeared briefly in two other French films.

10. STUDS TERKEL

Author and broadcaster Terkel played a sportswriter in the 1988 feature *Eight Men Out*.

11. REX REED

Film critic Reed played the role of Myron Breckenridge in *Myra Breckenridge* (1970).

NOTE: For more nonperformers who acted in movies, see *The Book of Lists #3*, pp. 215–16.

Henry Mancini's
10 Hardest Films to Score

Cleveland-born composer Henry Mancini won Academy Awards (with Johnny Mercer) for "Moon River," from *Breakfast at Tiffany's*, and "Days of Wine and Roses," from the film of the same title. He also won Academy Awards for best song and score for *Victor/Victoria*. He has been composing film scores since the early 1950s.

1. *Ghost Dad* (1990)
2. *The Great Imposter* (1960)
3. *Lifeforce* (1985)
4. *Mommie Dearest* (1981)
5. *Silver Streak* (1976)
6. *The Hawaiians* (1970)
7. *Soldier in the Rain* (1963)
8. *The Glass Menagerie* (1987)
9. *The Great Waldo Pepper* (1975)
10. *The White Dawn* (1974)

— Exclusive for *The Book of Lists*

11 Highest-Rated Episodes of TV Series

1. *M*A*S*H* Special (February 28, 1983)

   It is the summer of 1953 and the Korean War is winding down. Despite a last-minute escalation of fighting and increase of casualties, the members of the 4077th prepare themselves for leave-taking from one another and for their return to a life without war. Average audience: 60.2 percent.

2. *Dallas* (November 21, 1980)

   Oil magnate J. R. Ewing has collected so many enemies that when somebody shoots him, the list of suspects is almost endless. In this episode, the killer is revealed. Average audience: 53.3 percent.

3. *The Fugitive* (August 29, 1967)

   Dr. Kimble returns to the small Indiana town that he fled after his wife was murdered. Who really killed Helen Kimble? Was it the one-armed man, Kimble himself, or someone else? The answer is revealed at last. Average audience: 45.9 percent.

4. *Cheers* (May 20, 1993)

   Barmaid Diane Chambers returns tp Cheers but *doesn't* marry Sam; Rebecca Howe, to her horror, marries the plumber; and Woody takes his seat on the city council. The regulars go home, and Sam turns out the lights at the bar. Average audience: 45.5 percent.

5. *Ed Sullivan* (February 9, 1964)

   The Beatles make their live American television debut. Average audience: 45.3 percent.

6. *Beverly Hillbillies* (January 8, 1964)

   The Clampetts decide to have their dinner prepared for them. They call the Beverly Caterers, mistakenly believing that "Beverly" is a friendly widow who will happily prepare the "vittles" they want. Average audience: 44.0 percent.

7. *Gunsmoke* (February 13, 1960)

   Two cattle drives are racing toward Dodge, both trying to be the first to reach the town that season. Their paths are blocked by a rain-widened river. The two trail bosses meet there and find a ragged old cow that could guide one of the herds across. The bosses, however, can't agree which herd it will be. Average audience: 43.9 percent.

8. *Wagon Train* (January 20, 1960)

A widow, played by Jean Hagen, joins the wagon train. She is beautiful, but filled with bitterness. She distrusts all men and has raised her young son to look down on those who are weak. A fellow passenger seeks to discover the cause of her anger. Average audience: 43.7 percent.

9. *Bonanza* (March 8, 1964)

Working as an acting deputy, Hoss is sent to a town to pick up a prisoner. Unfortunately, he travels to the wrong town and finds himself charged with bank robbery. Average audience: 41.6 percent.

10. *The Cosby Show* (January 22, 1987)

Cliff gives Theo a lesson in negotiating when they go to replace the family station wagon. Vanessa advises Rudy on how to improve her report for school. Average audience: 41.3 percent.

11. *All in the Family* (January 8, 1972)

Edith goes through menopause with some interesting personality changes. Average audience: 40.7 percent.

10 Most Violent Television Series

The National Committee on Television Violence monitors television series and movies and calculates the number of acts of violence based on a weighted scale. For example, an angry push or shove counts as only ⅓ of an act of violence, whereas a murder, attempted murder, rape, or suicide counts as 1⅔ acts of violence.

Fall 1980	Violent Acts per Hour
1. *Enos*	22
1. *Sheriff Lobo*	22
3. *BJ and the Bear*	17
3. *Hart to Hart*	17
5. *The Incredible Hulk*	16
6. *Charlie's Angels*	14
6. *Hill Street Blues*	14
8. *Vegas*	13
9. *Dukes of Hazzard*	11
9. *Nero Wolfe*	11

Fall 1984	Violent Acts per Hour
1. *Hammer*	55
2. *A-Team*	54
3. *V*	52
4. *Matt Houston*	40
5. *Cover-Up*	38
6. *Fall Guy*	37
7. *Airwolf*	33
7. *Hunter*	33
9. *Street Hawk*	31
9. *Scarecrow & Mrs. King*	31

Fall 1992	Violent Acts per Hour
1. *Young Indiana Jones*	60
2. *Covington Cross*	45
3. *The Hat Squad*	42
3. *Raven*	42
5. *Angel Street*	41
6. *Top Cops*	38
7. *The Edge*	33
8. *FBI: The Untold Stories*	28
9. *Final Appeal*	27
10. *Secret Service*	24

16 Top-Rated Nonseries Shows on TV

	Average Audience (%)
1. *Roots*, pt. VIII (Jan. 30, 1977)	51.1
2. *Super Bowl XVI game* (Jan. 24, 1982)	49.1
3. *Super Bowl XVII game* (Jan. 30, 1983)	48.6
4. *Super Bowl XX game* (Jan. 26, 1986)	48.3
5. *Gone With the Wind*, pt. 1 (Nov. 7, 1976)	47.7
6. *Gone With the Wind*, pt. 2 (Nov. 8, 1976)	47.4
7. *Super Bowl XII game* (Jan. 15, 1978)	47.2
8. *Super Bowl XIII game* (Jan. 21, 1979)	47.1
9. *Bob Hope Christmas Show* (Jan. 15, 1970)	46.6
10. *Super Bowl XVIII game* (Jan. 22, 1984)	46.4

10.	*Super Bowl XIX game* (Jan. 20, 1985)	46.4
12.	*Super Bowl XIV game* (Jan. 20, 1980)	46.3
13.	ABC Theater — *The Day After* (Nov. 20, 1983)	46.0
14.	*Roots*, pt. VI (Jan. 28, 1977)	45.9
15.	*Super Bowl XXI game* (Jan. 25, 1987)	45.8
16.	*Super Bowl XXVII game* (Jan. 31, 1993)	45.1

SOURCE: A. C. Nielsen.

4 Performers Who
Have Won the Most Emmys

1. DINAH SHORE (8)

   Best Female Singer (1954); Best Female Singer (1955); Best Female Personality — Continuing Performance (1956); Best Continuing Performance (Female) in a Series by a Comedienne, Singer, Hostess, Dancer, MC, Narrator, Panelist, or any Person Who Essentially Plays Herself (1957, *The Dinah Shore Chevy Show*); Best Performance by an Actress (Continuing Character) in a Musical or Variety Series (1958–1959, *The Dinah Shore Chevy Show*); Outstanding Program Achievement in Daytime (1972–1973, *Dinah's Place*); Best Host or Hostess in a Talk, Service, or Variety Show (1973–1974, *Dinah's Place*); Outstanding Host or Hostess in a Talk, Service, or Variety Show (1975–1976, *Dinah!*).

2. EDWARD ASNER (7)

   Outstanding Performance by an Actor in a Supporting Role in Comedy (1970–1971, *The Mary Tyler Moore Show*); Outstanding Performance by an Actor in a Supporting Role in Comedy (1971–1972, *The Mary Tyler Moore Show*); Outstanding Continued Performance by a Supporting Actor in a Comedy Series (1974–1975, *The Mary Tyler Moore Show*); Outstanding Lead Actor for a Single Performance in a Drama or Comedy Series (1975–1976, *Rich Man, Poor Man*); Outstanding Single Performance by a Supporting Actor in a Comedy or Drama Series (1976–1977, *Roots*, part one); Outstanding Lead Actor in a Drama Series (1977–1978, *Lou Grant*); Outstanding Lead Actor in a Dramatic Series (1979–1980, *Lou Grant*).

3. ART CARNEY (6)

   Best Series Supporting Actor (1953, *The Jackie Gleason Show*); Best Supporting Actor in a Regular Series (1954, *The Jackie Gleason Show*); Best Actor in a Supporting Role (1955, *The Honeymooners*); Special Classification of Individual Achievement (1966–1967, *The Jackie Gleason Show*); Special Classification of Individual Achievement (1967–1968, *The Jackie Gleason Show*); Outstanding Supporting Actor in a Limited Series or a Special (1983–1984, *Terrible Joe Moran*).

3. MARY TYLER MOORE (6)

Outstanding Continued Performance by an Actress in a Series — Lead (1963–1964, *The Dick Van Dyke Show*); Outstanding Continued Performance by an Actress in a Leading Role in a Comedy Series (1965–1966, *The Dick Van Dyke Show*); Outstanding Continued Performance by an Actress in a Leading Role in a Comedy Series (1972–1973, *The Mary Tyler Moore Show*); Best Lead Actress in a Comedy Series (1973–1974, *The Mary Tyler Moore Show*); Actress of the Year — Series (1973–1974, *The Mary Tyler Moore Show*); Outstanding Lead Actress in a Comedy Series (1975–1976, *The Mary Tyler Moore Show*).

9 Recent Cases of TV Censorship

1. *Quantum Leap* (1991)

NBC objected to the script of an episode about a gay military cadet who contemplated suicide. A compromise was reached in which the character was made older so that at least the issue of teenage suicide could be avoided.

2. *Sisters* (1991)

The first episode of this NBC drama opened with four sisters in a steam bath discussing multiple orgasms. NBC deleted the dialogue even though Warren Littlefield, president of NBC Entertainment, had stated, "Corporately, we believe in orgasms."

3. *The Last Temptation of Christ* (1989)

This controversial film directed by Martin Scorsese was shown on the cable network Cinemax. However, under pressure from Christian fundamentalists, Multimedia Cablevision blacked out the showings in Kansas, Oklahoma, and North Carolina. The film was also kept off the air, after one showing, in Bossier City, Louisiana.

4. *Today* (1989)

NBC News officials deleted the following three sentences of a report about the use of substandard materials in U.S. industry: "Recently, General Electric engineers discovered they had a big problem. One out of three bolts from one of their major suppliers was bad. Even more alarming, GE accepted the bad bolts without any certification of compliance for eight years." NBC is owned by General Electric.

5. *Thirtysomething* (1989)

ABC censors forced producers to dub in new dialogue when main characters Hope and Michael argued politics and implied that car companies lobby against costly safety regulations, forsaking safety for profit. The censors did not want to alienate auto advertisers.

6. *Freedom Fest* (1988)

This rock concert on behalf of Nelson Mandela, who was then jailed in South Africa, was aired live in Great Britain. The BBC cut away frequently when the performers gave political speeches, but Fox Television went further, systematically deleting all political references when the program aired in the United States.

7. *Mighty Mouse* (1988)

This cartoon was among programs targeted by the Reverend Donald Wildmon and his pressure group, the Coalition of Christian Leaders for Responsible Television. Wildmon convinced CBS to edit out a scene in which the mouse sniffs a "powdery substance," an action that might be mistaken for snorting cocaine, although CBS contended he was sniffing flowers or cheese.

8. *Valerie* (1987)

An episode of this situation comedy was canceled by the NBC affiliate in Albany, New York, because the show dealt with a teenager who wanted to purchase condoms before a date.

9. *Spycatcher* (1987)

This nonfiction book by retired British spy Peter Wright was banned in Great Britain but became a best-seller in the United States. When Britain's Paul Nicholls began to read from the

Mighty Mouse — flying high?

book during the televised coverage of a Liberal Party meeting, BBC censors pulled the plug on the broadcast.

NOTE: For more cases of TV censorship, see *The Book of Lists #1*, pp. 216–17.

10 Classic Unsold TV Pilots

Each year the networks hear 4,000 ideas for TV series, commission hundreds of scripts, and greenlight about ninety pilots. Of those pilots, perhaps twenty will become series, and of those, less than five will survive to see their first birthdays. Here then are memorable pilots that *didn't* sell.

1. PESTS (NBC, 1992)

   The misadventures of a Nebraska man sharing a New York apartment with three three-foot-tall talking cockroaches.

2. *Steele Justice* (NBC, 1992)

   A tough cop (Robert Taylor) in a *Blade Runner*–like future is able to bring his dead son's favorite toy, a steel dinosaur, to life as a huge crime-fighter that likes to stomp bad guys.

3. *Danger Team* (ABC, 1991)

   The adventures of an inexperienced female private eye who solves crimes with the help of three animated clay figures.

4. *K-9000* (Fox, 1990)

   An irreverent cop (Chris Mulkey) is telepathically linked to his talking, bionic police dog, a canine partner who also doubles as a cellular phone.

5. *Poochinski* (NBC, 1990)

   Peter Boyle is Poochinski, an ill-mannered cop who is gunned down in the line of duty — and is reincarnated as a crime-fighting, flatulent, old English bulldog.

6. *Infiltrator* (CBS, 1987)

   Scott Bakula is a wacky scientist working on a transporter beam who inadvertently beams himself into a sexy female scientist's spy satellite — which is then absorbed into his molecules. Now, whenever he gets mad, he turns into a neon-and-metal Gobot that fights crime.

7. *Dr. Franken* (NBC, 1980)

   Robert Vaughn is a mad scientist who creates a monster out of body parts stolen from an organ bank. Now the sensitive monster (Robert Perault) gets "vibes" from his pilfered parts and seeks out the families of the organ donors to help them with their problems.

8. SAMURAI (NBC, 1979)

Joe Penny stars as a half-Asian, half-Caucasian district attorney by day and a sword-wielding samurai warrior by night.

9. *Ultimate Impostor* (NBC, 1979)

A secret agent (Joseph Hacker) whose brain is erased by the enemy has a computer implanted in his skull that allows him to be programmed with a new personality each week. There's just one catch — his personality fades after seventy-two hours.

10. *Where's Everett?* (CBS, 1966)

Alan Alda is a father who goes to fetch his morning paper and finds an invisible alien baby on his doorstep.

SOURCE: Lee Goldberg, author of the book *Unsold Television Pilots 1955–1990*, McFarland & Co. Publishers, Box 611, Jefferson, NC 28640.

15 Recording Artists with the Most Multiplatinum Albums

	No. of Albums
1. Elvis Presley	12
2. The Beatles	11
3. Led Zeppelin	9
4. Billy Joel	8
5. Aerosmith	7
5. Alabama	7
5. Journey	7
5. Bruce Springsteen	7
5. Barbra Streisand	7
10. AC/DC	6
10. Chicago	6
10. Earth, Wind & Fire	6
10. Heart	6
10. Madonna	6
10. The Rolling Stones	6

NOTE: A multiplatinum album is one that has sold 2 million copies.

SOURCE: Recording Industry Association of America, Inc., 1992.

Elvis the Pelvis.

14 Musical Artists Who Have Won the Most Grammys

1.	Sir George Solti	30
2.	Vladimir Horowitz	25
2.	Quincy Jones	25
4.	Henry Mancini	20
5.	Stevie Wonder	17
6.	Leonard Bernstein	16
7.	Aretha Franklin	15
7.	John Williams	15
9.	Itzhak Perlman	14
10.	Ella Fitzgerald	13
10.	Leontyne Price	13
10.	Robert Shaw	13
13.	Michael Jackson	12
13.	Paul Simon	12*

* Includes four Grammys earned as a member of Simon and Garfunkel.

NOTE: Sir George Solti, conductor of the Chicago Symphony, is the only person to win awards for ten straight years (1974–1983).

20 Musical Artists and Groups Who Have Never Won a Grammy

The Grammy Awards are decided by the 6,000 voting members of the National Academy of Recording Arts and Sciences. Some of the artists below received honorary prizes, but none of them won in a competitive category.

1.	The Beach Boys	11.	Van Morrison
2.	Chuck Berry	12.	Buck Owens
3.	Pablo Casals	13.	Santana
4.	Patsy Cline	14.	The Rolling Stones
5.	Sam Cooke	15.	Diana Ross
6.	Bing Crosby	16.	Rod Stewart
7.	Fats Domino	17.	The Supremes
8.	Benny Goodman	18.	The Talking Heads
9.	Jimi Hendrix	19.	Lawrence Welk
10.	Led Zeppelin	20.	Hank Williams, Sr.

NOTE: Elvis Presley won three Grammys — all in the religious categories, including Best Sacred Performance in 1967 for *How Great Thou Art*.

Dr. Demento's *11* Worst Song Titles of All Time

Radio personality Dr. Demento's private collection of more than 200,000 records is said to be one of the world's largest. He puts his library of discs to use on "The Dr. Demento Show," which is heard on 200 radio stations in the United States and on the Armed Forces Radio Network. All of the following are actual song titles from records in the Doctor's archives.

1. "Mama Get Your Hammer (There's a Fly on Baby's Head)," by the Bobby Peterson Quintet.
2. "When There's Tears in the Eyes of a Potato," by the Hoosier Hot Shots.
3. "I Like Bananas Because They Have No Bones," by the Hoosier Hot Shots.
4. "She Was Bitten on the Udder by an Adder," by Homer & Jethro.
5. "A Bowl of Chop Suey and You-ey," by Sam Robbins & His Hotel McAlpin Orchestra.
6. "I've Got Tears in My Ears from Lying on My Back in Bed While I Cry over You," by Homer & Jethro.
7. "Santa Claus Has Got the AIDS This Year," by Tiny Tim.
8. "I'd Rather Have a Bottle in Front of Me (Than a Frontal Lobotomy)," by Randy Hanzlick, M.D. (Dr. Demento adds: "[Hanzlick] is, or was as of 1980, a real internist, practicing in Atlanta, writing songs for a hobby. This record had little commercial success but became, and remains, an often requested item on my show.")
9. "It's So Hard To Say I Love You (When You're Sitting on My Face)," by Marty and the Muff Tones.
10. "Jesus Loves Me (But He Can't Stand You)," by the Austin Lounge Lizards.
11. "Kill a Tree for Christ," by Celtic Elvis.

— Exclusive for *The Book of Lists*

NOTE: For more awful song titles, see *The Book of Lists #1*, p. 178.

23 Early Names of Famous Music Groups

In the music business, you have to hit not only the right chords but also the right name. Here's a quiz to test your knowledge.

Carl and the Passions.

1. Angel and the Snakes
2. Composition of Sound
3. Big Thing
4. Artistics

5. Carl and the Passions
6. Primettes
7. Tom and Jerry
8. Johnny and the Moondogs

9. Caesar and Cleo
10. Honolulu Fruit Gum Band

11. Paramours
12. Earth
13. Bangs
14. Beefeaters
15. Falling Spikes

16. Sparrow
17. My Backyard

18. The New Journeymen
19. The Elgins
20. The Four Aces of Western Swing
21. The Golliwogs
22. The New Yardbirds
23. The Golden Gate Rhythm Section

a. Bangles
b. Beach Boys
c. Beatles
d. Bill Haley and His Comets
e. Black Sabbath
f. Blondie
g. Byrds
h. Champagne Music Makers (Lawrence Welk)
i. Chicago
j. Creedence Clearwater Revival
k. Depeche Mode
l. Journey
m. Led Zeppelin
n. Lynyrd Skynyrd
o. Mamas and the Papas
p. Righteous Brothers
q. Simon and Garfunkel
r. Sonny and Cher
s. Steppenwolf
t. Supremes
u. Talking Heads
v. Temptations
w. Velvet Underground

Answers: 1 (f), 2 (k), 3 (i), 4 (u), 5 (b), 6 (t), 7 (q), 8 (c), 9 (r), 10 (h), 11 (p), 12 (e), 13 (a), 14 (g), 15 (w), 16 (s), 17 (n), 18 (o), 19 (v), 20 (d), 21 (j), 22 (m), 23 (l).

Terry Riley's First Choice in *10* Categories of Twentieth-Century Music

California-born Terry Riley launched what is now known as the Minimalist movement with his groundbreaking classic *In C* composed in 1964. His work has been a seminal influence on the New Age movement and on many other musicians, both classical and pop. In 1970 he went to India to study Raga with the renowned vocal master Pandit Pran Nath, with whom he has frequently appeared in concert. Riley taught at Mills College in the 1970s, and began working with the Kronos string quartet, an association that has produced numerous critically acclaimed works. In 1989 he founded the new performance ensemble Khayal. A new major orchestral work written for the Saint Louis Symphony Orchestra, *The Jade Palace Orchestral Dances*, was commissioned by Carnegie Hall for their centennial celebration 1990/1991.

1. Best orchestral work: Bela Bartók's *Concerto for Orchestra*
2. Most innovative composer: LaMonte Young
3. Best American composer: George Gershwin
4. Best piano piece: Samuel Barber's *Piano Sonata*
5. Best songwriting team: Lennon/McCartney
6. Greatest piano improvisers: Art Tatum and Gonzalo Rubalcaba
7. Best vocalists: Bobby McFerrin and Pandit Pran Nath
8. Best conceptual musician: Adolf Woelfli
9. Best string quartets: Bela Bartók and Terry Riley
10. Greatest jazz musician: John Coltrane

— Exclusive for *The Book of Lists*

Dudley's Moore's *5* Greatest Classical Pianists

Originally known as a cabaret pianist in England, Dudley Moore became a famous television and film comedian. Among his most popular movies are *Bedazzled, 10,* and *Arthur.* He still plays the piano regularly.

1. VLADIMIR HOROWITZ (1904–1990)

   Russian-born, became U.S. citizen in 1944.

2. JOSEF LHEVINNE (1874–1944)

   Russian-born. Lived in New York City from 1919 until his death, taught at Juilliard.

3. SVYATOSLAV T. RICHTER (1915–   )

Russian. Named People's Artist of the USSR, 1961.

4. ARTUR SCHNABEL (1882–1951)

German. Left Nazi Germany for United States in 1939, returned to Europe after World War II. Foremost interpreter of Beethoven piano works.

5. DINU LIPATTI (1917–1950)

Romanian. Prodigy whose life was cut short by a rare disease at thirty-three.

— Exclusive for *The Book of Lists*

Steve Allen's
13 Favorite Songs

Best known as a comedian and television personality, Steve Allen has been a major entertainment figure for more than thirty-five years. His list of television credits is long and includes *The Tonight Show*, *The Steve Allen Comedy Hour*, and *Meeting of Minds*. The multitalented Allen has also made his mark as an award-winning playwright and the author of forty books. As a musician, he has more than thirty record albums to his credit and has written more than 4,000 songs. Once honored by the *Guinness Book of World Records* as the most prolific composer of modern times, Allen created such popular standards as "This Could Be the Start of Something Big" and "Impossible."

ALLEN NOTES: Although almost all lists are numbered, I wish to emphasize that I consider all the below melodies of equal quality.

1. "Stardust"
2. "Laura"
3. "Tenderly"
4. "Body and Soul"
5. "Misty"
6. "The Song Is You"
7. "I Can't Get Started with You"
8. "Yours Is My Heart Alone" (by Franz Lehar)
9. "Sophisticated Lady"
10. "You Go to My Head"
11. "After You've Gone"
12. "April in Paris"
13. "More Than You Know"

— Exclusive for *The Book of Lists*

Wynton Marsalis's
14 Greatest Jazz Musicians
in History

Wynton Marsalis, celebrated American jazz trumpeter, was the first musician ever to win Grammys in both the jazz and classical fields in one year. He is from a family of talented musicians — his father, Ellis, is a celebrated jazz pianist; his mother, Dolores, once sang with jazz groups; his older brother, Branford, is the well-known sax player who leads the band on *The Tonight Show*, with Jay Leno; one younger brother, Delfeayo, is a trombonist; and another younger brother, Jason, is a drummer. Marsalis has called jazz "America's classical music" and "the ultimate twentieth century music."

1. Duke Ellington (and his orchestra)
2. Louis Armstrong
3. Jelly Roll Morton
4.–5. Charlie Parker, Kenny Clarke
6. Art Tatum
7. Thelonious Monk
8.–9. Jo Jones, Lester Young
10.–11. John Coltrane, Elvin Jones
12.–13. Miles Davis, Paul Chambers
14. Charles Mingus

— Exclusive for *The Book of Lists*

Leonard Feather's
All-Star Jazz Band

One of the foremost authorities on jazz, Feather has written more than ten books and countless articles on the subject. In addition, he is an eminent composer who has written and arranged music for Duke Ellington, Louis Armstrong, and a host of other jazz notables. Feather is a frequent commentator on, and producer of, television and radio programs on jazz.

1. *Leader, composer:* Duke Ellington or Toshiko Akiyoshi (Akiyoshi, who co-leads a band with Lew Tabackin, is the most important new composer since Ellington).
2. *Trumpets:* Louis Armstrong, Bix Beiderbecke, Roy Eldridge, Dizzy Gillespie, Miles Davis, Wynton Marsalis.
3. *Trombones:* Jack Teagarden, J. J. Johnson.
4. *Saxes*: Benny Carter, Johnny Hodges, Charlie Parker, altos;

Charlie Parker (left) with Dizzy Gillespie (center) and John Coltrane (right), 1950.

Coleman Hawkins, Lester Young, John Coltrane, tenors; Harry Carney, baritone.

5. *Piano:* Art Tatum, Dick Hyman, Dorothy Donegan.
6. *Guitar:* Charlie Christian.
7. *Bass:* Charles Mingus, Nils Henning Orsted-Pedersen (the Danish virtuoso).
8. *Drums:* Sid Catlett.
9. *Singers:* Billie Holiday, Sarah Vaughan, Ella Fitzgerald, Joe Williams.
10. *Guest soloists:* Artie Shaw, Benny Goodman, clarinet; Joe Venuti, violin; Lionel Hampton, Red Norvo, Milt Jackson, vibraphone; Lew Tabackin, flute; Count Basie, organ; Toots Thielemans, harmonica.

— Exclusive for *The Book of Lists*

Kareem Abdul-Jabbar's
10 Greatest Jazz Artists
in History

At seven feet two inches, Kareem Abdul-Jabbar was a star of the Los Angeles Lakers for thirteen years, and remains one of the greatest basketball players of all time. Jazz has been Abdul-Jabbar's hobby ever since he first borrowed records from earlier basketball wizard Wilt Chamberlain's collection and frequented New York's leading jazz clubs.

1. Thelonious Monk
2. Miles Davis
3. John Coltrane
4. Dizzy Gillespie
5. Duke Ellington
6. Louis Armstrong
7. Lester Young
8. Billie Holiday
9. Charles Mingus
10. Charlie Parker

— Exclusive for *The Book of Lists*

Allen Ginsberg's
11 Greatest Blues Songs

Allen Ginsberg, one of the original Beat Generation poets, has taught, lectured, and read his poetry all over the world. Among his books are *Howl and Other Poems* (1955), *Reality Sandwiches* (1965), and *First Blues: Songs* (1982).

1. "James Alley Blues," by Richard "Rabbit" Brown
2. "Washington D.C. Hospital Center Blues," by Skip James
3. "Jelly Bean Blues," by Ma Rainey
4. "See See Rider Blues," by Ma Rainey
5. "Young Woman's Blues," by Bessie Smith
6. "Poor Me" (1934 version), by Charlie Patton
7. "Black Girl," by Leadbelly
8. "Levee Camp Moan Blues," by Texas Alexander
9. "Last Fair Deal Gone Down," by Robert Johnson
10. "I'm So Lonesome I Could Cry," by Hank Williams, Sr.
11. "Idiot Wind," by Bob Dylan

— Exclusive for *The Book of Lists*

Mitch Ryder's
11 All-Time-Favorite Songs

Mitch Ryder and the Detroit Wheels rocketed to the top of music charts in the 1960s with hits like "Devil with a Blue Dress On/Good Golly Miss Molly," "Jenny Take a Ride," and "Sock It to Me Baby." The all-action Mitch Ryder is considered one of the best of the white rhythm and blues singers. When the group broke up, Ryder temporarily retired but later staged a solo comeback with such recordings as "How I Spent My Vacation" and "Never Kick a Sleeping Dog."

1.–2. "The Night Tripper" and "Walk on Gilded Splinters," by Dr. John
   3. "I'm So Lonesome I Could Cry," by Hank Williams, Sr.
   4. "I've Got a Right to Trust My Baby," by Sonny Boy Williamson
   5. "Gimme a Pigfoot," by Bessie Smith
   6. "Fool in Love," by Ike and Tina Turner
   7. "Prisoner of Love," by James Brown
   8. "Fever," by Little Willie John
   9. "Bring It on Home," by Sonny Boy Williamson
  10. "That's How Heartaches Are Made," by Baby Washington
  11. "Way Over There," by Smokey Robinson and the Miracles

— Exclusive for *The Book of Lists*

Jonathan Richman's *11* Favorite Singers

Known primarily as a live performer, Jonathan Richman currently plays more than 150 shows a year worldwide, including standing-room-only performances to audiences in New York, Los Angeles, San Francisco, London, and Barcelona. While with his group the Modern Lovers, he wrote the song "Roadrunner" for which he is well known. His recent records include *I, Jonathan; Having a Party with Jonathan Richman*; and the unexpected *Jonathan Goes Country*, all on Rounder Records.

1. Van Morrison
2. Marty Robbins
3. Skeeter Davis
4. John Lee Hooker
5. Nicolas Reyes of the Gypsy Kings
6. Dion
7. Ted Hawkins (sings on the boardwalk in Venice, California)
8. Nana Mouskouri
9. Desmond Dekker
10. Maurice Chevalier
11. Mary Wells

RICHMAN NOTES: In limiting this list to eleven singers, I've left out many of my favorites. I've left out lead singers for vocal groups; for example, Jay Siegal of the Tokens, Frankie Lyman and the Teenagers, Nolan Strong and the Diablos, etc., because that would be a whole other category.

— Exclusive for *The Book of Lists*

Afrika Bambaataa's
10 Greatest African-Americans

Recording artist and former disc jockey Afrika Bambaataa is the Godfather of Hip-Hop (underground urban music, including break dancing, rap music, and funk). He calls himself "an elder statesman of ghetto affairs" with "the express intention of making music, not violence." Among his best-selling records are *Planet Rock* and *Looking for the Perfect Beat.*

1. Most Honorable Elijah Muhammad
2. Honorable Minister Louis Farrakhan
3. Minister Malcolm X
4. Reverend Martin L. King
5. Reverend Al Sharpton
6. James Brown
7. Sly Stone
8. Sister Souljah
9. Sojourner Truth
10. Huey P. Newton

— Exclusive for *The Book of Lists*

The Post-Music Careers of
10 Rock-and-Roll One-Hit
Wonders

According to Steven Rosen, editor and publisher of *One Shot: The Magazine of One-Hit Wonders*, a one-hit wonder had one song that made the Top 40 of *Billboard* magazine's pop singles chart and never made the top 100 again. Sample copies of *One Shot* are available for four dollars from One Shot Enterprises, Box 145, Contract Station 6, 1525 Sherman Street, Denver, CO 80203.

1. THE TUNE WEAVERS: "Happy, Happy Birthday Baby," number 5 in 1957.

   Gilbert Lopez, tenor singer: professional mediator.

2. WINK MARTINDALE: "Deck of Cards," number 7 in 1959. TV game-show host.

3. THE CAPRIS: "There's a Moon Out Tonight," number 3 in 1961.

Nick Santo (real last name Santamaria), lead singer: police officer (retired). Mike Mincieli, first tenor: bus driver.

4. JAN BRADLEY: "Mama Didn't Lie," number 14 in 1963. Social worker.

5. THE RAN-DELLS: "Martian Hop," number 16 in 1963.

Steve Rappaport, vocalist: owns company that makes discs that both play music and hold computer data.

6. BARRY MCGUIRE: "The Eve of Destruction," number 1 in 1965.

Christian music singer.

7. COUNT FIVE: "Psychotic Reaction," number 5 in 1966.

John Michalski, lead guitar: landscapist. Kenn Ellner, lead singer: lawyer.

8. LEMON PIPERS: "Green Tambourine," number 1 in 1968.

R. G. Nave, lead guitar: financial services.

9. PEOPLE: "I Love You," number 16 in 1968.

Robbie Levin: clothing manufacturer.

10. C. W. MCCALL: "Convoy," number 1 in 1976.

Real name William Fries: became mayor of Ouray, Colorado. (Note — had one preceding song, "Wolf Creek Pass," that made number 40 in 1975.)

Adam Block's Secret Subjects of *15* Pop Songs

Adam Block is a San Francisco–based investigative journalist and pop-culture critic whose work has been featured in the *London Observer*, *California* magazine, *Mother Jones*, *Image*, *Parenting*, and *Manshots*. He is also a columnist for the *The Advocate* and has contributed annotated lists of "homo-negative and pro-homo pop songs" to *The Alyson Almanac*.

1. "You've Got to Hide Your Love Away," THE BEATLES

In the spring of 1963, shortly after the birth of his son Julian, John Lennon took a brief holiday in Barcelona with the Beatles' gay manager, Brian Epstein. Epstein was clearly enamored of Lennon, and more than one biography (and a brilliant short film inspired by their speculations, *The Hours and Times*) suggests that there, in Spain, Epstein made a last, valiant effort to consummate their relationship. After they returned, Lennon wrote this ballad.

Although Lennon never addressed the subject, and the song wasn't recorded until February of 1965 (for the *Help* soundtrack), gay British singer/songwriter Tom Robinson was always convinced that it was Lennon's gift to Epstein — penned from the closeted manager's perspective. Robinson took its title for his cabaret show of "gay" pop songs.

2. "Sexy Sadie," THE BEATLES

In February 1968, with "Magical Mystery Tour" topping the U.S. charts, the Beatles flew to India to study meditation at the Maharishi Mahesh Yogi's ashram in Rishikesh. Ringo was the first to bail, comparing the place to "a Butkins Holiday camp." By the time a disillusioned Lennon packed his bags, he was already writing his pointed assault on the bubbly, rotund little holy man. Once he was dubbed Sexy Sadie, it was hard to think of him as anyone else.

3. "Went to See the Gypsy," BOB DYLAN

As one British critic astutely noted, "Bob Dylan wanted to be Elvis Presley — but there was an opening for a Woody Guthrie — so he took the gig." Indeed, Dylan was always a fan of the King's, claiming that his favorite cover of one of his own songs was the one Presley had done: "Tomorrow Is a Long Time," for the soundtrack of the movie *Spinout*. In 1970 Dylan recorded this probably apocryphal account of his meeting with Elvis. In Dylan's account, their conversation is epochally succinct: " 'How are you?' he said to me. I said it back to him."

4. "Chelsea Hotel," LEONARD COHEN

Though he has lately told interviewers that he regrets having let slip that this song was written to Janis Joplin, it's a detail he has regularly announced during concerts in recent years. The tawdry and faintly self-mocking account is set at the notorious New York Chelsea Hotel (where Bob Dylan wrote "Sad-Eyed Lady of the Lowlands," and Sid Vicious and Nancy Spungen both died). Cohen recalls, " 'You, giving me head on the unmade bed / While the limousines wait in the street' . . . That was called love for the workers in song — probably still is for those of them left . . . 'You told me again you preferred handsome men / But for me you would make an exception.' " Then he reminds Joplin, "You said, 'Well, never mind — / We are ugly — but we have the music.' "

5. "You're So Vain," CARLY SIMON

Upon release of this radio hit, the guessing game over who it was about became a hot topic in the pop press and gossip columns. The speculation fueled the song's success and undoubtedly encouraged Carly to remain cagey. A surprising number of people took it to be directed at Mick Jagger, which would signal a sense of humor in him hardly suggested by the lyrics, since he sang backup on the cut. After milking the mystery, Simon finally confessed, "Though it's about a lot of vain men I've known, there is nothing in the lyric which isn't true of Warren Beatty." As the song topped the charts, Simon wed James Taylor — who was himself the subject of many of singer Joni Mitchell's love (and hate) songs. In one, she wrote of "Dreaming of the pleasure I'm going to have/Watching your hairline recede (my vain darling)."

6. "How Do You Sleep?," JOHN LENNON

In the wake of the Beatles' split, Paul McCartney adopted a faintly pompous and condescending attitude toward John and Yoko. When he issued his LP *Ram*, the cover featured gentleman farmer Paul hugging a sheep, while in "Too Many People," he sang to his former partner as if he were chucking him under the chin: "You took your lucky break, and broke it in two. / Now what can be done for you?"

Lennon responded with venom. With laconic rage he punned off two of Paul's song titles, singing, "The only thing you've done was 'Yesterday,' / And since you've gone you're 'Just another day.' " With the LP, Lennon included a photo parodying *Ram*'s cover: Lennon hugging an immense hog.

James Taylor with his wife, Carly Simon. She wrote "You're So Vain" about actor Warren Beatty; singer Joni Mitchell wrote numerous songs to her own "vain darling" — James Taylor — on her album *Court and Spark.*

7. "Of Missing Persons" and "Rosie," JACKSON BROWNE

When Browne's friend Lowell George — the leader of Little Feat — died, Browne wrote the song "Of Missing Persons" to George's young daughter.

A more obscure and remarkable coded tune was written with his roadie, Donald Miller. At first blush, "Rosie" reads like a musician's touching ode to a loyal wife: "Rosie — you're alright / You wear my ring. / When you hold me tight, / I can almost sing . . . Looks like it's you and me again tonight, Rosie." But just who is Rosie? The singer's left hand.

8. "Space Monkey," PATTI SMITH

The godmother of punk, who twined the visionary poetry of Arthur Rimbaud with gutsy garage rock, penned this tune for a boyfriend who took his stage name from Rimbaud's male lover's: Tom Verlaine, founder of the band Television.

9. "Sweet Home Alabama," LYNYRD SKYNYRD

When Neil Young wrote the self-righteous whine "Southern Man," Ronnie Van Sant roared back with this barn-burning screed, blistering at the expatriate Canadian, "Mr. Young should remember / Southern man don't want him around." Van Sant's band was shattered in a plane crash. The song survives.

10. "New York," THE SEX PISTOLS

In an act of near-oedipal vengeance, the London punk combo took on the band that their manager, Malcolm McLaren, had previously handled: the New York Dolls. Johnny Rotten snarled in a pastiche of the New York Dolls' lyrics, "You're just an imitation — from New York . . . Poor little faggot: seal it with a kiss / Still high on those pills . . . looking for the dolls."

Ex-Dolls lead guitarist, Johnny Thunders (backed, appropriately, by Rotten's original Pistols sidemen Steve Jones and Paul Cook), responded with the song "London Boys" on Thunders's solo LP, *So Alone*. The guitarist drawled, "You need an escort to take a piss. / He holds your hand / And shakes your dick. You're a little London boy. / You think you're gonna fool me?," before unleashing a blithe copy of Rotten's sour cackle.

11. "Pretty Persuasion," R.E.M.

Asked about the inspiration for this cry of divided desire in which Michael Stipe pleads, "He's got pretty persuasion. She's got pretty persuasion. God damn my confusion . . . ," he claims it came to him in a dream "of an unknown Rolling Stones single. There was a picture on both sides of Brian

Jones looking very beautiful, sitting on the end of a pier. And as I watched the single rotate in space, on one side was written *Pretty*, and on the other — *Persuasion*." Hmmmm ... so that's what it's about.

12. "Vanz Kant Danz," JOHN FOGERTY

The founder of Creedence Clearwater Revival refused, for years, to perform any of the hits he wrote with that band — adamant that he wouldn't help send money to Creedence's label, Fantasy, and its president, Saul Zaentz. When Fogerty released this song — originally titled "Zanz Kant Danz" — which told of a remarkable pig named Zanz of whom Fogerty brayed, "Zanz can't dance — but he'll steal your money!," Zaentz took the singer to court.

Alleging libel and slander, Zaentz forced Fogerty to change the name of the porker in this dark, ebullient "children's song" by one letter, for future pressings and the history books.

13. "You Don't Move Me," KEITH RICHARDS

When Mick Jagger left the Rolling Stones to do a solo album, guitarist Richards was vocal in his criticism of what he called Jagger's Peter Pan complex. After Jagger's solo LP staggered, Richards issued his own, *Talk Is Cheap*, aimed at his past and future partner.

14. "No Vaseline," ICE CUBE

With "Message to B.A.," the outlaw rappers NWA took a shot at their former lead singer/songwriter, Ice Cube. His response helped fuel both an unprecedented editorial in *Billboard* magazine — condemning the disc's sentiments — and a call to retail chains (by Rabbi Abraham Cooper of the Simon Wiesenthal Center) asking that they refuse to carry the disc. Many were distressed by the song "Black Korea," which threatened the torching of Korean-owned stores in black neighborhoods. The Los Angeles riots (in the wake of the Rodney King verdict) delivered disturbingly on those chart-topping threats.

"No Vaseline" addressed Ice Cube's old band, but took sickening aim at NWA's manager, Jerry Heller. Cube advised his old posse, "Get rid of that devil real simple / Put a bullet in his temple / 'Cause you can't be a nigger for life, crew / With a white Jew telling you what to do." The singer insisted that the lyric was about Heller alone, and wasn't anti-Semitic.

In England, where police were prepared to destroy 23,000 copies of the record, Island Records spent $40,000 successfully defending the disc against obscenity charges, but only after dropping those two cuts from the British version.

15. "One," U2

The song seemed to be about two lovers trying to breach the distance between them, but Bono Hewson notes he "discovered" that the song was actually about a boy with AIDS addressing his father. A video, directed by Amton Corbijn, cast Bono in a black gown, singing to his own father. Upon completion, figures in management were disturbed by the sight and had Corbijn remove all shots of Bono singing in drag. The singer suggested that there were concerns that the video might imply that only gay people get AIDS.

The single was released with all proceeds earmarked for AIDS charities. The lyric "Did I disappoint you? / Or leave a bad taste in your mouth? / You act like you never had love, / And you want me to go without," makes powerful sense with the singer's explanation. The chorus — part accusation, part plea — "We're one, but we're not the same! / We've got to care for each other, carry each other," is an astonishingly potent cry against a fear so powerful it could sever a father from his ailing son. Unfortunately, shorn of its context, few have heard the song as the singer did.

— Exclusive for *The Book of Lists*

Stirring Opening Lines of *11* National Anthems

1. ALGERIA

We swear by the lightning that destroys,
By the streams of generous blood being shed
By the bright flags that wave,
Flying proudly on the high djebels
That we are in revolt . . .

2. BOLIVIA

Bolivians, propitious fate has crowned our hopes . . .

3. BURKINA FASO

Against the humiliating bondage of a thousand years
Rapacity came from afar to subjugate them
for a hundred years.
Against the cynical malice in the shape
Of neocolonialism and its petty local servants,
Many gave in and certain others resisted.

4. GUINEA-BISSAU

> Sun, sweat, verdure and sea,
> Centuries of pain and hope;
> This is the land of our ancestors.

5. LUXEMBOURG

> Where slow you see the Alzette flow,
> The Sura play wild pranks . . .

6. OMAN

> O Lord, protect for us Our Majesty the Sultan
> And the people in our land,
> With honor and peace.
> May he live long, strong and supported,
> Glorified by his leadership.
> For him we shall lay down our lives.

7. PARAGUAY

> To the peoples of unhappy America,
> Three centuries under a scepter
> oppressed.
> But one day, with their passion arising,
> 'Enough,' they said and broke the scepter.

8. SENEGAL

> Everyone strum your koras,
> Strike the balafons,
> The red lion has roared,
> The tamer of the bush with one leap,
> Has scattered the gloom.

9. TAIWAN

> The three principles of democracy our party does revere.

10. URUGUAY

> Eastern landsmen, our country or the tomb!

11. USSR

> Unbreakable union of freeborn republics,
> Great Russia has welded forever to stand;
> Thy might was created by will of our peoples,
> Now flourish in unity, great Soviet land!

Top **20** Longest-Running Broadway Plays

(as of June 1, 1993)

	Number of Performances
1. *Chorus Line* (M)	6,137
2. *Oh! Calcutta!* (M)	5,959
3. *Cats* (M)	4,445
4. *42nd Street* (M)	3,486
5. *Grease* (M)	3,388
6. *Fiddler on the Roof* (M)	3,242
7. *Life with Father*	3,224
8. *Tobacco Road*	3,182
9. *Hello, Dolly!* (M)	2,844
10. *My Fair Lady* (M)	2,717
11. *Les Miserables* (M)	2,534
12. *Annie* (M)	2,377
13. *Man of La Mancha* (M)	2,328
14. *Abie's Irish Rose*	2,327
15. *Phantom of the Opera* (M)	2,231
16. *Oklahoma!* (M)	2,212
17. *Pippin*	1,944
18. *South Pacific* (M)	1,925
19. *Magic Show*	1,920
20. *Deathtrap*	1,792

(M) denotes musical.
Source: *Variety.*

The chorus line from *Chorus Line*.

Ricky Jay's *10* Most Unusual Variety Acts of All Time

(In No Particular Order)

Ricky Jay is an author, actor, sleight-of-hand artist, and scholar of the unusual. Most of the performers listed here are included in his history of remarkable entertainers, *Learned Pigs & Fireproof Women* (New York: Villard Books, 1986).

1. TOMMY MINNOCK

   Shortly before the turn of the century this "human horse," a subject able to withstand excruciating pain, was literally nailed to a cross in a Trenton, New Jersey, music hall. While he was crucified he regaled the audience with his rendition of the popular tune *After the Ball Is Over*.

2. THEA ALBA

   This German schoolgirl wrote with both hands, both feet, and her mouth, simultaneously; for a finale she wrote ten different numerals at the same time with pieces of chalk extending from pointers on each of her fingers.

3. DANIEL WILDMAN

   This eighteenth-century equestrian beekeeper rode around the circus ring standing on the back of a horse while swarms of bees surrounded his face then moved away to specific locations at his command.

4. MATHEW BUCHINGER

   Born in Germany in 1674, this remarkable man was one of the most well known performers of his day. He played a dozen musical instruments, danced the hornpipe, and was an expert pistol shot, bowler, calligrapher, and magician. His accomplishments seem even more remarkable when one realizes he stood only twenty-eight inches high and had no arms or legs.

5. ORVILLE STAMM

   Billed as the "Strongest Boy in the World," he played the violin with an enormous bulldog suspended from the crook of his bowing arm. As an encore he lay on the ground and a piano was placed on his chest; a keyboardist stood on his thighs and pounded out the accompaniment as Orville sang "Ireland Must Be Heaven 'Cause Mother Comes from There."

6. SIGNORA GIRARDELLI

   Entertained audiences in the early nineteenth century by cooking eggs in boiling oil held in her palm, running a red-hot poker

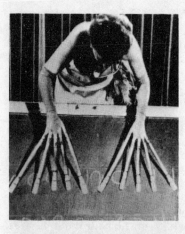

Thea Alba, "The Woman with 10 Brains," writing a different number with each of her ten fingers.

Thea Alba fashioning a different word with each hand and foot simultaneously.

over her limbs, and attending to baked goods while inside a blazing oven.

7. ARTHUR LLOYD

Astounded vaudeville fans by producing from his capacious pockets any item printed on paper. Admission tickets to the White House, membership cards to the Communist Party, and ringside tickets to the Dempsey-Carpentier championship fight were among the 15,000 items he could instantly retrieve from his clothing.

8. JEAN ROYER

A seventeenth-century native of Lyon, he swallowed an enormous quantity of water and then spewed it out in continuous graceful arcs for as long as it took to walk 200 paces or recite the Fifty-first Psalm.

9. CLARENCE WILLARD

As "Willard, the Man Who Grows," he had an act that consisted of his growing six inches in height while standing next to a volunteer from the audience. A master of manipulating his body, Willard used no trick apparatus of any kind.

10. JOSEPH PUJOL

"Le Petomane," as he was called, was the legendary French musical farter who issued sonorous but odorless notes from his body's most secret orifice.

9 Celebrities Who Were in the Circus

1. WALLACE BEERY (1885–1949), actor

While still in his teens, Beery joined the Forepaugh-Sells circus as an elephant handler. He later became head elephant trainer for the Ringling Brothers Circus. He left the circus in 1904 to embark on a stage career.

2. JOE E. BROWN (1892–1973), actor

At the age of nine, as one of the Five Marvelous Ashtons with the Sells and Downs Circus, Brown was tossed back and forth forty feet in the air. Several broken bones and bruises later, he tried professional baseball, then went into vaudeville and films.

3. YUL BRYNNER (1917–1985), actor

Brynner's early career included work as a folk singer with a traveling gypsy troupe in France. That led to an engagement as an acrobat with the French Cirque d'Hiver. For three years he performed on the high trapeze, touring with the circus in France, Switzerland, and Italy. His circus career ended when he was injured in a fall.

4. W. C. FIELDS (1880–1946), stage and film comedian

Fields began working as a comic juggler with a circus at age fourteen. He traveled with circus shows before becoming a vaudeville headliner at age twenty.

5. BEN HECHT (1894–1964), screenwriter

Hecht and his younger brother, Peter, learned trapeze routines from their landlady's son. They practiced in the barn behind their Racine, Wisconsin, home for three summers, then joined a circus in 1908, billing themselves as the "Youngest Daredevils in America." The act was short-lived, but Hecht later used what he had learned in the screenplays for *Trapeze* (1956), *Jumbo* (1962), and *Circus World* (1964).

6. BURT LANCASTER (1913–   ), actor

Billed as Lang of the Lang and Cravat acrobatic act, Lancaster at first earned three dollars a week in 1931 to set up tents and do odd jobs for the Kay Brothers Circus while honing his skills. He and his parents became experts and eventually toured with the Ringling Brothers and Barnum and Bailey Circus. A hand injury forced him to retire from the circus in 1939.

7. WILL ROGERS (1879–1935), stage and film star

Rogers began his show business career as a rope-throwing cowboy with the Mulhall Circus in 1899. He later toured South Africa with Texas Jack's Wild West Circus, and Australia and New Zealand with the Wirth Brothers Circus.

8. RED SKELTON (1913–   ), film and TV comedian

Before he was fifteen, Skelton had followed in his father's shoes as a clown in the Hagenbeck and Wallace Circus. He had wanted to be a lion tamer but gave up that idea when he saw Clyde Beatty get mauled by one of his charges.

9. TINY TIM (1932–   ), singer and performer

In 1959, under the name Larry Love, the Singing Canary, Tiny Tim played Hubert's Museum and Live Flea Circus of New York. The singer, later famed for his high-pitched rendition of "Tiptoe Through the Tulips," left Hubert's when he was asked to sing in a lower register.

Anthony Quinn's
12 All-Time-Favorite Artists

Actor Anthony Quinn has appeared in more than a hundred motion pictures. He has won two Academy Awards, for his supporting roles in *Viva Zapata!* and *Lust for Life* (he played artist Paul Gauguin). His other notable films include *The Hunchback of Notre Dame*, *The Guns of Navarone*, *Zorba the Greek*, *Barabbas*, *Requiem for a Heavyweight*, and *The Shoes of the Fisherman*. An accomplished painter, Quinn is also an avid art collector.

1. Rembrandt
2. Michelangelo
3. da Vinci
4. Titian
5. Goya
6. Velázquez

7. Picasso
8. Matisse
9. Tamayo

10. Siqueiros
11. Orozco
12. Miró

— Exclusive for *The Book of Lists*

8 Great Finds

1. IN A FARMER'S FIELD

In 1820 a Greek peasant named Yorgos was digging in his field on the island of Milos when he unearthed several carved blocks of stone. He burrowed deeper and found four statues — three figures of Hermes and one of Aphrodite, the goddess of love. Three weeks later, the Choiseul archaeological expedition arrived by ship, purchased the Aphrodite, and took it to France. Louis XVIII gave it the name *Venus de Milo* and presented it to the Louvre in Paris, where it became one of the most famous works of art in the world.

2. BENEATH A STREET

On February 21, 1978, electrical workers were putting down lines on a busy street corner in Mexico City when they discovered a twenty-ton stone bas-relief of the Aztec night goddess, Coyolxauhqui. It is believed to have been sculpted in the early fifteenth century and buried prior to the destruction of the Aztec civilization by the Spanish conquistadors in 1521. The stone was moved 200 yards from the site to the Museum of the Great Temple.

3. IN A HOLE IN THE GROUND

In 1978 more than 500 motion pictures dating from 1903 to 1929 were dug out of a hole in the ground in Dawson City, Yukon. Under normal circumstances, the 35mm nitrate films would have been destroyed, but the permafrost preserved them perfectly.

4. UNDER A BED

Joanne Perez, the widow of vaudeville performer Pepito the Spanish Clown, cleaned out the area underneath her bed and discovered the only existing copy of the pilot for the TV series *I Love Lucy*. Pepito had coached Lucille Ball and had guest-starred in the pilot. Ball and her husband, Desi Arnaz, had given the copy to Pepito as a gift in 1951 and it had remained under the bed for thirty-nine years.

5. ON A WALL

A middle-aged couple in a suburb of Milwaukee, Wisconsin, asked an art prospector to appraise a painting in their home. While he was there he examined another painting that the couple had thought was a *reproduction* of a work by Vincent van Gogh. It turned out to be an 1886 original. On March 10, 1991, the painting *Still Life with Flowers* sold at auction for $1,400,000.

6. IN A TRUNK IN AN ATTIC

In 1961 Barbara Testa, a Hollywood librarian, inherited six steamer trunks that had belonged to her grandfather James Fraser Gluck, a Buffalo, New York, lawyer who died in 1895. Over the next three decades she gradually sifted through the contents of the trunks, until one day in the fall of 1990 she came upon 665 pages that turned out to be the original handwritten manuscript of the first half of Mark Twain's *Huckleberry Finn*. The two halves of the great American novel were finally reunited at the Buffalo and Erie County Public Library.

7. AT A FLEA MARKET

A Philadelphia financial analyst was browsing at a flea market in Adamstown, Pennsylvania, when he was attracted by a wooden picture frame. He paid four dollars for it. Back at his home, he removed the old torn painting in the frame and found a folded document between the canvas and the wood backing. It turned out to be a 1776 copy of the Declaration of Independence — one of only twenty-four known to remain. On June 13, 1991, Sotheby's auction house in New York sold the copy for $2,420,000.

8. ABOVE A COPYING MACHINE

For sixty years a painting of Niagara Falls had hung unappreciated in Eno Memorial Hall in Old Lyme, Connecticut, most recently above a copying machine. In April 1991, a local gallery owner walked into the building and recognized it as a previously unknown work by John Frederick Kensett. The 1855 oil is estimated to be worth almost $1 million.

Vincent van Gogh's *Still Life with Flowers* hung on a wall in a Milwaukee suburban home before it was discovered to be an original. It was auctioned for $1,400,000.

HEALTH AND FOOD

Tom Dodds's **17** Unusual Accidents

Tom Dodds is a retired writer and editor for the National Safety Council.

1. RUMP STEAK

   In 1990, a 64-year-old Hartsville, Tennessee, woman entered a hospital for surgery for what doctors diagnosed as a tumor on her buttocks. What surgeons found, however, was a four-inch pork chop bone, which they removed. They estimated that it had been in place for five to ten years. The woman could not remember sitting on it, or eating it, for that matter.

2. KNOCKOUT BLOW

   Daniel Caruso was preparing for his bout in the New York Golden Gloves in January 1992 and was building up his punching resistance by pounding his gloves into his face just before the introductions. Unfortunately, Caruso scored a hit with one punch, breaking and bloodying his own nose. The bout was canceled when the doctor would not allow him to box.

3. ATTACKED BY PASTA

   A Michigan housewife hurt herself trying to clean her kitchen sink: she was stabbed by a shard of pasta. The noodle was left over from some soup her husband had poured in the sink the day before. Lying in the sink, the noodle dried out, regaining its sharpness and rigidity. When the woman reached in the sink she struck the noodle at an angle that drove it into her finger beneath the fingernail. Not only was it painful, but the finger started to swell. The next morning the pain was so great she went to the hospital, where part of her fingernail had to be removed so the doctor could get at the noodle.

4. BEWARE OF SAFETY CAMPAIGNS

   The Consumer Products Safety Commission was forced to recall 80,000 buttons it had distributed to promote toy safety because they were found to be hazardous to children. The buttons, which said "For kids' sake think toy safety," could be swallowed by a child and were painted with a paint that had a dangerously high lead content.

5. SUPERMAN

In New York City, in 1990, Angel Santana was shot with a .357-magnum pistol during a struggle with one of three men holding up the store where he worked. The robbers were so shocked when Santana failed to fall that all three of them fled. Santana was no Superman — the bullet had become lodged in the zipper of his trousers, thus failing to hurt him.

6. BEE-LATED

Maddie Mix was late for work, but she had an excuse that had her bosses buzzing. More than 10,000 bees lost their queen and commandeered Mix's car as she drove to work in Baton Rouge, Louisiana. Driving her car through a car wash didn't work, but then fate intervened. A former beekeeper, Terry Tillman, just happened to be getting his car washed at the same time. Tillman succeeded in luring most of the bees into a honeycomb trap.

7. OEDIPAL ACCIDENT

In September 1991, Joe Copeland, a Dallas police officer, slowed his vehicle to avoid an object in the road. Seconds later, a car rammed into his from behind. That kind of collision happens every day, but this accident had an unusual twist. The other car was driven by Copeland's mother. Dazed, both remained in their cars until police arrived, at which time Mrs. Copeland asked officers to notify her son that she had been in an accident.

8. LOVE BITE

The University of Arizona poison control center's 1990 study of 218 rattlesnake bites turned up one weird case. A man was bitten on his tongue while kissing a snake.

9. NOSE JOB

A motorist who was shot in the right temple during a traffic dispute dislodged the bullet by blowing his nose in the hospital emergency room. The bullet had apparently lodged in a sinus, said a spokeswoman from the Chandler, Arizona, Desert Samaritan Hospital. The victim was treated and released.

10. DRIVING WITHOUT A LICENSE

When Jodie Brown's car was rear-ended at a stop sign in Naperville, Illinois, she looked in the rearview mirror but couldn't see anyone behind the wheel of the truck that had plowed into her. Jodie thought maybe the driver had had a heart attack and slipped down in the driver's seat, so she got out to investigate. What she found was no human driver inside, only a German shepherd puppy that had apparently knocked the gear shift of the idling truck into drive.

11. LEFT BEHIND

Khaled Kamadan, an Egyptian injured in Kuwait during the Gulf War, was operated on to repair his injuries. The operation was successful — almost. Within two weeks Kamadan was back in the hospital for another operation in exactly the same spot. This time it was to remove the surgical scissors left inside him during the first operation.

12. BRUSHING UP AND GETTING DOWN

Kerry Shea of De Pere, Wisconsin, was brushing the back of her tongue because she had seen it recommended on TV. "My toothbrush was slippery because I had just washed my hands," explained the youngster. "It just slipped and I swallowed it." Doctors removed the toothbrush without surgery, using a long tube with a hook on the end.

13. STUCK IN TRAFFIC

When motorists said they were stuck in traffic near Brighton, England, they really meant it. A truck had spilled 1,000 gallons of glue on the road.

14. STOPPED COALED

In 1984, a Pittsburgh, Pennsylvania, man parked his car on a street with a downhill grade and left to run an errand. When he came back, he found his car wedged between a loaded coal truck and another car that was snug up against his car's rear bumper. Being resourceful, the man figured he would release the coal truck's emergency brake and let the truck roll forward a few feet, giving him room to get his car out of its cramped parking space. He climbed into the truck's cab and was confronted by a variety of levers. He wasn't sure which was the brake, so he guessed — wrong! He grabbed the dump lever and instantly buried his car under five tons of coal.

15. THE TOILET BOWL

In Salt Lake City, Utah, a rupture in a sixteen-inch water main was blamed on an implosion caused by a massive rush to bathrooms at halftime during the telecast of Super Bowl XVIII.

16. POOR TIMING

In Oakland, California, Roy Johnson failed his driver's test after his car crashed through a window of the Motor Vehicle

Department. Johnson had just finished the test and had an examiner sitting on the passenger side when he stopped in front of the building. His foot slipped off the brake pedal and hit the accelerator. His car leapt forward and smashed into the window.

17. A TOUGH JOB, BUT SOMEBODY HAS TO DO IT

Liz Villagomez of San Jose, California, was trying on a pair of designer jeans when the zipper snagged. After a long struggle she gave up and called the fire department. Firefighters arrived on the scene quickly, but it took one of the firefighters about twenty minutes to remove the zipper, tooth by tooth, using a surgical scissors.

NOTE: For more unusual accidents, see *The Book of Lists #3*, pp. 366–67.

10 Afflictions and Their Patron Saints

1. CANCER

A young fourteenth-century Italian, Peregrine Laziosi, once demonstrated against the papacy, but was converted and became famous for his preaching and his holiness. When he developed a cancer on his foot and doctors were about to amputate, he prayed all night and was miraculously cured. He became the patron saint of cancer victims.

2. EPILEPSY

St. Vitus expelled an evil spirit from a Roman emperor's child, and so he became the patron of people suffering from diseases typified by convulsions — epilepsy, chorea (or St. Vitus's dance), and other neurological disorders. He is also considered the patron saint of dancers, comedians, and actors.

3.–4. HEMORRHOIDS AND VENEREAL DISEASE

St. Fiacre, a seventh-century holy man who set up a hospice for travelers in France, was known for miraculously healing his visitors of a variety of ills, including venereal disease and hemorrhoids. In addition, cabdrivers call on him as their protector because the Hôtel St. Fiacre in Paris was the first establishment to offer coaches for hire.

5. MENTAL ILLNESS

The remains of St. Dympna, a seventh-century Irish princess murdered by her father when she tried to escape his incestuous desires, are kept in a church in Gheel, Belgium. Dympna became the patron saint of the mentally ill when many insane or retarded people were cured after visiting her shrine.

6. PARALYSIS

St. Giles, a hermit who lived near Arles, France, in the seventh century, became the patron of the lame and the crippled. He had protected a deer that was being hunted and took an arrow that had been meant for the animal.

7. RABIES

According to legend, St. Hubert (eighth century) converted to Christianity when during a hunt he saw a stag bearing a cross in its antlers. He became the patron saint of hunters and, because of his connection with wild animals, rabies victims.

8. SKIN DISEASES

The patron saint of pig herders, St. Anthony, was also the fourth-century Egyptian monk who established the world's first Christian monastery. Because pork fat was used to dress wounds, he became the intercessor for people with skin problems. One type of skin inflammation is known as St. Anthony's fire.

9. THROAT INFECTIONS

St. Blaise (fourth century) cured a young boy who was near death from a fish bone caught in his throat. To this day, Catholics celebrate the blessing of throats. Blaise is also the patron saint of wool combers (his enemies used iron combs on his flesh) and of wild animals (he once lived in a cave among the animals).

10. TOOTHACHES

The intercessor for those with toothaches (and the patron saint of dentists) is St. Apollonia. She lived in Alexandria, Egypt, during the third century, at a time when gangs roamed the city and

St. Apollonia, patron saint of toothaches and dentists, won the honor because her teeth were pulled out by an Egyptian mob when she refused to give up Christianity.

tortured Christians. When artists draw Apollonia, they show her either holding a gold tooth or a set of pincers — her teeth were pulled out by a mob when she refused to give up her Christianity.

8 Really Unusual Medical Conditions

"Nothing is too wonderful to be true."

— *Michael Faraday*

1. ART ATTACK

Fine art can really make you sick. Or so says Dr. Graziella Magherini, author of *The Stendhal Syndrome*. She has studied more than a hundred tourists in Florence, Italy, who became ill in the presence of great works. Their symptoms include heart

Many people, upon coming face-to-face with Michelangelo's *David*, are overcome by anxiety, dizziness, and stomach disorders.

palpitations, dizziness, and stomach pains. The typical sufferer is a single person between the ages of twenty-six and forty who rarely leaves home. Dr. Magherini believes the syndrome is a result of jet lag, travel stress, and the shock of an overwhelming sense of the past. "Very often," she says, "there's the anguish of death." The disorder was named after the nineteenth-century French novelist who became overwhelmed by the frescoes in Florence's Santa Croce Church. Particularly upsetting works of art include Michelangelo's statue of David, Caravaggio's painting of Bacchus, and the concentric circles of the Duomo cupola. Dr. Magherini is presently studying the syndrome in other art-rich cities such as Venice and Jerusalem.

2. HULA-HOOP INTESTINE

On February 26, 1992, Beijing worker Xu Denghai was hospitalized with a "twisted intestine" after playing excessively with a Hula-Hoop. His was the third such case in the several weeks since a Hula-Hoop craze had swept China. The Beijing *Evening News* advised people to warm up properly and avoid Hula-Hooping immediately after eating.

3. CARROT ADDICTION

In its August 1992 issue, the highly respected *British Journal of Addiction* described three unusual cases of carrot dependence. One forty-year-old man had replaced cigarettes with carrots, ate as much as five bunches a day, and thought about them obsessively. According to two Czech psychiatrists, when carrots were withdrawn he and the other patients "lapsed into heightened irritability."

4. CUTLERY CRAVING

The desire to eat metal objects is comparatively common. Occasionally there is an extreme case, such as that of forty-seven-year-old Englishman Allison Johnson. An alcoholic burglar with a compulsion to eat silverware, Johnson has had thirty operations to remove strange things from his stomach. As of 1992, he had eight forks and the metal sections of a mop head lodged in his body. He has repeatedly been jailed and then released, each time going immediately to a restaurant and ordering lavishly. Unable to pay, he would then tell the owners to call the police, and eat cutlery until they arrived. Johnson's lawyer said of his client, "He finds it hard to eat and obviously has difficulty going to the lavatory."

5. DR. STRANGELOVE SYNDROME

Officially known as alien hand syndrome, this bizarre neurological disorder afflicts several thousand Americans. It is caused by damage to certain parts of the brain, and causes one of a person's hands to act independently of the other and of its owner's wishes. For example, the misbehaving hand may do the opposite of what the normal one is doing: if a person is trying to button a shirt with one hand, the other will follow along and undo the buttons. If one hand pulls up trousers, the other will pull them down. Sometimes the hand may become aggressive — pinching, slapping, or punching the patient; in at least one case, it tried to strangle its owner. Says neurologist Rachelle Doody, "Often a patient will sit on the hand, but eventually it gets loose and starts doing everything again."

6. MUD WRESTLER'S RASH

Twenty-four men and women wrestled in calf-deep mud at the University of Washington. Within thirty-six hours, seven wrestlers were covered with patches of "pus-filled red bumps similar to pimples," and the rest succumbed later. Bumps were on areas not covered by bathing suits — one unlucky victim had wrestled in the nude. The *dermatitis palastraie limosae,* or "muddy wrestling rash," may have been caused by manure-tainted mud.

7. ELECTRIC PEOPLE

According to British paranormalist Hilary Evans, some people are "upright human [electric] eels, capable of generating charges strong enough to knock out streetlights and electronic equipment." Cases of "electric people" date back to 1786; the most famous is that of fourteen-year-old Angelique Cottin, whose presence caused compass needles to gyrate wildly. To further investigate this phenomenon, Evans has founded SLIDE, the Street Lamp Interference Data Exchange. To contact SLIDE, write to 59 Tranquil Vale, London SE3 OBS, England.

8. MARY HART EPILEPSY

The case of Dianne Neale, forty-nine, appeared in the *New England Journal of Medicine:* In a much-publicized 1991 incident, Neale apparently suffered epileptic seizures at hearing the voice of *Entertainment Tonight* co-host Mary Hart. Neale experienced an upset stomach, a sense of pressure in her head, and confusion. Laboratory tests confirmed the abnormal electrical discharges in her brain, and Neale held a press conference to insist that she was not crazy and resented being the object of jokes. She said she bore no hard feelings toward Hart, who apologized on the air for the situation.

In another bizarre case, the theme from the show *Growing Pains* brought twenty-seven-year-old Janet Richardson out of a coma. She had been unresponsive for five days after falling out of bed and hitting her head, until, according to her sister, the TV theme "woke her up."

Phobias of
15 Famous People

*"Am I afraid of high notes? Of
course I am afraid! What sane
man is not?"*

— *Luciano Pavarotti*

1. AUGUSTUS CAESAR (Roman emperor) — fear of sitting in the dark (achluophobia).
2. HOWARD HUGHES (millionaire businessman) — fear of public places (agoraphobia) and germs (mysophobia).
3. ELIZABETH I (British queen) — fear of roses (anthophobia).
4. SIGMUND FREUD (father of psychoanalysis) — fear of train travel (siderodromophobia).
5. RICHIE VALENS (singer) — fear of airplanes (aerophobia). He died in a plane crash.
6. DAVID STEINBERG (comic) — fear of snakes (ophidiophobia).
7. MARILYN MONROE (actress) — fear of public places (agoraphobia).
8. HENRI III (French king) — fear of cats (ailurophobia).
9. GRAHAM GREENE (novelist) — fear of blood (hematophobia) and birds (ornithophobia).
10. ARNOLD SCHÖNBERG (composer) — fear of the number 13 (triskaidekaphobia). He died on a Friday the 13th, 13 minutes before midnight.
11. SID CAESAR (comedian) — fear of haircuts (tonsurphobia).
12. MALCOLM LOWRY (novelist) — fear of choking on fish bones (pnigophobia).

Sid Caesar (center) coming to terms with his phobia by performing with Carl Reiner and Howard Morris as The Haircuts.

13. JOHN CHEEVER (novelist) — fear of crossing bridges (gephyrophobia).
14. NATALIE WOOD (actress) — fear of water (hydrophobia). She died by drowning.
15. ALAN LADD (actor) — fear of birds (ornithophobia).

12 Unusual Support Groups

1. AMERICAN ASSOCIATION OF DENTAL VICTIMS

   People who have had trouble with dentists "brace" each other through a self-advocacy movement and pen-pal network. (Eighty-seven branches in the United States and Canada; write to 3320 E. 7th St., Long Beach, CA 90804.)

2. CONSUMER-CREDIT COUNSELING SERVICES (formerly Debtors Anonymous)

   Assistance for people suffering from compulsive indebtedness. (Check your local directory or write to the National Foundation for Consumer Credit, 8611 2nd Ave., Suite 100, Silver Spring, MD 20910.)

3. FUNDAMENTALISTS ANONYMOUS

   Help for dissatisfied fundamentalists who wish to leave fundamentalist religions. (More than 50,000 members in the United States and Canada; write to P.O. Box 20324, Greeley Square Station, New York, NY 10001.)

4. IMPOTENTS ANONYMOUS

   Self-help for men suffering from sexual impotence; also offers help to spouses. (More than a hundred groups in the United States alone; for information, send a large SASE and $1.00 for handling to 119 S. Ruth St., Maryville, TN 37801.)

5. MESSIES ANONYMOUS

   Aid for the disorganized homemaker. (Fifty groups organized, more or less, across the United States; write Sandra Felton, founder, for an introductory newsletter: 5025 S.W. 114th Ave., Miami, FL 33165.)

6. **PET LOSS SUPPORT**

Comfort for those who have lost a special pet. (For support and/or information on group meetings in your location, write to the Human-Animal Program, School of Veterinary Medicine, University of California, Davis, CA 95616.)

7. **PMS HOTLINE**

Number to call for support for women who suffer premenstrual tension. (Groups across the United States and Canada. Write to PMS Access, P.O. Box 9326, Madison, WI 53715.)

8. **PROSTITUTES ANONYMOUS**

For men and women who want to leave the "sex life." (Groups hold meetings in several locales; for information, send an SASE to 11225 Magnolia Blvd., Box 181, North Hollywood, CA 91601.)

9. **SEXAHOLICS ANONYMOUS**

Help for the person seeking "sexual sobriety" in a twelve-step program. (More than a thousand chapters in the United States and Canada; for information, send a business-size SASE to P.O. Box 300, Simi Valley, CA 93062.)

10. **WORKAHOLICS ANONYMOUS**

Support for the compulsive overworker and affected family and friends. (Ten groups in the United States; write to National Workaholics Anonymous, P.O. Box 661501, Los Angeles, CA 90066.)

11. **FALSE MEMORY SYNDROME FOUNDATION**

Support for parents falsely accused by their adult children of abuse, incest, and Satanic rituals. (Write to 3401 Market Street, Suite 130, Philadelphia, PA 19104, or call 800-568-8882.)

12. **NATIONAL CHASTITY ASSOCIATION**

Provides information and support for people who choose to reject premarital sex, kissing, or even handholding. (Send an SASE to P.O. Box 402, Oak Forest, IL 60452.)

13. **LOW-FREQUENCY NOISE SUFFERERS ASSOCIATION**

This organization has been lobbying on behalf of people who hear a hum inside their heads but do not suffer from a hearing disorder. They are acutely sensitive to certain types of environmental noise. (Write c/o Elizabeth Griggs, Hyatt Place, Old World Road, Shepton Mallet BA 4 5XY, England.)

NOTE: For more information on support organizations, check local listings, or send a self-addressed stamped envelope (SASE) to the National Self-Help Clearinghouse, 25 W. 43rd St., Room 620, New York, NY 10036.

12 Famous Men Who Were Injured in Battle

1. MUHAMMAD (War Against Mecca)

   The prophet of Islam was wounded by a stone in the very first battle in which he personally took part: the Battle of Uhud on March 23, A.D. 625.

2. MIGUEL DE CERVANTES (Defeat of the Turkish Fleet)

   The author of *Don Quixote* was wounded three times at the naval battle of Lepanto against the Turks on October 7, 1571. He took two gun wounds in the chest, and then a ball bruised and shattered his left hand, leaving it lame.

3. TOM MIX (Spanish-American War; Boxer Uprising)

   The son of a cavalry officer, the future cowboy star enlisted in the artillery at age eighteen, following the outbreak of the Spanish-American War. After the Spanish surrender in Cuba, Mix and other scouts were sent to round up the remaining Spanish sharpshooters. One of them shot Mix in the mouth. The bullet came out the back of his neck and he spent a month in the hospital before being sent home. He rejoined the army in time to be sent to China for the Boxer Uprising in 1900. This time he was injured by an exploding shell.

4. BELA LUGOSI (World War I)

   Although he was exempt from military service because he was an actor with the National Theater, Lugosi enlisted in the Hungarian army in June 1914 and was commissioned a second lieutenant. Five months later he was hospitalized with a gunshot wound in the shoulder. Back in action in the northern Carpathian mountains, the future star of *Dracula* was shot through the thigh during a Russian ambush. Returning to the front, he was saving an injured comrade when an exploding shell threw him into the air. When he landed, his head hit a jagged rock, and he woke up in a field hospital with a serious concussion.

5. PAUL LUKAS (World War I)

   Lukas enlisted in the Hungarian army before he could be drafted, and then the war broke out. He was wounded by Russian shrapnel in 1915 and was discharged after suffering shell shock. He went on to a long career in Hollywood and won an Academy Award for his portrayal of an anti-Nazi hero in *Watch on the Rhine* (1943).

6. JEAN RENOIR (World War I)

While on patrol between the lines in April 1915, the great French director was shot in the leg. His femur was fractured and gangrene set in. His mother raced to his hospital bedside and convinced the doctors not to amputate her son's leg. A newly invented procedure was tried on Renoir — draining the wound and irrigating it with water. The experiment succeeded and Renoir returned to service.

7. ADOLF HITLER (World War I)

Rejected for military service in 1914, Hitler was able to join the 16th Bavarian Reserve Infantry Regiment after war broke out. He was wounded in the leg on October 7, 1916, and gassed and temporarily blinded on October 14, 1918. He was still hospitalized when the war ended.

8. ERNEST HEMINGWAY (World War I)

After being rejected by the military because of an eye defect, Hemingway became an ambulance driver for the American Red Cross and was sent to Italy. On July 8, 1918, less than two months after his arrival, Hemingway was hit by fragments of an Austrian trench mortar shell. The soldier nearest him was killed. Hemingway was dragging another wounded soldier to safety when he was injured again, this time by machine gun bullets in the knee. Hemingway spent three months in a hospital in Milan, where he turned nineteen, fell in love with a nurse, and underwent a dozen operations to remove more than two hundred shell fragments from his legs and body. The experience left him with insomnia and the inability to sleep in the dark.

9. FRANÇOIS MITTERRAND (World War II)

In May 1940, the future president of France was in charge of a munitions dump when the German army swept through the French defenses. Mitterrand was badly wounded in the chest by shrapnel. His retreating comrades dumped him in a cart and dragged him along for two days before they reached a French military hospital. His wounds were treated, but soon he was taken prisoner by the Germans.

10. TONY CURTIS (World War II)

Curtis, then known as Bernie Schwartz, enlisted in the U.S. Navy in 1944, six months before he was scheduled to graduate high school. He served as a signal man on the submarine USS *Dragonette.* While he was loading torpedoes in Guam, a winch chain snapped and hit him. His legs were paralyzed for four weeks and he spent several months receiving treatment before he was discharged.

11. LEE MARVIN (World War II)

Marvin dropped out of high school and joined the Marine Corps. While fighting on Saipan in 1944, a wound just below the spine severed his sciatic nerve. He was hospitalized for thirteen months before being discharged.

12. ROCKY BLEIER (Vietnam War)

Bleier was drafted by the Pittsburgh Steelers and the U.S. Army at about the same time. In 1969 he was sent to Vietnam, where an exploding grenade maimed his right foot and left more than a hundred pieces of shrapnel in both legs. Although he was told that he would be lucky to walk again, Bleier returned to football and gained more than a thousand yards in 1976.

Effectiveness of
14 Contraceptive Methods

Method	Accidental Pregnancies in First Year of Use (%)
1. Implants	
Norplant-2 (2 rods)	0.03
Norplant (6 capsules)	0.04
2. Male sterilization	0.15
3. Female sterilization	0.4
4. Injectable progestogen	
Depo-Provera	0.3
Norethindrone eninthate	0.4
5. Pill	3
6. IUD	3
7. Condom	12
8. Diaphragm	18
9. Cap	18
10. Withdrawal	18
11. Sponge	
Nulliparous women (have not given birth)	18
Parous women (have given birth)	28
12. Periodic abstinence	20
13. Spermicides	21
14. Chance	85

SOURCE: Population Council from James Trussell, Robert Hatcher, Willard Cates, Felicia Stewart, and Kathryn Kost, "Contraceptive Failure in the United States: An Update," *Studies in Family Planning* 21 (1), January/February 1990, Table 1.

Andrew Weil's
11 Medical Practices to Avoid

A graduate of Harvard Medical School, Dr. Weil is associate director of the Division of Social Perspectives in Medicine of the College of Medicine, University of Arizona. He teaches courses on alternative medicine, mind/body interactions, and medical botany. His general practice in Tucson focuses on natural and preventive medicine and diagnosis of difficult health problems. Among his books are *Natural Health, Natural Medicine* and *Health and Healing.*

1. CHOLECYSTECTOMY(REMOVAL OF GALLBLADDER) BY OPEN ABDOMINAL SURGERY

   This operation is frequently performed when unnecessary. A recently developed alternative — laparoscopic cholecystectomy — is much safer. The new operation requires special training, so many surgeons are reluctant to give up the old one. Sometimes gallbladder surgery can be avoided altogether by making dietary changes, such as drastically cutting down on fat consumption.

2. PROPHYLACTIC APPENDECTOMY

   It is common for surgeons to remove the appendix if they happen to have the patient's abdomen open for some other reason. Often the patients don't know it happened until they get the hospital bill. Many doctors believe it is an unnecessary organ that might as well be gotten rid of to avoid future trouble. This is a fallacy — the appendix is a functioning part of the immune system.

3. HYSTERECTOMY FOR UTERINE FIBROIDS

   Uterine fibroids are growths in the womb that can cause painful periods and heavy blood loss. Hysterectomy for this condition is a bread-and-butter operation for many surgeons, but in fact uterine fibroids can be treated by laser surgery or by lowering the estrogen levels of the blood.

4. RADICAL MASTECTOMY

   This procedure for breast cancer involves removing the entire breast and surrounding muscle. It is disfiguring and painful, and research has demonstrated that it is no more effective against the return of cancer than simple mastectomy or removal of the tumor (lumpectomy) with follow-up treatments such as chemotherapy. A woman should never consent to this obsolete procedure.

5. Back Surgery for Slipped Discs and Chronic Pain

Two frequently recommended operations — laminectomy and spinal fusion — are far from guaranteed to eliminate chronic back pain. The vast majority of cases will respond to nonsurgical treatments, including exercise, rest, hypnosis, and stress reduction.

6. Long-Term Corticosteroid Treatment

Cortisone and similar drugs used to relieve allergies and inflammation seem to have almost magical effects as pain relievers. However, the price is high: when used for more than two or three weeks, they can cause depression, weight gain, ulcers, weakened bones, eye cataracts, and more.

7. Long-Term Treatment with Valium, Halcion, and Other Benzodiazepines

Valium and its many relatives are highly addictive, and the addiction is one of the hardest to break. While it is all right to use them for occasional bouts of insomnia or jet lag, long-term use interferes with memory and intellectual functioning.

8. Antibiotic Treatment for Viral Respiratory Conditions

Most common respiratory infections, including colds, flus, sore throats, and bronchitis, are caused by viral infections. Antibiotics work against bacteria, but have no antiviral activity. Nonetheless, patients often demand antibiotics, and doctors comply, justifying their prescriptions by saying they are treating secondary bacterial infections. Studies show that in most cases, however, the infections are purely viral. Taking antibiotics unnecessarily weakens immunity and can lead to more illness.

9. Sinus Surgery

Surgery for chronic sinusitis — the scraping away of infected tissue lining the sinuses — is expensive, painful, and rarely effective. The condition almost always returns full-blown. Alternative methods of treatment include dietary changes (such as milk-free diet) and nasal hygiene (inhaling a saline solution daily).

10. Prostatectomy

Surgical removal of the prostate gland is another expensive and painful operation, frequently resulting in impotence and urinary dysfunction. It is done as treatment for benign prostate hypertrophy (BPH) and early stages of prostate cancer. In the case of cancer, removal of the gland is often unnecessary if the cancer is not aggressive. Alternatively, some new pharmaceutical drugs and some herbal medicines can help control BPH or reverse the condition.

11. DELIVERY BY CESAREAN SECTION

The rate of cesarean delivery in the United States now approaches 25 percent of all births. Cesareans are more expensive, and in many cases more dangerous, than vaginal delivery. Most C-sections are done as "defensive medicine" to avoid perceived threats of malpractice actions.

5-Year Relative Survival Rates for 19 Types of Cancer

In 1991 the National Cancer Institute published the five-year survival rate for cancer patients diagnosed between 1981 and 1987. This rate is defined as the probability of escaping death from cancer for five years following its diagnosis. The listing gives survival rates, where appropriate, for males and females combined.

		Total Survival (%)
1.	Thyroid gland	94
2.	Corpus uteri	83
3.	Melanoma of skin	81
4.	Urinary bladder	78
5.	Breast	77
6.	Prostate gland	74
7.	Cervix uteri	66
8.	Larynx	66
9.	Colon, except rectum	57
10.	Rectum and rectosigmoid	54
11.	Kidney and renal pelvis	53
12.	Oral cavity and pharynx	51
13.	Ovary	39
14.	Brain and nervous system	25
15.	Stomach	17
16.	Lung and bronchus	13
17.	Esophagus	8
18.	Liver and intrahepatic	5
19.	Pancreas	3

SOURCE: *Cancer Patient Survival Experience* (U.S. Department of Health and Human Services, June 1991).

Baseball star Jackie Robinson suffered from diabetes.

33 Famous Diabetics

More than one person out of twenty has diabetes; about half of those affected don't know it. Some early symptoms include excessive urination, excessive thirst, extreme hunger, weight loss, irritability, and weakness. For information, contact the Juvenile Diabetes Foundation at 800-JDF-CURE, or the American Diabetes Association at 800-ADA-DISC.

1. Yuri Andropov (1914–1984), Soviet premier
2. Arthur Ashe (1943–1993), U.S. tennis star
3. Hafiz al-Assad (1928–   ), Syrian general and dictator
4. Menachem Begin (1913–1992), former Israeli prime minister
5. Jack Benny (1894–1974), U.S. entertainer
6. James Cagney (1904–1986), U.S. entertainer
7. Paul Cézanne (1839–1906), French painter
8. Bobby Clarke (1949–   ), U.S. hockey player
9. Miles Davis (1926–1991), U.S. jazz musician

10. François Duvalier (1907–1971), Haitian dictator
11. Thomas Edison (1847–1931), U.S. inventor
12. William Fox (1879–1952), U.S. motion picture executive
13. Jerry Garcia (1942–   ), U.S. rock-and-roll musician
14. Ernest Hemingway (1899–1961), U.S. writer
15. Jim "Catfish" Hunter (1946–   ), U.S. baseball player
16. Charles Ives (1874–1954), U.S. composer
17. Mahalia Jackson (1911–1972), U.S. gospel singer
18. Nikita Khrushchev (1894–1971), Soviet premier
19. Stanley Kramer (1913–   ), U.S. motion picture producer/director
20. Fiorello La Guardia (1882–1947), U.S. politician
21. George Lucas (1944–   ), U.S. motion picture producer/director
22. George Minot (1885–1950), U.S. physician and Nobel Prize winner
23. Mary Tyler Moore (1937–   ), U.S. actress
24. Gamal Abdel Nasser (1918–1970), Egyptian politician
25. Gary Owens (1935–   ), U.S. radio and TV performer and announcer
26. Giacomo Puccini (1858–1924), Italian opera composer
27. Mario Puzo (1920–   ), U.S. author
28. Jackie Robinson (1919–1972), U.S. baseball player
29. Dan Rowan (1922–1987), U.S. TV personality
30. Ron Santo (1940–   ), U.S. baseball player
31. Spencer Tracy (1900–1967), U.S. actor
32. David Viscott (1939–   ), U.S. psychiatrist and author
33. H. G. Wells (1866–1946), English writer

25 Famous People Who Had Tuberculosis

Tuberculosis is often thought of as a disease that, like polio, has practically been wiped out. Between 1988 and 1990, though, TB cases increased by 14 percent in the United States and, between 1988 and 1989, by about 4 percent in Canada. Drug-resistant cases in the United States have also been on the rise. Symptoms of TB include coughing, fevers, night sweats, fatigue, and weight loss. Tuberculosis is usually curable with early detection and proper treatment, and many people who contract it go on to lead active, productive lives. For further information about tuberculosis, contact the Lung Association in your area.

1. Paul Anka, singer
2. Alexander Graham Bell, inventor
3. Judy Collins, singer

4. Noel Coward, actor and playwright
5. Marie Curie, scientist
6. W. C. Fields, actor and comedian
7. Charles Finley, baseball executive
8. Mahatma Gandhi, political and religious leader of India
9. Paul Gauguin, artist
10. Ulysses S. Grant, U.S. president
11. Adolf Hitler, dictator of Germany
12. Andrew Jackson, U.S. president
13. Al Jolson, entertainer and singer
14. Jean-Claude Killy, skier and co-president of the Albertville Olympic organizing committee
15. Vivien Leigh, actress
16. W. Somerset Maugham, author
17. Napoleon I, military leader and emperor of France
18. George Orwell, author
19. Jack Paar, television talk-show host
20. Louella Parsons, syndicated columnist
21. Anthony Perkins, actor
22. Walter Pidgeon, actor
23. Robert Louis Stevenson, author
24. Henry David Thoreau, naturalist and author
25. H. G. Wells, author

SOURCE: American Lung Association.

8 Notable Dyslexics

Dyslexia, a learning disability that is often inherited, affects an estimated 15 out of 100 schoolchildren. A dyslexic's brain routinely transposes symbols, making spelling or math difficult to learn. For more information, write to the Orton Dyslexia Society, 724 York Road, Baltimore, MD 21204 (a three-dollar donation is requested for literature).

1. HANS CHRISTIAN ANDERSEN, storyteller

Although he could read, Andersen never learned to spell, even after five years with a tutor. Spelling errors in his tales such as *The Emperor's New Clothes* and *The Ugly Duckling* were fixed by his publishers.

2. RICHARD CHAMBERLAIN, actor

Chamberlain dreaded school because of his disability. Finally, in his late teens, he "learned the pleasures of study." While breaking into acting, reading for parts traumatized him, but he persisted. He is now known for his roles in film and television as well as in Shakespearean plays.

3. CHER, actress

Cher dropped out of school in the eleventh grade — she could not read until she was eighteen. Although her problem was finally diagnosed at age thirty, she still has trouble reading billboards and dialing long-distance. Her daughter, Chastity, also has dyslexia.

4. TOM CRUISE, actor

Cruise, his mother, and his three sisters are dyslexic. In learning to read, he had trouble telling which way letters like *c* or *d* curved. Singled out by his peers, he sought to prove himself in sports, but an injury sidelined him, and he found an alternative outlet in acting. In 1992 he caused a stir in the medical community by stating that his dyslexia had been "cured" by Scientology.

5. GREG LOUGANIS, Olympic diver

Classmates teased Louganis about his reading disability, so he spent his leisure time working out at a gym and a dance studio. There he learned some of the techniques that helped his development as a champion diver.

6. LEE HARVEY OSWALD, accused assassin of U.S. president John F. Kennedy

Oswald's dyslexia caused him to reverse letters and punctuation marks when he wrote. His problem went undiagnosed, and some writers have suggested that it led to his low self-esteem and disruptive behavior in school.

7. GEORGE S. PATTON, general

Because of his erratic spelling and difficulties with math, it took Patton five years to finish West Point. He once admitted, "I have trouble with the *a, b,* and — what do you call that other letter?"

8. NELSON ROCKEFELLER, politician

Rockefeller transposed numbers, got words mixed up, and nearly failed ninth grade. His political speech writers found that he disliked "that fancy stuff," preferring to use clichés because he stumbled on unfamiliar phrases.

14 Famous Stutterers

1. JAMES EARL JONES, actor

   As a young man, Jones stammered so badly that at times he was reduced to writing notes. He overcame the affliction with speech therapy and by joining his high school debating team.

2. BRUCE WILLIS, actor

   Willis began stuttering at the age of eight. In high school he joined a drama club and found that his stammer vanished whenever he spoke in front of an audience.

3. ERASMUS DARWIN, eighteenth-century physician and grandfather of Charles Darwin

   Darwin was a good speaker, in spite of his stutter. When asked whether he found his speech impediment inconvenient, he replied, "No, sir, it gives me time for reflection, and saves me from answering impertinent questions."

4. CHARLES I, British king

   A lifetime stutterer, Charles addressed his first Parliament when he ascended the throne in 1623. He said, "I am unfit for speaking." Then he sat down.

5. CHARLES DARWIN, naturalist

   Plagued by a lifetime of nervous disorders, Darwin turned to science because he stuttered too badly to become a minister.

6. BEN JOHNSON, runner

   Johnson "learned" to stutter by teasing his brother, who stuttered. Unfortunately, the habit stuck and he couldn't get rid of his stammer.

7. BOB LOVE, basketball player

   The former NBA all-star believes he began to stammer in imitation of an uncle he loved deeply. His inability to communicate caused him to turn to basketball. After arduous speech therapy, Love has virtually conquered his disorder. He now gives lectures, because, he says, "I really want to be an inspiration to other people. I have forty years of words inside me."

8. COTTON MATHER, Puritan

   Although he desperately wanted to become a clergyman, he nearly abandoned all hope because he suffered from a bad stammer. He felt sure nobody would understand his sermons. He took heart from the knowledge that Moses stammered and went on to become one of the greatest preachers of his day.

9. CHARLES LAMB, writer

Lamb was disqualified from entering university because of his disability. His alcoholism exaggerated his stammer, and he described himself as "a drunken dog, ragged head, seldom shaven, odd-eyed and stuttering."

10. MARION DAVIES, actress

Fifty-two-year-old publishing magnate William Randolph Hearst was smitten the first time he saw eighteen-year-old Marion Davies in a chorus line. A year later, when she was given one speaking line in *Ziegfeld's Follies,* she botched it. Hearst, determined to make her a star, provided coaches to work day and night on her stammer. She improved, and starred in a number of films.

11. HENRY LUCE, publisher, founder of *Time* magazine and *Sports Illustrated*

Luce, the child of missionary parents, was born in China. He was sent to boarding school at age fifteen, where he was called Chink. He began to stammer, and became surly and aloof. Eventually, he conquered his stutter by participating in the Yale debating society.

12. WINSTON CHURCHILL, statesman

Churchill once said, "Personally, I like short words." Certain stutterers use starters prior to speaking to keep their vocal cords from seizing up; according to one specialist, Churchill used long *m*s for that purpose, as in "MmmmmmEngland will never surrender." He also suffered a lifelong inability to enunciate the letter *s*. He wrote all his speeches — which he often rehearsed in the bath — with the terminal *s* carefully eliminated.

13. W. SOMERSET MAUGHAM, novelist

Maugham's stutter was so severe that it deeply scarred his life. It was much worse when he was nervous, and only in the company of his closest friends did it disappear. His childhood was full of humiliating moments, such as the time he stuttered in school and the whole class screamed with laughter until the teacher pounded the desk and called him a fool. As an adult, he turned down frequent invitations to speak publicly and read on the radio. Only twice, as part of the war effort, did he struggle through two talks on the BBC.

14. KING GEORGE VI, king of England

King George first began to stammer after his teachers insisted he write with his right hand rather than his more natural left. In private he spoke normally, but he could barely speak in public. Before his speeches he was rehearsed by a famous Austrian voice therapist, but even so he stuttered heavily, particularly when he declared war with Germany. His speeches were later pruned to remove difficult words.

10 Short Sleepers

1. THOMAS EDISON, U.S. inventor

When he was young, Edison sometimes worked for several days in a row, catching up on sleep later. On one such occasion he slept for thirty-six hours straight, waking briefly to eat steak, potatoes, and apple pie. Said Edison, "Sleep is an acquired habit. Cells don't sleep. Fish swim in the water all night. Even a horse doesn't sleep. A man doesn't need any sleep."

2. CLORIS LEACHMAN, U.S. actress

The Academy Award–winning star sleeps only three or four hours a night because she has "so many things to do." She often starts her day at 4:30 A.M., works until 8:00 or 9:00 P.M., then goes out. When she finally gets home, she plays the piano or reads before bed.

3. MARGARET THATCHER, former British prime minister

While she was prime minister, Thatcher began her eighteen-hour workday when the BBC was still broadcasting the farm report. She often cooked a light supper for herself and her husband when she got home (usually around 11:00 P.M.), then did a few hours of paperwork. She believes "it is a sin to be idle."

4. ROCK HUDSON, U.S. actor

After a wild night and a mere three or four hours of sleep, Hudson would bound out of bed, according to a biographer, "bright-eyed and bushy-tailed, raring to go." He would work a full day starting at six in the morning and look clear-eyed and fresh-faced, with not a sign of a hangover marring his good looks.

5. BORIS YELTSIN, president of Russia

Yeltsin is another four-hour-a-night sleeper. Rising at 5:00 A.M., he reads contemporary authors for two hours, then does his morning exercises.

6. DAVID BRENNER, U.S. comedian

At the age of eight, Brenner figured out that by cutting his sleep down to four hours maximum a night, he could save up 1,456 more waking hours a year than the average person. In this way, he believes he has acquired numerous "extra years of life." Says Brenner, "I'm now a hundred and seven years old — and feeling fine . . . a little sleepy, but fine."

7 . GEORGE OHSAWA, Japanese philosopher

Ohsawa, the founder of macrobiotics, slept no more than four hours a night, and for one period slept only two. Said one of his students, explaining why Ohsawa died at age seventy-four of a heart attack, "That's stressful, and stress, as we know, is not good for the heart."

8 . DUKE OF WELLINGTON, British general and statesman

Wellington, a man of Spartan habits, slept between three and six hours a night, often in his clothes. He rose at 6:00 A.M., wrote steadily for three hours, and did not breakfast until 9:00 A.M. When asked each day what he wanted for dinner, Wellington invariably replied, "Cold meat."

9 . ISAAC ASIMOV, U.S. science fiction writer

Not surprisingly, the prolific author didn't lounge around in bed. "I never use an alarm clock," he said. "I can hardly wait till five A.M. In the army I always woke before reveille. I hate sleeping. It wastes time."

10 . NAPOLEON BONAPARTE, emperor of France

Napoleon was said to get by on only three or four hours of sleep. Sometimes he would wake at three in the morning and would dictate to his secretary until dawn, snapping impatiently at the sleepy aide, "What's the matter with you? You're sleeping on your feet."

10 Famous Insomniacs and *1* Honorable Mention

1 . MARLENE DIETRICH, German actress

Dietrich said that the only thing that lulled her to sleep was a sardine-and-onion sandwich on rye.

2 . AMY LOWELL, U.S. poet

Whenever she stayed in a hotel, Lowell would rent five rooms — one to sleep in, and empty rooms above, below, and on either side, in order to guarantee quiet.

3. W. C. Fields, U.S. actor

The aging Fields resorted to unusual methods to woo sleep. He would stretch out in a barber's chair (he'd always enjoyed getting haircuts) with towels wrapped around him, until he felt drowsy. Sometimes he could only get to sleep by stretching out on his pool table. On his worst nights, he could only fall asleep under a beach umbrella being sprinkled by a garden hose. He told a friend that "somehow a moratorium is declared on all my troubles when it is raining."

W. C. Fields preparing for mosquitoes and other enemies of sleep.

4. Alexandre Dumas, French author

Dumas suffered from terrible insomnia, and after trying many remedies, he was advised by a famous doctor to get out of bed when he couldn't sleep. He began to take late-night strolls, and eventually started to sleep through the night.

5. Judy Garland, U.S. actress

As a teenager, Garland was prescribed amphetamines to control her weight. As the years went by she took so many that she sometimes stayed up three or four days running. She added sleeping pills to her regime, and her insomnia and addiction increased. She eventually died of a drug overdose.

6. TALLULAH BANKHEAD, U.S. actress

Bankhead suffered from severe insomnia. She hired young homosexual "caddies" to keep her company, and one of their most important duties was to hold her hand until she drifted off to sleep.

7. FRANZ KAFKA, Austrian author

Kafka, miserable with insomnia, kept a diary detailing his suffering. For October 2, 1911, he wrote, "Sleepless night. The third in a row. I fall asleep soundly, but after an hour I wake up, as though I had laid my head in the wrong hole."

8. THEODORE ROOSEVELT, U.S. president

His insomnia cure was a shot of cognac in a glass of milk.

9. GROUCHO MARX, U.S. comic actor

Marx first began to have insomnia when the stock market crashed in 1929 and he lost $240,000 in forty-eight hours. When he couldn't sleep, he would call people up in the middle of the night and insult them.

10. MARK TWAIN, U.S. author

An irritable insomniac, Twain once threw a pillow at the window of his bedroom while he was a guest in a friend's house. When the satisfying crash let in what he thought was fresh air, he fell asleep at last. In the morning he discovered that he had broken a glass-enclosed bookcase.

Honorable Mention:
Tomas Izquierdo, a Cuban born in 1933, has not slept since World War II. He is the only person in medical literature proven to have this condition. Izquierdo believes his problem resulted from a terrifying tonsillectomy he had as an adolescent, which left him with horrible nightmares and the desire to avoid sleep. He meditates in

Groucho Marx suffering through a sleepless night.

order to relax, and used to work double shifts in a textile factory. He is known in his hometown of San Antonio de los Bānos as "Tomas who doesn't sleep."

7 Researchers Who Used Themselves as Guinea Pigs

1. JONAS SALK

   Salk, noted for developing a polio vaccine, has tested influenza serums on himself. He and his staff at the Immune Response Corporation (Carlsbad, California) worked to develop an AIDS vaccine. Salk once contended that when it was ready for human testing, "actions speak louder than words," and that he would be one of the first to try it.

2. PAUL NIEHANS

   This Swiss surgeon popularized a form of "rejuvenation" therapy consisting of cells from the crushed organs of lambs. Niehans often used the concoctions on himself, once with near-tragic results. He died in 1971, in his early nineties. Many scientists assert that cell therapy is quackery, but people seeking to restore their youth still flock to the Niehans clinic in Vevey, Switzerland.

3. WERNER FORSSMANN

   Forssmann, a German surgeon, pioneered the technique of cardiac catheterization in 1929 by threading a thin rubber tube through a vein in his left arm and pushing it two feet into his body. An X ray proved that the tube reached his heart. In 1956 Forssmann was awarded the Nobel Prize for his work.

4. ELIE METCHNIKOFF

   This pioneering bacteriologist and Nobel Prize winner was also widely known for his search for a cure for old age. Noting that many Bulgarian peasants lived to be 110 or 120, he was a proponent of their "sour milk" (yogurt) diet and was convinced that death before age eighty was unnatural. In 1912 he injected himself with microbes that he hoped would extend life. He died four years later, at age seventy-one.

5. CLARA MAASS

   The head of a nursing school in New Jersey, Maass took part in Walter Reed's yellow fever studies in Cuba in 1900, allowing herself to be bitten by an infected mosquito. She was supposed to contract a mild case of the disease and then recover, immune. She became the only woman to die as a result of the experiments.

6. ELIHU THOMSON

An electrical engineer second only to Thomas Edison in number of patents held, Thomson was also a pioneer in the field of radiology. Before the dangers of X rays were fully understood, workers were being burned by the radiation. In 1896, using two of his own fingers, Thomson discovered that lead shields stopped the rays but aluminum did not. The experiments left his fingers stiff and scarred.

7. HORATIO C. WOOD

This botany professor set out in 1869 to prove that American hemp (marijuana), then grown primarily for use as a rope fiber, was a psychoactive drug. He tested Kentucky hemp himself in various doses, finding it quite potent. By the end of the nineteenth century, hemp cultivation for rope-making had declined dramatically.

11 Prominent People Who Died While Exercising

1. RON COPELAND (1957–1975)

Copeland, an NCAA hurdles champ and All-American track and field star, died at age twenty-eight of an apparent heart attack after he ran a sixty-yard dash challenge match against a young college athlete.

2. BING CROSBY (1904–1977)

The Crooner, an avid golfer, had just completed seventeen holes of golf at La Moralejo Golf Club in Spain when he fell to the ground. His golf partners thought he had merely slipped, but he had had a massive heart attack. He died en route to a hospital in Madrid.

3. JIM FIXX (1932–1984)

A 220-pound, two-pack-a-day smoker until age thirty-five, Fixx became the guru of marathoners in the 1970s when he wrote

The Complete Book of Running. He died of a massive heart attack, at age fifty-two, during one of his daily ten-mile runs.

4. ZANE GREY (1875–1939)

This famous author suffered a fatal heart attack after working out on weight equipment in his home. As a record-holding deep-sea fisherman, he used the weights to stay in shape for his fishing expeditions.

5. HAROLD E. HOLT (1908–1967)

Holt, prime minister of Australia, drowned near his home outside Melbourne while skin diving in the ocean in search of crayfish. His doctor had earlier advised him to cut down on swimming and tennis.

6. BRIAN JONES (1944–1969)

Guitarist Jones had quit the Rolling Stones only one month before taking what turned out to be a fatal midnight swim. Friends who found him at the bottom of his pool were unable to revive him.

7. NICO (1938–1988)

Nico, the German-born vocalist who sang with the Velvet Underground, died of a cerebral hemorrhage while riding her bicycle in Ibiza, Spain. She had performed in Berlin four weeks before her death.

8. THEODORE ROETHKE (1908–1963)

Though overweight, the Pulitzer Prize–winning poet was a good swimmer, tennis player, and dancer. However, a few minutes after he dived into a swimming pool, friends found him floating facedown, dead of a heart attack.

9. CARROLL ROSENBLOOM (1907–1979)

Sports entrepreneur and owner of the Rams football team, Rosenbloom drowned while swimming in the surf near his rented Florida vacation home. He had been caught in a severe undertow.

10. RICHARD TREGASKIS (1916–1973)

This U.S. journalist and author (best known for *Guadalcanal Diary*) had a heart attack while swimming in the ocean near Honolulu. He was found in the water, dead.

11. JEAN TROISGROS (1926–1983)

Troisgros, one of the great chefs of Europe, died of a heart attack while playing tennis at Vittel, a French spa.

Addictive Potential of
18 Drugs

In Health magazine asked a panel of experts to rank commonly used drugs by their potential for addiction. Two factors were used: how easily people become addicted and how difficult it is for most people to quit. A score of 100 represented a high potential for addiction, 1 a low potential. Because each individual reacts differently, based on physiology, psychology, and social pressures, the rankings reflect addictive potential only.

	Potential for Addiction
1. Nicotine	100.00
2. Ice, glass (methamphetamine smoked)	98.53
3. Crack	97.66
4. Crystal meth (methamphetamine injected)	94.09
5. Valium (diazepam)	85.68
6. Quaalude (methaqualone)	83.38
7. Seconal (secobarbital)	82.11
8. Alcohol	81.85
9. Heroin	81.80
10. Crank (amphetamine taken orally)	81.09
11. Cocaine	73.13
12. Caffeine	72.01
13. PCP (phencyclidine)	55.69
14. Marijuana	21.16
15. Ecstasy (MDMA)	20.14
16. Psilocybine mushrooms	17.13
17. LSD	16.72
18. Mescaline	16.72

SOURCE: Researched by John Hastings. Reprinted from IN HEALTH. Copyright © 1990.

15 Most Popular Ice Cream Flavors

		Percent Preferring
1.	Vanilla	29.0
2.	Chocolate	8.9
3.	Butter pecan	5.3
3.	Strawberry	5.3
5.	Neapolitan	4.2
6.	Chocolate chip	3.9
7.	French vanilla	3.8
8.	Cookies and cream	3.6
9.	Vanilla fudge/ripple	2.6
10.	Praline pecan	1.7
11.	Cherry	1.6
11.	Chocolate almond	1.6
11.	Coffee	1.6
14.	Rocky road	1.5
15.	Chocolate marshmallow	1.3
	All others	23.7

SOURCE: International Ice Cream Association, 888 16th Street N.W., Washington, D.C., 20006.

11 Foods and Their Filth Levels

These are some of the sample levels of filth which are considered acceptable by the U.S. Food and Drug Administration.

1. CHOCOLATE; CHOCOLATE LIQUOR

    Up to 60 microscopic insect fragments per six 100-gram samples or up to 90 fragments in one sample; or an average of more than one rodent hair in a set of six samples or up to four hairs in any one sample.

2. COFFEE BEANS

    Ten percent insect-infested, insect-damaged, or moldy.

3. FIG PASTE

    Thirteen insect heads in two 100-gram samples.

4. FISH (FRESH FROZEN)

Five percent of fish or fillets with "definite odor of decomposition" over 25 percent of fish area; or 20 percent of the fish fillets with "slight odor of decomposition" over 25 percent of fish area.

5. MUSHROOMS (CANNED)

Up to 20 maggots per 100 grams of drained mushrooms; up to 5 maggots 2 millimeters (about one-twelfth of an inch) or longer; or 75 mites.

6. PEANUT BUTTER

Average of 30 or more insect fragments per 100 grams. Average of one or more rodent hairs per 100 grams.

7. PEPPER

Average of 1 percent insect-infested or moldy by weight; or 1 percent of excreta per pound.

8. POPCORN

Either one rodent pellet per sample or one rodent hair per two samples; or two rodent hairs per pound or 20 gnawed grains per pound, and hairs in 50 percent of samples. Popcorn may contain up to 5 percent field corn by weight.

9. SPINACH (CANNED OR FROZEN)

In 100-gram samples, either 50 aphids, thrips, or mites, or 8 leaf miners; or, in 24 pounds, 2 spinach worms, or worm fragments, whose total length is 12 millimeters (about one-half inch).

10. STRAWBERRIES (FROZEN, WHOLE, SLICED)

Mold count of 55 percent in half of the samples.

11. TOMATO PASTE (PIZZA AND OTHER SAUCES)

In 100-gram samples, either 30 fly eggs or 15 eggs plus one larva; two larvae per twelve samples; or mold count averaging 40 percent (30 percent for pizza sauce) in six samples.

10 Foods You Should Never Eat

A 2,000-calorie daily diet should include no more than 30 percent of calories from fat (about 67 grams); no more than 10 percent (about 22 grams) should come from saturated fats. Salt intake should be limited to no more than 6 grams (or the equivalent of about three teaspoons) per day. Some products on the market come close to the upper limits for a whole day's allowance of salt and fat. As of early 1993 the Center for Science in the Public Interest recommended avoiding the following foods. (The CSPI publishes the Nutrition Action Healthletter, 1875 Connecticut Avenue, N.W., Washington, D.C. 20009.)

1. QUAKER 100% NATURAL CEREAL — high in fat; low in fiber (compared to other cereals); ¼ cup serving contains 6 grams of fat and 2 grams of fiber
2. CONTADINA ALFREDO SAUCE — high in fat and saturated fat; ½ cup serving contains 34 grams of fat, 20 of them saturated
3. NISSIN CHICKEN CUP O' NOODLES — high in fat and sodium; one serving contains 14 grams of fat, 1700 milligrams (1.7 grams) of sodium
4. TACO BELL'S TACO SALAD WITH SHELL — 61 grams of fat (19 of them saturated) and 941 calories; even without the taco shell, this salad has more fat than a McDonald's Quarter Pounder with cheese
5. STOUFFER'S CHICKEN ENCHILADA — high in fat; 31 grams of fat per serving
6. SWANSON GREAT STARTS SCRAMBLED EGGS AND SAUSAGE WITH HASH BROWNS — high in fat; 34 grams of fat
7. OSCAR MAYER LUNCHABLES — high in fat and sodium; the average is 26 grams of fat, 1556 milligrams of sodium per 4.5-ounce serving package
8. HÄAGEN-DAZS ICE CREAM — most "premium" ice creams are high in fat; a ¾ cup serving of Häagen-Dazs vanilla contains 26 grams of fat
9. CAMPBELL CHUNKY SOUPS — high in sodium; the average sodium content for a single-serving "Individual Size" can is 1135 milligrams
10. SWANSON HUNGRY MAN TURKEY POT PIE — high in fat; 36 grams of fat

15 Common Fruits
with Lowest Available Sugar

	Total Available Glucose per Ounce
1. Casaba melon	1.92
2. Strawberries	2.12
3. Watermelon	2.17

15 Common Fruits with Lowest Available Sugar (Cont.)

	Total Available Glucose per Ounce
4. Grapefruit	2.42
5. Cantaloupe	2.54
6. Honeydew melon	2.70
7. Lemons	2.85
8. Pricklypear	2.87
9. Avocado	2.88
10. Papaya	2.91
11. Gooseberries	3.07
12. Limes	3.13
13. Peaches	3.29
14. Tangerines	3.31
15. Apricots	3.42

15 Common Vegetables with Highest Available Sugar

	Total Available Glucose per Ounce
1. Taro	9.97
2. Yams, cooked	8.14
3. Corn, sweet	7.76
4. Potatoes, baked	7.59
5. Sweet potatoes (baked in skin)	7.23
6. Parsnips	5.81
7. Artichokes	3.33
8. Carrots, cooked	3.18
9. Butternut squash, winter	3.15
10. Carrots, raw	3.07
11. Brussels sprouts	2.91
12. Acorn squash, winter	2.62
13. Peas, edible-podded	2.56
14. Rutabagas	2.40
15. Leeks	2.32

NOTE: Total available glucose (TAG) is a value calculated by using 58 percent of the amount of protein, 10 percent of the fat, and 100 percent of the carbohydrates in 100 edible grams of food. That number is divided by 3.5 to arrive at the TAG per ounce.

SOURCE: Mary Joan Oexmann, *Total Available Glucose: A Diabetic Food System* (New York: William Morrow, 1989).

11 Food Repair Tips

Cookbook authors are always telling us how to prepare the perfect meal, but how many give us advice when we've ruined the perfect meal or when we're having trouble in the kitchen? In their book *How to Repair Food,* Marina and John Bear provide all the necessary solutions.

1. *Butter: burning while sautéing or frying.* Add a small amount of oil to the butter when you see that it is browning too quickly.
2. *Ketchup: won't pour.* Put a drinking straw down to the bottom of the bottle — the air channeled to the bottom allows the ketchup to pour.
3. *Marshmallows: hard or stale.* Seal marshmallows and a piece of fresh bread in a plastic bag for 3 days. This yields soft marshmallows and stale bread.
4. *Milk: going sour.* Adding 2 teaspoons of baking soda to a quart of milk will make it last an extra day or two.
5. *Olives: hard to pit.* Place on paper towel or wax paper and roll gently with a rolling pin. Next, push down on the olive with the heel of your hand, and the pit will come out.
6. *Popcorn: won't pop.* Popcorn may not pop if it has dried out. Put the kernels in water for 5 minutes, then drain. Still no action? Freeze the kernels for 24 hours, then pop them while still frozen. (Some people store popcorn in the freezer.)
7. *Potato chips: soggy.* Put chips under the broiler briefly, but don't let them brown. Or, microwave on high setting for 30 to 60 seconds, then let stand for 3 minutes.
8. *Radishes: wilted, soft, soggy.* Soak in ice water for 2 or 3 hours. Optional: Add 1 tablespoon of vinegar or the juice of 1 lemon to the water.
9. *Rice: burned.* Turn off the heat, place the heel of a loaf of bread on top of the rice, cover for 5 minutes. The bread absorbs the scorched taste.
10. *Soup: too salty.* Add a can of tomatoes, if appropriate to the type of soup; or, a few pinches of brown sugar; or, a thin-sliced raw potato.
11. *Broccoli: smelly.* Put a piece of bread or a small piece of red pepper into the pot as it cools.

Alice Waters's
10 Best Cookbooks of All Time

Alice Waters, known as "the mother of the new American cuisine," opened her restaurant, Chez Panisse, in Berkeley, California, in 1971. In 1992 she was honored with two James Beard Awards — the Oscars of the eatery industry — for Best Chef in America and Best Restaurant in America. Her philosophy has always remained the same: use the freshest, purest, most seasonal ingredients; the best food is the simplest food. Her books include *Chez Panisse Menu Cookbook, Chez Panisse Cooking,* and a children's book, *Fanny at Chez Panisse.*

1. *French Provençal Cooking,* by Elizabeth David
2. *French Menu Cookbook,* by Richard Olney
3. *Traditional Recipes of the Provences of France,* by Curnonsky
4. *Serve It Forth,* by M. F. K. Fisher
5. *Almanach des Gourmands,* by Gimond de la Reyniere
6. *Passionate Epicure,* by Marcel Rouff
7. *Delights and Prejudices,* by James Beard
8. *Larousse Gastronomique,* by Prosper Montagne
9. *The Auberge of the Flowering Hearth,* by Andres Roy DeGroot
10. *Les Plats Regionaux de France,* by Austin de Croze

— Exclusive for *The Book of Lists*

14 Nations with More Sheep Than Humans

		Sheep	Humans
1.	Australia	162,774,000	17,800,000
2.	New Zealand	57,000,000	3,400,000
3.	Uruguay	25,986,000	3,100,000
4.	Syria	15,321,000	3,700,000
5.	Mongolia	15,083,000	2,300,000
6.	Somalia	13,800,000*	8,300,000
7.	Bolivia	12,300,000*	7,800,000
8.	Namibia	6,700,000*	1,500,000
9.	Libya	6,500,000*	4,500,000
10.	Ireland	6,001,000	3,500,000
11.	Mauritania	4,200,000*	2,100,000
12.	Iceland	700,000*	250,000
13.	Djibouti	420,000*	400,000
14.	Faeroe Islands	67,000*	50,000

World sheep population: 1,202,920,000

*F.A.O. estimate

SOURCE: Food and Agriculture Organization of the United Nations, *F.A.O. Yearbook*, volume 45, 1991.

10 Nations with More Cattle Than Humans

		Cattle	Humans
1.	Brazil	152,000,000*	150,800,000
2.	Argentina	50,080,000*	33,100,000
3.	Australia	23,430,000	17,800,000
4.	Uruguay	8,869,000	3,100,000
5.	Paraguay	8,260,000	4,500,000
6.	New Zealand	8,200,000	3,400,000
7.	Ireland	6,029,000	3,500,000

10 Nations with
More Cattle Than Humans (Cont.)

	Cattle	Humans
8. Mongolia	2,849,000	2,300,000
9. Botswana	2,600,000†	1,400,000
10. Namibia	2,131,000	1,500,000

World cattle population: 1,294,604,000

*Unofficial figure

†F.A.O. estimate

SOURCE: Food and Agriculture Organization of the United Nations, *F.A.O. Yearbook,* volume 45, 1991.

5 Nations with
More Goats Than Humans

	Goats	Humans
1. Somalia	20,500,000*	2,300,000
2. Mongolia	5,126,000	2,300,000
3. Mauritania	3,310,000*	2,100,000
4. Namibia	1,400,000	1,500,000
5. Djibouti	504,000*	400,000

World goat population: 94,266,000
* F.A.O. estimate

SOURCE: Food and Agriculture Organization of the United Nations, *F.A.O. Yearbook,* volume 45, 1991.

3 Nations with
More Pigs Than Humans

	Pigs	Humans
1. Denmark	9,489,000	5,200,000
2. Wallis and Futuna	25,000	17,000
3. Tuvalu	12,000	9,000

World pig population: 857,099,000

SOURCE: Food and Agriculture Organization of the United Nations, *F.A.O. Yearbook,* volume 45, 1991.

11 Nations with the Most Camels

	Camels (1991 estimates)
1. Somalia	6,860,000
2. Sudan	2,757,000
3. India	1,490,000
4. Ethiopia	1,060,000
5. Pakistan	1,005,000
6. Mauritania	920,000
7. Kenya	820,000
8. Chad	565,000
9. Mongolia	562,000
10. China	463,000
11. Saudi Arabia	390,000

World camel population: 19,627,000

NOTE: Egypt ranks 16th with 200,000.

SOURCE: Food and Agriculture Organization of the United Nations, *F.A.O. Yearbook*, volume 45, 1991.

8 Examples of Strange Animal Behavior

1. GENTLE CROCODILES

Nile crocodiles, although physically and morally capable of killing humans, are tender guardians of their own babies. Newborn crocodiles average twenty-eight centimeters (eleven inches) in length and weigh 100 grams (three and a half ounces) — tempting prey for a wide range of predators. To protect them when they emerge from their shells, a mother crocodile delicately picks up the hatchlings with her deadly jaws and slips them into a pouch inside her mouth. Then she carries the chirping babies to the water where they are greeted by a roaring chorus from the adult males.

2. TRANSFORMER FROGS

The female gastric brooding frog *(Rheobatrachus silus)*, which flourished in Queensland, Australia, until its recent extinction, swallowed her fertilized eggs, transformed her stomach into a uterus, carried the developing tadpoles in her stomach, and then gave birth to fully formed young through her mouth.

3. Farmer Ants

Aphids produce a sugary excrement which has come to be known as honeydew. Some ants obtain this honeydew by licking the leaves and stems on which it has fallen. But some ant species have learned to gather the aphids into their nests, feed them, and then when the ants are hungry, to stroke the aphids with their feelers so that they produce the honeydew, which the ants then drink fresh.

4. Incestuous Mites

The female mite known as *Histiostoma murchiei* creates her own husband from scratch. She lays eggs that turn into adults without needing to be fertilized. The mother then copulates with her sons within three or four days of laying the eggs, after which the sons die rather quickly.

5. Non-nurturing Cuckoos

Female cuckoos deposit their eggs in the nests of other birds, who then incubate the eggs and raise the offspring until they are able to fly away on their own. Curiously, each individual cuckoo mother chooses the same species to adopt all of her children and is able to lay eggs that resemble the eggs of the foster family.

6. Codependent Angler Fish

As soon as they mature sexually, male angler fish begin a desperate search to find a mate in the dark waters 6,000 feet below the surface. As soon as they locate likely prospects, certain species of angler fish attach themselves to the females — literally. The male latches on to the much larger female and never lets go

Angler fish couple.

for the rest of his life. In fact, their vascular systems become united and the male becomes entirely dependent on the female's blood for nutrition. In exchange, the male provides the female with sperm.

7. CHILD-LABORING ANTS

Several species of tree ants in southeast Asia have evolved a bizarre method for building their nests. While one brigade of ants holds together two leaves, another brigade grabs hold of ant larvae and squeezes out of their young bodies a sticky thread that is used to hold together the edges of the leaves.

8. TORTURING, MURDEROUS WASPS

Ichneumon wasps are the sort of beings that inspire horror films. At the worst, an ichneumon mother picks a victim, usually a caterpillar, and injects her eggs into the host's body. Often she also injects a poison that paralyzes the victim without killing it. When the eggs hatch, the wasp larvae begin eating the caterpillar. Because a dead caterpillar would be useless to developing wasps, they contrive to keep the unfortunate victim alive as long as possible by eating its fatty deposits and digestive organs first and saving the heart and central nervous system for last.

9 Unusual Animal Mating Habits

This has been condensed from *How They Do It,* by Robert A. Wallace (New York: William Morrow, 1980), which is highly recommended for anyone wishing to learn more about animal amours.

1. GEESE

Two male geese may form a homosexual bond and prefer each other's company to any females. Sometimes, however, a female may interpose herself between them during such a courtship, and be quickly fertilized. They will accept her, and weeks later the happy family of three can be seen attending to its tiny newborn goslings.

2. DOLPHINS

Dolphins engage in extensive foreplay, nuzzling, rubbing, and giving love bites. The male inserts only the tip of his penis — which is attached to the shaft by a kind of swivel and rotates independently — into his partner. Captive dolphins masturbate freely, even when there are females present. One woman keeper made news by occasionally masturbating her male dolphins when they approached her with an erection.

3. PENGUINS

Penguins prefer to be "married," but they suffer long separations due to their migratory habits. When reunited, a pair will stand breast to breast, heads thrown back, singing loudly, with outstretched flippers trembling. Two weeks after a pair is formed, their union is consummated. The male makes his intentions known by laying his head across his partner's stomach. They go on a long trek to find privacy, but the actual process of intercourse takes only three minutes. Neither penguin will mate again that year.

4. RHINOCEROS

Not surprisingly, rhino mating is a dangerous business. As the female enters her mating period, her vulva swells and she makes shrill whistling noises in the presence of a male. He responds with deep, heaving sighs. Next, he charges her head-on, and she meets the attack. Again and again they rush each other, bellowing with anger and butting fiercely. They continue for an hour, risking serious injury. If the female finally decides the male is worthy, she presents her rear to him, and he enters her with his two-foot-long penis. He remains mounted for over an hour, ejaculating every ten minutes.

5. TICKS

A female tick needs at least one blood meal in order to form her eggs. While she is feeding on a bird or animal, the male sneaks under her belly and prepares to make love. Unfortunately, he doesn't have a penis, so he wiggles around inside her vagina with his nose. When her opening is large enough, he turns around and deposits a packet of sperm from his rear onto the entrance of her orifice. Then he uses his snout to push it deeply into her vagina.

6. SKUNKS

The male skunk makes an aggressive attack on the female, following her around, licking her genitals, and then holding her down by the scruff of the neck. In spite of all his efforts, she won't mate with him until she's ready, so he stimulates her by scratching vigorously at her vulva with his rear legs. This technique does the trick, and he then enters her with his tiny penis — an inch-and-a-half long, and no thicker than a pencil lead. When the female's heat ends, she refuses to mate further, even though the male attempts (unsuccessfully) to rape her. Miffed, she may temporarily move her bedding out of their nest and sleep elsewhere.

7. BEDBUGS

The male bedbug does not penetrate the female's vagina with his large, warped penis. Instead, he uses it to break the shell on her back and deposit his sperm, which migrates to special pouches in her body for storage. A female who mates with more than six males is likely to die from her wounds. Furthermore, homosexuality is rampant among bedbugs, and some males have special organs to receive the sperm of other males. An inseminated male bedbug may then ejaculate both his own sperm and that of his homosexual partner into a female.

8. DUCKS

Male ducks become sex maniacs in the spring, trying to force themselves on any female they see. Once mated, they stay "married" to a female for a season. A "husband" may not try to prevent his "wife" from being chased by suitors, but he may follow her to be sure he doesn't lose her. The female duck apparently would rather die than be unfaithful, and may hide in the grass all day to avoid her suitor.

9. PIGS

The term *screwing* may have originated with observation of pigs' mating habits. The male's penis is a foot and a half long, and the tip is spirally twisted into a kind of corkscrew. When he enters the female, the tip rotates until it is tightly lodged inside her. His repeated ejaculations are spectacular — each time, he injects her with up to a *pint* of semen.

Average Erect Penis Lengths for *10* Species

Animal	Average Erect Penis Length
1. Humpback whale	10 ft.
2. Elephant	5 to 6 ft.
3. Bull	3 ft.
4. Stallion	2 ft. 6 in.
5. Rhinoceros	2 ft.
6. Pig	18 to 20 in.
7. Man	6 in.
8. Gorilla	2 in.
9. Cat	¾ in.
10. Mosquito	1/100 in.

SOURCE: Leigh Rutledge, *The Gay Book of Lists* (Boston: Alyson Publications, 1987).

Bandleader Kay Kyser and comedian Bob Hope reviewing their assets.

Maximum Recorded Life Span
of **27** Animals

	Age
1. Lake sturgeon	152 yrs.
2. Human being	120 yrs. 7 mos.
3. Tortoise	116 yrs.
4. Whale	87 yrs.
5. Condor	72 yrs.
6. Elephant	70 yrs.
7. Chimpanzee	59 yrs. 4 mos.
8. Hippopotamus	59 yrs. 1 mo.*
9. Orangutan	59 yrs.
10. Monkey	53 yrs.
11. Gorilla	47 yrs. 6 mos.
12. Horse	46 yrs.
13. Rhinoceros	46 yrs.
14. Hyena	41 yrs. 1 mo.
15. Dolphin	39 yrs. 8 mos.*
16. Brown Bear	38 yrs. 1 mo.
17. Giraffe	36 yrs. 2 mos.
18. Camel	35 yrs. 5 mos.
19. Tapeworm	35 yrs.
20. Cat	34 yrs.
21. Bat	31 yrs. 5 mos.

22. Sumatran porcupine	27 yrs. 3 mos.
23. Jaguar	24 yrs. 5 mos.*
24. Raccoon	20 yrs. 7 mos.
25. North American porcupine	13 yrs. 9 mos.
26. Ant (queen)	13 yrs.
27. Slug	1 yr. 6 mos.

*Still alive as of June 1993.

SOURCE: M. L. Jones, Zoological Society of San Diego.

The Cat Came Back:
11 Cats Who Traveled Long Distances to Return Home

1. SUGAR — 1,500 miles

   Sugar, a two-year-old part-Persian, had a hip deformity, which made her uncomfortable during car travel. Consequently, she was left behind with a neighbor when her family left Anderson, California, for Gage, Oklahoma. Two weeks later, Sugar disappeared. Fourteen months later, she turned up in Gage on her old owner's doorstep — having traveled 100 miles a month to reach a place *she had never been.* The case was investigated in person by the famous parapsychologist J. B. Rhine, who observed pussy and interviewed witnesses.

2. MINOSCH — 1,500 miles

   In 1981 Mehmet Tunc, a Turkish "guest worker" in Germany, went home with his cat and family for a vacation. At the Turkish border, Minosch disappeared. Sixty-one days later, back on the island of Sylt, in northern Germany, the family heard a faint scratching at the door. It was a bedraggled Minosch.

3. SILKY — 1,472 miles

   Shaun Philips, sixteen, and his father, Ken, lost Silky at Gin Gin, about 200 miles north of Brisbane, Australia. That was in the summer of 1977. On March 28, 1978, Silky turned up at Mr. Philips's house in a Melbourne suburb. According to his owner, "He was as thin as a wisp and stank to high heaven."

4. HOWIE — 1,200 miles

   In 1978 this three-year-old Persian walked home from the Gold Coast in Queensland, Australia, to Adelaide — a trip that took a year. Said his owner, Kirsten Hicks, fifteen, "Although its white coat was matted and filthy and its paws were sore and bleeding, Howie was actually purring."

5. RUSTY — 950 miles

Rusty distinguished himself by setting an American all-time speed record for a cat return. In 1949 this ginger tom traveled from Boston, Massachusetts, to Chicago, Illinois, in eighty-three days. It is speculated that he hitched rides on cars, trucks, and trains.

6. GRINGO — 480 miles

The Servoz family lost their pet tom, Gringo, from their home in Lamarche-sur-Seine, France, in December 1982. The following July they learned that the cat had moved to the French Riviera. Wishing to escape the cold winter, he had made the journey south in a week and appeared at their summer home, where neighbors took care of him.

7. MUDDY WATER WHITE — 450 miles

On June 23 or 24, 1985, Muddy Water White jumped out of a van driven by his owner, Barbara Paule, in Dayton, Ohio. Almost exactly three years later, he returned to his home in Pennsylvania. "He came and just flopped down like he was home," said Ms. Paule. She fed him for three days before realizing he was Muddy Water White, an identification that was confirmed by the local vet.

8. MURKA — 400 miles

In 1987 Murka, a stray tortoiseshell, was adopted by Vladimir Donsov in Moscow. Murka killed his canary; a year later, she unlocked the bird cage and killed another one. She was banished to live with Mr. Donsov's mother in Voronezh, but disap-

Murka, who took a year to walk the 400 miles from Voronezh to Moscow.

peared after two years. A year later, on October 19, 1989, Mr. Donsov found her in his Moscow apartment building, hungry, dirty, pregnant, and missing the tip of her tail. She ate a large meal and slept for three days.

9. CHICHI — 300 miles

The Reverend J. C. Cox of Blanchard, Louisiana, gave his seventeen-year-old cat to his granddaughter, who lived in a suburb of New Orleans. ChiChi missed Reverend Cox, and to everyone's astonishment, crossed the Mississippi and Red rivers in three weeks and arrived home in time for Christmas.

10. POOH — 200 miles

The Reverend and Mrs. James Daves moved from Long Island to Georgia in 1973. Because their daughter was allergic to animal fur, her two-year-old white tom, Pooh, was given to a friend, but soon ran away. In May, the family moved to South Carolina. On April 18, 1975, Pooh showed up at the home he had never been to before.

11. BORIS — 8 miles

Boris trekked back twice in 1990 to his old home in Berkshire, England — a short trip, but one that involved crossing two superhighways, the M4 and the A34.

PRIMARY SOURCE: *Fortean Times,* number 61 (February–March 1992).

6 Ways Cats Talk with Their Tails

1. A VERTICAL TAIL

He likes you — maybe. If his tail is completely straight, the cat is thrilled to see you, but a tip tilted into the shape of a question mark says the verdict on your character is still out.

2. SOFT CURVES

He's interested. The curious cat carries his tail just slightly raised and curved outward.

3. A LOWERED TAIL

He's not taking any chances. If his tail is lowered and fluffed out, this cat's afraid. In surrender, he tucks his tail between his hind legs.

4. A TWITCHING TIP

The cat is miffed. This tiny tail gesture means he's mildly irritated. Don't bug him.

5. A WAGGING TAIL

He's weighing his options. You may shift from foot to foot when you're making a decision; a cat wags his tail. Look out when it whips up speed: he's probably really angry.

6. AN ARCHED, BRISTLED TAIL

He's all set to duke it out. The angry cat bristles his coat to scare off enemies. He may take a swipe at you if you try to interfere.

SOURCE: Reprinted with permission from *Pet Care Report.* Copyright 1991, Whittle Communications L. P.

The Top 25 Cat Names

1. Kitty	10. Princess	19. Blackie
2. Smokey	11. Patches	20. Coco
3. Shadow	12. Sam	21. Bandit
4. Tiger	13. Max	22. Lady
5. Boo (Boo Boo)	14. Mickey	23. Misty
6. Boots	15. Samantha	24. Morris
7. Molly	16. Wiskers	25. Casey
8. Tigger	17. Fluffy	
9. Spike	18. Katie	

SOURCE: Renee Cowing, *The Complete Book of Pet Names* (San Mateo: Fireplug Press, 1990).

The Top 25 Dog Names

1. Brandy	10. Bear	19. Buddy
2. Lady	11. Misty	20. Buffy
3. Max	12. Duke	21. Rusty
4. Rocky	13. Pepper	22. Nicky
5. Sam	14. Princess	23. Toby
6. Heidi	15. Coco	24. Sandy
7. Sheba	16. Prince	25. Dusty
8. Ginger	17. Charlie	
9. Muffin	18. Daisy	

SOURCE: Renee Cowing, *The Complete Book of Pet Names* (San Mateo: Fireplug Press, 1990).

9 Winners of the Dog Hero of the Year Award

In 1954 Ken-L Ration began honoring exceptional canines by awarding the Dog Hero of the Year medal. The program is currently sponsored by Kibbles 'n' Bits. The stories of eleven pre-1980 winners can be found in *The Book of Lists #3*.

1. WOODIE (1980)

   A collie mix owned by Rae Anne Knitter of Cleveland, Woodie leapt off an eighty-foot cliff to rescue Knitter's fiancé, Ray Thomas, from drowning. One afternoon, Rae Anne, Ray, and Woodie were walking along a nature trail in the Rocky River Reservation when Ray, an amateur photographer, decided to capture a spectacular view from atop a steep shale cliff. Rae Anne and Woodie waited on the path while Ray disappeared over the top of the hill. Suddenly, the usually well-behaved Woodie began twisting and tugging to escape from Rae Anne. She let go of Woodie, who raced ahead. When Rae Anne reached the brink she saw Ray lying unconscious in a stream eighty feet below. Woodie, who broke both hips in jumping down, was by his side, nudging Ray's face to keep it out of the water. Both Ray and Woodie survived.

2. KING (1981)

   On the morning of December 26, 1981, the Carlson family of Granite Falls, Washington, was asleep when a fire broke out in their utility room. King, a German shepherd mix, was sleeping in the adjoining family room. Instead of escaping through a door that had been left open for him, King clawed and chewed his way through the plywood door that separated him from the utility room. Then he charged through the burning room into the bedroom where sixteen-year-old Pearl Carlson was sleeping. He woke her and the two rushed to her parents' bedroom to alert them. Howard Carlson had a lung condition and could not move as quickly as his wife and daughter, but King remained by him until the man was safely outside. King was badly burned on his paws, had a gash on his back, and splinters in his mouth, but made a full recovery.

3. BO (1982)

   Bo, a Labrador retriever, was rafting on the Colorado River with a puppy named Dutchess and their owners, Laurie and Rob Roberts of Glenwood Springs, Colorado, when an eight-foot wave flipped the raft over. Rob and Dutchess were thrown free, but Laura and Bo were trapped underneath. Bo finally emerged, but then dived back under the raft. He reappeared towing Laurie by the hair. Once she was free of the raft, Laurie grabbed Bo's tail and let the dog pull her across the strong current to shore.

4. VILLA (1983)

During a severe blizzard in Villas, New Jersey, eleven-year-old Andrea Anderson was blown into a large snowdrift about forty feet from her home. Disoriented, blinded by snow being blown by sixty-mile-an-hour winds, and unable to pull herself out, she began to scream for help. Villa, a one-year-old black Newfoundland puppy belonging to Mrs. Lynda Veit, heard Andrea's cries and, for the first time in her life, leapt over the five-foot fence surrounding her run. Villa ran eighty feet to the snowdrift, found Andrea, and licked her face reassuringly. Then she circled the girl to clear the snow entrapping her. Once Andrea was free, Villa cleared a path for her through the blinding snow and led her to the front door of Andrea's house.

5. LEO (1984)

Leo, a four-year-old standard poodle from Hunt, Texas, was playing near the Guadalupe River with eleven-year-old Sean Callahan and Sean's nine-year-old sister, Erin. Suddenly, Leo and the two children stumbled upon a five-and-a-half-foot diamondback rattlesnake. Leo lunged between the snake and Sean, allowing his young master to escape. Leo received six poisonous bites to the head. He almost died, but made a remarkable recovery.

6.–7. CHAMP AND BUDDY (1986)

Champ, a terrier, and Buddy, a mixed breed, from Dickinson, North Dakota, saved an injured truck driver one blustery winter night. The pair led their owners, Harvey and Anneliese Schmidt, to a deserted warehouse where Marvin Dacar was trapped and injured beneath a 2,680-pound scraper tire. Doctors said that Dacar would have died from shock due to loss of blood and the cold if Champ and Buddy hadn't saved him.

8. REONA (1989)

On October 17, 1989, a devastating earthquake hit northern California. After the first jolt, Reona, a two-and-a-half-year-old rottweiler owned by Jim Patton of Watsonville, heard screams from across the street. Reona bolted out the door, jumped three fences (something she had never done), and raced into the home of five-year-old Vivian Cooper. The terrified child was standing in the kitchen when Reona pushed her against the cabinets and sat on her. Seconds later, a large microwave oven

Reona, a 2½-year-old rottweiler, saved the life of 5-year-old Vivian Cooper during an earthquake.

on top of the refrigerator came crashing down where Vivian had been standing.

9. WILLY (1991)

Betty Souder of Los Alamos, New Mexico, was sleeping soundly when she was awakened by her nine-year-old weimaraner, Willy. "I couldn't seem to wake up," she later recalled. But Willy persisted. When Souder finally stood, she felt dizzy and she noticed that Willy was weaving too. Almost too weak to pick up the telephone, Souder finally managed to place a call to a friend. It turned out that a faulty furnace had leaked, filling the house with poisonous carbon monoxide gas. Had Souder slept a few minutes longer, she probably would not have been able to make her life-saving call.

17 Dog Terms

1. *Apple head:* A rounded head, instead of flat on top.
2. *Brisket:* The part of the body in front of the chest.
3. *Butterfly nose:* A spotted nose.
4. *Button ear:* Where the tip falls over and covers the orifice.
5. *Cat foot:* A short round foot, knuckles high and well developed.
6. *Chops:* The pendulous lip of the bulldog.
7. *Dew claw:* Extra claw, found occasionally on all breeds.
8. *Dewlap:* Pendulous skin under the throat.
9. *Dish-faced:* When nose is higher than muzzle at the stop.

10. *Dudley nose:* A yellow or flesh-coloured nose.
11. *Flews:* The pendulous lips of the bloodhound and other breeds.
12. *Haw:* Red inside eyelid, shown in bloodhounds and St. Bernards.
13. *Hucklebones:* Tops of the hip joints.
14. *Pig jaw:* Exaggeration of overshot.
15. *Rose ear:* Where the tip of the ear turns back, showing interior.
16. *Smudge nose:* A nose which is not wholly black, but not spotted.
17. *Tulip ear:* An erect or pricked ear.

SOURCE: "Dog," *Encyclopaedia Britannica*, 11th edition (1910–11), 8:379.

Killer Bees and
9 Other Mistakes

1. GIANT AFRICAN SNAIL (1990s)

   A crate of 1,000 giant African snails was recently smuggled from Lagos, Nigeria, to the United States. The baseball-size slugs were then sold to exotic-pet dealers in twenty-five states. If it escapes into the wild, a single slug can reproduce itself (they're hermaphrodites) 16 quadrillion times in five years. The snail, which weighs up to a pound, can eat an entire head of lettuce in one sitting. "It eats anything," said one zoologist — including house paint, rats, and beer.

2. WALKING CATFISH (1967)

   Imported originally from southeast Asia as an aquarium fish, the catfish escaped from breeding tanks in Florida. Able to breathe and crawl on land, this fish is aggressive and can eat other fish up to seven inches long.

3. NILE PERCH (1962)

   Officials of Ugandan and Kenyan fisheries, hoping to increase Lake Victoria's output of food, stocked it with the Nile perch. But the voracious perch killed off many of the indigenous fish. Overfishing and pollution contributed to the problem, and now 300 species of fish have vanished from the lake.

4. AFRICANIZED BEE (1957)

   Thirty-five years after it was introduced into Brazil and escaped from a breeding experiment, the killer bee arrived in Texas. It is believed that by the mid-1990s, swarms may reach Los Angeles. On its migration north, the bee has killed hundreds of people and has caused a falloff in honey production. The best way to cope with a killer bee attack is to run in a zigzag motion.

5. NUTRIA (1940)

One hundred fifty of these three-foot-long, twenty-pound rodents, imported from South America for their fur, escaped from a Louisiana fur ranch. This aggressive animal, which eats crops and aquatic plants, has spread across the United States and as far as western Canada.

6. GIANT TOAD (1930s)

This eight-inch toad was introduced into Australia to aid farmers in controlling the sugar cane beetle. But the toad, which secretes a deadly poison, became a menace to dogs, cattle, sheep, and other domestic animals. By the 1970s the Australian government was offering a bounty for the toad.

7. STARLING (1890)

Sixty of the birds were released in New York's Central Park by a group that planned to bring to the United States all of the birds mentioned in Shakespeare's works. The starlings multiplied and by the late 1950s they had invaded all of North America, taking over the nests of songbirds and damaging grain and fruit crops.

8. CARP (1870s)

Long raised for food in Asia and Europe, the carp was imported to the United States for that purpose and was successfully established in the 1870s. This giant cousin of the goldfish, though, muddies its waters by uprooting aquatic plants, rendering its environment uninhabitable for other species.

9. GYPSY MOTH (1866, 1991)

A French scholar visiting Harvard University allowed several caterpillars to escape. They soon multiplied and spread throughout New England, attacking trees and stripping their leaves. In 1991 thirty-five Asian gypsy moths entered the United States and British Columbia, apparently as stowaways aboard a group of Russian freighters. The newly hatched caterpillars climbed up to the highest point on the ship and were blown ashore. They are far more destructive than the European moth, which defoliates 4 million acres annually in the American Northeast. The Asian moths could cause $35 billion dollars of damage over the next forty years.

10. EUROPEAN WILD RABBIT (1859)

An Australian farmer freed these creatures, hoping to turn a profit from their pelts and meat. Within three years, the rabbit was a national catastrophe, turning grassland into desert, rendering it useless to livestock and to many native marsupials. Today, the rabbit population is still uncontrolled.

10 Safe Ways to Control Pests

In their 1991 book, *Tiny Game Hunting: Environmentally Healthy Ways to Trap and Kill the Pests in Your House and Garden,* authors Hilary Dole Klein and Adrian M. Wenner give us an all-around program for *safe* pest removal. Here are a few of their tips:

1. ANTS

   To block ants out, make barriers of cayenne pepper or lemon juice, rub the doorsill with oil of cloves or camphor, and smear petroleum jelly over entrance cracks. Some ants are repelled by cucumber slices, coffee grounds, or handfuls of crushed mint.

2. COCKROACHES

   The cockroach is known as the rat of the insect world. They are noted for their learning ability and are clever enough to shun poisons. The best way to be free of cockroaches is to keep your house clean and dry. Also, try strategically placed bay leaves, cucumbers, and slit garlic cloves. To make a cockroach trap, dampen a rag with beer and put it on the floor in an out-of-the-way place. Cockroaches like beer, and will gather under the cloth. If nothing else works, you can buy a gecko — a species of tropical lizard that will devour your roaches. But not if you have a cat — cats eat geckos.

3. FLEAS

   The Egyptians used to smear a slave with the milk of asses and make him stand in the room as a human flea trap; if you don't have a slave handy, there are other methods. The best is to comb your pet regularly with a fine-tooth flea comb, then dip the comb, bugs and all, into a glass of soapy water. Or, score the skin of an orange to release the citrus oil and rub the fruit right into the infested animal.

4. BEES

   Troublesome swarms of bees call for professional help, but if you have a lone bee in your house, open one window, pull the curtains, shut the remaining windows, and close the door. The bee will be attracted to the light and will hopefully fly out. To minimize your chances of getting stung, don't wear perfumes or brightly colored clothing. If you do get stung, don't pull out the stinger, but scrape at it with a finger or credit card to dislodge it. Bees, by the way, are at their most irritable after a rain, because pollen and nectar have been washed away.

5. FLIES

Natural fly repellents include mint, camphor, and a crushed potpourri of eucalyptus leaves, bay leaves, cloves, and pennyroyal. Spiders make great fly catchers, so don't kill them! So do frogs, toads, and birds.

6. MOSQUITOES

If you're getting attacked at night, try eating a dinner made with lots of garlic, or rub apple-cider vinegar on your skin. Pennyroyal and citronella are the best repellents, and you can buy citronella-scented candles at camping stores. To make a mosquito barrier, plant tansy or basil near doorways and patios.

7. BEETLES AND OTHER PANTRY PESTS

We all know how yucky it is to find moths or larvae in a bag of flour or a box of cereal. Bay leaves are an excellent repellent, or try unwrapping sticks of spearmint gum and putting them on the shelves. These pests hate cold, and you can safeguard your flour by storing it in the refrigerator. Also, these insects don't like to be disturbed. Try rummaging through your pantry and giving boxes and containers a good thump.

8. DEER

Pretty as they are, deer can do a lot of damage to a garden, eating everything from vegetables to roses. Stuff nylon stockings with human hair and hang them among the plants — the scent will repel them. Or, go to the zoo and get manure from members of the cat family — this makes an excellent repellent.

9. GOPHERS

These voracious animals can drive gardeners crazy. One way to rout them is to put a foul-smelling substance — such as rotting garbage, dead fish, or sponges soaked in urine — into their tunnels. Another trick is to take a small battery-operated radio, wrap it securely inside a plastic bag, and set it on loud static. Put this inside the tunnel and the noise will discourage the gophers.

10. RACCOONS

If raccoons are raiding your garbage, try sprinkling ammonia, Lysol, or Tabasco sauce on top of the garbage cans. If they're climbing over a fence into your garden, hang a few articles of sweaty clothing over it, replacing them when the odor wears off. You can also go to a pet groomer and get the hair trimmings from dogs, put them into a mesh bag, and set them around your property.

Odd Jobs of
35 Celebrities

1. Warren Beatty — dishwasher and cocktail-lounge pianist
2. Marlon Brando — department-store elevator operator (He quit after four days because having to call out "Lingerie" embarrassed him.)
3. Danny DeVito — hairdresser in his sister's beauty salon
4. Whoopi Goldberg — applied makeup to corpses in mortuary (She said it was "great work," because clients "never complained about how they looked.")
5. Gene Hackman — ladies' shoe salesman at Saks in New York
6. Pee-Wee Herman — Fuller Brush salesman
7. Gregory Hines — karate instructor
8. Cyndi Lauper — cleaned dog kennels
9. Steve Martin — eight years at Disneyland selling Mousketeer ears and Davy Crockett coonskin hats
10. Groucho Marx — cleaned wigs for a theatrical-wig maker
11. Gregory Peck — carnival barker at the World's Fair and tour guide at New York's Rockefeller Center
12. Telly Savalas — Peabody Award–winning executive with ABC News, and State Department employee
13. Sylvester Stallone — gym instructor and dorm bouncer at a girls' boarding school in Switzerland
14. Brad Pitt — worked as a giant chicken in front of El Pollo Loco, a fast-food chain
15. Benny Hill — milkman
16. Sinéad O'Connor — singing kiss-o-gram French maid in Dublin
17. Luther Vandross — defective-merchandise clerk at S&H trading stamps
18. Dan Aykroyd — wrote a manual for penitentiary guards
19. Ho Chi Minh — snow shoveler, photo retoucher, pastry chef's assistant in New York

20. Allen Ginsberg — merchant seaman, accountant
21. Ralph Lauren — tie salesman at Brooks Brothers
22. Sir Arthur Conan Doyle — wrote for vaudeville shows
23. Agatha Christie — dispenser in pharmacy
24. Frank Zappa — greeting-card designer, encyclopedia salesman
25. Sean Connery — milkman, coffin polisher
26. Jerry Hall — manure shoveler at stables
27. Danny Glover — social worker
28. Rod Stewart — grave digger
29. Elvis Costello — computer programmer
30. Joe Cocker — plumber
31. Chuck Berry — hairdresser
32. Charles Dickens — court reporter
33. Harry Truman — haberdasher
34. Lawrence Welk — farmer
35. Cleo Laine — pawnshop clerk, cobbler

12 Postal Workers
Who Became Celebrities

1. DAN AYKROYD, actor, comedian

In the early 1970s, Aykroyd worked as a mail sorter for Canada's national postal service.

2. CHARLES BUKOWSKI, poet, author

Portrayed as an itinerant writer in the 1987 film *Barfly*, Bukowski actually held jobs in Los Angeles as a mail carrier from 1952 to 1955 and postal clerk from 1958 to 1970. The experience became grist for his book *Post Office* (1970).

3. BING CROSBY, singer, actor

As one of his many jobs before hitting it big as a crooner, Crosby was a postal clerk in Spokane, Washington, from 1920 to 1921.

4. WALT DISNEY, cartoonist, film producer

During World War I, Disney tried to enlist in both the U.S. and Canadian armies, but was refused because he was just sixteen. So he worked temporarily as a postal clerk in Chicago, then went to France as a Red Cross ambulance driver. On his return from Europe, he again worked briefly as a postal clerk, this time in Kansas City.

5. WILLIAM FAULKNER, Pulitzer Prize–winning novelist

As postmaster at the University of Mississippi's post office from 1921 to 1924, Faulkner often ignored customers and tossed some of their mail in the garbage. He entertained friends on the job, even inviting them to read patrons' magazines, which he displayed in a "reading room."

6. SHERMAN HEMSLEY, actor

Before he was George Jefferson on *All in the Family* and *The Jeffersons,* Hemsley spent eight years as a postal clerk in New York and Philadelphia.

7. CONRAD HILTON, hotel owner

From 1910 to 1911, Hilton served as postmaster of the tiny New Mexico town of San Antonio, where his father owned a general store and a bank building. The postal service rented space from the Hiltons for four dollars a month.

8. ROCK HUDSON, actor

In 1946, after two years in the U.S. Navy, Hudson was a mailman in his hometown of Winnetka, Illinois.

9. ABRAHAM LINCOLN, U.S. president

The odd jobs of Lincoln's early life included rail splitter, flatboatman, surveyor, and postmaster in the town of New Salem, Illinois.

10. CHARLES LINDBERGH, aviator

Lindbergh operated an airmail run from St. Louis to Chicago under contract with the postal service between 1926 and 1927.

11. KNUTE ROCKNE, football coach

From 1907 to 1910, Rockne often had to hoist seventy-five-pound mail sacks. With his earnings (about a thousand dollars) he was able to attend Notre Dame.

12. RICHARD WRIGHT, author

Wright, the author of *Native Son* (1940), worked at the central post office in Chicago from 1928 to 1930, but lost his job when the staff was cut back in the Depression.

18 Waiters Who Became Movie Stars

1. RUDOLPH VALENTINO (1895–1926)

   Shortly after his arrival in the United States in 1913, the future matinee idol waited on tables in Brooklyn.

2. RAMON NOVARRO (1899–1968)

   When his father died, young Novarro supported his family as a singing waiter in a Los Angeles restaurant.

3. JAMES CAGNEY (1899–1986)

   During World War I the teenage James Cagney and his two brothers worked as waiters in a restaurant on 114th Street in New York.

4. KIRK DOUGLAS (1916–   )

   So broke one Thanksgiving Day in 1940 that he could only afford a twenty-cent bowl of stew from a lunch wagon, young Izzy Demsky quickly got a job waiting on tables from 9:00 P.M. to 1:00 A.M. at Schrafft's restaurant. The pay — which helped defray his tuition at the American Academy of Dramatic Arts — was fifteen dollars a week plus tips and an occasional stolen sandwich.

5. PETER FINCH (1916–1977)

   At sixteen Finch borrowed a waiter's suit from a sick friend and got a job at the Astra Hotel in the Bondi section of Sydney. Years later he recalled: "I had to get up at five in the morning to polish acres of bloody brass work and sweat it out until seven-thirty at night." He was sacked after two weeks for uncorking a bottle of champagne and showering the contents on a dinner party, including a woman in a very elegant Parisian gown.

6. MICHAEL CAINE (1933–   )

   Between the ages of sixteen and eighteen, Maurice Micklewhite, the son of a cockney fish-market porter and a charlady, worked at a variety of jobs, including that of tea waiter — he served tea in a London theater.

7. MALCOLM MCDOWELL (1943–   )

   After graduating from secondary school, he worked as a waiter in his father's pub in Liverpool.

8. JAMES CAAN (1939–   )

   Dropping out of Hofstra University in the late 1950s, Caan was a waiter on weekends at the Tuxedo Ballroom dance palace in

New York before enrolling as a drama student at the Neighborhood Playhouse.

9. JAMES COCO (1929–1987)

In the late 1940s Coco was a waiter at a milk bar in Grand Central Station. He called it "a terrifying experience because hundreds of ravenous little people kept pouring out of those train tunnels, and I'd get petrified that I wouldn't be able to fill their orders fast enough. One morning I overturned a hot-water urn, scalding twelve businessmen who were standing at the counter having coffee. . . . I was fired immediately."

10. GENE HACKMAN (1931–   )

In 1956 Hackman was a counterman at a Howard Johnson's restaurant in New York.

11. DUSTIN HOFFMAN (1937–   )

For seven lean years between 1958 and 1965 Hoffman was employed in numerous capacities, including several brief waiting jobs in Manhattan.

12. BUDDY HACKETT (1924–   )

After graduating from New Utrecht High School in Brooklyn, Leonard Hacker broke into show business as a combination waiter-entertainer in various Catskill resorts along the "borscht belt."

13. JAMES GARNER (1928–   )

Among nearly fifty jobs the young Korean War veteran held between 1952 and 1953 was a short-lived waiter's position in his hometown of Norman, Oklahoma.

14. EDDIE CANTOR (1892–1964)

As a teenager, Banjo Eyes was a singing waiter in Carey Walsh's saloon in Coney Island, where the piano player was Jimmy Durante.

15. YVES MONTAND (1921–   )

To help support his family, the fifteen-year-old Italian refugee, Ivo Livi, was a *garçon du café* in Marseilles.

16. WILLIAM BENDIX (1906–1964)

Apparently in spite of his gravelly voice, Bendix was a singing waiter in Brooklyn in the 1920s.

17. JACK LEMMON (1925–   )

The young Harvard graduate was a performer-waiter at the Old Knickerbocker Music Hall at 2nd Avenue and 54th Street in New York, where he "did everything from old-time melodramas to waiting on tables." Lemmon did a deliberately corny pitchman routine — dressed in a straw boater and blazer — that was favorably mentioned by several columnists and which helped get him his first TV job.

18. BILL "BOJANGLES" ROBINSON (1878–1949)

During a lull in his dancing career, Bojangles was a waiter in a Richmond, Virginia, beanery, where he spilled a plate of hot oyster stew down the neck of Marty Forkins, a booking agent. When told that Robinson was a hoofer, Forkins caught his act, and a few years later became Bojangles's manager — for the next forty years, until the dancer's death in 1949.

NOTE: For movie stars who worked as waitresses, see *The Book of Lists #3*, pp. 305–307.

SOURCE: Marc E. Paavola.

20 Lawyers Who Became Famous in Other Professions

1. Rossano Brazzi (1916–   ), film actor
2. Hoagy Carmichael (1899–1981), songwriter, whose works include "Stardust" and "Georgia on My Mind"
3. Fidel Castro (1927–   ), Cuban premier
4. Howard Cosell (1920–   ), sportscaster
5. Henry Fielding (1707–1754), author of *Tom Jones* and other novels
6. Terry Louise Fisher (1946–   ), television writer and producer of *L.A. Law*
7. Mohandas Gandhi (1869–1948), political and spiritual leader
8. Erle Stanley Gardner (1889–1970), detective story writer, creator of Perry Mason
9. Sir William Gilbert (1836–1911), playwright, author of *The Pirates of Penzance* and *The Mikado*
10. John Wesley Hardin (1853–1895), outlaw, murderer
11. Washington Irving (1783–1859), author of *Rip Van Winkle* and *The Legend of Sleepy Hollow*
12. Francis Scott Key (1779–1843), poet and author of "The Star-Spangled Banner"
13. Vladimir Ilyich Lenin (1870–1924), Russian Communist leader
14. James Pike (1913–1969), Episcopal bishop
15. Otto Preminger (1906–1986), film producer and director
16. Geraldo Rivera (1943–   ), broadcast journalist and entertainer
17. Charlie Rose (1942–   ), broadcast journalist
18. Scott Turow (1949–   ), author of *Presumed Innocent*
19. Lew Wallace (1827–1905), soldier and author of *Ben-Hur*
20. Noah Webster (1758–1843), lexicographer

Percentage of Blacks
in *16* Jobs

	Blacks (%) (1992)
1. Winding and twisting machine operators	41.8
2. Nursing aides, orderlies, and attendants	31.4
3. Taxicab drivers and chauffeurs	29.5
4. Maids and housemen	27.3
5. Pressing machine operators	27.1
6. Postal clerks, except mail carriers	26.6
7. Correctional institution officers	25.7
8. Concrete and terrazzo finishers	25.4
9. Athletes	9.7
10. Dentists	1.1
11. Farmers	.9
12. Geologists and geodesists	.8
13. Chemical engineers	.7
14. Dental hygienists	.6
14. Fishers	.6
16. Surveying and mapping technicians	.3

NOTE: Black Americans make up 12.1 percent of the population and 10.1 percent of the work force.

SOURCE: *Employment and Earnings* (January 1993). U.S. Department of Labor, Bureau of Labor Statistics.

Percentage of Hispanics
in *15* Jobs

	Hispanics (%) (1992)
1. Farm workers	27.8
2. Nonagricultural graders and sorters	26.8
3. Cleaners and servants	24.6
4. Pressing machine operators	23.6
5. Butchers and meat cutters	23.2
6. Textile sewing machine operators	22.4
7. Packing and filling machine operators	21.0
8. Members of U.S. Congress	4.6
9. Lawyers	1.9
10. Farmers	1.7

	Hispanics (%) (1992)
11. Aerospace engineers	1.3
12. Authors	.9
12. Dental hygienists	.9
14. Speech therapists	.3
15. Winding and twisting machine operators	.1

NOTE: Americans of Hispanic origin make up 9.7 percent of the population and 7.6 percent of the work force.

SOURCE: *Employment and Earnings* (January 1993). U.S. Department of Labor, Bureau of Labor Statistics.

Percentage of Women in *15* Jobs

	Female (%) (1992)
1. Dental hygienists	99.0
1. Secretaries	99.0
3. Prekindergarten and kindergarten teachers	98.6
4. Receptionists	97.3
5. Household child-care workers	97.1
6. Real estate sales	50.4
7. Painters, sculptors, craft artists, and artist printmakers	50.3
8. Editors and reporters	49.7
9. United States senators	7.0*
10. Firefighters	2.4
11. Carpenters	1.0
12. Automobile mechanics	.8
13. Heating, air-conditioning, and refrigeration mechanics	.6
14. Heavy equipment mechanics	.3
14. Electrical power installers and repairers	.3

* 1993

NOTE: Women make up 51.2 percent of the U.S. population and 45.7 percent of the work force.

SOURCE: *Employment and Earnings* (January 1993). U.S. Department of Labor, Bureau of Labor Statistics.

20 Jobs with the Highest Unemployment Rates

At the end of 1992, according to government statistics, there were 8,422,000 unemployed persons in the United States. Below are the occupations with the highest percentages of people out of work. (These rates are for occupations in which more than 50,000 workers are employed.)

	Workers Unemployed (%)
1. Graders and sorters in agricultural products	34.0
2. Structural metal workers	30.3
3. Concrete and terrazzo finishers	28.0
4. Construction helpers	25.2
5. Construction laborers	22.9
6. Drywall installers	21.1
7. Production helpers in industrial occupations	19.9
8. Graders and sorters in industries other than agricultural	18.4
9. Insulation workers	18.2
10. Brickmasons and stonemasons	17.7
11. Roofers	16.3
12. Pressing machine operators	16.2
13. Vehicle washers and equipment cleaners	15.3
14. Carpenters	14.5
15. Garage- and service-station-related occupations	14.2
16. Painters in construction and maintenance	14.1
17. Packaging and filling machine operators	13.8
18. Laborers in industries other than construction	13.7
19. Actors and directors	13.5
20. Hand packers and packagers	13.4

Some other occupations with high jobless rates include maids and housemen (12.4 percent), cashiers (11.8 percent), cooks (10.5 percent), and electricians (10.1 percent).

SOURCE: Unpublished tabulation, "Current Population Survey, 1992," U.S. Department of Labor, Bureau of Labor Statistics.

15 Jobs with the Lowest Unemployment Rates

	Workers Unemployed (%)
1. Speech therapists	0.1
2. Respiratory therapists	0.1
3. Stenographers	0.1
4. Farmers	0.3
5. Clergy	0.4
6. Physicians	0.5
7. Supervisors of police and detectives	0.5
8. Dental hygenists	0.5
9. Dentists	0.6
10. Radiologic technicians	0.7
11. Pharmacists	0.8
12. Funeral directors	0.9
13. Dental laboratory and medical appliance technicians	0.9
14. Registered nurses	1.1
15. Lawyers	1.2

SOURCE: Unpublished tabulation,"Current Population Survey, 1992," U.S. Department of Labor, Bureau of Labor Statistics.

18 Very Odd Jobs

1. ANT CATCHER
   Digs up live ants for use in plastic Ant Farms.

2. BACK WASHER
   Tends machine that washes, rinses, and dries fiber (called sliver) in the textile industry.

3. CAR CHASER
   Directs the movement of grain-freight railroad cars.

4. DEBUBBLIZER
   Tends high-pressure heating equipment that removes internal solvent bubbles from nitrocellulose rod stock in the plastics industry.

5. EGG BREAKER
   Separates yolk and white of eggs for use in food products by striking eggs against a bar. Pours contents of broken eggs into an egg-separating device.

6. FLUSH TESTER

Tests flush channels of toilet bowls by flushing rags down the channels.

7. IMPREGNATOR

Tends vacuum or pressure tank that impregnates powdered-metal parts with lubricating oil or molten plastic.

8. LINGO CLEANER

Cleans metal lingos (weighted heddles) used in Jacquard loom harnesses.

9. LUMP INSPECTOR

Inspects lumps of tobacco for defects in wrapper leaf and re-pairs tears and holes with glue and leaf.

10. MANGLER

Tends a machine that shapes and smooths knitted garments.

11. MASHER

Operates cooker and mashing tub to combine cereal and malt in the preparation of beer.

12. PILLOWCASE TURNER

Tends machine that turns pillowcases right side out and stretches material to remove wrinkles.

13. SNIFFER

Sniffs people's body parts to test the effectiveness of foot and underarm deodorants.

14. SWEATBAND SHAPER

Places hats on heated metal blocks to shape sweatbands. Re-moves hats and places them on racks.

15. TOE PUNCHER

Tends toe-punching machine that flattens toe seams of knitted seamless socks.

16. UPSETTER

Sets up and operates a closed-die forging machine that ex-pands the ends of hot metal bars.

17. WEED FARMER

Grows weeds for sale to universities and chemical companies to be used in herbicide research.

18. WORM PICKER

Gathers worms to be used as fish bait.

NOTE: For more very odd jobs, see *The Book of Lists #2*, pp. 278–79 and *The Book of Lists #3*, pp. 397–98.

Alan Caruba's
10 Most Boring Things to Do

Alan Caruba, "expert in boredom," is the head of the Boring Institute in Maplewood, New Jersey. Since starting the institute in 1984, he has polled people across the country to determine what they find most monotonous. For further information, contact him at the Boring Institute, Box 40, Maplewood, NJ 07040.

1. Standing in line
2. Laundry
3. Commuting
4. Meetings
5. Diets
6. Exercise
7. Weeding lawn or garden
8. Housework
9. Political debates
10. Opening junk mail

5 Unfortunate Product Names
and *1* Honorable Mention

A corporate or product name can symbolize more than intended, especially when that name is used in other lands. Today's multinational markets require sensitivity to other cultures, as many companies have learned the hard way.

1. NOVA

   Latin American buyers were a bit reluctant to purchase this Chevrolet; in Spanish, *no va* means "doesn't go." So for those markets, the car was renamed Caribe.

2. GROS JOS

   Hunt-Wesson introduced its Big John products in Canada before realizing that the name, which translated to *Gros Jos,* was French Canadian slang for "big breasts." However, sales did not suffer from the translation.

3. PINTO

   The Ford Pinto suffered image problems when it went on sale in Brazil — *pinto* is Portuguese slang for "small male genitals." For Brazilian buyers, Ford changed the name to Corcel, which means "horse."

4. Bite the Wax Tadpole

When Coca-Cola expanded into China in the 1920s, the company chose Chinese characters which, when pronounced, would sound like the English name for the drink. Those particular Chinese letters, though, actually translated to "bite the wax tadpole" or "wax-flattened mare." The company now uses characters that mean "good mouth, good pleasure" or "happiness in the mouth."

5. Pledge

The Johnson Company retained the American name of the wax product when it was introduced in the Netherlands. Unfortunately, in Dutch it means "piss," making it difficult for shoppers to ask for Pledge. The product survived because most Dutch retail stores converted to self-service.

Honorable Mention:
The Yokohama Rubber Company was forced to withdraw hundreds of tires from the sultanate of Brunei when Islamic authorities complained that the tread design resembled the word for Allah.

20 Ill-Fated Foreign Products

The following was compiled by Charles Brymer of Interbrand Corporation (14 E. 60th Street, New York, NY 10022) and by Reinhold Aman, the editor of *Maledicta*, the irregular "Journal of Verbal Aggression." *Maledicta* can be purchased through P. O. Box 14123, Santa Rosa, CA 95402-6123.

1. Ass Glue (blood tonic from donkey parts; China)
2. Blue Peter (canned fish; Norway)
3. Colon Plus (liquid detergent; Spain)
4. Fockink (liqueur; the Netherlands)
5. Green Piles (lawn fertilizer; Japan)
6. Homo Sausage (beef jerky; Japan)
7. Hornyphon (video recorder; Austria)
8. Krapp (toilet paper; Sweden)
9. Last Climax (paper tissues; Japan)
10. Mucos (soft drink; Japan)
11. Pansy (men's underwear; China)
12. Pipi (orangeade; Yugoslavia)
13. Plopp (chocolate bar; Sweden)
14. Polio (detergent; Czechoslovakia)
15. Pshitt (soft drink; France)

16. Shitto (hot spiced pepper sauce; Ghana)
17. Skinababe (baby cleanser; Japan)
18. Superglans (car wax; the Netherlands)
19. Trim Pecker (trousers; Japan)
20. Zit (lemon-lime soft drink; Greece)

6 Costly Rumors

1. THE PROCTER & GAMBLE DEVIL

For a decade, on TV, radio, and in newspapers, Procter & Gamble battled rumors that its logo — a man-in-the-moon face and cluster of thirteen stars — represented Satan or that it symbolized a corporate takeover by the Reverend Sun Myung Moon's Unification Church. In 1991 Procter & Gamble won a $75,000 lawsuit against James and Linda Newton of Parsons, Kansas, who were found responsible for spreading rumors that the company supported the church of Satan. The two were distributors of Amway products, a competitor of Procter & Gamble.

2. RECIPE FOR SALE

Rumor had it that a woman phoned Mrs. Fields's headquarters to ask for their cookie recipe and was told that it would cost "two-fifty." She was so incensed at receiving a bill for $250 that, in retaliation, she passed copies of the recipe to everyone she knew. By 1987 Mrs. Fields's stores were displaying notices that their formula had never been sold to anyone. Mrs. Fields is not the only company burned by the recipe rumor. Since the 1940s, it has been rumored that the Waldorf-Astoria Hotel, Marshall Fields, and other stores have sold their cake or fudge recipes at a high price to customers who later took revenge.

3. BURT REYNOLDS'S PHONE NUMBER

When actor Burt Reynolds won a $1 million lawsuit in 1981, so the story went, he chose to share his award with the public by offering free use of his telephone credit-card number. The number given out by the rumormongers wasn't Reynolds's, but it was a working number — it belonged to a small Illinois phone company that was hit with about $100,000 in charges. This rumor has resurfaced often during the past twenty years, each time with a different actor as the subject.

4. WORMS IN THE BIG MAC

In the summer of 1978, a novel twist was put on the growing concern over food additives: the rumor was that red worms were being added to fast-food hamburgers to boost their volume and protein content. Business dropped off at about 20 percent of McDonald's outlets and the company spent a year, and a small fortune in advertising, to lay this rumor to rest.

5. EXPLODING CANDY

When General Foods introduced a carbonated candy called Pop Rocks in 1978, stories immediately began to circulate that the candy exploded in the digestive system. One boy, it was said, died after eating three bags of the candy and drinking a soda. General Foods was forced to launch an expensive media campaign to counter the rumors.

6. CIGARETTES CAUSE LEPROSY

Cigarettes are linked to many diseases, but in 1934, they were said to be associated with leprosy also. That year, a rumor was spread that a leper was employed by the Chesterfield factory in Richmond, Virginia. Sales of Chesterfields plummeted. The company offered a substantial reward for the identity of the rumormongers, but they were never apprehended.

12 Examples of the Dark Side of Disney

1. ACADEMY OF MOTION PICTURE ARTS AND SCIENCES

Walt Disney Company threatened the academy with a lawsuit when an actress dressed as Snow White was used in the opening number of the 1989 Academy Awards show. Disney holds the copyright on the Snow White character. The academy apologized for using her without permission.

2. DAY-CARE CENTERS

Murals of Mickey Mouse, Minnie Mouse, and other characters painted on the walls of three Hallandale, Florida, preschools made Disney very grumpy. In 1989 Disney argued that the paintings infringed on its copyrights and implied support of the schools. The pictures came down. Hanna Barbera Productions, a Disney rival, donated to the schools new murals portraying their own characters, including Pebbles and Dino of *The Flintstones,* and also threw a party for the children.

3. WINNIE THE POOH STATUE

White River, Ontario, claims to be the birthplace of the black bear cub upon which A. A. Milne based his Winnie the Pooh

The controversial statue of Winnie the Pooh in White River, Ontario.

character. But in 1989, Walt Disney Company, which holds the copyright to Pooh, refused to allow the townsfolk to erect a statue of their famous resident. The bad publicity brought by the refusal eventually forced Disney to relent.

4. GAY DANCING

Three homosexual men were stopped from slow-dancing by a Disneyland security guard who said that "touch dancing is reserved for heterosexual couples." The men sued, claiming that their civil rights were violated, but dropped the case in 1989 when Disneyland reaffirmed that it has a policy against such discrimination. In 1980 another gay man, Andrew Exler of Palm Springs, had brought a successful suit against the Magic Kingdom for being prevented from fast-dancing.

5. WILD BIRDS

Walt Disney World, in Florida, and five of its employees were charged in 1989 with abusing and killing wild birds at the park. The birds, including vultures, hawks, and falcons, were accused by Disney of freeloading at Discovery Island, making too much noise, and defecating on the walkways.

6. MUSICIANS

The American Federation of Musicians went to court in 1989 to get back pay for its musicians. The union claimed that Disney had not been paying them when snippets of pre-1960 Disney movies were used in recent films and TV shows.

7. HAZARDOUS WASTE

In 1988 the Florida Department of Environmental Regulation fined Walt Disney World more than $150,000 for hazardous-waste leaks. And, according to the Environmental Protection Agency, the park faced possible fines for dumping treated sewage into a creek. Two years later, Disneyland, in California, agreed to pay a $550,000 fine for allowing 14,000 gallons of toxic garbage to be hauled to disposal facilities in Wyoming and Utah that were not permitted to handle the waste. It was the largest penalty ever paid by a toxic-waste producer in the United States.

8. LONGHAIRS

Disneyland instituted a "grooming policy" in 1970, the day after about a dozen mostly long-haired youths were arrested for disturbing the peace at the park. Plainclothes police were hired to cull from the ticket line any young man whose hair was too long, whose attire was too "unorthodox," or who was judged to have a "chip on his shoulder."

9. *LADY AND THE TRAMP*

Jazz singer Peggy Lee provided the voices for four of the characters in the popular 1955 Disney cartoon feature *Lady and the Tramp.* She also cowrote six songs for the movie. Lee received $3,500 for her voiceovers, and she and her songwriting partner, Sonny Burke, earned $1,000 for the songs. When the film was released in videotape and became the biggest-selling video of 1987, Lee sued Disney for violating her contract, in which she retained rights to transcriptions. Disney fought the seventy-year-old wheelchair-ridden singer tooth and nail, but in 1991 a Los Angeles judge awarded her $2,300,000.

10. EMPLOYEE DRESS CODE

Protectors of French culture were outraged in 1991 when Euro Disneyland issued a written set of guidelines for prospective employees which included the following prohibitions: Men must wear their hair cut above the collar and ears, with no beards or mustaches. Neither men nor women can wear more than one ring on each hand. Women can wear only one earring in each ear, and the diameter of each earring must not exceed two centimeters (three-fourths of an inch). Fingernails must not pass the ends of the fingers. Women are required to wear "appropriate undergarments," and transparent pantyhose only, not black or anything with a lacy or fancy design.

11. THE SEVEN-YEAR TRICK

When Disney first moved into Florida in the 1960s, the state legislature agreed to allow the company to create its own self-contained government, known as the Reedy Creek Improvement District. In 1989 Disney agreed to pay Orange County, Florida, $14 million for road improvements in exchange for a promise not to challenge Disney's government powers for the next seven years. A few weeks later Disney announced, for the first time, its full plans for those seven years: 7 new hotels, 29 new attractions, 19,000 more employees, and a fourth amusement park.

12. THE GRINCH THAT STOLE AFFORDABLE HOUSING

In January 1990, $57 million in Florida state tax-free bonds became available to local governments on a first-come, first-served basis. Orange County, which includes Disney World, had planned to use its share to build low-income housing. But Disney, which had had a profit of $703 million the previous year, got in line first and took all the money for their sewer system. An *Orlando Sentinel* editorial dubbed Disney "the grinch that stole affordable housing."

11 Celebrity Inventors

1. EDIE ADAMS, model and actress

In 1963 the widow of television comic Ernie Kovacs invented, and later patented, a cigar-holder ring. It was the one she used in her famous Muriel Cigar commercials, in which she said, "Why don't you pick one up and smoke it sometime?"

2. JOHN DOS PASSOS, author

Best known for such works as *The Manhattan Transfer* and *U.S.A.*, Dos Passos is listed as the coinventor of the soap-bubble gun in 1959.

3. ZEPPO MARX, comic actor

In the 1940s, bombardiers depended on coupling devices built by a company founded by Herbert "Zeppo" Marx to release atomic bombs over Japan. Zeppo, of the Marx Brothers, later invented and patented an alarm system worn on the wrist to measure the heartbeat.

4. YAKOV SMIRNOFF, comedian

Among the hot-selling items at gift shows in 1989 were Shower Notes, invented by the Russian-born comic and his wife. The invention consists of a pad with waterproof paper for jotting down notes in the shower.

5. MARK TWAIN, author

Under his real name, Samuel Clemens, the writer held three patents. One was a pegboard game — Mark Twain's Memory-Builder — to help players learn world history. The others were a scrapbook with preglued pages and an adjustable strap for the back of a vest. Throughout his life, Twain lost money on patent schemes. On one occasion, when he had lost $42,000 on a patent, he wrote "I gave it away to a man whom I had long detested and whose family I desired to ruin."

6. JULIE NEWMAR, actress and dancer

In 1975 Newmar invented a new design for pantyhose. She said it created a "balloon look for the buttocks," instead of flattening and lowering them like other brands. They were called Cheeky Derriere pantyhose.

7. VASLAV NIJINSKY, dancer

Nijinsky invented a windshield wiper, an "eversharp" pencil, and a system of notation for dance.

8. DANNY KAYE, comedian

In 1952 Kaye patented a party favor called a blowout — a noisemaker that unrolls in three directions when a person blows into the mouthpiece.

Mark Twain's Memory-Builder — a pegboard game invented by the author of *Huckleberry Finn*

9. DONNA DOUGLAS, actress

Douglas, known for years as Elly May Clampett on *The Beverly Hillbillies,* invented Critter Country Classics pet cologne. The line consisted of Miss Tabby, for cats, and Timber Wolf, for dogs.

10.–11. HEDY LAMARR, actress, and GEORGE ANTHEIL, concert pianist and composer

During World War II, the sultry film star worked on her idea for a device to direct remote craft such as torpedoes. The machine, consisting of two synchronized transmitting and receiving player-piano rolls, would allow a technician to switch control frequencies so a torpedo could escape enemy tracking. Lamarr's friend Antheil assisted her, and they received a patent in 1942. They were shocked when the War Department declined to use it. Years later, when their patent had expired, Sylvania adapted the invention for use in satellite communications without crediting or thanking Lamarr.

7 Unsung Inventors of Everyday Objects

1. GEORGE DE MESTRAL — Velcro

One day in 1941 De Mestral, a Swiss mechanical engineer, went hunting in the Jura Mountains with his Irish pointer. When he tried to remove the cockleburs that had stuck to his dog's coat and to his own wool pants, he was amazed by the strength of the seedpods. He took one home, examined it under a microscope, and discovered that the burrs contained hundreds of tiny hooks. Ten years later he patented the Velcro fastener, which gained wide success in the fashion industry and was used to keep the boots of astronauts stuck to the floor in a weightless environment. The name *Velcro* is derived from two French words: *velour,* a kind of fabric, and *crochet,* or hook.

2. LUIS MARCUS — bobby pin

Marcus was a cosmetics manufacturer in San Francisco when he designed the bobby pin to hold in place the bobbed hair of flappers after World War I.

3. JOSHUA PUSEY — paper matchbook

Pusey, a lawyer in Lima, Pennsylvania, created the paper matchbook in 1892. The first advertisement on a match cover — for a local opera in Cloquet, Minnesota — appeared in 1896. Pusey is also credited with inventing the roller coaster.

4. ERMAL CLEON FRAZE — pull-tab opener

In 1959 Fraze, an engineer, was on a family picnic near his hometown of Dayton, Ohio, when he had to use a car bumper to open a beer because he had forgotten to bring a can opener. Thinking that there must be an easier way to open cans, he invented the pull tab and obtained a patent in 1963. By 1990 over 150 billion pull-tab cans were being manufactured every year.

5. JOHAN VAALER — paper clip

Vaaler, a Norwegian, patented the paper clip in Germany in 1900. In 1989, a twenty-two-and-a-half-foot-tall paper clip was erected in his honor in Oslo.

6. WALTER JAMES ALCOCK — perforated toilet paper

Alcock, an English manufacturer, came up with the idea of perforated toilet paper in the 1880s, but it took him several years to convince a dubious public of the usefulness of his product.

7. CHESTER GREENWOOD — earmuffs

Greenwood was only fifteen years old when he came up with the idea for earmuffs in 1873, after his ears turned blue while he was skating on a pond in Farmington, Maine. At age eighteen, he obtained a patent for his invention and began produc-

A 22½-foot-tall paper clip erected in Oslo, Norway, in honor of inventor Johan Vaaler.

ing Greenwood's Champion Ear Protectors. Greenwood also invented a cotton picker, a washing machine, a folding bed, and a doughnut hook.

NOTE: For more unsung inventors of everyday objects, see *The Book of Lists #2*, pp. 233–36.

10 Patented Inventions Whose Time Has Not Yet Come

1. LIGHTER-THAN-AIR FURNITURE

   (Inventor: William A. Calderwood; Peoria, Arizona; 1989; U.S. Patent 4,888,836)

   Filled with helium or any other lighter-than-air gas, the furniture levitates to the ceiling when not in use. When needed, it is pulled down to the floor by means of a tether.

   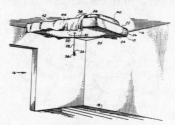

2. HALITOSIS DETECTOR DEVICE

   (Inventor: Katumori Nakamura; Iwatsuki, Japan; 1989; U.S. Patent 4,823,807)

   After determining the chemical makeup of an exhalation sample, it produces a signal appropriate to the degree of malodorousness.

3. PAT ON THE BACK APPARATUS

   (Inventor: Ralph Pire; Lindenhurst, New York; 1986; U.S. Patent 4,608,967)

   For use during self-congratulatory moods.

   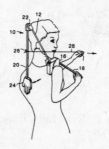

4. METHOD AND APPARATUS FOR MOLDING FRUIT

(Inventor: Richard Tweddell III; Cincinnati, Ohio; 1989; U.S. Patent 4,827,666)

The mold is attached to the ground in such a way that a growing plant, for example a squash or a cucumber, assumes the shape of the mold.

5. FRESH-AIR BREATHING DEVICE AND METHOD

(Inventor: William O. Holmes; Belmont, California; 1982; U.S. Patent 4,320,756)

In case of a fire in a high-rise hotel, the user inserts a breathing tube through the water trap of a toilet until it reaches a vent pipe connected to a sewer line of the toilet. The user then breathes "fresh" air until rescued.

6. ANIMAL TOILET GARMENT

(Inventor: Samuel Andrisani; Los Angeles, California; 1963; U.S. Patent 3,090,356)

Used to eliminate exposed and strewn deposits of animal waste products in public places and on farms. Can also be used as a birth-control device.

7. SMOKER'S HAT

(Inventor: Walter C. Netzchert; Buena Park, California; 1989; U.S. Patent 4,858,627)

A portable hat system that allows the user to smoke tobacco without affecting the environment. Includes a purification and deionization system, a filtration system to allow intake of ambient air, and an exhaust system for expelling deodorized, deionized, and optionally scented air from the hat.

8. FEMALE BODY SUIT

(Inventor: Lyndola M. Storie; Caseyville, Illinois; 1986; U.S. Patent 4,627,111)

Made of skintight material closely simulating skin texture. Allows the wearer to eliminate psychological barriers resulting from mastectomy and to be more satisfied with personal appearance during coitus.

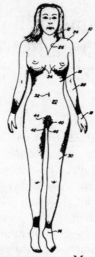

9. STABILIZING APPARATUS FOR MALE AND FEMALE PARTNERS

(Inventor: Luther C. Oxendine, Jr.; Maxton, North Carolina; 1982; U.S. Patent 4,343,299)

A strap apparatus to be mounted on both partners during coitus to stabilize the action of each.

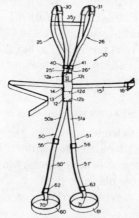

10. FORCE-SENSITIVE, SOUND-PLAYING CONDOM

(Inventor: Paul Lyons; Southbridge, Massachusetts; 1992; U.S. Patent 5,163,447)

Contains a chip-controlled sound transducer that, when activated by contact, plays a melody or voice message. Suggested melodies include *The 1812 Overture* and Beethoven's "Ode to Joy."

SOURCE: U.S. Patent Office, courtesy of Longacre & White, Arlington, Virginia.

NOTE: For more patented inventions whose time has not yet come, see *The Book of Lists #2*, pp. 232–33.

8 People Who Put Their Dreams to Work

1. SAMUEL TAYLOR COLERIDGE, British poet

History's most celebrated episode of dream inspiration occurred on an English summer day in 1797, when the young poet dozed off while reading a history book about Kublai Khan. An opium addict, Coleridge was probably in a pleasantly drugged state when the immortal verses came to him. Waking up, he began to write feverishly. He had reached the fifty-fourth line — one-sixth of the poem as he envisioned it — when he was interrupted by the infamous "person on business from Porlock." An hour later, when his visitor had left, Coleridge had forgotten the rest of the poem.

2. GAY BALFOUR, American inventor

This Colorado inventor started a successful business vacuuming prairie dogs from their burrows. The idea for Dog-Done came to him in a dream: "I saw a large yellow vehicle and there were green hoses running from it. I was putting the hoses in the ground, sucking out prairie dogs." The vacuum system he built doesn't hurt the animals, but deposits them alive if "somewhat confused" in a large tank in his truck. He is trying to develop a market in Japan for prairie dogs as pets.

3. ROBERT LOUIS STEVENSON, Scottish author

Stevenson had a rich and complicated dream life, full of nightmares and inspirations. He read entire imaginary books in his sleep and traveled to distant places, but most important, he received visits from his "little people." They dictated stories to him, "piece by piece, like a serial," especially when he needed money. Sometimes he dreamed stories without their help. According to his wife, Fanny, "In the small hours of one morning, I was awakened by cries of horror from Louis. Thinking he had a nightmare, I awakened him. He said angrily, 'Why did you wake me? I was dreaming a fine bogey tale.'" The bogey tale was to become a classic, *The Strange Case of Dr. Jekyll and Mr. Hyde.* Though he was seriously ill,, his publishers were pressuring him to produce a popular "shilling shocker." He had been racking his brains for two days for an idea when on the second night he wrote, "I dreamed the scene at the window . . . in which Hyde, pursued for some crime, took the powder and underwent the change in the presence of his pursuers. All the rest was made awake, and consciously."

4. FREDRICH A. KEKULÉ, German chemist

For years, Kekulé had tried unsuccessfully to find the molecular structure of benzene. One night in 1865 he fell asleep in front of the fireplace and dreamed of atoms swirling in long chains. In his dream "everything was moving in a snake-like and twisting manner. Suddenly, what was this? One of the snakes got hold of its own tail and the whole structure was mockingly twisting in front of my eyes. As if struck by lightning, I awoke . . ." As a result of this vision, Kekulé realized that the structure of benzene is a closed carbon ring, a discovery that revolutionized modern chemistry. Announcing his breakthrough at a scientific convention in 1890, Kekulé told his colleagues, "Let us learn to dream, gentlemen, and then we may perhaps find the truth."

5. WILLIAM BLAKE, English poet, artist, and engraver

Blake's beloved brother Robert died in 1787, at the age of nineteen. Blake believed that Robert continued to advise him from beyond the grave, in dreams and waking visions. While William was seeking a less expensive method of engraving his illustrated songs, his brother appeared to him in a dream and explained the process of copper engraving, an alternative to the ordinary method of intaglio painting. In the morning Mrs. Blake went out with all their money (half a crown) and spent it on the materials needed to conduct the experiment. The technique was successful, and Blake produced numerous magnificent illustrations using this method.

6. OTTO LOEWI, German-American physiologist

The night before Easter Sunday in 1921, the scientist awoke from a dream and "jotted down a few notes on a tiny slip of paper." In the morning he couldn't read his handwriting. The next night, at 3:00 A.M., the idea returned. "It was of the design of an experiment to determine whether or not the hypothesis of chemical transmission that I had uttered 17 years ago was correct. I got up immediately, went to the laboratory, and performed a simple experiment on a frog heart according to nocturnal design." Loewi's experiment proved that it is not nerves but the chemicals they release that directly affect the heart. This discovery led to his winning the Nobel Prize in 1936.

7. GIUSEPPE TARTINI, Italian violinist and composer

At the age of twenty-one, Tartini had a dream in which he sold his soul to the Devil. He handed his violin to Satan, "but how great was my astonishment when I heard him play with consummate skill a sonata of such exquisite beauty as surpassed the flights of my imagination. I felt enraptured, transported, enchanted; my breath was taken away, and I awoke. Seizing my violin, I tried to retain the sounds I had heard. But it was in vain. The piece I then composed, the 'Devil's Sonata,' was the best I ever wrote, but how far below the one I had heard in my dream!"

8. HERMANN V. HILPRECHT, German archaeologist

Professor Hilprecht had one of the most extraordinary dream breakthroughs ever recorded. In 1893 he was trying to decipher the cuneiform writing on two small fragments of agate, which he thought were Babylonian finger rings found in temple ruins. The fragments were housed in separate cases in an Istanbul museum, and Hilprecht was working with facsimiles. One night he went to bed around midnight, and dreamed that "a tall, thin priest of the old pre-Christian Nippur . . . led me to a treasure chamber of the temple." The priest told him that the two stones were not rings but rather a votive cylinder that had been cut into three pieces, two of them serving as earrings for the statue of the god Ninib. The priest then told Hilprecht to put the pieces together and explained what the inscription would read. When Hilprecht woke up he told his wife the dream, examined the fragments, and found it all to be true, including the reference to Ninib. When he visited the original pieces in Constantinople, they fit together perfectly. The 3,000-year-old cuneiform tablet that Hilprecht deciphered came to be known as the Stone of Nebuchadnezzar.

In payment for his soul, the Devil teaches Giuseppe Tartini what was to become his most famous sonata.

7 FAMILY AND RELATIONSHIPS

30 Famous People's Thoughts About Marriage

1. "Marriage, *n.* The state or condition of a community consisting of a master, a mistress and two slaves, making in all, two." — *Ambrose Bierce*

2. "A man may be a fool and not *know it — but not if he is married.*" — *H. L. Mencken*

3. "For a while we pondered whether to take a vacation or get a divorce. We decided that a trip to Bermuda is over in two weeks, but a divorce is something you always have." — *Woody Allen*

4. "My parents want me to get married. They don't care who anymore, as long as he doesn't have a pierced ear, that's all they care about. I think men who have a pierced ear are better prepared for marriage. They've experienced pain and bought jewelry." — *Rita Rudner*

5. "The happiest time of anyone's life is just after the first divorce." — *John Kenneth Galbraith*

6. *Heinrich Heine bequeathed his estate to his wife on the condition that she marry again, because, according to Heine,* "There will be at least one man who will regret my death."

7. "American women expect to find in their husbands a perfection that English women only hope to find in their butlers." — *W. Somerset Maugham*

8. "I've only slept with the men I've been married to. How many women can make that claim?" — *Elizabeth Taylor*

9. "Take it from me, marriage isn't a word — it's a sentence." — *King Vidor*

10. "Marrying a man is like buying something you've been admiring for a long time in a shop window. You may love it when you get it home, but it doesn't always go with everything else in the house." — *Jean Kerr*

11. "I don't think I'll get married again. I'll just find a woman I don't like and give her a house." — *Lewis Grizzard*

12. "The only charm of marriage is that it makes a life of deception necessary for both parties." — *Oscar Wilde*

13. "By all means marry; if you get a good wife, you'll be happy. If you get a bad one, you'll become a philosopher." — *Socrates*

14. "Marriage is neither heaven nor hell; it is simply purgatory." —*Abraham Lincoln*

15. "It destroys one's nerves to be amiable every day to the same human being." — *Benjamin Disraeli*

16. "Marriage is based on the theory that when a man discovers a brand of beer exactly to his taste he should at once throw up his job and go to work in the brewery." — *George Jean Nathan*

17. "We would have broken up except for the children. Who were the children? Well, she and I were." — *Mort Sahl*

18. "She has buried all her female friends; I wish she would make friends with my wife." — *Martial*

19. "Wives are people who feel they don't dance enough." — *Groucho Marx*

20. "A man's mother is his misfortune, but his wife is his fault." — *Walter Bagehot*

21. "My wife doesn't care what I do when I'm away, as long as I don't have a good time." — *Lee Trevino*

22. "If you want to sacrifice the admiration of many men for the criticism of one, go ahead, get married." — *Katharine Hepburn*

23. "Married men live longer than single men. But married men are a lot more willing to die." — *Johnny Carson*

24. "Why do Jewish divorces cost so much? Because they're worth it." — *Henny Youngman*

25. "Gettin' married's a lot like getting into a tub of hot water. After you get used to it, it ain't so hot." — *Minnie Pearl*

26. "Sex when you're married is like going to a 7-Eleven. There's not as much variety, but at three in the morning, it's always there." — *Carol Leifer*

27. "Sex in marriage is like medicine. Three times a day for the first week. Then once a day for another week. Then once every three or four days until the condition clears up." — *Peter De Vries*

28. "My wife and I were happy for twenty years. Then we met." — *Rodney Dangerfield*

29. "It is a sad fact that fifty percent of marriages in this country end in divorce. But hey, the other half end in death. You could be one of the lucky ones!" — *Richard Jeni*

30. "Only choose in marriage a woman whom you would choose as a friend if she were a man." — *Joseph Joubert*

PRIMARY SOURCE: *A Curmudgeon's Garden of Love,* compiled and edited by Jon Winokur, copyright 1991 by Jon Winokur. Reprinted by permission of the author.

George Burns's
5 Tips for Meeting Women

George Burns began his entertainment career singing on street corners in New York City at the age of seven. After more than thirty years of comedy partnership with Gracie Allen, George Burns went on alone after her death in 1964. In 1976, at the age of eighty, he won an Academy Award for his work in *The Sunshine Boys*.

1. Be sure to wear a good cologne, a nice aftershave lotion, and a strong underarm deodorant. And it might be a good idea to wear some clothes, too.
2. If a real beauty comes your way walking her dog, stop and pet it. That makes you her friend, and before you know it she'll be introducing herself and shaking your hand — unless her dog is a pit bull. Then she'll just introduce herself.
3. Bump into her rear end. I mean, if she's driving ahead of you. This may cost you a hundred, but you'll have her name, address, and phone number. The rest is up to you.
4. Making the scene in a sporty convertible with the top down still gets results. I was doing fine last week until the girl had to jump out to bring my hair back.
5. If all of the above fails, book yourself on a cruise. And if you strike out there, forget my tips on how to meet women, but I've got some great ones on how to make a fortune in the stock market.

— Exclusive for *The Book of Lists*

How 8 Famous People
Met Their Mates

1. JOHN LENNON AND YOKO ONO

According to biographers, avant-garde artist Ono pursued Lennon relentlessly. At the time they met, she was showing her work at London's Indica Gallery. Lennon saw the show, which impressed him, but did not respond immediately to her advances, which included pleas for sponsorship of her art, hanging around outside his door, and bombarding him with notes. Eventually the couple divorced their respective spouses and married in 1969 on the Rock of Gibraltar.

Oliver Hardy fell in love with future wife Lucille Jones while she was unconscious.

2. OLIVER HARDY AND VIRGINIA LUCILLE JONES

Jones was a script girl on *The Flying Deuces,* starring Laurel and Hardy. One day on the set, she tripped over a rolled-up carpet, struck her head on an arc light, and was taken to the hospital. While she was unconscious, Hardy was struck by her beauty. He courted her by sending flowers and notes to the hospital. They were married in 1940.

3. LYNDON BAINES JOHNSON AND CLAUDIA "LADY BIRD" TAYLOR

Johnson met Lady Bird in the office of a friend in Austin, Texas, in 1934. Within three minutes of their introduction, Johnson asked her for a date. She turned him down. He barraged her with telegrams and phone calls until she relented, and two months later they were married.

4. OZZY OSBOURNE AND SHARON ARDEN

Heavy-metal rocker Osbourne met his wife-to-be when she was working as a receptionist for her father, a London music agent. He walked into her office barefoot, with a water faucet dangling from his neck, and sat on the floor. "I was terrified," she recalled. The couple wed two years later, in 1981, and now have three children.

5. RUTH WESTHEIMER AND MANFRED "FRED" WESTHEIMER

The diminutive sex therapist met her third husband on a ski trip in the Catskills in 1966. Her then boyfriend, Hans, was six feet tall, and an uncomfortable match on the ski-lift T-bar. At the top she told Hans, "I'm going up with that short man," pointing to the five-foot Westheimer. They married less than a year later. Westheimer sometimes calls his wife "my little skiing accident."

6. THE DUKE OF WINDSOR AND MRS. WALLIS SIMPSON

The Duke of Windsor was introduced to Mrs. Wallis Simpson — the woman for whom he eventually gave up the throne — at a house party. He asked whether she missed American central heating. She replied, "I'm sorry, sir, but you disappoint me. . . . Every American woman who comes to your country is always asked the same question. I had hoped for something more original from the Prince of Wales."

7. DWIGHT D. EISENHOWER AND MAMIE DOUD

In 1915 Eisenhower met his future wife, Mamie Doud, at a dinner dance. When he asked her for a date, she told him to call in a month. Instead, he called her every fifteen minutes the next day, until she agreed to see him that night. He arrived four hours early and they were engaged within three months.

8. BOB CUMMINGS AND JANE BERZYNSKY

In 1989 Jane Berzynsky was standing in a supermarket checkout line in Tennessee, reading a tabloid's account of actor Bob Cummings's latest divorce. She went home and wrote him a fan letter — with photo enclosed — saying that she was available. After receiving the okay from Cummings's astrologer (Jane's an Aquarius, Bob was a Gemini), he flew her to Los Angeles. Four days later, the seventy-nine-year-old Cummings proposed, and Jane became the actor's fifth wife.

16 Most Married Stars

1.	Zsa Zsa Gabor	8
2.	Mickey Rooney	8
3.	Liz Taylor	8
4.	Lana Turner	8
5.	Dick Haymes	7
6.	Arline Judge	7
7.	Stan Laurel	7
8.	Jennifer O'Neill	7*
9.	Martha Raye	7
10.	Arlene Dahl	6
11.	Rex Harrison	6
12.	John Huston	6
13.	Hedy Lamarr	6
14.	Tom Mix	6
15.	Claude Rains	6
16.	Gloria Swanson	6

*O'Neill was only forty-four years old when she married her seventh husband.

Artie Shaw's
10 Women in History He
Would Like to Have Married

Artie Shaw, the clarinet-playing bandleader of the Big Band era, is almost as famous for his many marriages to some of Hollywood's most glamorous women as he is for his music. Among the seven women with whom he had what he calls "legal love affairs" were Lana Turner, Ava Gardner, and Evelyn Keyes.

1. Lucrezia Borgia (sixteenth-century Italian patron of the arts; rumored to have joined her brother Cesare Borgia in a variety of crimes and immoralities)
2. Zasu Pitts (actress and comedienne; films include *It's a Mad Mad Mad Mad World*)
3. Lizzie Borden (central suspect in the unsolved murder in 1892 of her wealthy father and stepmother)
4. Catherine de Médicis (sixteenth-century queen of France who provoked religious wars to keep herself in power)
5. Marie Dressler (American actress, born in Canada; films include *Dinner at Eight*)
6. Ruth Snyder (American murderess; electrocuted in 1928 for the brutal murder of her husband)
7. The Fat Lady — "who sings when it's over"
8. Queen Victoria — "soft and cuddly" (nineteenth-century queen of Great Britain and Ireland and empress of India)
9. Eva Braun — "she must have had *some*thing" (mistress of Adolf Hitler; married to him on the eve of their mutual suicide in a German bunker)
10. Fay Wray — "King Kong was crazy about her!" (American film actress; most noted for *King Kong*)

— Exclusive for *The Book of Lists*

36 Long Hollywood Marriages

Couple and Date of Marriage	Years Married*
1. James Cagney/Frances "Bill" Vernon (September 28, 1922–March 30, 1986)	63
2. Annette Kellerman/James R. Sullivan (November 26, 1912–October 30, 1975)	62
3. Dennis Morgan/Lillian Vedder (December 5, 1933–)	59

Couple and Date of Marriage	Years Married*
4. Bob Hope/Dolores Reade (February 19, 1934–)	59
5. Jack Haley/Florence McFadden (February 25, 1921–June 6, 1979)	58
6. Jane Wyatt/ Edgar Bethune Ward (November 9, 1935–)	57
7. Ray Bolger/Gwendolyn Rickard (July 9, 1929–January 15, 1987)	57
8. Bud Abbott/Betty Smith (September 17, 1918–April 24, 1974)	55
9. Sir Alec Guinness/Merula Salaman (June 20, 1938–)	55
10. Danny Thomas/Rose Marie Cassaniti (January 15, 1936–February 6, 1991)	55
11. Karl Malden/Mona Graham (December 18, 1938–)	54
12. Robert Mitchum/Dorothy Spencer (March 16, 1940–)	53
13. Walter Pidgeon/Ruth Walker (December 12, 1931–September 25, 1984)	52
14. Pat O'Brien/Eloise Taylor (January 23, 1931–October 15, 1983)	52
15. John Mills/Mary Hayley Bell (January 16, 1941–)	52
16. Phil Harris/Alice Faye (May 12, 1941–)	52
17. Richard Widmark/Ora Jean Hazelwood (April 5, 1942–)	51
18. Hume Cronyn/Jessica Tandy (September 27, 1942–)	51
19. Sid Caesar/Florence Levy (July 17, 1943–)	50
20. Dorothy McGuire/John Swope (July 18, 1943–)	50
21. Charlton Heston/Lydia Clarke (March 17, 1944–)	49
22. Melvyn Douglas/Helen Gahagan (April 5, 1931–June 28, 1980)	49
23. Craig Stevens/Alexis Smith (June 18, 1944–June 9, 1993)	48
24. Richard Attenborough/Shelia Sim (January 22, 1945–)	48
25. Eddie Cantor/Ida Tobias (June 9, 1914–August 8, 1962	48
26. Gene Autrey/Ina Mae Spivey (April 1, 1932–May 20, 1980)	48

Couple and Date of Marriage	Years Married*
27. Jack Benny/Sadye Marks (Mary Robinson) (January 25, 1927–December 26, 1974)	47
28. Fredric March/Florence Eldrige (May 30, 1927–April 14, 1975	47
29. Barbara Hale/Bill Williams (June 22, 1946–)	47
30. Danny Kaye/Sylvia Fine (January 3, 1940–March 3, 1987)	47
31. W. C. Fields/Harriet Hughes (August 8, 1900–December 25, 1946)	46
32. George Arliss/Florence Montgomery (September 16, 1899–February 5, 1946)	46
33. Paul Muni/Bella Finkel (May 8, 1921–August 25, 1967)	46
34. Dick Van Dyke/Marjorie Willetts (February 12, 1948–)	45
35. Eli Wallach/Anne Jackson (March 5, 1948–)	45
36. Ossie Davis/Ruby Dee (December 9, 1948–)	44

* As of October 1, 1993.

6 Couples Married *6* Weeks or Less

1. Jean Arthur and Julian Anker — 1 day
2. Patty Duke and Michael Tell — 13 days
3. Carole Landis and Irving Wheeler — 3 weeks
4. Debra Paget and Budd Boetticher — 22 days
5. George Brent and Constance Worth — 35 days
6. Greer Garson and Edward Snelson — 5 weeks

NOTE: For more unusually brief marriages, see *The Book of Lists #3*, pp. 277–79.

8 Women Who Had Much Younger Lovers

1. DINAH SHORE AND BURT REYNOLDS — 19-year difference

Reynolds first met Shore as a guest on her show *Dinah's Place* and spent most of his segment trying to convince her to go to

Palm Springs with him. Though this famous pair eventually broke up after a long love affair, Reynolds said in an interview, "Dinah was the great love of my life."

2. YOKO ONO AND SAM HAVADTOY — 19-year difference

Ono says of her relationship with Havadtoy, a New York interior designer, "Why can't a powerful woman have a relationship with a younger man? I need someone if I'm not going to crawl up the wall. I'm not eighty, you know."

3. LOUISE FLETCHER AND MORGAN MASON — 19-year difference

The forty-two-year-old actress had a three-and-a-half-year affair with Mason, the son of actors James and Pamela Mason. Said Fletcher, "I never called him 'You punk kid,' and he never called me 'You old bag.' "

4. EDITH PIAF AND THEO SARAPO — 20-year difference

The French singer was forty-seven when she married the twenty-seven-year-old Sarapo. Contrary to rumor, Piaf was poor and Sarapo was from a well-off family. They were happily married until her death in 1963.

5. CHER AND ROB CAMILLETTI — 23-year difference

When the forty-six-year-old Cher began to date the muscular twenty-three-year-old bartender and bagel maker, gossip was lively. "At one time," she said, "I wanted to marry Robert badly, but he needed time to go off and find himself."

6. MERLE OBERON AND ROBERT WOLDERS — 25-year difference

In 1975 the then sixty-three-year-old actress married the thirty-eight-year-old actor Wolders. He was her fourth husband, and they were married until her death five years later.

7. AYN RAND AND NATHANIEL BRANDEN — 25-year difference

In 1955 the fifty-year-old author began an affair with her twenty-five-year-old protégé. The relationship lasted fourteen years, with the full knowledge of their respective spouses. Eventually Branden fell in love with a younger woman and ended the relationship.

8. MARTHA RAYE AND MARK HARRIS — 33-year difference

Harris, forty-three, claims not to be bothered by the negative publicity surrounding his marriage to the seventy-six-year-old actress. Harris, a would-be show business promoter, eloped to Las Vegas with Raye a few weeks after their first meeting, and stands to inherit her $2.4 million estate. Says Raye of her critics, "It's none of their goddamn business."

When she was 63 years old, Merle Oberon married 38-year-old Robert Wolders.

11 Men Who Were at Least *33* Years Older Than Their Wives

1. **MILTON BERLE AND LORNA ADAMS** — 33-year difference

   The eighty-three-year-old comedian married the fifty-year-old fashion designer in 1991.

2. **BILL WYMAN AND MANDY SMITH** — 34-year difference

   After one marriage and "relations" with more than a thousand women, the fifty-two-year-old Rolling Stone married eighteen-year-old Mandy Smith. They first met when she was a thirteen-year-old Catholic-school girl, and for a time he paid her school fees. "It's great to be Mrs. Wyman," said the bride, "it's what I wanted for so long." The Wymans were divorced after seventeen months.

   In 1993, Wyman's thirty-year-old son, Stephen, became engaged to Mandy Smith's forty-six-year-old mother, Patsy. Their marriage would make Bill Wyman his own grandfather-in-law.

3. **CHARLIE CHAPLIN AND OONA O'NEILL** — 36-year difference

   Chaplin married his fourth wife when he was fifty-four and she was eighteen. The bride's father, playwright Eugene O'Neill, objected vigorously. In fact, Chaplin's sons had courted the girl,

Bill Wyman, 52, with his 18-year-old fiancée, Mandy Smith.

but she preferred their father. The happy marriage produced eight children, the last one fathered by Chaplin when he was seventy-three.

4. TONY CURTIS AND LISA DEUTSCH — 37-year difference

   Curtis, sixty-seven, married Deutsch, a thirty-year-old Los Angeles lawyer, in 1993. The actor has six children by his previous three wives.

5. HUGH HEFNER AND KIMBERLY CONRAD — 37-year difference

   The sixty-three-year-old founder of *Playboy* magazine married for the first time in 1989. His bride, who had been Miss January 1988, was twenty-six — ten years younger than Hefner's daughter. She announced at the wedding, "I'm writing a book and I'll let all you ladies know my secret."

6. T. S. ELIOT AND VALERIE FLETCHER — 39-year difference

   When the poet was sixty-nine, he married the thirty-year-old Fletcher, who had been his devoted secretary for eight years. By all accounts this was a happy marriage that brought Eliot rejuvenation and contentment.

7. GROUCHO MARX AND EDEN HARTFORD — 40-year difference

   In 1954, when Marx was sixty-four, he married a twenty-four-year-old former model. They were divorced after fifteen years.

8. GENE KELLY AND PATRICIA WARD — 41-year difference

   While starring in a television special, Kelly met writer Patricia Ward. After dating for five years, the pair married in 1990. He was seventy-seven, she thirty-six.

T. S. Eliot returning from his honeymoon with Valerie Fletcher.

9. LEOPOLD STOKOWSKI AND GLORIA VANDERBILT — 42-year difference

The conductor's third marriage, at sixty-three, was to the twenty-one-year-old heiress Vanderbilt. They had two sons before their divorce ten years later. Stokowski continued to have occasional affairs until his death at ninety-five.

10. SAUL BELLOW AND JANICE FRIEDMAN — 43-year difference

Nobel Prize–winning author Bellow wed for the fifth time in 1989. His wife, Janice Friedman, had been his student at the University of Chicago. The groom was seventy-four, the bride thirty-one.

11. SENATOR STROM THURMOND AND NANCY MOORE — 44-year difference

When the sixty-six-year-old Thurmond married a twenty-two-year-old former beauty queen, he boasted that he was still in great shape. Indeed, he fathered four children. The couple were separated in 1991, after twenty-two years of marriage.

7 Unlikely Couples

1. DANNY KAYE AND LAURENCE OLIVIER

Kaye met Olivier and his wife, Vivien Leigh, at a Hollywood party in 1940. From then on he visited and entertained them constantly, lavishing attention on his new friend, whom he nicknamed Lally. Kaye was married, but apparently had an arrangement with his wife. The Olivier-Leigh marriage was more volatile, with Olivier finding his wife too sexually demanding. When the two men began an affair, according to biographer Donald Spoto, it was no secret to Leigh. Nevertheless, the Oliviers continued to socialize with Kaye. On one occasion, Kaye disguised himself as a Customs inspector in order to strip-search Olivier when he entered the United States on a 1953 trip. Their liaison lasted ten years, until Olivier's next wife, Joan Plowright, strongly objected to it.

2. JIM BROWN AND GLORIA STEINEM

Brown, football hero and actor, claims in one of his memoirs to have had a fling with feminist Steinem. They met in 1968, when she interviewed him for a magazine profile. The affair caused Brown's then girlfriend, Eva Bohn-Chin, to become jealous, which in turn led to a quarrel during which Brown was arrested for allegedly throwing Bohn-Chin off a balcony.

3. GYPSY ROSE LEE AND OTTO PREMINGER

Lee, the famous and flamboyant stripper, instigated an affair with the Hollywood filmmaker in order to have a child by him. She selected him over other men "in spite of his reputation" for being a brute. She "sensed he was a good man" and admired his mind. Once she was pregnant, she brushed off Preminger. Their son, Erik, did not know who his real father was until he was an adult. After Lee's death, Preminger legally adopted Erik, and the two became close friends.

4. AIMEE SEMPLE MCPHERSON AND MILTON BERLE

In 1930, four years after her infamous "kidnapping," the flamboyant evangelist met Berle — then a rising young comic — at a charity show. The two had a brief affair, and Berle remembers her as a worldly, passionate woman who enjoyed making love in her apartment in front of a homemade altar, complete with candles and crucifix.

5. IMELDA MARCOS AND BENIGNO AQUINO, JR.

When she won the Miss Manila beauty contest in 1953, Imelda Romualdez attracted several suitors. Among them was the young journalist Benigno Aquino, whom she dated for a time. But it was another of her suitors, politician Ferdinand Marcos, whom she married. Nearly thirty years later, the assassination of Aquino brought down the Marcos government and swept the widowed Corazon Aquino into power.

6. BARBARA WALTERS AND ROY COHN

Cohn, a rabid "red-baiter" during the anti-Communist witch hunts of the 1950s, dated Walters when she was in college. Friends believe that, at the time, she was unaware of Cohn's homosexuality. Said one, "Barbara felt that the only problem

General George S. Patton and Marlene Dietrich.

with Roy was that he was very tied to his mother." Acquaintances believe that the affair was never consummated, even though Cohn asked Walters more than once to marry him.

7. MARLENE DIETRICH AND GENERAL GEORGE S. PATTON

During World War II, Dietrich devoted herself wholeheartedly to entertaining the Allied troops at the front. Traveling together, Patton and Dietrich began an intense affair. This unlikely passion was eventually replaced by an even hotter liaison — that between Dietrich and the handsome General James A. Gavin. Among her other lovers were Yul Brynner, Frank Sinatra, Fritz Lang, Kirk Douglas, Maurice Chevalier, Gary Cooper, George Raft, Jean Gabin, Douglas Fairbanks, Jr., Josef Von Sternberg, Adlai Stevenson, and Burt Bacharach. John Wayne was among the few to have declined her offer of intimate friendship. Dietrich also had numerous affairs with women, including Edith Piaf and writer and feminist Mercedes De Acosta, who was also a lover of Greta Garbo's.

12 Unlikely Roommates

1.–2. SHELLEY WINTERS AND MARILYN MONROE

When the two young actresses were starting out in Hollywood, they decided to share an apartment together. They found a place for $227 a month and furnished it in what Winters called "early relative." They became best friends, staying up late listening to jazz, and making lists of famous men they wanted to sleep with. (Winters's included Cary Grant and Eric Sevareid; Monroe's included Charles Laughton and Albert Einstein.) Sometimes they entertained, but Marilyn couldn't cook at all. When they had poet Dylan Thomas over to dinner, she did make a pitcher of gin martinis, which she served in a milk bottle. Winters recalled, "Once I asked her to wash a salad while I went to the store. When I came back an hour later she was still scrubbing each leaf. Her idea of making a salad was to scrub each lettuce leaf with a Brillo pad."

3.–4. MARLON BRANDO AND WALLY COX

Cox and Brando had been good friends since they were ten. "It wasn't an unlikely friendship," Brando insisted, "because Wally didn't resemble in the remotest his Mr. Peepers character." He had, rather, "the mentality of an ax murderer." They were sometimes roommates during their early acting days, living in true bachelor-pigsty style. Even when Wally had his own apartment in New York's Hell's Kitchen, Brando brought girls over and Cox slept in the living room. They ribbed each other constantly, yodeled and whistled in harmony at parties, and read *Scientific American* cover to cover. They talked incessantly about the Big Questions — marriage, life and death. After Cox died in 1973, Brando told a reporter that he kept Wally's ashes in the house and talked to him all the time, adding, "I can't tell you how I miss and love that man."

5.–6. SPENCER TRACY AND PAT O'BRIEN

O'Brien and Tracy had been teenage friends, and when they ran into each other in New York, the two struggling actors decided to share a room. It was a drab, sparsely furnished twelve-by-twelve with twin iron beds, twin washstands, and, Tracy said, "twin cracks." They were so poor that they lived on pretzels, rice, and water, and soled their shoes with cardboard. Finally they got a break playing robots in the play *R.U.R.* (the word *robot* originated in this show). They made fifteen dollars a week until Tracy got a line to read and then their income went up to twenty dollars.

Marlon Brando and his roommate Wally Cox read *Scientific American* magazine together.

7.–8. Dennis Wilson and Charles Manson

One late night in 1968, Beach Boy Dennis Wilson returned to his home on Sunset Boulevard. He was greeted by a strange, scruffy man who had broken into his house, and who dropped to his knees and kissed Wilson's sneakers. Inside were over a dozen young girls drinking and smoking pot. Two of them knew Wilson and had brought the thirty-three-year-old Manson and his "Family" for a visit. They moved in immediately, and orgies — carefully choreographed by Charlie — began that night. Manson believed that everyone should have sex seven times a day.

The Family stayed for the summer, and cost Wilson over $100,000 in food, clothing, cars, and doctors' bills (usually to cure his guests of gonorrhea). Wilson encouraged Manson's musical ambitions, and one of his songs, "Cease to Exist," appeared on the Beach Boys' album *20/20,* under the title "Never

Learn Not to Love." Wilson, too intimidated to evict his guests, eventually moved out of his own house. Not long after, Manson and the Family committed the Tate-LaBianca murders.

9.–10. DAVID NIVEN AND WILLIAM F. BUCKLEY, JR.

Niven and Buckley were close friends in Niven's last years. They roomed together briefly in 1975, renting a studio in Switzerland for the winter in order to paint. Niven described his friend as "the worst amateur painter in the world . . . He knocks off nine [paintings] a night and they all look like the bottom of Lake Erie." When the celebrated Marc Chagall came to visit them, Niven begged Buckley not to display his work. Undaunted, Buckley brought out a series of paintings, and when Chagall came upon a blank canvas, he remarked, "I like that one best." In his youth, Niven had another famous roommate: Errol Flynn.

11.–12. CARY GRANT AND RANDOLPH SCOTT

In 1933 the two successful actors rented the first of many houses together in Los Angeles. The fan magazines dubbed their second home — a spacious mansion in the Hollywood Hills — Bachelor's Hall, and made much of the eligibility of the two stars. However, it didn't take long for tongues to wag about the nature of their relationship. Photographs appeared of them wearing matching aprons, washing their dishes together, making their beds, and cavorting in the pool. One columnist decided that they were "carrying the buddy business a bit too far."

Over the years, they had affairs, married, and divorced, but usually returned to living together. When Grant was dating actress Virginia Cherrill, she was warned away from him by a friend, Jack Kelly: "He told me that I should be very cautious indeed before entering into a committed affair with Cary; he added that Cary was the lover of Randolph Scott." For the sake of appearances, when Grant and Cherrill married, Scott moved out of Grant's house and into the house next door. As soon as they divorced, Scott moved back in.

9 Names Celebrities Gave Their Children

1. Dandelion (daughter of Keith Richards)
2. Free (son of Barbara Hershey)
3. Satchel (son of Woody Allen)
4. Moon Unit (daughter of Frank Zappa)
5. Dweezil (son of Frank Zappa)
6. Rain (daughter of Richard Pryor)
7. Zowie (son of David Bowie)
8. Sage Moonblood (son of Sylvester Stallone)
9. God (daughter of Grace Slick)

9 Successful People Who Were Educated at Home

1. ALEXANDER GRAHAM BELL, inventor of the telephone

   Until the age of ten, Bell was educated by his hearing-impaired mother, who taught him the manual alphabet to facilitate communication. He attended school for five years, but was an undistinguished student. When he turned fifteen, Bell went to live with his seventy-two-year-old grandfather, who took charge of the boy's education and inspired him to challenge himself academically.

2. PEARL BUCK, Nobel Prize–winning novelist

   The daughter of American missionaries in China, Buck was given a Western education by her mother in the mornings. In the afternoons she was tutored in Chinese studies by a Mr. Kung, who did not come on rainy days because his mother feared he would wet his feet and fall ill. He was in his late forties at the time. Nevertheless, he died of cholera when Buck was thirteen, and she was sent, two or three times a week, to a mission school for girls.

3. AGATHA CHRISTIE, mystery writer

   Christie's mother believed that it was bad for the brain for children to be taught to read before the age of eight, so the future novelist taught herself before she was five. Her father then instructed her in writing and arithmetic. Another of her mother's beliefs was that girls should be allowed to run free instead of being sent to school, so Christie immersed herself in the contents of the large family library. She received less than two years of formal education from age thirteen to fifteen and later commented that if she had continued, she would have probably ended up "a third- or fourth-rate mathematician" instead of a successful author.

4. THOMAS EDISON, inventor of the phonograph and the electric light bulb

Edison began school when he was eight years old, but did not respond well to the harsh methods of the schoolmaster. After three months he overheard the teacher refer to his mind as "addled." Edison stormed out of the schoolroom and never returned. His mother took over his education and by the age of nine he was reading literary classics, including Shakespeare and Dickens. That same year, his mother brought home a textbook on physical science. Edison completed every experiment in the book. From then on, his mother encouraged him to study whatever he wanted.

5. C. S. LEWIS, literary critic and author

Lewis grew up in a house filled with books and was allowed to read anything he wished. His mother taught him French and Latin, and his governess all other subjects, until he was sent to boarding school at the age of ten.

6. GEORGE BERNARD SHAW, Nobel Prize–winning playwright and critic

Shaw was taught by a governess until he was ten years old, although he learned Latin from an uncle. When he finally started school, he hated it. As an adult he believed that children should be allowed to come and go to school as they pleased, with adults present only to assist them. "Abolish the schoolmaster," he declared. "Education will never get anywhere while the schoolmaster is there."

7. WOODROW WILSON, president of the United States

Wilson's mother believed that children should not be confined to schoolrooms. Consequently, he did not enter one until he was almost twelve. Although he could not read comfortably until he was eleven, his father taught him literature, science, and theology. Once a week, father and son visited city shops or country farms and factories so that Wilson could learn firsthand how the economy worked. He went on to become president of Princeton University before moving to politics.

8. ANDREW WYETH, painter

A sickly child, Wyeth was educated at home by a tutor and by his father, the famous artist and illustrator N. C. Wyeth.

9. BRIGHAM YOUNG, religious leader

Raised in a poor, frontier family, the future president of the Mormon Church received only eleven days of formal schooling. Instead, he learned practical skills, such as farming, gardening, carpentry, painting, masonry, and boatbuilding.

7 Famous People Who Were Victims of Child Abuse

1. MARY McCARTHY (1912–1989), novelist, essayist

McCarthy, best known for her novel *The Group,* was orphaned at the age of six. She and her three younger brothers were sent to live with their sadistic aunt Margaret and uncle Meyers. They were beaten regularly — for being "bad," or for being good, as a preventive measure against becoming stuck-up. When she was ten, McCarthy won first prize in an essay contest and was viciously beaten with a razor strop afterward. The children were sent to bed with their mouths taped shut — to prevent "mouth breathing" — fed a diet of root vegetables, and locked outside in subzero weather, where they would stand in the snow and cry. Wrote McCarthy of her guardians, "It was as though these ignorant people, at sea with four frightened children, had taken a Dickens novel — *Oliver Twist,* perhaps, or *Nicholas Nickleby* — for a navigation chart." Her grandparents rescued her when she was eleven.

2. ROD McKUEN (1933–   ), poet and author

McKuen was both battered and raped as a child. Though his stepfather broke both his arms and several ribs, McKuen claims that his sexual molestation at the hands of an aunt and uncle scarred him more deeply. While baby-sitting for the seven-year-old McKuen, his aunt fondled his genitals. He screamed, and finally she stopped. Two weeks later, her husband took him camping. He convinced the boy to get into his sleeping bag, where he sodomized him. McKuen said he "thought about what happened almost every day until I was in my thirties." Finally, at forty-nine, McKuen spoke out, telling his story for the first time to 600 people at a meeting of the National Committee for the Prevention of Child Abuse. He advises victimized children to "tell somebody immediately."

3. DIRK BOGARDE (1921–   ), actor

In his autobiography, Bogarde describes his very bizarre childhood molestation. One day, at a matinee showing of *The Mummy,* he was befriended by a Mr. Dodd, who "was almost entirely beige. A beige raincoat, beige face, beige hair and freckles." He bought Bogarde ice cream, took him to tea the following week, and described to him his studies in medical school. Offering to show Bogarde how mummies were bandaged, he invited him to his apartment. As the demonstration proceeded, young Bogarde was "straitjacketed in strips of thin cotton bandage ... trussed like a fowl." Mr. Dodd tightly swathed everything but Bogarde's genitals, then threw him on the bed and masturbated him. Bogarde "never set foot in a cinema alone for many years to come."

4. BRIAN WILSON (1942–   ), musician, former member of the Beach Boys

Wilson's father was a vicious tyrant who regularly beat and humiliated his three sons. Brian was the most severely victimized, and he lived in terror of his father. He was constantly berated, and when he was nine was thrashed with a splintered two-by-four. On one occasion, Murry Wilson threw a newspaper on the floor and ordered his son to defecate on it, in front of his mother, who did not intervene.

5. OPRAH WINFREY (1954–   ), television personality

Winfrey was born out of wedlock, and was given to her grandmother's care shortly after birth. At nine she was sent to live with her mother. She was repeatedly raped by a teenage cousin, and later sexually abused by other family members. Says Winfrey, "I was, and still am, severely damaged by the experience. I unconsciously blamed myself for those men's acts." Since telling her story publicly in 1985, Winfrey has been active in promoting education about child abuse and has spoken on the subject before the Senate Judiciary Committee.

6. SINÉAD O'CONNOR (1966–   ), singer and songwriter

When O'Connor's parents separated she went to live with her mother, whom she describes as "a very unhappy woman who was very, very violent . . . Merely the sound of my mother's feet on the hearth ceiling were enough to send us into spasms of complete terror." O'Connor was often locked out of the house overnight, and "was beaten up very severely with every kind of implement you can imagine yourself being beaten with. And I was starved, I was locked in my room for days at a time without being fed, with no clothes." Eventually, O'Connor returned to live with her father, and "took it all out on him."

7. MAYA ANGELOU (1928–   ), poet, author, director

When she was eight, Angelou was raped by her mother's boy-friend, a Mr. Freeman. He told her, "If you scream, I'm gonna kill you. And if you tell, I'm gonna kill Bailey [her brother]." She wrote, "There was the pain. A breaking and entering when even the senses are torn apart. The act of rape on an eight-year-old body is a matter of the needle giving because the camel can't." Angelou was hospitalized with injuries, Freeman was arrested, and the stunned and humiliated eight-year-old was cross-examined at his trial. Freeman was convicted, though never jailed; shortly after the trial, he was found kicked to death.

9 Famous Fathers

1. Father of Chop Suey — Li Hung-chang (1823–1901)
2. Father of Frozen Foods — Clarence Birdseye (1886–1956)
3. Father of the Mail-Order Catalog — Benjamin Franklin (1706–1790)
4. Father of the One-Way Ride — Earl "Hymie" Weiss (1898–1926)

Earl "Hymie" Weiss, Father of the One-Way Ride.

5. Father of Landscape Gardening — André Le Nôtre (1613–1700)
6. Father of Power Steering — Francis W. Davis (1887–1978)
7. Father of the Brillo Pad — Milton E. Loeb (1889–1972)
8. Father of the Cosa Nostra — Salvatorre Maranzano (1868–1931)
9. Father of Courtesy — Richard de Beauchamp, earl of Warwick (1382–1439)

13 Famous People With Jewish Fathers and Christian Mothers

1. William Cohen (1940–   ), U.S. senator
2. Joan Collins (1933–   ), actress
3. Jamie Lee Curtis (1958–   ), actress
4. Werner Erhard (1935–   ), cult founder
5. Carrie Fisher (1956–   ), actress
6. Kathie Lee Gifford (1954–   ), TV host
7. John Houseman (1902–1988), actor
8. Kevin Kline (1947–   ), actor
9. Michael Landon (1936–1991), actor
10. Paul Newman (1925–   ), actor
11. Jerry Orbach (1935–   ), actor
12. Joseph Pulitzer (1847–1911), newspaper owner
13. Jane Seymour (1951–   ), actress

6 Famous People Whose Families Were Not What They Seemed

1. ART BLAKEY, drummer, bandleader

Blakey's father left his mother shortly after their shotgun marriage. His mother died when he was six months old, and a cousin, Sarah Parran, raised him. Blakey grew up believing Parran was his mother, and when he found out the truth, at age thirteen, he ran away from home. Blakey married when he was fourteen years old and became a father by age fifteen.

2. MICHAEL CAINE, actor

For more than forty years, Caine's mother, Ellen Maria Burchell, paid periodic visits to a "cousin" in a mental hospital. When she died in 1989 Caine learned that the cousin was really his older brother, named David.

3. ERIC CLAPTON, guitarist, singer

Clapton's mother left him in the care of his grandparents until he was about twelve. At that time she returned to the family, and for a while they all pretended she was the boy's sister. Keeping this secret made him, in his own words, "moody and nasty," and he failed exams for secondary school.

4. JACK NICHOLSON, actor

Nicholson was raised in Neptune, New Jersey, by his beautician mother, Ethel May, and her two daughters, Lorraine and June, who were fifteen and seventeen years older than Jack. When he was thirty-seven years old, Nicholson learned the bizarre truth about his family from a *Time* magazine researcher: Ethel May was really his grandmother. The woman who actually gave birth to him was his "sister" June.

Four-year-old Jack Nicholson with his real mother (left) and the woman he thought was his mother (second from left).

5. ERIK LEE PREMINGER, author, screenwriter

Gypsy Rose Lee told her son, Erik, who was born in 1944, that his father was her second husband, Alexander Kirkland, an art gallery operator. When Erik was seventeen, Kirkland asked Erik's psychiatrist to explain to Erik that he was not the boy's biological father. His real father was producer/director Otto Preminger, but Lee swore both father and son to secrecy. Preminger finally adopted Erik in 1971, after Lee's death.

6. BUFFY SAINTE-MARIE, folksinger, songwriter

Sainte-Marie was raised in Maine and Massachusetts believing she was white. When she was a teenager, she unexpectedly met someone who knew her true background: she was a Cree Indian, born in Canada, who was adopted by a white family and raised as white after her mother had died in an accident. The adoption agency had effectively kidnapped her and had not told her relatives of her whereabouts. Learning the truth, Sainte-Marie quickly left her adoptive family and joined her extended Cree family.

12 Famous Orphans

1. INGRID BERGMAN (1915–1982)

Bergman's mother died when she was three years old. When her father died ten years later, Bergman went to live with her aunt and uncle. Lonely and shy and self-conscious because she was tall, she retreated into a world of fantasy, making up plays in which she acted all of the parts. In the 1940s she became one of the world's most popular actresses, starring in such films as *Casablanca, For Whom the Bell Tolls, Gaslight,* and *Notorious.*

2. SIMÓN BOLÍVAR (1783–1830)

Bolívar's father passed away when he was three and his mother died of tuberculosis when he was nine. After his grandfather died a short time later, his uncle became his guardian and took charge of his education. Bolívar learned his lessons well and became a soldier and statesman, known as the "Liberator of South America."

3. RALPH BUNCHE (1904–1971)

Bunche's parents died within three months of each other when Bunche was eleven years old. After that he was raised by his grandmother and two maternal aunts. A good student, he graduated from UCLA and Harvard, became a professor of political science, and devoted the better part of his adult life to the United Nations. In 1950 he was awarded the Nobel Peace Prize for mediating the 1949 dispute between Israel and its Arab neighbors.

4. GABRIELLE "COCO" CHANEL (1883–1971)

After her mother died of consumption, six-year-old Gabrielle and her sister were dropped off at an orphanage by their peddler father. Eventually claimed by aunts, she became a seamstress and ultimately built a fashion empire that included a textile business, perfume laboratories, and a workshop for costume jewelry.

5. HERBERT HOOVER (1874–1964)

Orphaned at the age of ten, Hoover moved in with an aunt and uncle who ran a prep school in Oregon. He later became the thirty-first president of the United States. Hoover's vice-president, Charles Curtis, was also an orphan.

6. BORIS KARLOFF (1887–1969)

Karloff's parents died when he was a child. The youngest of eight sons, he was raised by his older brothers and a stepsister, who pushed him toward a career in government service. However, he quickly turned to acting, gaining his greatest fame as the monster in *Frankenstein.*

7. JAMES MICHENER (1907–   )

The future novelist was abandoned as an infant in Doylestown, Pennsylvania. He was raised, along with other abandoned children, by a poor Quaker widow named Mabel Michener. He has said that because he knew nothing about his parents, "I've never felt in a position to reject anybody. I could be Jewish, part Negro, probably not Oriental, but almost anything else."

8. MUHAMMAD (570–632)

His father died before Muhammed was born and his mother died when he was six. He was placed in the care of his grandfather, who died two years later. Thereafter he was raised by the family of his uncle Abu Talib.

9. EDGAR ALLAN POE (1809–1849)

Poe's alcoholic father abandoned his family shortly after Edgar's birth. When Edgar was two and a half, his mother died of tuberculosis. Poe was raised by Frances Allan, the wife of a Richmond, Virginia, merchant who never legally adopted him.

10. ELEANOR ROOSEVELT (1884–1962)

Roosevelt's mother died when she was eight and her father when she was nine. She grew up with her grandmother Hall, her mother's mother. In 1905 she married her cousin, Franklin Roosevelt. When Franklin became president of the United States, Eleanor became the most active and one of the most popular First Ladies in U.S. history.

11. BARBARA STANWYCK (1907–1990)

Born Ruby Stevens in Brooklyn, Stanwyck was four years old when her mother was killed by a drunk who pushed her off a moving streetcar. Devastated by the death of his wife, Ruby's bricklayer father abandoned his five children. Stanwyck grew up in a series of foster homes before finding work as a chorus girl at age fifteen. In the 1930s she became a movie star, famed for her portrayal of strong women.

12. LEO TOLSTOI (1828–1910)

Tolstoi's mother died before his second birthday and his father dropped dead in the middle of the street when Leo was eight years old. After the death of his grandmother less than a year later, he and his four siblings were split up. Tolstoi, his older brother Dmitri, and his younger sister Marya went to live in the country with their aunt Toinette, who had once promised their father to look after his children as if they were her own.

53 Parents of Adopted Children

According to WAIF, an organization founded by Jane Russell and devoted to finding a permanent family for every child, there are more than 500,000 children in need of adoption in the United States alone. For further information, write to WAIF, P.O. 878, New York, NY 10159.

1. Eddie Albert
2. June Allyson
3. Don Ameche
4.–5. Julie Andrews and Blake Edwards
6. Eve Arden
7. Pearl Bailey
8. Senator Lloyd Bentsen
9. Art Buchwald
10. George Burns
11.–12. Tom Cruise and Nicole Kidman

13. Jamie Lee Curtis
14. Ted Danson
15. Bette Davis
16. Sammy Davis, Jr.
17. Oscar De La Renta
18. John Denver
19.–20. Mia Farrow and Woody Allen
21. Mia Farrow and André Previn
22. Henry Fonda
23. Connie Francis
24. Louis Gossett, Jr.
25. Valerie Harper
26.–27. Helen Hayes and Charles MacArthur
28. Senator Jesse Helms
29. Bob Hope
30.–31. Jill Ireland and Charles Bronson
32. Patti LaBelle
33. Jerry Lewis
34. Art Linkletter
35. Willie Mays
36. Ed McMahon
37.–38. Paul Newman and Joanne Woodward
39. Carroll O'Connor
40. Patti Page
41. Estelle Parsons
42. Della Reese
43.–44. Burt Reynolds and Loni Anderson
45.–46. Roy Rogers and Dale Evans
47. Dinah Shore
48. Senator Paul Simon
49. Gloria Swanson
50. Kurt Vonnegut
51. Barbara Walters
52.–53. Jane Wyman and Ronald Reagan

15 Famous People Who Were Adopted

1. John J. Audubon, naturalist
2. Richard Burton, actor
3.–4. Peter and Kitty Carruthers, Olympic figure skaters
5. Bill Clinton, U.S. president
6. Faith Daniels, newscaster

7. Ted Danson, actor
8. Eric Dickerson, football player
9. Gerald Ford, U.S. president
10. Scott Hamilton, Olympic figure skater
11. Steven Paul Jobs, electronics engineer and computer developer
12. Greg Louganis, Olympic diver
13. Jim Palmer, baseball player
14. Nancy Reagan, actress and U.S. First Lady
15. Dave Thomas, comic actor

NOTE: For more famous people who were adopted, see *The Book of Lists #3*, p. 289.

14 Famous Men Who Have Publicly Denied Being Gay

1. BOY GEORGE (1961–), English pop singer

   The androgynous pop star told a London newspaper in 1984, "I'm not gay, and I'm not a transvestite, no matter what anybody thinks. I'm basically very much a man." At other times, Boy George has variously described himself as "bisexual," "very confused," "not confused," and "not really all that keen on sex." In 1993, he finally acknowledged his homosexuality, stating, "I always wanted to be a gay songwriter who can write gay love songs."

2. ROY COHN (1927–1986), U.S. attorney

   The controversial New York attorney, former counsel for Senator Joseph McCarthy and an assistant prosecutor in the case that sent Ethel and Julius Rosenberg to the electric chair in 1953, was asked on *60 Minutes* about rumors that he was gay and dying of AIDS. "It's a lie as far as I'm concerned," Cohn replied. Cohn said he was suffering from liver cancer. Later, on the *Larry King Live* show, a phone caller asked if he was gay. "No," Cohn flatly replied. After Cohn's death, in July 1986, it was revealed that he had, in fact, been gay, and had AIDS. "He denied his homosexuality," wrote one of his friends, conservative columnist William Safire, "because he could never reconcile it with his self-image of political masculinity."

3. TROY DONAHUE (1936–), U.S. actor

   Donahue told *People* magazine in 1984, "I am not gay. Once in a while people get me confused with another blond, blue-eyed actor who was around at the same time, but it's no big deal. I love women. Sometimes, I guess, too much." Donahue has been married four times, once to actress Suzanne Pleshette.

4. BLAKE EDWARDS (1922–   ), U.S. film director

In a 1983 *Playboy* magazine interview, Edwards was asked if after writing and directing *Victor/Victoria* he was worried people would start whispering he was coming out of the closet. Edwards replied that despite having done some typical homosexual experimentation as a child, and despite some fears early in his life that he might be gay, he was nonetheless, in his words, "very heterosexual." He is married to actress Julie Andrews.

5. THOMAS S. FOLEY (1929–   ), U.S. Speaker of the House

In 1989 officials of the Bush White House sought to destroy the political power of Speaker of the House Thomas Foley (Democrat from Washington) by publicly insinuating that he was a homosexual. Foley vehemently denied any suggestion that he was gay, calling such assertions "a very cheap smear." "I am not a homosexual," he said in a nationally televised interview on CNN. "I have been married for twenty-one years." The White House later apologized for its campaign to discredit Foley.

6. DARYL HALL (1948–   ), U.S. pop singer

In a 1984 *Rolling Stone* magazine interview, Hall denied persistent rumors that he was gay and that he and singing partner John Oates were lovers. "The idea of sex with a man doesn't turn me off," he said, "but I don't express it. I satisfied my curiosity about that years ago. I had lots of sex between the ages of three or four and the time I was fourteen or fifteen. Strange experiences with older boys. But men don't particularly turn me on. And, no, John and I have never been lovers. He's not my type. Too short and dark."

7. MICHAEL JACKSON (1958–   ), U.S. pop singer

Jackson held a national press conference in 1984 to refute insinuations that he was a homosexual. Calling the rumors a "terrible slander," he threatened to sue any periodical that printed "new fantasies." Michael's brother Jermaine told one newspaper, "Even to say that he's not gives people the idea that he is. People want to hear ugliness." The *Los Angeles Times* later commented: "There does not appear to be any precedent for a celebrity going to such lengths to proclaim his or her heterosexuality."

8. JACK KEMP (1935–   ), U.S. politician

As an aide to California governor Ronald Reagan, Kemp worked for an official who resigned from office in 1967 amid allegations of homosexual conduct. "My name got mixed in tangentially," Kemp told *Newsweek* several years later, "and that little piece of poison just stays there." Kemp has flatly denied rumors that he is gay.

9. PERRY KING (1948–), U.S. actor

After playing a gay man in the 1978 movie *A Different Story*, King denied that he was himself gay. "It's funny," he remarked. "Audiences don't think you're a murderer if you play a murderer, but they do think you're gay if you play a gay."

10. ED KOCH (1924–), New York City mayor

During the 1977 mayoral primary between Mario Cuomo and Ed Koch, posters appeared throughout New York City with the slogan "Vote for Cuomo, not the homo." Reacting to long-standing rumors that he was a homosexual, Koch told one magazine in 1982: "No, I am not a homosexual. If I were a homosexual, I would hope I would have the courage to say so. What's cruel is that you are forcing me to say I am not a homosexual. This means you are putting homosexuals down. I don't want to do that." Asked if he had ever had a homosexual experience, Koch replied that he would not discuss his private life in public.

11. LIBERACE (1919–1987), U.S. entertainer

In 1959 Liberace sued the London *Daily Mirror* and one of its journalists for libel for implying that he was a homosexual. On the witness stand, Liberace flatly denied that he was a homosexual and stated that he had never in his life indulged in homosexual practices. The trial lasted only six days, and Liberace won the suit and a $24,000 settlement. In 1982 Liberace himself became the defendant in a highly publicized lawsuit that once again called his sexual orientation into question. The suit was filed by his former chauffeur and bodyguard, twenty-three-year-old Scott Thorson, who sought $113 million in palimony after claiming that he and Liberace had had "an intimate sexual and emotional relationship" for more than six years. Liberace again denied he was gay, and issued a statement asserting that Thorson's suit was "an outrageous, ambitious attempt to assassinate my character." Liberace eventually paid Thorson an out-of-court settlement. After Liberace died in 1987, it was revealed that he had had AIDS. His homosexuality — an open secret within the entertainment industry — became widely known. Shortly after the entertainer's death, the London *Daily Mirror* asked for a refund of the $24,000 libel settlement it had paid the pianist back in 1959.

12. JOE NAMATH (1943–), U.S. football star

After he appeared wearing nylons in a series of nationally televised commercials for women's pantyhose, Namath publicly denied being gay. He told *Esquire* magazine in 1979, "Not only am I not gay, I am not even bisexual . . . I'm sure thirty years from now, if I'm still a bachelor, people will be asking me if I'm gay."

13. POPE PAUL VI (1897–1978)

When Italian magazine *Tempo* published an article in 1967 asserting that he was a homosexual, Pope Paul VI took the unusual step of issuing a denial in a public speech from his balcony overlooking St. Peter's Square. He called the magazine's assertions "a horrible and slanderous insinuation," and implored Catholics to "pray for our humble person, who has been made the target of scorn . . . by a certain press lacking dutiful regard for honesty and truth." Soon afterward, Italian police began mass confiscations of the magazine, on grounds that it had libeled the Catholic Church.

14. RANDY TRAVIS (1963–), U.S. country music singer

The popular singer angrily denied a 1991 supermarket tabloid story asserting he was a homosexual. "I usually let things slide," he said, "but I couldn't this time. There is not a man alive that can prove that statement, because it isn't true." Travis later joked, "I guess it could have been worse. They could've said I wasn't country."

SOURCE: Leigh W. Rutledge, author of *The Gay Book of Lists* (Boston: Alyson Publications, 1987).

Pope John Paul VI issued a public denial after being accused of homosexuality.

15 Famous People Who Acknowledged Having Had at Least *1* Homosexual Experience in Their Lives

1. VOLTAIRE (1694–1778), French philosopher

   The great French author, one of the leading figures of the Enlightenment, acknowledged to friends that when he attended the Catholic college Louis-le-Grand in Paris, "those damned Jesuits buggered me to such a degree that I shall never get over it as long as I live." Later, he wrote explicitly passionate poems to both Frederick the Great and the noted English homosexual Lord John Hervey, leading some biographers to speculate that he may have been actively bisexual.

2. GIOVANNI GIACOMO CASANOVA (1725–1798), Italian adventurer and memoirist

   The famed libertine rarely passed up an opportunity to sample any sort of sexual encounter, and acknowledged having had at least two homosexual experiences in his adult life.

3. LEO TOLSTOI (1828–1910), Russian author

   When he was twenty-three, Tolstoi confided to his diary, "I have never been in love with a woman ... but I have quite often fallen in love with a man." Detailing one encounter involving a close male friend, Dimitri Dyakov, he wrote: "I shall never forget the night we left Pirogovo together, when, wrapped up in my blanket, I wanted to devour him with kisses and weep. Sexual desire was not totally absent ..." Later in life, Tolstoi became so enamored of one of his disciples, Vladimir Chertkov, that Tolstoi's wife, Sonya, publicly accused the two of being homosexual lovers.

4. WINSTON CHURCHILL (1875–1961), British prime minister

   Churchill acknowledged to novelist W. Somerset Maugham that he'd once had sex with a man "to see what it was like." His partner turned out to be Ivor Novello, a dashingly handsome homosexual and one of the most popular musical-comedy stars of his day. "And what was it like?" Maugham inquired. "Musical," Churchill replied. Churchill also acknowledged the experience to his friend Lord Beaverbrook.

5. TALLULAH BANKHEAD (1903–1968), U.S. actress

   Bankhead was outspoken about her attraction to both men and women, and admitted having had several lesbian relationships

Winston Churchill tried homosexuality once "to see what it was like."

in her life. "I don't know what I am, darling," she told a friend. "I've tried several varieties of sex. The conventional position makes me claustrophobic. And the others give me either stiff neck or lockjaw." She once cheerfully referred to herself as "ambisextrous."

6. ARTHUR C. CLARKE (1917–), British author

The distinguished science fiction writer was asked by *Playboy* magazine in 1986 whether he'd ever had any "bisexual experiences." "Of course," Clarke replied. "Who hasn't? Good God! If anyone had ever told me that he hadn't, I'd have told him he was lying. But then, of course, people tend to 'forget' their encounters."

7. CARSON MCCULLERS (1917–1967), U.S. author

The author of *The Heart Is a Lonely Hunter* and *The Ballad of the Sad Café* became feverishly infatuated with numerous women during her life — including Katherine Anne Porter and Greta Garbo — and was unusually candid with friends about her various bisexual experiences. She liked to say of herself, in regard to sex, "Anything a man can do, I can do better."

8. MARLON BRANDO (1924–), U.S. actor

In 1976, in a publicity interview for his film *The Missouri Breaks,* Brando told a French newspaper, "Homosexuality is so much in fashion it no longer makes news. Like a large number of men, I, too, have had homosexual experiences, and I am not ashamed." In the same interview, Brando went on to respond to rumors that he and co-star Jack Nicholson were having a homosexual affair. "I have never paid much attention to what people think of me," said Brando. "But if there is someone who is convinced that Jack Nicholson and I are lovers, may they continue to do so. I find it amusing."

9. RICHARD BURTON (1925–1984), British actor

After portraying a homosexual in the 1969 film *Staircase,* Burton privately acknowledged to friends that he had "tried" homosexuality once, just for the experience. He never offered any details of the encounter. Shortly before his death, he told *People* magazine, "Perhaps most actors are latent homosexuals and we cover it with drink. I was once a homosexual, but it didn't work."

10. JAMES DEAN (1931–1955), U.S. actor

Dean bragged to a friend that he'd performed homosexual acts with "five of the big names in Hollywood." He also claimed to have worked, with his friend Nick Adams, as a street hustler when he first came to Hollywood. When asked if he was gay, he replied, "Well, I'm certainly not going through life with one hand tied behind my back."

11. JOAN BAEZ (1941–   ), U.S. folk singer and political activist

In a 1972 interview with a Berkeley newspaper, Baez mentioned in passing that she'd had a brief but "wonderful" sexual relationship with another woman when she was twenty-two. As a result of her candor, she was besieged by reporters demanding to know if she was a lesbian. She was also, in her words, "absolutely inundated at my concerts with homosexual women; and really, I am not interested." The affair, she has said, was an isolated episode in her life.

12. BILLIE JEAN KING (1943–   ), U.S. tennis pro

As the result of a multimillion dollar palimony suit filed against her in April 1981, King acknowledged that she'd once had a sexual relationship with her former secretary and hairdresser, Marilyn Barnett. However, King denied that she was by nature a homosexual. "If you have one gay experience, does that

When asked if he was gay, James Dean replied, "Well, I'm certainly not going through life with one hand tied behind my back."

mean you're gay?" she told reporters. "If you have one hetero-sexual experience, does that mean you're straight? Life doesn't work quite so cut-and-dried."

13. JANIS JOPLIN (1943–1970), U.S. blues singer

Joplin's offstage life was as unabashed as her on-stage perfor-mances, and she readily acknowledged sleeping with women as well as men — or sometimes both at the same time.

14. DAVID BOWIE (1947–   ), British rock star

The King of Camp Rock told *Melody Maker* magazine in 1972 that he was bisexual. Shortly afterward, he told another mag-azine that he and his wife, Angela, had first met when they were dating the same man. So overwhelming was the amount of publicity that these disclosures received that Bowie began to worry he'd be assassinated on stage, and for a time he hired a small phalanx of bodyguards to protect him. After Bowie tried, in 1983, to recant the acknowledgments about his sex life — "The biggest mistake I ever made was telling that *Melody Maker* writer that I was bisexual," he said — one music col-umnist observed, "The former King of Glitter Rock, once the very symbol of rock and roll decadence, has anointed himself the Yuppie King."

15. MARIA SCHNEIDER (1952–   ), French actress

When she was twenty, the co-star of the controversial 1973 film *Last Tango in Paris* told the *New York Times,* "I've had quite a few lovers for my age. More men than women. Proba-bly fifty men and twenty women. Women," she said, "I love more for beauty than for sex. Men I love for grace and intelli-gence."

SOURCE: Leigh W. Rutledge, author of *The Gay Book of Lists* (Boston: Alyson Publica-tions, 1987).

7 Religious Sex Scandals

1. JIM BAKKER

Starting from scratch, Assemblies of God minister Jim Bakker and his wife, Tammy Faye, built up a huge empire that included a cable-TV network with 13 million subscribers, and Heritage USA, a $172 million, 2,300-acre Christian theme park. Their PTL (Praise the Lord) organization brought in $129 million in 1986 alone. But in 1987, the Bakkers' kingdom began to fall apart when it was revealed that Jim Bakker had committed adultery six years earlier with a twenty-one-year-old church secretary named Jessica Hahn. Bakker paid out $265,000 in exchange for Hahn's promise to keep quiet for twenty years. Bakker's troubles snowballed, and by 1989 he was serving a prison term for bilking his followers out of $150 million.

2. EAMONN CASEY

Casey, for sixteen years the bishop of Galway, was one of Ireland's most popular bishops, known for his championing of the poor at home and abroad. But in 1992, Casey was forced to resign when he confessed to being the father of a seventeen-year-old boy. Over national radio, he told about a "magical" love affair he had had with an American woman named Annie Murphy. He also confessed to having given $120,000 in church funds to Murphy for the care of their son.

3. EUGENE MARINO

In 1988 Eugene Marino of Atlanta was installed as the first black archbishop in the United States. But two years later he resigned his post, stating that he needed "psychological ther-

Tammy Faye and Jim Bakker —before the fall.

apy and medical supervision." It soon came out that Marino had been carrying on a two-year affair with Vicki Long, a twenty-seven-year-old lay minister. Their relationship began when she went to him for comfort after she had an affair with a different priest. In fact, she filed a paternity suit against the first priest, and even though a blood test absolved him, the church paid her child support. Within five months of the public exposure of their affair, both Marino and Long attempted suicide.

4. JAMES PORTER

A long suppressed story of sexual abuse exploded to the surface in 1992 when former parish priest James Porter confessed to dozens of cases of child molestation in Massachusetts, New Mexico, and Minnesota. Eventually more than a hundred men and women came forward to accuse Porter of attacks that took place between 1960 and 1974. Most of the victims were age ten, eleven, or twelve at the time of the assaults. In one case, Porter sexually abused a young boy who was immobilized by a body cast. The number of complaints against Porter made it the largest sexual abuse case in the history of the Roman Catholic Church. What made the scandal particularly appalling was that Porter was repeatedly caught, treated, and reassigned to new parishes, where he started fondling and abusing children all over again. In December 1992, a financial settlement was reached between the diocese of Fall River, Massachusetts, and a group of sixty-eight men and women calling themselves the Victims of Father Porter. That same month, Porter was convicted of molesting a fifteen-year-old baby-sitter in 1987.

5. JIMMY SWAGGART

When Jim Bakker was exposed as an adulterer, fellow Assemblies of God minister Jimmy Swaggart self-righteously called the scandal "a cancer that needs to be excised from the body of Christ." Swaggart also accused Louisiana rival Marvin Gorman of adultery and managed to get Gorman defrocked. But Gorman struck back. He hired a private investigator who, in October 1987, photographed Swaggart at a New Orleans motel with prostitute Debra Murphree. Murphree told WVUE-TV that she had been meeting with Swaggart for a year, but that they never had sexual intercourse. He preferred to have her pose naked for him and talk about "perverted" subjects. "I wouldn't want him around my children," she added. Gorman sued Swaggart for defamation of character and won a $10 million judgment. Swaggart, meanwhile, made an emotional but nonspecific public confession and returned to his pulpit. However, in 1991, he was stopped for a traffic violation in Indio,

California, and again found to be in the company of a prostitute.

6. SANTIAGO "HENRY" TAMAYO

In 1978 forty-three-year-old Los Angeles priest Henry Tamayo began an affair with sixteen-year-old Rita Milla. After the affair ended, three years later, Tamayo got her a job answering phones in his rectory and introduced her to six other priests, with whom she had sex. When Milla became pregnant by one of the priests, Tamayo took her to the Philippines to give birth in his brother's medical clinic. In 1983 Milla went to her local archdiocese in California asking for child support and demanding that the priests be punished. She got the money, but the priests were not reprimanded. Tamayo by this time had met another woman and eventually married. Meanwhile, the archdiocese paid Tamayo to stay in the Philippines and keep quiet about the case. However, in 1991 Tamayo came forward and, with Milla beside him, held a press conference at which he confessed everything. Both Tamayo and Milla expressed their wish that the other priests do the same, but they never did.

7. OZEL TENDZIN

Tendzin, who was born Thomas Rich, was the first Westerner to lead an international Buddhist sect. He became regent of the Boulder, Colorado–based Vajradhatu Buddhist organization following the death of its founder, Chogyam Trungpa Rinpoche, in 1987. In 1985 Tendzin, who was bisexual, learned that he had been infected with the AIDS virus. However, he kept his condition a secret. "Thinking that I had some extraordinary means of protection, I went ahead with my business as if something would take care of it for me." Instead, he infected a male companion, who infected a woman friend. It is not known how many people in all were given the deadly disease as a result of Tendzin's arrogance. Tendzin himself died of AIDS in 1990.

The *12* Most
Prolific Serial Killers

1. PEDRO LOPEZ (Peru, Ecuador, Colombia)

   Lopez was the son of a Colombian prostitute who abandoned him at the age of eight, whereupon he was raped for the first time. Ten years later, in 1967, while he was in prison for auto theft, he was raped by three fellow inmates, whom he then killed in revenge. After he was released from prison, Lopez began raping and strangling Indian girls between the ages of eight and twelve. In northern Peru a group of Ayachuco Indians caught him trying to kidnap a nine-year-old girl. They beat him and tortured him and were about to bury him alive when he was saved by an American missionary who turned him over to police. Peruvian authorities, not wanting to be bothered with prosecuting Lopez, deported him instead. Lopez continued to kill children in Colombia and Ecuador until April 1980, when he was caught trying to abduct a twelve-year-old Indian girl in Ecuador. Lopez led authorities to fifty-three graves. He estimated that he had killed at least 110 girls in Ecuador, about 100 in Colombia, and more than 100 in Peru.

2. HERMANN MUDGETT (United States)

   Using the alias H. H. Holmes, Mudgett lured young women to his Chicago hotel, seduced them with offers of marriage, and then murdered them. After he was arrested in 1894, Chicago police searched Mudgett's building and discovered that he had turned it into a Murder Castle, complete with chutes, hidden gas pipes, a kiln, and peepholes. It was reported that the remains of more than 150 women were removed from the "castle." While in prison, Mudgett wrote detailed descriptions of 27 murders, but was hanged on May 7, 1895, before he could complete his confessions.

3. BRUNO LÜDKE (Germany)

Sterilized by the Nazis because he was mentally defective and a suspected rapist, Lüdke claimed to have killed 85 women between 1928 and 1943, when he was finally caught. Because other men had already been arrested for many of Lüdke's crimes, his case was hushed up. Instead of being charged, he was sent to a hospital in Vienna, where he died on April 8, 1944, as a result of a Nazi medical experiment.

4.–5. DELFINA AND MARIA DE JESÚS GONZALEZ (Mexico)

These two sisters ran a brothel where young women were enslaved and tortured. When the victims became ill, pregnant, or uncooperative, the Gonzalez sisters had them killed. In 1964 they were finally arrested. The remains of between 50 and 80 bodies were found on their property, a fact that the Gonzalezes tried to explain away by saying "maybe the food didn't agree with them."

6. DANIEL BARBOSA (Ecuador, Colombia)

In 1985 Barbosa escaped from a prison in Colombia where he was serving a life sentence for rape and murder. He fled across the border into Ecuador, where he raped and murdered 71 girls and women. Barbosa preferred child victims, whom he lured away with candy and ballpoint pens.

7. JANE TOPPIN (United States)

Between 1880 and 1901, Toppin worked as a private nurse in New England — and poisoned approximately 70 of her patients with morphine and atrophine. She lived out the last thirty-seven years of her life in an asylum for the criminally insane.

8. KAMPATIMAR SHANKARIYA (India)

On May 16, 1979, Shankariya was hanged in Jaipur after confessing to the murders of at least 70 victims over a two-year period.

9. RANDY KRAFT (United States)

Arrested in California in 1983, Kraft is thought to have killed 63 men after having sex with them. He specialized in seducing and murdering Marines.

10. ANDREI CHIKATILO (Russia)

Between 1978 and 1990, Chikatilo, a former teacher, sexually attacked and murdered 55 young people of both sexes in and around the port city of Rostov.

11. DONALD HARVEY (United States)

Harvey is thought to have killed at least 50 people while working as an orderly and aide at various hospitals in Kentucky and

Ohio. In 1987 he was convicted of 37 murders, a United States record.

12. GEORG KARL GROSSMAN (Germany)

During World War I, Grossman, who already had a long criminal record, raped and murdered young women and sold their flesh on the streets, claiming it was beef or pork. He was arrested in 1921 and committed suicide in prison. His victims are thought to have numbered about 50.

The FBI's 7 Most Wanted Women Plus 2

Since the FBI began publishing its "10 Most Wanted Fugitives" list in 1950, seven women and two female impersonators have been included. Their stories are reported in Michael and Judy Ann Newton's *FBI Most Wanted: An Encyclopedia* (New York: Garland Publishing, 1989).

1. RUTH EISEMANN-SCHIER

The first woman on the FBI's roster was a partner to kidnapping in Atlanta, Georgia, in 1968. The victim survived being buried alive by her abductors. Eisemann-Schier was captured in March 1969 in Norman, Oklahoma, where she had applied for a job as a nurse. She served a prison term and was then deported to her native Honduras.

2. MARIE ARRINGTON

A convicted murderess, Arrington escaped from prison in Florida and threatened to kill the judge who had sentenced her to death. She was on the "Most Wanted" list from May 1969 to December 1971, when she was rearrested in New Orleans.

3. ANGELA DAVIS

Davis, a black activist and a Communist, had purchased guns that her bodyguard, Jonathan Jackson, later used to try to free a friend on trial. Jackson and three others were killed in the escape attempt. In August 1970, Davis was placed on the FBI roll for murder, kidnapping, and unlawful flight. She was arrested two months after that and was later acquitted by an all-white jury.

4. BERNADINE DOHRN

Dohrn, a member of the revolutionary Weather Underground group, was indicted in 1970 in Chicago and Detroit for conspir-

ing to incite riots and for carrying explosives across state lines.
Placed on the FBI list in October 1970, she was removed in 1973
when the FBI dropped the charges rather than reveal sensitive
information about its investigation.

5.–6. KATHERINE POWER AND SUSAN SAXE

These Brandeis University radicals were placed on the FBI roster
in 1970. Saxe and three ex-convicts robbed a Philadelphia bank
and shot and killed a patrol officer while Power waited in a get-
away car a mile away. The men were quickly caught, but Saxe
was not arrested until 1975. Power was dropped from the FBI's
list in 1984 because the case against her was weak.

7. DONNA WILMOTT

At large since 1986, Wilmott has been on the FBI list since May
1987. She and a companion, Claude Marks, both listed as members of the Puerto Rican terrorist group F.A.L.N. (in English, the
Armed Forces of National Liberation), allegedly tried to free a
radical compatriot from federal prison in Leavenworth, Kansas.

2 MEN WHO DRESSED AS WOMEN

1. ISAIE BEAUSOLEIL

Beausoleil, originally from Ontario, Canada, was a bootlegger,
robber, and murderer who had escaped prison in 1939 and managed to elude police until he was added to the "Most Wanted"
list in 1952. Beausoleil was caught in 1953 when officers in Chicago, answering a call about a "pervert," arrested a "Rita Bennett." Since Beausoleil's face had first appeared on "Most
Wanted" posters, he had been dressing as a woman in public to
avoid being recognized.

2. LESLIE ASHLEY

Ashley, a female impersonator known for quoting scripture and
wearing tacky jewelry, killed a Houston realtor during a sex
party in 1961. Ashley was captured in New York, dressed as a

Isaie Beausoleil
and "Rita Ben-
nett."

woman, and he was sent to a mental hospital. In 1964 he escaped from the hospital and joined a carnival. His name had been on the "Most Wanted" list for about two weeks when he was arrested while working as "Bobo the Clown."

Alan Dershowitz's
10 Defendants from History
He Would Like to Have Defended

Professor Alan Dershowitz of Harvard Law School has been described as a "feisty civil libertarian," "defense attorney extraordinaire," and "the top lawyer of last resort in the country." His high-profile clients have included Claus von Bulow, Leona Helmsley, Michael Milken, Jim Bakker, Christian Brando, Mike Tyson, John DeLorean, and Patricia Hearst. A frequent guest on television and radio shows, Dershowitz is also the author of numerous books, including *Contrary to Popular Opinion* and *Taking Liberties: A Decade of Hard Cases, Bad Laws and Bum Raps.*

1. JESUS OF NAZARETH

   Think how much difficulty would have been avoided if a Jewish lawyer had successfully defended Jesus.

2. SOCRATES

   I would have urged him to appeal rather than taking the hemlock.

3. GALILEO GALILEI

   Whose innocence for espousing the heliocentric theory — that the earth revolves around the sun — was finally acknowledged by the Catholic Church, 350 years after he copped a plea to avoid being burned.

4. SHOELESS JOE JACKSON

   The baseball star who took the fall for Charles Comiskey, the crooked owner of the Chicago Black Sox, who knew the World Series of 1919 was fixed.

5. JOHN BROWN

   Who was hanged for trying to free the slaves, but whose truth goes marching on.

6. OSCAR WILDE

   I would have advised him not to sue for defamation unless he was willing to come out of the closet.

Galileo: shouldn't have copped a plea.

7. THE SALEM WITCHES

What a challenge! To defend in front of judges who genuinely believed in witches!

8. JOHN T. SCOPES

I would have loved to make monkeys out of politicians who forbade teachers from teaching evolution.

9. MENDEL BEILIS

A Jew charged with the "blood libel" — that Jews kill Christian children to use their blood for ritual purposes — in Russia in 1911. What a great opportunity to expose one of the most pernicious frauds in history.

10. KING CHARLES I OF ENGLAND

I always wanted to defend a king.

— Exclusive for *The Book of Lists*

18 Celebrities Who Went to Jail

1. ARLETTY

The great French film star of the 1930s and 1940s is best known for her portrayal of Garance in the 1944 classic *Children of Paradise*. After World War II she was jailed for two months as a collaborator because she had had a love affair with a Nazi officer.

2. CHUCK BERRY

At the height of his fame as a rock-and-roll singer, Berry was convicted of transporting a fourteen-year-old girl across state lines for immoral purposes. He served two years in the federal penitentiary in Terre Haute, Indiana, and was released in February 1964.

3. JAMES BROWN

At the age of fifteen, the future "Godfather of Soul" was arrested for stealing clothes out of parked cars. Tried as an adult in Georgia, he was sentenced to a minimum of eight years, but served three years and one day. In 1978 he spent three days in a Baltimore jail for defying a court order to stay in the United States during an investigation related to radio stations that he owned. Ten years later Brown was arrested again, following an incident in which he carried a shotgun into an office building he owned and demanded to know who had used his private toilet. Convicted of failing to stop for a police car with flashing lights and for aggravated assault, Brown commented, "I aggravated them and they assaulted me." The fifty-eight-year-old singer was released in 1991 after serving two and a half years of a six-year sentence.

4. DAVID CROSBY

The singer was in and out of prison for drug and weapon charges in the early 1980s. In 1986 he turned himself in to the FBI and served eleven months in Texas jails, including four months in solitary confinement.

5. KELSEY GRAMMER

After being arrested for drunk driving, Grammer, best known for his role in the TV series *Cheers,* was ordered to attend an alcohol-abuse program. When he failed to show up for the program in 1990, he was sentenced to thirty days in jail and ten days roadside cleanup. His jail term was reduced to two weeks because of jail overcrowding. Two months later he pleaded guilty to possession of cocaine and was placed on probation.

6. BILLIE HOLIDAY

Legendary jazz great Billie Holiday was imprisoned for prostitution when she was very young. A heroin addict, she was sent to prison on narcotics charges in 1947. Upon her release, she performed at Carnegie Hall.

7. RICK JAMES

In August 1991 the "King of Funk" was arrested with his girlfriend on charges of torturing another woman with a hot cocaine pipe and forcing her to have sex with his girlfriend. James spent three weeks in jail before being released on bail. The case is still pending, but in the meantime, James was returned to jail after he was arrested again for assaulting another woman.

8. STACY KEACH

In 1985 the star of TV's *Mickey Spillane's Mike Hammer* spent six months in England's Reading Gaol after being arrested at Heathrow Airport for smuggling 1.3 ounces of cocaine.

9. SOPHIA LOREN

At the age of forty-seven, Loren spent seventeen days in a women's prison in Italy in 1982 for a tax evasion incident that had occurred eighteen years earlier.

10. DENNY MCLAIN

The last major-league pitcher to win thirty games in one season, McLain was sentenced in 1985 to twenty-three years in prison for racketeering, extortion, and possession of cocaine. He was released from federal prison in Talladega, Alabama, after serving thirty months.

11. ROBERT MITCHUM

As a teenager, Mitchum was sentenced to a Georgia chain gang on a charge of vagrancy. In 1949, already a major movie star, he served seven weeks in prison on a charge of possession of marijuana.

12. EUGENE "MERCURY" MORRIS

The former Miami Dolphins football star served three years of a fifteen-year sentence for cocaine trafficking before being released in 1986.

Sophia Loren spent 17 days in prison for tax evasion.

13. O. HENRY (WILLIAM SIDNEY PORTER)

Before O. Henry became a world-famous short-story writer, he was convicted of embezzling funds from a Texas bank where he worked as a teller. He entered prison in 1898 and served three years of a five-year sentence.

14. RYAN O'NEAL

In 1960 actor O'Neal served fifty-one days of a sixty-day sentence for assaulting a stranger during a New Year's Eve party in Los Angeles.

15. SEAN PENN

In June 1987 Penn was sentenced to sixty days for probation violations including reckless driving and assault. The sentence was reduced to thirty-three days "in anticipation of good behavior." Penn served five days, was released to film a movie, and then served out the remainder of his sentence in private jail facilities for which he paid an extra eighty dollars per day.

16. PETE ROSE

In April 1990 baseball's "Charlie Hustle" pleaded guilty to two counts of failure to report income from gambling and memorabilia sales. He served five months in prison, three months in a halfway house, and a thousand hours of community service assisting gym teachers in Cincinnati's schools.

Sean Penn served 33 days in jail for probation violations including assault and reckless driving. By paying an extra $80 a day, he was allowed to serve all but the first five days in private facilities.

In 1927, Mae West was convicted of "producing an immoral play" and sentenced to jail in New York City.

17. MIKE TYSON

Former heavyweight boxing champion Mike Tyson was sentenced to six years in an Indiana prison for raping a teenage beauty pageant contestant in 1991.

18. MAE WEST

In April 1927 West was convicted of "producing an immoral play," the title of which was *Sex*. She was sentenced to ten days in jail in New York City, but was given one day off for good behavior.

18 Unusual
Stolen Objects

1. MARLA MAPLES'S SHOES

When the girlfriend of entrepreneur Donald Trump discovered that more than forty pairs of her high-heeled shoes were missing, she installed a video camera in her bedroom closet to catch the culprit. On July 15, 1992, the camera reportedly recorded Maples's publicist, Chuck Jones, filching another pair. New York police raided Jones's office and recovered the shoes, as well as a copy of *Spike*, a pornographic magazine for shoe fetishists. Jones pleaded not guilty to the charges.

2. GEORGE WASHINGTON'S WALLET

One hundred ninety-one years after his death in 1799, George Washington's battered wallet was stolen from an unlocked case in the Old Barracks Museum in Trenton, New Jersey. The wallet was later returned to police. In a separate incident in 1986, a lock of Washington's hair was taken from a museum in France

Five years later it was recovered, along with a lock of hair belonging to the Marquis de Lafayette, by French police during a raid on a drug dealer's hideout.

3. BULL SEMEN

In October 1989, $10,000 worth of frozen bull semen and embryos was taken from the dairy building at California Polytechnic University in San Luis Obispo, California. The embryos were later found, but despite a $1,500 reward, the semen was never recovered.

4. CHURCH PULPIT

On August 2, 1992, congregation leaders of the First Missionary Baptist Church in Houston, Texas, voted to oust their pastor, the Reverend Robert L. White. The Reverend White retaliated by loading most of the church's property into three cars, a pickup, and a fourteen-foot-long U-haul truck. Included in his haul were furniture, an organ, curtains, speakers, amplifiers, and even the pulpit. He left behind the church's piano because it was still being paid for.

5. HALF A HUMAN HEAD

Jason Paluck, a premedical student at Adelphi University, was arrested in May 1992 after his landlord discovered half of a human head in a plastic bag while evicting Paluck from his Mineola, New York, apartment. Paluck admitted that he had taken the head from one of his classes.

6. KATEY SAGAL'S PUSH-UP BRA

On the night of April 30, 1992, Jim B., a twenty-four-year-old art student in Los Angeles, drove into Hollywood to observe the fires and looting that followed the acquittal of four police officers in the beating of Rodney King. Jim B. joined the crowd looting Frederick's of Hollywood, the famous purveyor of exotic lingerie. He headed straight for their lingerie museum, intent on grabbing Madonna's bustier. It had already been stolen, so Jim B. settled for Ava Gardner's bloomers and a push-up bra worn by Katey Sagal on the television comedy *Married . . . With Children*. A couple of days later, a repentant Jim B. handed over the stolen items to the Reverend Bob Fambrini, the pastor at the Church of the Blessed Sacrament, who returned them to Frederick's. Madonna's bustier is still on the missing list.

7. TWENTY-FOOT INFLATABLE CHICKEN

To mark the March 1990 debut of a new franchise in Sherman Oaks, California, the El Pollo Loco fast-food chain installed a twenty-foot tall inflatable rubber chicken in front of the restaurant. Two weeks later, it was stolen. "Don't ask me what

Rev. Bob Fambrini of the Church of the Blessed Sacrament, with Katey Sagal's push-up bra. (Jim Wilson/NYT Pictures)

someone would do with it," said Joe Masiello, director of operations for Chicken Enterprises, Ltd. "If you put it in your yard, someone would notice it." The restaurant's owners offered a reward of twelve free chicken combos for its return, but the thieves didn't bite.

8. BUTTONS

Felicidad Noriega, the wife of Panamanian dictator Manuel Noriega, was arrested in a Miami-area shopping mall in March 1992. She and a companion eventually pleaded guilty to stealing $305 worth of buttons, which they had removed from clothes in a department store.

9. FIFTEEN-TON BUILDING

In August 1990, businessman Andy Barrett of Pembroke, New Hampshire, reported the unexpected loss of an unassembled fifteen-ton prefabricated structure, complete with steel girders and beams thirty-five feet long and three feet thick.

10. MANHOLE COVERS

In July 1990, Los Angeles police broke the case of the Great Manhole Theft Caper when they arrested two culprits who later confessed to stealing 300 manhole covers weighing as much as 300 pounds each. The Manhole Men were selling the covers for six dollars each to scrap-material dealers. They could have made thirty times as much money by recycling the same weight in aluminum soft-drink cans.

Two years later manhole mania hit Lillehammer, Norway,

site of the 1994 Winter Olympics, after local officials began stamping the covers with the Olympic logo. Three of the 140-pound covers were stolen, but one was returned after the thief "sobered up."

11. SACRED CHIN

Saint Anthony's jawbone and several teeth were taken from a basilica in Padua, Italy, in October 1991, but were later found near Rome's international airport at Fiumicino.

12. BIRDS' NESTS

Burglars in Hong Kong stole $250,000 worth of birds' nests from a restaurant during the night of May 1, 1992. The nests are a main ingredient in a popular Chinese soup.

13. GODZILLA

In March 1992 a 132-pound rubber model of Godzilla was stolen from a Tokyo movie studio. Ten days later it was found in a bamboo thicket outside the city.

14. VINTAGE AIRPLANE

Israeli Air Force Reserve Major Ishmael Yitzhaki was convicted in February 1992 of stealing a World War II Mustang fighter plane and flying it to Sweden, where he sold it for $331,000. He had managed to remove the plane from the Air Force museum by saying that it needed painting.

15. GENE KELLY'S LAMPPOST

Bryan Goetzinger was part of the labor crew that cleared out the Metro-Goldwyn-Mayer film company vaults when MGM ceded its Culver City, California, lot to Lorimar Telepictures, in 1986. Among the items scheduled to be trashed was the lamppost that Gene Kelly swung on in the Hollywood musical classic *Singin' in the Rain.* Goetzinger brought the lamppost home and installed it in the front yard of his Hermosa Beach home. Four years later it was stolen. It was never recovered.

6. MARY'S LITTLE LAMB

A life-size statue of Mary's famous little lamb was erected in Sterling, Massachusetts, the hometown of Mary Sawyer, who was the inspiration for the nursery rhyme written in 1830 by Sarah J. Hale. During the night of June 30, 1990, the unfortunate lamb was stolen from the town commons. Fortunately, it was later returned.

7. SOFA BALLOON

When Nadar Almasi, the manager of Krause's Sofa Factory in Fremont, California, reported the theft of a sofa from his store,

Fremont police laughed. The sky blue sofa, known as Maxine, was actually a thirty-one-foot, 500-pound forced-air balloon that had adorned the store's rooftop until the Independence Day weekend of 1989. Maxine was recovered a few weeks later.

9 Stupid Thieves

1. SAFE AT LAST

   On the night of June 12, 1991, John Meacham, Joseph Plante, and Joe Laattsch were burgling a soon-to-be-demolished bank building in West Covina, California, when Meacham came upon an empty vault. He called over his accomplices and invited them inside to check out the acoustics. Then he closed the vault door so they could appreciate the full effect. Unfortunately, the door locked. Meacham spent forty minutes trying to open it, without success. Finally he called the fire department, who called the police. After seven hours, a concrete-sawing firm was able to free the locked-up robbers, after which they were transported to *another* building they couldn't get out of.

2. BIG MOUTH

   Dennis Newton was on trial in 1985 for armed robbery in Oklahoma City. Assistant District Attorney Larry Jones asked one of the witnesses, the supervisor of the store that had been robbed, to identify the robber. When she pointed to the defendant, Newton jumped to his feet, accused the witness of lying, and said, "I should have blown your ——— head off!" After a moment of stunned silence, he added, "If I'd been the one that was there." The jury sentenced Newton to thirty years in prison.

3. INCONVENIENCE STORE

   In December 1989, three fifteen-year-old boys stole a car in Prairie Village, Kansas, and stopped off at the nearest convenience store to ask directions back to Missouri. Except that it wasn't a convenience store — it was a police station. At the same moment, a description of the stolen vehicle was broadcast over the police station public address system. The car thieves tried to escape, but were quickly apprehended.

4. A REAL DRAG

   When Silver's lock and safe shop of Canoga Park, California, moved in October 1990, they had to leave behind a 6,000-pound safe until they could rent a forklift to transport it. In the meantime, a rumor spread that the safe contained $6,000. This was too much of a temptation for James Richardson and Jeffrey Defalco, who got the brilliant idea of stealing the safe. In the dead of night they tied a nylon strap around the safe and attached the strap to their car. Then they made their getaway. Unfortunately for Richardson and Defalco, the scraping of the safe on the asphalt street created showers of sparks that could be seen for blocks, not to mention a deafening roar that woke up the entire neighborhood. The two would-be thieves were easily tracked and arrested. The safe turned out to be empty.

5 · WRONG FENCE #1

Stephen Le and two juvenile companions tried to break into a parked pickup truck in Larkspur, California, on the night of September 27, 1989. But the owner caught them in the act, chased them, and hailed a police car. Le and one of his friends climbed a fence and ran. It soon became apparent that they had chosen the wrong fence — this one surrounded the property of San Quentin prison. The suspects were booked for investigation of auto burglary and trespassing on state property, although charges were never filed. "Nothing like this has ever happened here before," said Lieutenant Cal White. "People just don't break into prison every day."

6 · WRONG FENCE #2

On the morning of March 1, 1990, James Innis and Tyrone Thomas of Queens traveled to Harlem and robbed a grocery store of $207. Two police officers saw them running away and cornered Innis with their patrol car. Innis tried to jump a metal fence, but got stuck and ended up hanging upside down by his pants. When his pants ripped apart and fell off, Innis fell to the ground. He jumped up and tried to run, but found himself surrounded by twenty policemen. The fence he had tried to jump led to the backyard of the Thirty-second Precinct police station.

7 · MURPHY'S LAW

On June 3, 1984, Charles Murphy of Long Beach, California, tried to hold up a Safeway supermarket. But he became so nervous that he ran out of the store without a penny and went straight home. It didn't take a Sherlock Holmes to find Murphy. Twenty-five minutes before his bungled robbery attempt, he had entered the same store, gone up to the same window, and filled out an application for a check-cashing identity card, using his correct name and address.

8 · STUPID GANG OF THIEVES

This complex and well-planned robbery took place in the Silverlake district of Los Angeles on June 7, 1990. A gang of ten to twelve men from Chula Vista, some of them armed with guns, drove up to the lot of The Shipping Company, a company that shipped cars across the United States. The robbers kidnapped the security guard, picked out nine cars, and drove them away. What the thieves failed to realize was that each car had been drained of all but a gallon of gasoline. The gang raced to the freeway, but one by one they ran out of gas, sputtered, and stopped. One of them even suffered a flat tire.

9. MOST PHOTOGENIC

Vernon Brooks, thirty-four, thought he was being a clever thief when he robbed a Radio Shack in Raleigh, North Carolina, in July 1992. Before leaving the store, he disconnected the video surveillance camera and took it with him. However, he forgot to take the recorder to which the camera had been connected. Police found a perfect full-face shot of Brooks on the tape and had little difficulty identifying him.

Note: For more stupid thieves, see *The Book of Lists #3*, pp. 49–53.

20 Unusual Lawsuits

1. COKE ISN'T IT

Amanda Blake of Northampton, Massachusetts, had been working for Coca-Cola Bottling Company for eight years when, in 1985, Coca-Cola discovered that she had fallen in love with and become engaged to David Cronin, who worked for Pepsi. Blake was ordered to break off her engagement, persuade Cronin to

Amanda and David Cronin: the Romeo and Juliet of the soft-drink industry.

quit his job, or quit herself. She refused, and was fired for "conflict of interest." Blake sued Coca-Cola for damages and won a $600,000 settlement.

2. CORPORATE SPY?

For six weeks in the summer of 1989, Maritza and Stephen French of Costa Mesa, California, rented a room in their house to Takashi Morimoto, an employee of the Nissan Motor Company who had been sent from Japan to study American automotive habits. Three months later, the French family read in an article in the *Los Angeles Times* that Mr. Morimoto's research had included a detailed study of the Frenches themselves, about whom he had taken copious notes. Feeling violated, the Frenches sued Morimoto and Nissan, claiming fraud, invasion of privacy, trespassing, and unfair business practices. However, they eventually dropped the lawsuit rather than face the stress of continued litigation.

3. TOO BIG TO BOOST

When seventeen-year-old Vicki Ann Guest was not chosen for the 1986 cheerleading squad at Fountain Valley High School in southern California, she asked Jean Clower, the teacher in charge of the squad, what she had done wrong. Clower explained that Guest's problem was that her breasts were too large. She suggested that Guest, who had already received a scholarship to study dance, should undergo breast reduction surgery. Guest sued the school district, citing sex discrimination and emotional distress. The suit was settled out of court.

4. FALSE PREGNANCY

"World's Oldest Newspaper Carrier, 101, Quits Because She's Pregnant" read the headline in a 1990 edition of the *Sun,* a supermarket tabloid. The accompanying article, complete with a photograph of the sexually active senior, told the story of a newspaper carrier in Stirling, Australia, who had to give up her job when a millionaire on her route impregnated her. The story was totally false. Stirling, Australia, didn't even exist. But as it turned out, the photo was of a real, living person — Nellie Mitchell, who had delivered the Arkansas *Gazette* for fifty years. Mitchell wasn't really 101 years old — she was only 96, young enough to be humiliated when friends and neighbors asked her when her baby was due. Mitchell sued the *Sun,* charging invasion of privacy and extreme emotional distress. John Vader, the editor of the *Sun,* admitted in court that he had chosen the picture of Mitchell because he assumed she was dead. Dead people cannot sue. A jury awarded Mitchell $850,000 in punitive damages, but a further judgment for $650,000 in compensatory damages is still being appealed.

5. BOTTOM LINES

Krandel Lee Newton, a street artist in Dallas's West End, thought he had a pretty good thing going. Unlike other street artists, Newton specialized in drawing people's rear ends. He even registered a trademark for his business: Butt Sketch. Then in 1992 along came another street artist, Mark Burton, who decided to add rear-end sketches to his repertoire. Burton called his business Fanny Sketch. Newton filed a federal lawsuit accusing Burton of threatening his business. The suit was settled out of court when Burton agreed to stop using the name Fanny Sketch and to refrain from engaging in any act which could cause the public to confuse his work with Mr. Newton's "custom-artistry services."

6. THE WRONG CHANNEL

New Age channeler J. Z. Knight made a fortune claiming she could pass on the thoughts of Ramtha, a warrior who lived 35,000 years ago on the lost continent of Atlantis. Besides charging for sessions with Ramtha, Knight and her husband, Jeffrey, marketed books, tapes, and survival gear. When the couple divorced in 1989 Jeffrey came away with a meager $120,000. He later claimed that Ramtha had bullied him into accepting the settlement. In 1992 Judge Bruce Cohoe of the Pierce County, Washington, Superior Court, rejected the charge of coercion, but did order J. Z. Knight to pay her ex-husband $792,000 — one-half of the "goodwill value" of the Ramtha business, which had not been taken into account as part of the original settlement.

7. ACTING LIKE AN ASS

Former sex symbol Brigitte Bardot has devoted her post-film career years to promoting the rights of animals. Among the members of her personal menagerie in St. Tropez, France, was a thirty-two-year-old mare named Duchesse and a young donkey named Mimosa. In the summer of 1989, Bardot invited her neighbor's donkey, a three-year-old male named Charly, to graze alongside Duchesse and Mimosa. When Charly began to display a sexual interest in Duchesse, Bardot feared that if Charly was allowed to have his way with the elderly mare, it might prove fatal to Duchesse. So she called in her vet and had Charly castrated. Charly's owner, Jean-Pierre Manivet, was out of town at the time. When he returned to St. Tropez, he was outraged by what had happened. Manivet sued Bardot, claiming that Charly had really been interested in Mimosa, not Duchesse. Bardot countersued, alleging that the bad publicity had harmed her reputation. Both suits were eventually rejected by the courts.

8. Blaming the Victim

S. Brian Willson served as an intelligence and security officer during the Vietnam War. His experiences in Vietnam transformed him into a peace activist. On September 1, 1987, Willson and two other activists decided to protest U.S. support of the Nicaraguan Contras by sitting down on a railroad track in order to stop a military munitions train from leaving the Concord Naval Weapons Station in northern California. However, the train did not stop for them. The other two demonstrators escaped uninjured, but Willson was run over by the train and dragged along the tracks. His skull was fractured and his right leg was severed. His left leg was later amputated as well. Four months later, the conductor of the train, Ralph Dawson; the engineer, David Humiston; and the brakeman, Robert Mayfield sued *Willson*, claiming they had suffered mental anguish because of the incident. Willson, who until that point had taken no legal action himself, now countered with a lawsuit against the U.S. Navy. The U.S. government agreed to pay Willson $940,000. The suit brought by the railroad crew was dismissed.

9. Child Divorces Parents

In a widely publicized case that was televised live in 1992, twelve-year-old Gregory Kingsley of Florida filed suit to sever his legal relationship with his biological parents and asked to be adopted by his foster parents, George and Lizabeth Russ. Gregory's natural father, Ralph Kingsley, did not contest the lawsuit, but his natural mother, Rachel Kingsley, did. Circuit judge Thomas Kirk ruled that Mrs. Kingsley had been a neglectful parent and allowed Gregory to be adopted by the Russes.

10. Sprinting to the Courts

On August 28, 1988, the world-championship cycling road race, held in Robse, Belgium, came down to a sprint between Steve Bauer of Canada and 1984 world champion Claude Criquielion of Belgium. But a mere seventy-five meters from the finish line, the two crashed, allowing Maurizio Fondriest of Italy to snatch an unexpected victory. In a case without precedent in professional cycling, Criquielion sued Bauer for assault and asked for more than $1.5 million in damages. Criquielion alleged that Bauer had swerved in front of him and elbowed him, thus denying him the glory and financial rewards that come with a world championship. The case dragged through the courts, but finally, three and a half years later, a Belgian judge ruled in favor of Bauer.

11. L-A-W-S-U-I-T

The two finalists to decide who would represent Los Altos School in the 1987 Ventura County, California, spelling bee were Steven Chen, thirteen, and Victor Wang, twelve. Victor spelled *horsy* H-O-R-S-Y, while Steven spelled it H-O-R-S-E-Y. Contest officials ruled that Steven's spelling was incorrect and advanced Victor to the county finals. But when Steven went home, he found both spellings in his dictionary and returned to the school to lodge a protest. It turned out that the officials had used an inadequate dictionary, so it was decided that both boys could advance. At the county finals, Steven defeated defending champion Gavin McDonald, thirteen, and advanced to the national spelling bee. Gavin's father sued the county event's sponsor, the Ventura County *Star–Free Press,* charging mental distress, and asked for $2 million in damages. He claimed that Steven Chen should not have been allowed to compete because each school was only allowed one entrant. A superior court judge and a state court of appeals dismissed the suit, stating that the major reason Gavin McDonald lost the Ventura County spelling bee was not that the contest was poorly run, but that he had misspelled *iridescent.*

12. AN ARM AND A LEG

On the night of April 10, 1989, dishwasher Francisco Merino became so drunk that he fell onto the subway tracks at the 183rd Street IRT station in the Bronx and was hit by a northbound train. He lost his left arm in the accident and filed suit against the New York Transit Authority for failing to remove him from the platform when they noticed that he was intoxicated. Incredibly, in 1990 a jury decided that the Transit Authority was responsible for all disabled passengers, including those disabled by alcohol. They awarded Merino $9.3 million in damages. The court threw out the judgment, declaring that the jury had acted "irrationally." The case is still being appealed.

13. PSYCHIC VISION

When thirty-nine-year-old shipping clerk Etta Louise Smith of Pacoima, California, led police to the body of a missing nurse, Melanie Uribe, she told them she had seen the rural location in a psychic vision. Detectives questioned Smith for ten hours and then arrested her on suspicion of murder. She was released four days later after someone else confessed to the killing. Smith sued the city of Los Angeles for lost wages, as well as pain and suffering, on the grounds that her arrest was illegal. Although the police contended that she had learned about the body's location from neighborhood gossip or other natura means, a jury believed Smith's story about the psychic vision and in 1987 awarded her $26,184: a year's salary plus lawyers' fees.

14. SORE LOSER

Toshi Van Blitter of El Macero, California, was not a good gambler. Playing blackjack at two Harrah's casinos in Nevada, she ran up $350,000 in debts. In 1985 Van Blitter filed suit to have her debts canceled, charging that Harrah's had been negligent in failing to inform her that she was incompetent and in failing to suggest that she attend classes on how to play blackjack. Two federal courts rejected her claim.

15. NERDS NOT ALLOWED

Two cases filed in Los Angeles challenged the right of fashionable nightclubs to deny entrance to would-be patrons because they are not stylishly dressed. In the first case, settled in 1990, Kenneth Lipton, an attorney specializing in dog-bite cases, was barred from entering the Mayan nightclub because a doorman judged his turquoise shirt and baggy olive pants to be "not cool." Owners of the club were forced to pay Lipton and three companions $1,112 in damages. The following year, the California State Department of Alcoholic Beverage Control won its suit against Vertigo, another trendy club that refused admittance to "those people with no fashion sense." Administrative-law judge Milford Maron ruled that Vertigo could continue to exclude customers only if they published a written dress code with specific requirements rather than leaving the decisions to the whim of doormen.

Kenneth Lipton appearing in court wearing his "not cool" clothes.

16. Loss of Paranormal Powers

Penny Pellito of Miramar, Florida, filed a personal-injury lawsuit against the Hollywood Home Depot hardware store after she was struck in the head by three eight-foot planks while shopping in April 1987. Pellito claimed that the accident caused her to lose the unusual ability to block out pain. Although witnesses testified to having witnessed a doctor saw Pellito's toe bone without benefit of anesthesia before the accident, a jury rejected her claim. They also decided that she was 80 percent responsible for the accident, but they did award her $1,200 for normal physical damages.

17. Back-Door Man and Woman

In 1989 a Ft. Lauderdale, Florida, couple, Henrietta and Alfred Binns, were forced to file a lawsuit to seek permission to use their back door. The property manager for the Bonaventure Condominium ordered the Binns to stop using their back door because they were wearing a path in the lawn between their condo and the parking lot. NCSC Housing Management Corporation told the Binns that they were destroying the landscaping and creating an eyesore. The case was dismissed when NCSC sent the Binns a letter of apology, paid their legal fees, and agreed to let them continue to use their back door.

18. Hell Hath No Fury Like a Lawyer Scorned

When Maria Dillon broke off her engagement to Chicago corporate lawyer Frank Zaffere in 1992, the forty-five-year-old Zaffere responded by suing the twenty-one-year-old restaurant hostess. He demanded that she repay the $40,310.48 he had spent courting her. The amount covered the costs of a fur coat, a car, a typewriter, a ring, and even the champagne he had used to toast her. Zaffere dropped the suit three months after he filed it.

19. Lack of Foresight

In 1982 Charles Wayne Brown of Newton, Iowa, was struck in the right eye by a golf ball stroked by car salesman Bill Samuelson. The accident caused permanent damage to Brown's eye. Brown sued Samuelson for failing to yell "Fore" before he hit the ball. The case was dismissed in 1984.

20. The Big Spin

On December 30, 1985, Doris Barnett of Los Angeles appeared on television to try her luck at the California lottery's Big Spin. Barnett spun the lottery wheel and watched as her ball settled into the $3 million slot. Show host Geoff Edwards threw his hands in the air and shouted "Three million dollars!" Barnett's

Left: Doris Barnett celebrating her $3 million prize in the California lottery "Big Spin." Note that the ball, unbeknownst to Barnett, has fallen out of the $3 million slot and into the $10,000 slot. Right: Barnett learns of her change of fortune from a conciliatory Geoff Edwards.

children rushed out of the audience and joined her in celebration, whooping and jumping for joy. Then Edwards tapped Barnett on the shoulder and turned her attention back to the wheel. The ball had slipped out of the $3 million slot and into the $10,000 slot. Edwards explained that lottery rules required the ball to stay in the slot for five seconds. Barnett was hustled offstage, but she did not go meekly. She sued the California lottery. In 1989, after watching endless videos of other contestants being declared winners in less than five seconds, a jury awarded Barnett the $3 million, as well as an extra $400,000 in damages for emotional trauma. But the California lottery didn't go meekly either: they refused to pay. Eventually, though, "a mutually satisfactory settlement" was reached, with the agreement that the amount not be made public.

NOTE: For more unusual lawsuits, see *The Book of Lists #3*, pp. 69–74.

8 Creative Legal Defenses

1. RAP MUSIC MADE THEM DO IT

On April 16, 1991, five drunk and stoned teenagers attacked and shot to death at random a twenty-six-year-old stranger in Dodge

City, Kansas. Defense attorneys for the accused claimed that their clients had been hypnotized by the music of the Geto Boys, a Houston-based rap group. The case is believed to be the first in which music-prompted insanity was used as a defense in a murder trial.

2. THE OUIJA BOARD MADE THEM DO IT

Vance Davis and five other U.S. Army intelligence analysts went AWOL from their Augsburg, Germany, base in July 1990. The six soldiers, all of whom had top-secret security clearances, were arrested five days later for driving with a broken taillight in Gulf Breeze, Florida. They refused to explain why they left their posts, and they were discharged from the army two weeks later. In 1992 Davis finally broke his silence. He revealed that a spirit had visited them through a Ouija board and told them to leave and to assume their role of preparing people for an impending world cataclysm.

3. DAN RATHER MADE HIM DO IT

James Campbell, a chemist at Virginia Tech, was caught in 1991 making methamphetamines — speed — in a university laboratory. He told police in Christiansburg, Virginia, that he needed the money to pay off debts. While watching TV's *48 Hours,* he saw Dan Rather explain how to make speed, and decided to try it. Campbell received probation.

4. PMS MADE HER DO IT

One night in May 1979, Sandie Craddock was working in a pub west of London when she stabbed a fellow barmaid to death. Craddock had previously been convicted of thirty lesser crimes. When a doctor, Katharina Dalton, studied the pattern of Craddock's transgressions, she identified the outbursts as premenstrual syndrome. Craddock's charge was reduced to manslaughter and she was released on probation with the stipulation that she receive progesterone treatment. However, she continued to commit crimes whenever her doses were reduced.

5. PHILADELPHIA MADE HIM DO IT

At a 1992 hearing before the Illinois Attorney Registration and Disciplinary Commission, Kenneth Solomon confessed to submitting 154 fake expense reports between 1982 and 1990. His excuse, supported by a psychologist's report, was that his behavior had been triggered by a "deep-seated resentment" at having to make frequent business trips to Philadelphia. A sympathetic hearing board voted two to one to suspend Solomon's law practice for only one year instead of the two years sought by prosecutors.

6. It Was Really Buried Treasure

When former First Lady Imelda Marcos returned to the Philippines in November 1991, the Filipino government filed fifty-four civil and criminal suits against her and accused her and her husband, Ferdinand, of stealing $5 billion from the country. Mrs. Marcos claimed that it was all a misunderstanding. She and Ferdinand had not really robbed and looted the nation's treasury through graft and corruption; the source of the family fortune that the Marcoses so gaudily displayed was actually the fabled Yamashita treasure, which had been buried by Japanese general Tomoyuki Yamashita during World War II. Marcos claimed that her husband had found the treasure while he was a guerrilla fighting the Japanese. Filipino authorities were not convinced, and refused to drop the charges.

7. The Twinkie Defense

On November 27, 1978, Dan White, a former policeman and a member of San Francisco's board of supervisors, shot and killed the city's mayor, George Moscone, and its first openly homosexual supervisor, Harvey Milk. At White's trial the following year, his attorneys brought in a battery of psychiatrists to testify on his behalf. One psychiatrist contended that White had taken his revolver and extra ammunition to City Hall that tragic morning not because he planned to murder Moscone and Milk, but because the gun represented a "security blanket" at a time when he felt emotionally threatened. Another psychiatrist stated that White entered the building by crawling through a basement window rather than going through the front door because White "didn't want to embarrass the police officer" at the door. Another expert testified that White shot Moscone because he was too moral to punch him in the nose, shooting being a more impersonal and, thus, a more moral expression of anger. Yet another psychiatrist discussed White's near-addiction to junk food, especially Twinkies, Coca-Cola, and potato chips, and how the resultant extreme variations in blood-sugar levels exacerbated his manic depression and led to the killings. On May 21, 1979, White, who had been charged with murder, was instead convicted of involuntary manslaughter. He later committed suicide.

8. The Burrito Defense

Less well known than Dan White's Twinkie defense was the burrito defense of Edward Vasquez, a student of criminal justice and sociology at California State University, Los Angeles. In September 1988, Vasquez was accused of shooting to death a security guard in a parking lot in central Los Angeles. The perpetrator was described as wearing a white T-shirt; Vasquez claimed that he had been wearing a green jacket, and that when the shooting took place he was actually on the other side of the parking lot buying a burrito from a canteen truck. Vasquez's jacket was seized as evidence and kept in law-enforcement custody until his trial, which did not begin until almost two years later.

At the trial, Vasquez claimed that he had been wounded in the rear by a stray bullet. The prosecution contended that if Vasquez had been wearing the jacket, it would have been covered with blood, when, in fact, it was blood-free. Vasquez's lawyer, Jay Jaffe, noted that the jacket only reached to Vasquez's waist, and had his client try on the jacket in front of the jury to prove his point. While the jury was deliberating the case, Vasquez contacted Jaffe and told the lawyer that when he had tried on the jacket, he had felt "something heavy in the right pocket." The jury was brought back into the courtroom, the jacket was recalled from custody, and from out of the right pocket Jaffe produced an object wrapped in foil. The foil was unwrapped and the two-year-old burrito was revealed. Vasquez was acquitted.

19 Innocent Americans Who Were Almost Executed

1.–2. WILLIAM JENT AND EARNEST MILLER — 16 hours

Half brothers Jent and Miller were convicted of rape and murder in 1980. Three years later they came within sixteen hours of being executed before a federal judge issued a stay. In 1986 the victim's identity was finally established and suspicion shifted to her boyfriend. In 1988 Jent and Miller were released from prison and in 1991 they were judged to be victims of corruption of witnesses and incompetent police. They were awarded $65,000 in compensation by the Pasco County, Florida, sheriff's department.

3. JOSEPH GREEN BROWN — 13 hours

In 1974 Brown and a partner, Ronald Floyd, committed a robbery together in Florida. Brown turned himself in and implicated Floyd. As revenge, Floyd claimed that Brown had confessed to a murder that took place the day after the robbery. Brown was convicted of first-degree murder and sentenced to death. A new trial was ordered in 1986, thirteen hours before Brown was due to be executed. A year later, the state dropped all charges and Brown was released.

4. EDWARD LARKMAN — 10 hours

Larkman was convicted of the August 12, 1925, murder of the paymaster of the Art Metal Shop in Buffalo, New York. Ten hours before his scheduled execution, Governor Alfred Smith commuted Larkman's sentence to life imprisonment. Two years later, a Buffalo gangster confessed to the crime. However, it wasn't until 1933 that Larkman was pardoned, after it was revealed that the police, knowing the killer had worn sunglasses, forced Larkman to put on a pair of sunglasses and to stand alone at the lineup, where an eyewitness identified him.

5. WILLIAM LINDLEY — several hours

On August 18, 1943, thirteen-year-old Jackie Hamilton was raped and murdered in Yuba City, California. As she lay dying, she turned to her father and whispered, "Don't let that old red-headed man get me, Daddy." There were two redheaded men living nearby. Local police chose forty-nine-year-old "Red" Lindley, an illiterate farm worker who had served time in a Texas prison for burglary. Although the trial was delayed a year on the grounds that Lindley was mentally incompetent, he was eventually tried, convicted, and sentenced to death. While Lindley was awaiting execution, the famous mystery writer, Erle Stanley Gardner, began researching the case and discovered that Lindley had an excellent alibi that was never presented in court — he was with the victim's father at the time of the crime! Despite this new evidence, Lindley was almost executed on three occasions in 1946. Once, he was reprieved a few hours before he was to enter the gas chamber, and another time two days before. Finally, in April 1947, Governor Earl Warren commuted his sentence to life imprisonment. Unfortunately, by this time Lindley's ordeal had destroyed him emotionally. He lived out his days in a prison for the criminally insane.

6. AYLIFF DRAPER — several hours

Draper and a friend, Roy House, committed a robbery in which the victim was murdered. House claimed that Draper had done the killing. Both men were convicted and sentenced to death. In 1936, with a few hours to go before their execution, House confessed that he, not Draper, had committed the murder, and proved it by directing police to the murder weapon. House was executed, but in 1938 Draper was pardoned and released.

7. LLOYD MILLER — 7½ hours

In November 1955 Miller was arrested for the murder of an eight-year-old girl in Canton, Illinois. Two days later, after intense police pressure, he signed a confession. Between 1958 and 1963, Miller was scheduled for electrocution seven times. Once, he came within seven and a half hours of execution. A crucial piece of evidence used against Miller was the discovery of bloodstained jockey shorts. Reexamination of the evidence showed not only that Miller did not wear jockey shorts, but also that the "blood" was really paint, a fact that the prosecution had known but never revealed. Miller was finally released in 1967.

8. RALPH RENO — 7 hours

Reno was convicted of a 1925 double murder in Illinois and sentenced to death; however, the judge considered the evidence insufficient and ordered a new trial. Again Reno was convicted and sentenced to death. Seven hours before his scheduled execution, Reno was granted a stay and allowed an appeal, thanks to the efforts of the first judge, who considered him innocent. At a third trial he was finally acquitted when the only witness changed her testimony. Reno was released from prison in 1928.

9. TOM JONES — 5 hours

In 1936 Jones was convicted of murdering his wife, even though he claimed that the gun had gone off while he was struggling to prevent her from committing suicide. Five hours before his scheduled execution, a stay was granted. Two thousand citizens of Kentucky, including the original jurors, signed petitions for clemency, and the conviction was eventually reversed.

10. GANGI CERO — 4 hours

Cero was convicted of the June 11, 1927, Boston murder of Joseph Fantasia. Cero claimed mistaken identity. Sentenced to death, Cero was reprieved four hours before his execution because his brother found a witness who identified Cero's boss, Samuel Gallo, as the murderer. Gallo was tried and convicted. Then both men were tried together in a bizarre trial during which they each implicated the other. Eventually both Cero and Gallo were acquitted.

11. ANASTACIO VARGAS — 4 hours

Vargas of Austin, Texas, was convicted of murder in 1925 and sentenced to life imprisonment. The conviction was reversed on appeal. At the retrial Vargas was again found guilty, but this time he was sentenced to death. Vargas's head had already been shaved and he had already been served his last meal when a look-alike confessed to the murder. Vargas was pardoned and released in 1929. Thirty-five years later he sued the state for damages and was awarded $20,000.

12.–13. EDGAR LABAT AND CLIFTON PORET — 3 hours

Labat and Poret, both of whom were black, were convicted of raping a white woman in Louisiana in 1953. After their lawyers gave up on them, the two men smuggled out an appeal for help that ran as an ad in the *Los Angeles Times*. A reader hired a new attorney on their behalf, and in 1960 their ninth stay of execution was granted, this one a mere three hours before the end. At this point, the state's case began to unravel and a new trial was ordered. To avoid the embarrassment of an acquittal, the Louisiana courts resentenced Labat and Poret to time served and released them — after they had spent sixteen years on death row for a crime they didn't commit.

14. ISADORE ZIMMERMAN — 2 hours

In 1937 Zimmerman was sentenced to death in New York for providing the guns that were used in a robbery during which a police detective was killed. Zimmerman was barely mentioned during the high-profile trial, which included five defendants, twelve defense attorneys, and eighty-four witnesses. Nonetheless, he was convicted and sentenced to death. On January 26, 1939, Zimmerman ate his last meal, had his head shaved, and said good-bye to his family. Then, two hours before he was to be electrocuted, Zimmerman learned that Governor Herbert Lehman had commuted his sentence to life imprisonment. But Zimmerman continued to maintain his complete innocence. Finally, in 1962, he won the right to a new trial and was subsequently released. Still, he demanded compensation for the twenty-four years he had spent in prison. On June 30, 1983, Zimmerman was vindicated at last when he won an award for $660,000 (after expenses). Three and a half months later he died of a heart attack.

15. CHARLES STIELOW — 40 minutes

A farmhand in Shelby, New York, Stielow was convicted of the 1915 murder of his boss and the boss's housekeeper. He received five stays of execution. Once, on July 29, 1916, he had already been sent to the execution chamber and was forty minutes away from electrocution. Two weeks later another man confessed to the killings, but it was another twenty months before Stielow was finally released from prison.

16. GUS COLIN LANGLEY — 25 minutes

In 1932 Langley was convicted of killing a gas station attendant in Asheville, North Carolina, even though he was 400 miles away at the time of the crime. Langley came so close to being executed that when the chaplain appeared at his cell door, Langley thought he was being led away to the electric chair. Instead, he was granted a stay because of a technical error. After six more reprieves, including another one with only minutes to spare, the state of North Carolina admitted that Langley was innocent. He was pardoned and released in 1936.

17. CHARLES BERNSTEIN — several minutes

In 1919 Bernstein was convicted of a robbery he didn't commit. He spent nine years in prison. Four years after his release, Bernstein was again arrested for a crime he didn't commit. This time it was the April 21, 1932, murder of a gambler in Washington, D.C. Despite the testimony of six witnesses who said that Bernstein was in New York at the time of the crime, the unfortunate Bernstein was convicted and sentenced to death by electrocution. Minutes before his scheduled execution in 1935, President Franklin Roosevelt commuted his sentence to life in prison. In 1940 Roosevelt commuted the sentence to time served, and on April 30, 1945, Bernstein was granted a full pardon by President Harry Truman.

18. WILLIAM WELLMAN — 2 minutes

Wellman, who was black, was sentenced to death for the 1941 rape of an elderly white woman in Iredell County, North Carolina. In fact, Wellman was at work in Virginia, 350 miles away, at the time of the crime. Wellman was already seated in the electric chair when Governor J. Melville Broughton issued a reprieve upon learning that another man had confessed to the crime. After an investigation showed that Wellman had signed a payroll receipt in Virginia on the day of the rape, he was granted a full pardon and released from custody.

19. J. B. BROWN — 1 minute

A railroad worker, Brown was convicted of murdering an engineer in Florida on October 17, 1901. As Brown was standing on the gallows with a rope around his neck, the death warrant was read and it was discovered that, by mistake, the name of the jury foreman had been written in instead of Brown's name. The hanging was canceled, and in 1902 Brown's sentence was commuted to life imprisonment. In 1913 the real murderer confessed and Brown was granted a pardon. In 1929 the state of Florida awarded Brown a relief fund of $2,492.

PRIMARY SOURCE: Michael Radelet, Hugo Bedau, and Constance Putnam, *In Spite of Innocence* (Boston: Northeastern University Press, 1992).

Simon Wiesenthal's
9 Most Wanted Nazi Fugitives

Founder and director of the Jewish Documentation Center in Vienna, Wiesenthal is a concentration camp survivor who has spent decades meticulously piecing together evidence that has led to the discovery of about a thousand Nazis, including Alfred Eichmann. The Laurence Olivier character in the film *The Boys from Brazil* was based on Wiesenthal.

1. HEINRICH MÜLLER, chief of the Gestapo. Fate and whereabouts unknown.
2. RICHARD GLÜCKS, inspector general of all concentration camps. Fate and whereabouts unknown.
3. ALOIS BRUNNER, one of Eichmann's deputies, lives under the name of Fisher in Damascus, Syria. He was responsible for the deaths of thousands of Jews in Czechoslovakia and Greece.
4. FRANZ ABROMEIT, member of the staff of Eichmann, involved in many crimes, especially in Hungary. Fate and whereabouts unknown.
5. FRIIEDRICH WARTZOG, commander of the concentration camp Lemberg-Janovska, USSR. He ordered the killing of at least 40,000 people; whereabouts unknown.
6. ANTON BURGER, assistant of Eichmann, deputy commander of Theresienstadt. Escaped from prison in 1948; whereabouts unknown.
7. DR. ARIBERT HEIM, doctor of the concentration camp Mauthausen. Lives somewhere in Europe under a false name.

Heinrich Müller was chief of the Gestapo. Presumed dead in 1945, his tomb was opened in 1963 and found to be empty.

8. GERHARD THIELE, responsible for the death by burning of more than a thousand prisoners, who were murdered on his order only a few days before the end of the war in 1945. Whereabouts unknown.

9. OLESH SOKOLYSHYN, commander of the Ukrainian police of Lemberg (Lviv), coresponsible for the death of many thousands of Jews. Whereabouts unknown.

— Exclusive for *The Book of Lists*

10 Nazi Criminals Still Sought by Serge Klarsfeld

Klarsfeld is a lawyer, historian, and president of the Association of Sons and Daughters of French Deported Jews, and is involved with numerous similar organizations. He and his wife found Nazi Klaus Barbie in 1971 in Peru, and obtained his forced return from Bolivia. His list is in alphabetical order.

1. ALOIS BRUNNER, commandant of the concentration camp in Drancy, France, from June 1943 to August 1944. He deported 25,000 Jews from France, 45,000 Jews from Austria, 45,000 Jews from Salonika, and 13,000 Jews from Czechoslovakia. The Klarsfelds found him in Damascus, where he lived at one time as Dr. Fisher and was under the protection of President Hafiz al-Assad. After three tries, the Klarsfelds were expelled from Syria.

2. ERNST BRUCKLER, adjutant to Alois Brunner in Austria, Greece, and France. He participated in the terror at the Drancy camp.

3. ANTON BURGER, adjutant to Eichmann, commander of the camp at Theresienstadt. He escaped in 1948 and has since disappeared.

4. RICHARD GLÜCKS, inspector general of various concentration camps.

5. ROLF GÜNTHER, assistant to Eichmann; participated efficiently in the accomplishment of the "final solution."

6. HANS GÜNTHER, brother of Rolf, an active member of Eichmann's staff.

7. ERICH HASSE, head of the Gestapo in Bourges, France. He was responsible for the massacre of Guerry in 1944, in which about forty Jews were thrown into a well.

8. ARIBERT HEIM, a doctor, undertook criminal experiments in the Mauthausen camp, where he executed numerous inmates. It is possible that he lives in Europe under a false name.

9. RUDOLF LANGE, one of the Nazis responsible for the special SS extermination group, Einsatz gruppe A, in the Baltic countries.

10. HEINRICH MÜLLER, head of the Reich's Gestapo. He was presumed dead in 1945, but his tomb was opened in 1963 and there was no skeleton inside. He is said to have gone to Cordoba, Argentina, in 1974.

"Facts Are Stupid Things" and *16* Other Slips of the Tongue by U.S. Politicians

1. "Facts are stupid things." — *Ronald Reagan, addressing the Republican National Convention in 1988. He was misquoting John Adams, who in 1770 wrote "Facts are stubborn things." Reagan repeated the mistake several times.*

2. "I hope I stand for antibigotry, anti-Semitism, antiracism. That is what drives me." — *George Bush in 1988. New York governor Mario Cuomo remarked that Bush at least had not offended Italians by declaring himself antipasto.*

3. "We have had triumphs, we have made mistakes, we have had sex." — *George Bush in 1988, speaking of his eight years as vice-president under Reagan, meant to say "we have had setbacks."*

4. "If Lincoln were alive today, he'd roll over in his grave." — *Newly inaugurated president Gerald Ford*

5. "My first qualification for mayor of the city of New York is my monumental ingratitude to each and all of you." — *Fiorello La Guardia, on the night of his first election victory*

6. "Outside of the killings, we have one of the lowest crime rates." — *Marion Barry, mayor of Washington, D.C., in 1989*

7. "I think we're on the road to coming up with answers that I don't think any of us in total feel we have the answers to." — *Kim Anderson, mayor of Naples, Florida, in 1991*

8. "Now, the simple truth is those Democrats who are here are probably here because like millions I've met across the country, they have found they can no longer follow the leadership of the Republican Party, which has taken them down a course that

leads to ruin." — *Ronald Reagan in 1986, campaigning on behalf of Republican candidate Jim Santini*

9. "I have opinions of my own — strong opinions — but I don't always agree with them." — *George Bush*

10. "Now we are trying to get unemployment to go up, and I think we are going to succeed." — *Ronald Reagan in 1982*

11. "The first black president will be a politician who is black." — *L. Douglas Wilder, governor of Virginia, in 1992*

12. "This is Pearl Harbor Day. Forty-seven years ago to this very day, we were hit and hit hard at Pearl Harbor." — *George Bush, addressing the American Legion in Louisville, Kentucky, on September 7, 1988, three months off target*

13. "I didn't go down there with any plan for the Americas, or anything. I went down to find out from them and {learn} their views. You'd be surprised. They're all individual countries." — *Ronald Reagan in 1982, responding to a question about whether his Latin American trip had changed his outlook on the region*

14. "Boy, they were big on crematoriums, weren't they?" — *George Bush in 1987, after a visit to the Auschwitz death camp*

15. "{Republicans} understand the importance of bondage between parent and child." — *Dan Quayle in 1988, on bonding between parents and children*

16. "What a waste it is to lose one's mind — or to not have a mind. How true that is." — *Dan Quayle in 1989, addressing the United Negro College Fund*

17. "I stand by all the misstatements." — *Dan Quayle in 1989, on his oratorical slipups*

PRIMARY SOURCE: David Olive, *Political Babble* (New York: John Wiley & Sons, copyright © 1992). Reprinted by permission of John Wiley & Sons, Inc.

NOTE: For more slips of the tongue by U.S. politicians, see *The Book of Lists #2*, pp. 38–39, and *The Book of Lists #3*, pp. 393–95.

13 Actors Who Became Politicians

1. HELEN GAHAGAN DOUGLAS

A Broadway star, Gahagan moved to Hollywood after marrying film actor Melvyn Douglas. Her brief movie career was highlighted by her leading role in the cult classic *She* (1935). After several years' involvement in Democratic Party politics, she was elected to Congress in 1944 and served three terms. Gahagan Douglas ran for the U.S. Senate in California in 1950, facing up-and-coming right-winger Richard Nixon. Nixon scared voters by calling her "red hot" and "pink right down to her underwear" and by insinuating that she had slept with President Truman. Nixon won the election and went on to further political success. Gahagan Douglas never ran for office again.

2. CLINT EASTWOOD

The star of such films as *A Fistful of Dollars* (1964), *Dirty Harry* (1971), and *Sudden Impact* (1983), Eastwood took time off from his film career to serve two years as mayor of Carmel, California (pop. 4,800). Elected on a pro-development platform in 1986, Eastwood nonetheless stopped greedy developers from buying the twenty-two-acre Mission Ranch by buying it himself for $5 million.

3. JOSEPH ESTRADA

Known as the "Filipino Ronald Reagan" because he starred in so many B movies, Estrada built his reputation by playing the role of the common man fighting the system. Elected mayor of San Juan, a suburb of Manila, Estrada moved on to become the only senator without a college degree. In 1992 he was elected vice-president of the Philippines.

4. CHARLES FARRELL

During the late 1920s and the early 1930s, Farrell and Janet Gaynor made twelve pictures together and were known as "America's Favorite Lovebirds." When his career began to decline, Farrell became a land developer in Palm Springs, California, and served as the city's mayor from 1947 to 1955. Television allowed Farrell an opportunity to stage a successful comeback as an actor. He co-starred in *My Little Margie* (1952–

Clint Eastwood, mayor of Carmel, California.

1956), and *The Charlie Farrell Show* (1956–1960), before retiring again to the desert.

5. FRED GRANDY

Although he has appeared on Broadway and in the movies, Grandy, a Harvard graduate, is best known for his portrayal of Gopher in the TV series *The Love Boat* (1977–1986). In 1986 he returned to his earlier interest in politics, winning election from Sioux City, Iowa, to the U.S. House of Representatives. A Republican, Grandy describes himself as a "knee-jerk moderate."

6. GLENDA JACKSON

Jackson won two Academy Awards for her performances in *Women in Love* (1970) and *A Touch of Class* (1972). Running as a Labour Party candidate, the bricklayer's daughter won election to Parliament in 1992 in the Hampstead and Highgate sections of north London.

7. BEN JONES

Best known for his portrayal of the mechanic Cooter Davenport in *The Dukes of Hazzard,* Jones, a Georgia Democrat, won election to the U.S. Congress in 1988. He was reelected in 1990, but in 1992 he was defeated in the Democratic Party primary.

8. MELINA MERCOURI

The star of *Never on Sunday* (1959), Mercouri entered Greek politics as soon as democracy was restored in 1974. A member of the Pan-Hellenic Socialist movement, she was elected to Parliament in 1977 and has represented the working-class district of Piraeus ever since. She also served as minister of culture from 1981 until 1990. In 1990 she ran for mayor of Athens, but was defeated.

9. GEORGE MURPHY

After several years on Broadway, Murphy moved to Hollywood, where he specialized in musicals such as *Little Miss Broadway* (1938), and war films such as *This Is the Army* (1943), in which he appeared with Ronald Reagan. From 1944 to 1946 he served two terms as president of the Screen Actors' Guild. A Democrat turned Republican, Murphy was elected U.S. senator from California in 1968. An ineffective legislator, he was defeated when he ran for reelection in 1974.

10. ALESSANDRA MUSSOLINI

No one was surprised or upset when the beautiful niece of actress Sophia Loren became a film actress herself, appearing in such films as *White Sister* (1973) and *A Special Day* (1977). But she did cause a stir when, at the age of thirty, she followed in the footsteps of her grandfather, dictator Benito Mussolini, by entering politics. In 1992 she was elected to Parliament as the representative of the neo-Fascist party from Naples.

11. **N. T. RAMA RAO**

Known as the "Saffron Caesar" because he usually appeared in an orange costume, Rama Rao, the star of more than 300 Indian films, capitalized on his widespread popularity to enter politics. He rose to become chief minister of Andhra Pradesh state. After leaving office, he remained the leader of the Hindu Telegu Desam Party, and in 1991, at the age of sixty-nine, he was arrested in the midst of a hunger strike to protest an attack on his house by supporters of the ruling Congress Party.

12. **RONALD REAGAN**

Like George Murphy before him, Reagan was a movie actor, a president of the Screen Actors' Guild, and a Democrat-turned-Republican. When he announced that he planned to run for governor of California in 1966, studio head Jack Warner commented, "No, no, no! Jimmy Stewart for governor, Ronald Reagan for best friend." When he won the election, Reagan was asked what he planned to do when he took office. "I don't know," he replied, "I've never played a governor." Reagan was reelected in 1970 and later served two terms as president of the United States (1981–1989). Nevertheless, he never lost his

Porn star Ilona Staller — a member of the Party of Love — was elected to the Italian Parliament in 1987.

basic actor's mentality. At the 1987 economic summit in Venice, Italy, Reagan startled the leaders of the world's industrial nations by showing up with cue cards, not just for important meetings, but even at an informal cocktail party.

13. ILONA STALLER

Hungarian-born pornographic film star Ilona Staller, better known by her stage name, Cicciolina, was elected to the Italian Parliament in 1987. A member of the Radical Party and the Party of Love, Staller represented her Rome constituency until retiring in 1992.

10 Presidents Ranked By Popularity

	Average Approval Rating for Entire Presidency (%)	Most Recent Approval Rating (1990) (%)
1. John Kennedy	70	84
2. Franklin Roosevelt	68	75
3. Dwight Eisenhower	65	70
4. George Bush	60	56[*]
5. Lyndon Johnson	55	40
6. Ronald Reagan	52	48[†]
7. Richard Nixon	48	32
8. Jimmy Carter	47	50[†]
9. Gerald Ford	46	55
10. Harry Truman	43	68

SOURCE: The Gallup Poll.

[*] At end of term.

[†] Figures for 1992.

Historians Rate *37* Presidents

In 1991 almost 500 history professors were asked to rate each U.S. president from 1 (great) to 6 (failure). George Bush was not included in the survey because his term was not yet completed. William Henry Harrison and James Garfield were also left off the list because they died within six months of their inauguration.

	Mean
GREAT	
1. Abraham Lincoln	1.13
2. Franklin Roosevelt	1.22
3. George Washington	1.27
4. Thomas Jefferson	1.70
NEAR GREAT	
5. Theodore Roosevelt	1.93
6. Woodrow Wilson	2.07
7. Andrew Jackson	2.32
8. Harry Truman	2.45
ABOVE AVERAGE	
9. John Adams	2.85
10. Lyndon Johnson	2.87
11. Dwight Eisenhower	2.99
12. James Polk	3.06
13. John Kennedy	3.13
14. James Madison	3.30
15. James Monroe	3.35
16. John Q. Adams	3.42
17. Grover Cleveland	3.43
AVERAGE	
18. William McKinley	3.78
19. William Taft	3.87
20. Martin Van Buren	3.97
21. Herbert Hoover	4.03
22. Rutherford Hayes	4.05
23. Chester Arthur	4.24
24. Gerald Ford	4.32
25. Jimmy Carter	4.36
26. Benjamin Harrison	4.40
BELOW AVERAGE	
27. Zachary Taylor	4.45
28. Ronald Reagan	4.46
29. John Tyler	4.46
30. Millard Fillmore	4.64
31. Calvin Coolidge	4.65
32. Franklin Pierce	4.95
FAILURE	
33. Andrew Johnson	5.00
34. James Buchanan	5.15

	Mean
35. Richard Nixon	5.18
36. Ulysses Grant	5.25
37. Warren Harding	5.56

SOURCE: Tim H. Blessing, Director of Presidential Performance Study, Penn State, Berks Campus, Tulpehocken Road, Reading, PA 19610.

NOTE: Grover Cleveland served two nonconsecutive terms as president.

5 U.S. Presidents Who Were Injured in Horseback-Riding Accidents

1. FRANKLIN PIERCE

Pierce began the Mexican War as a private but moved up quickly to brigadier general. While leading an attack near Mexico City on August 19, 1847, his horse, frightened by artillery fire, jumped up and threw him. Pierce's pelvis was fractured and his knee severely wrenched. Pierce fainted from the pain, but regained consciousness and resumed fighting. The next day he twisted his injured knee and fainted from the pain again.

2. ULYSSES S. GRANT

Grant was known as a daring horseman who tamed unruly horses and was never thrown. After Mexico City had been taken during the Mexican War and the fighting had ended, Grant was riding back from an afternoon of merrymaking with his fellow officers when his horse, racing at full speed, was startled by the shriek of a locomotive whistle. The horse lost its footing and fell, knocking Grant unconscious, pinning him to the ground, and injuring his left side and leg. Grant recuperated at a local inn, but the pain he experienced "was almost beyond endurance."

3. RUTHERFORD B. HAYES

At the Battle of Cedar Creek on October 19, 1864, Hayes received a concussion when his horse was killed.

4. THEODORE ROOSEVELT

An avid — and reckless — horseman, Roosevelt fell off horses at least five times. On May 13, 1879, the twenty-year-old Roosevelt and his horse fell while galloping downhill. He recovered quickly, but the horse almost died. In 1883 he was hunting buffalo when his horse spun suddenly and tossed his head, knocking Roosevelt's rifle against his forehead and causing a deep gash. A few days later, his horse pitched him forward into a bed of sharp bushes. In 1885 Roosevelt was working as a cowboy, assisting with the Badlands spring cattle roundup, when his horse fell over backward on him, cracking the point of his left shoulder. Later that year, he took up fox hunting with hounds. On October 26 he rode his horse so hard that it tripped over a wall and landed in a pile of stones. Roosevelt's face smashed against something sharp and his left arm snapped beneath the elbow. Nevertheless, he remounted and finished the hunt with blood pouring down his face and his arm dangling at his side. That night, with his arm in splints, he presided over the Hunt Ball.

5. RONALD REAGAN

By the time Ronald Reagan earned his spurs, buffalo hunting was illegal in the United States. So, on his first Fourth of July since leaving the presidency, Reagan traveled across the border into Mexico for an unofficial buffalo hunt on the private ranch of longtime friend William A. Wilson. On a rocky downhill slope, Reagan's horse bucked wildly and then stumbled and threw his rider. The seventy-eight-year-old Reagan was flown by military helicopter to an Army hospital in Arizona. But he'd received only minor abrasions and was released after five hours. Reagan often said, "There's nothing better for the inside of a man than the outside of a horse."

9 People Misquoted by Ronald Reagan

1. JIMMY CARTER

QUOTE: *"Our concept of human rights is preserved in Poland."* Candidate Reagan claimed that President Carter made this statement while visiting Communist Poland in 1977. Carter never said anything of the sort.

2. WINSTON CHURCHILL

QUOTE: *"The idea that a nation can tax itself into prosperity is one of the cruelest delusions which has ever befuddled the human mind."* Although Reagan used this strong statement in a speech on March 9, 1982, there is no evidence that Churchill ever said or wrote such a thing.

3. OLIVER WENDELL HOLMES, JR.

QUOTE: *"Keep government poor and remain free."*
Reagan quoted Holmes in a speech on June 15, 1982. But Holmes scholars have been unable to find such a statement in the Supreme Court justice's writings.

4. HAROLD ICKES

QUOTE: *"What we were striving for was a kind of modified form of communism."*
Ickes was secretary of interior under President Franklin Roosevelt. Reagan used the quote in a December 1981 speech in an attempt to discredit Roosevelt's New Deal policies. Not only does the quote not appear in any of Ickes's writings, but there is nothing in his diaries to indicate that he supported communism at all.

5. ANDREW JACKSON

QUOTE: *"One man with courage makes a majority."*
Reagan used this quotation on October 10, 1987, to support his nomination of Robert Bork to the U.S. Supreme Court. Although it does reflect the *spirit* of the seventh U.S. president, there is no record of Jackson actually having said it.

6. HENRY KISSINGER

QUOTE: *"The day of the United States is past, and today is the day of the Soviet Union. . . . My job as secretary of state is to negotiate the most acceptable second-best position available."*
This shocking false quotation was delivered by Reagan during a televised speech in the spring of 1976.

7. V. I. LENIN

QUOTE: *"First, we will take eastern Europe, then the masses of Asia, then we will encircle the United States, which will be the last bastion of capitalism. We will not have to attack. It will fall like an overripe fruit into our hands."*
There is nothing in the voluminous *Complete Works* of Lenin that even comes close to this statement, which was first "quoted" by Reagan in a speech in the spring of 1985. In 1988 Reagan was challenged by Soviet journalists to divulge the source of the quote. Reagan's reply began "Oh my!" and went on for 200 words, but did not answer the question.

8. ABRAHAM LINCOLN

QUOTE: *"You cannot strengthen the weak by weakening the strong. You cannot help the wage earner by pulling down the wage payer. You cannot help the poor by destroying the rich. You cannot help men permanently by doing for them what they could and should do for themselves."*

This popular misquotation, used by Reagan at the 1992 Republican National Convention, originally comes from a 1916 leaflet entitled "Lincoln on Private Property." On one side were quotes from Lincoln; on the other side were maxims written by the Reverend William John Henry Boetcker. The quote used by Reagan came from Boetcker's side of the pamphlet.

9. ALEXIS DE TOCQUEVILLE

QUOTE: *"You know, in America someone sees a problem that needs solving. And they cross the street and talk to a neighbor about it. And the first thing you know, a committee is formed. Finally, the problem is solved. You won't believe this. But not a single bureaucrat had anything to do with it."*

When Reagan used this "quote" in a speech on November 11, 1982, critics pointed out that the word *bureaucrat* didn't exist in 1835 when Tocqueville wrote *Democracy in America*. A White House spokeswoman admitted, "The president changed it a little."

PRIMARY SOURCE: *They Never Said It: A Book of Fake Quotes, Misquotes, and Misleading Attributions*, edited by Paul F. Boller, Jr., and John George. Copyright © 1989 by Paul F. Boller, Jr., and John George. Reprinted by Oxford University Press, Inc.

Walter Mondale's *10* Things He Would Have Done If Elected President

Walter Mondale, Democratic vice-president under Jimmy Carter, ran unsuccessfully against Ronald Reagan for the presidency in 1984. If given the chance, these are some of the things he would like to have done.

1. RAISED TAXES

Higher taxes had to be part of any real solution to America's fiscal crisis, which instead only got worse. In 1984 the budget deficit was $186 billion and the total federal debt was $1.6 trillion. By 1992 the budget deficit had grown to $320 billion and the total debt was more than $4 trillion.

2. TOLD THE TRUTH

See #1.

3. OBEYED THE LAW

One of the most disturbing developments in modern American government is that some presidents seem to think they do not have to obey the law like everyone else. Thus, the Watergate and Iran-Contra scandals.

4. IMPROVED THE FAIRNESS OF THE TAX SYSTEM

During the 1980s, the tax burden on low- and moderate-income Americans went up, while the tax burden on the richest Americans went down.

5. CONTROLLED AMERICA'S RUNAWAY HEALTH-CARE COSTS

In 1984 total health-care spending was $390 billion — about 10.3 percent of the gross national product. By 1992 health-care costs had grown to more than $800 billion — almost 14 percent of GNP.

6. STOOD UP TO THE WORLD'S DICTATORS

For too many years, there was an insidious distinction in American foreign policy between dictators who were "friendly" or "unfriendly." Any ruler who terrorizes his own citizens should not be considered a friend of the United States.

7. HALTED AMERICA'S ILLEGAL WAR AGAINST NICARAGUA

This not-so-secret "covert war" shamed the United States in the eyes of the world community and showed our government in blatant violation of its own stated commitment to the rule of law in international affairs.

8. ELIMINATED THE STAR WARS STRATEGIC DEFENSE INITIATIVE

As its name suggests, Star Wars was never anything but a fantasy — a very dangerous and expensive fantasy.

9. WORKED TO RESTORE PUBLIC TRUST IN GOVERNMENT

Lincoln once said: "With public trust, everything is possible; without it, nothing is possible."

10. ENROLLED IN A CLASS ON HOW TO SPEAK ON TV

This is one thing I learned from Ronald Reagan.

— Exclusive for *The Book of Lists*

Harrison Salisbury's
10 Greatest Leaders
of the Twentieth Century

Beginning his career in 1928 at age twenty, Salisbury worked for the *Minneapolis Journal* and United Press International before becoming the *New York Times* Moscow correspondent in 1949. His *Russia Re-Viewed* won him the 1955 Pulitzer Prize for international reporting. An associate editor for the *Times* since 1972, Salisbury has written nearly twenty books on Russia, China, and the United States.

1. Franklin D. Roosevelt
2. Winston Churchill
3. Vladimir I. Lenin
4. Mao Tse-tung
5. Joseph Stalin
6. Mohandas K. Gandhi
7. Chou En-lai
8. Dwight D. Eisenhower
9. Charles de Gaulle
10. Woodrow Wilson

— Exclusive for *The Book of Lists*

Shirley MacLaine's
5 Greatest Spiritual Political Leaders

Actress Shirley MacLaine won an Academy Award in 1984 for her role in *Terms of Endearment*. She has starred in dozens of motion pictures, and has written several best-sellers, including *Out on a Limb* (1983) and *Dancing in the Light* (1985).

1. Anwar Sadat
2. Mohandas K. Gandhi
3. Martin Luther King, Jr.
4. Lech Walesa
5. Corazon Aquino

— Exclusive for *The Book of Lists*

4 Long-Held Prisoners of Conscience

1. ### ABDELHAQ ROUISSI (Morocco)

   Abdelhaq Rouissi, a former bank employee and activist in the Moroccan labor union, has apparently been held in secret detention since he disappeared on October 4, 1964. Before his disappearance, he had opposed government policies. Experience has shown that people who have disappeared in Morocco may still be alive and held in secret detention centers; hundreds of prisoners were released in 1991 after having disappeared for many years. Former disappearance victims who have recently been released from detention have confirmed that Abdelhaq Rouissi is being secretly detained.

2. ### NGUYEN KHAC CHINH (Vietnam)

   Nguyen Khac Chinh, a lawyer, writer, and former member of the Nationalist Party of Vietnam, has been held in detention without charge or trial since his arrest in December 1975. He was allegedly tortured and spent a few years in solitary confinement before being sent to a "reeducation" camp. Nguyen Khac Chinh was among a group of Catholic intellectuals reportedly arrested because they opposed the Communist government.

3. ### WEI JINGSHENG (People's Republic of China)

   Wei Jingsheng was arrested in March 1979 for placing a poster promoting democracy on Beijing's Democracy Wall. Formerly a

In 1979 Wei Jingsheng received a fifteen-year prison sentence for placing a poster promoting democracy on Beijing's Democracy Wall.

staunch Communist, Mr. Wei developed a deep belief in democracy after witnessing atrocities committed in the name of communism during China's Cultural Revolution.

4. RIAD AL-TURK (Syria)

Riad al-Turk, a lawyer, has been imprisoned since October 1980, without charge or trial, for his nonviolent political activities. He is reported to have been severely tortured at various stages during his detention, resulting in his being repeatedly hospitalized.

SOURCE: Amnesty International, 740 West Peachtree Street, N.W., Atlanta, Georgia 30308.

15 Nations with the Most Human Suffering

The Population Crisis Committee (1120 19th Street, NW, Suite 550, Washington, D.C. 20036) ranks 140 nations based on life expectancy, daily calorie supply, clean drinking water, infant immunization, secondary-school enrollment, gross national product per capita, rate of inflation, communications technology, political freedom, and civil rights, and creates a composite Human Suffering Index (0 = best, 100 = worst).

	Human Suffering Index
1. Mozambique	93
2. Somalia	92
3. Afghanistan	89
3. Haiti	89
3. Sudan	89
6. Zaire	88
7. Laos	87
8. Angola	86
8. Guinea	86
10. Ethiopia	85
10. Uganda	85
12. Cambodia	84
12. Sierra Leone	84
14. Chad	82
14. Guinea-Bissau	82

16 Nations with the Least Human Suffering

	Human Suffering Index
1. Denmark	1
2. Belgium	2
2. Netherlands	2
4. Canada	3
4. Switzerland	3
6. Australia	4
6. Norway	4
8. United States	5
9. Austria	6
9. Germany	6
11. France	7
11. Iceland	7
11. Japan	7
11. Luxembourg	7
15. Finland	8
15. New Zealand	8

NOTE: The United Kingdom ranked twenty-second with 16 points.

9 Deposed Dictators . . . After the Fall

1. IDI AMIN (Uganda)

Amin seized power in 1971 and launched a reign of terror that led to the deaths of an estimated 300,000 people. Deposed in 1979, Amin was offered asylum in Saudi Arabia, with all living expenses paid. In 1989 he tried to return to Uganda using a false passport. He got as far as Zaire, where he was recognized and arrested and then sent back to Saudi Arabia.

2. JEAN-BEDEL BOKASSA (Central African Republic)

Bokassa seized power in 1965. In 1976 he declared himself emperor and a year later staged an elaborate coronation celebration that used up one-fourth of the nation's annual earnings. He was overthrown in 1979, but not before he had committed a series of horrible outrages, including ordering the massacre of schoolchildren who refused to buy uniforms made in a factory owned by Bokassa's wife. After his ouster, he lived lavishly in Paris. Then, incredibly, he returned to the CAR, where he was arrested upon arrival and charged with murder and cannibalism. He was convicted of the former charge and now lives in "comfortable confinement" in the capital city of Bangui.

3. JEAN-CLAUDE DUVALIER (Haiti)

When longtime Haitian dictator François "Papa Doc" Duvalier died in 1971, the mantle of power passed to his nineteen-year-old son Jean-Claude, better known as "Baby Doc," who also inherited the dreaded *Tonton Macoutes* secret police. Baby Doc was finally forced out of office in 1986 after widespread protests and flown out of the country on a U.S. Air Force plane. Baby Doc and his wife, Michelle, not content with stuffing an Air Haiti cargo plane with plunder, bumped eleven passengers off their escape flight — including Michelle's grandparents — to make room for more loot. The Duvaliers settled on the French Riviera and spent millions of dollars a year before divorcing in 1990.

4. ERICH HONECKER (East Germany)

As head of East German security, Honecker supervised the construction of the Berlin Wall in 1961. Ten years later he assumed leadership of the Communist Party. Among his most odious acts was ordering all border areas to be mined and equipped with automatic shooting devices. With the fall of communism in 1989, Honecker was put under house arrest. In 1991 he was flown from a Soviet military hospital near Berlin to Moscow itself. However, on July 29, 1992, the seventy-nine-year-old Honecker was expelled from the Chilean embassy where he had sought refuge and was flown back to Berlin to face charges of corruption and manslaughter. Because he was diagnosed as dying from liver cancer, Honecker was allowed to leave for Chile in January 1993.

Jean-Claude Duvalier and his wife Michelle fleeing Haiti in 1986. They forced Michelle's grandparents off their escape plane in order to make room for more loot.

5. MENGISTU HAILE MARIAM (Ethiopia)

Mengistu was a member of the military junta that ousted Haile Selassie in 1974. By 1977 Mengistu had consolidated his personal power. While the Ethiopian people were suffering through a series of droughts and famines, Mengistu concentrated on brutally suppressing his opponents. Bodies of political prisoners who had been tortured to death were displayed in public and shown on television. Mengistu's ability to beat back various secessionist armies finally failed, and on May 21, 1991, he resigned and fled the country. He settled in Zimbabwe, where he was welcomed by that country's dictator, Robert Mugabe.

6. MANUEL NORIEGA (Panama)

Noriega was raised in a poor family of Colombian background. Something of an ugly duckling, he found his place in the military. He rose rapidly to become head of Panama's intelligence service. In 1983 he took command of the national army and, with it, the nation. A devious manipulator who played all sides, Noriega cooperated with the U.S. government and the CIA while at the same time making huge profits from drug trafficking. He also suspended civil rights in his own country and tortured and murdered his opponents. In 1988 Noriega was indicted in the United States on charges of drug trafficking, money laundering, and racketeering. When Noriega refused to abide by the results of a free election, President Bush ordered the invasion of Panama, and troops seized Noriega and brought him back to Miami to stand trial. He was convicted and sentenced to forty years in prison. In December 1992, U.S. District Court Judge William Hoeveler declared Noriega a prisoner of war, entitled to the rights guaranteed by the third Geneva Convention.

7. AUGUSTO PINOCHET (Chile)

As commander in chief of Chile's armed forces, Pinochet led the 1973 coup that overthrew the elected government of Salvador Allende. For the next seventeen years he ruled Chile with an iron fist, suspending Parliament and ordering the abduction and

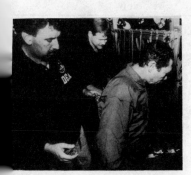

Panamanian dictator Manuel Noriega being taken into custody by agents of the U.S. Drug Enforcement Administration.

murder of 2,000 political opponents. He did, however, agree to democratic elections in 1988, which he lost. In 1990 he stepped down as president, but retained control of the armed forces, a position that he still holds.

8. POL POT (Cambodia)

Pol Pot was one of the few modern dictators whose genocidal policies were so horrible that they rivaled those of Adolf Hitler. As leader of the notorious Khmer Rouge, Pol Pot launched a four-year reign of terror (1975–1979) that turned the country into one large forced-labor camp and led to the death of an estimated 1 million people. When Vietnamese forces finally drove the Khmer Rouge from power, Pol Pot and his followers set up shop in Thailand. They continue to retain a large military force and threaten the restoration of peace in Cambodia. Pol Pot's whereabouts are unknown, although he is thought to be living on the Thai-Cambodian border.

9. ALFREDO STROESSNER (Paraguay)

Stroessner seized power in a 1954 military coup and held on for over thirty-four years, thus setting a record as the longest-ruling head of state in the Western Hemisphere. He was finally deposed in February 1989. He flew to exile in Brazil, with one of his sons, while the rest of his family moved to Miami.

20 New Names for Old Places

Some place names are changed when the people of an area escape colonial rule. Some changes represent a shift away from glorifying military or political heroes. Occasionally, it is simply a matter of streamlining the spelling.

Old	New
1. Abyssinia	Ethiopia
2. Belgian Congo	Zaire
3. British Honduras	Belize
4. Burma	Myanmar
5. Byelorussia	Belarus
6. Ceylon	Sri Lanka
7. Constantinople	Istanbul
8. Custer Battlefield National Monument	Little Bighorn Battlefield National Monument

Old	New
9. Fort Dearborn, Indian Territory	Chicago, Illinois
10. Gorky	Nizhny Novgorod
11. Leningrad	St. Petersburg
12. Lvov	Lviv
13. New Amsterdam, New Netherland	New York, New York
14. Peking	Beijing
15. Persia	Iran
16. Rangoon	Yangon
17. Siam	Thailand
18. Sverdlovsk	Yekaterinburg
19. Tanganyika and Zanzibar	Tanzania
20. Tenochtitlán	Mexico City

Percent of Women in **20** National Legislatures

The Inter-Parliamentary Union, an international organization that works to foster representative government and world peace, reports that women are appallingly underrepresented in their national parliaments. In 1991 the number of female legislators dropped to 11 percent. Yet women account for 52 percent of the world's population. The figures below are for 1993, except where noted. (The IPU can be contacted by writing to Place du Petit Saconnex, Case Postale 438, 1211 Geneva 19, Switzerland.)

THE 6 NATIONS WITH THE HIGHEST PERCENT OF WOMEN IN THEIR LEGISLATURES . . .

1. Finland	38.5
2. Norway	35.8
3. Sweden	33.5
4. Denmark	33.0
5. Iceland	23.8
6. Cuba	22.7

. . . COMPARED TO 14 OTHERS

1. Germany	20.5
2. China	20.1
3. Canada	15.3

4. Spain	14.6*
5. Australia	14.0
6. Mexico	12.4*
7. Iraq	10.8
8. Bangladesh	10.3
9. United States	10.1
10. United Kingdom	9.2
11. Israel	9.1
12. Japan	7.2
13. France	6.0
14. Kuwait	0

* 1991 data

10 Underreported Stories

Since 1976, a panel of media experts has each year selected important news stories that were inadequately covered by the U.S. national press, their goal being better coverage of vital issues. The following are some of Project Censored's most underreported stories of recent years.

1. UNITED STATES: THE WORLD'S LEADING MERCHANT OF DEATH (1992)

During the 1980s, worldwide weapons sales skyrocketed to almost $1 trillion a year — about $2 million a minute. By far the leading arms dealers were the United States and the USSR. With the collapse of the Soviet Union and the end of the Cold War, there was hope that the trafficking in weapons would decline and that U.S. arms plants could be converted to civilian factories. Instead, the United States has led the way in filling the gap left by the USSR. In the last decade, the United States has provided $128 billion in weapons and military assistance to more than 125 countries.

2. OPERATION CENSORED WAR (1991)

The Bush administration, aided by the press, kept from the American public several stories that might have decreased support for the Persian Gulf War. Among them were these items: 70 percent of Allied bombs missed their targets; U.S. tanks with plows buried alive thousands of Iraqi soldiers; U.S. Marines used napalm bombs; "friendly fire" caused four times as many casualties as were originally admitted; and, unlike their European counterparts, U.S. television networks refused to show graphic footage of the mass destruction of retreating Iraqi troops during the "Turkey Shoot" on the road to Basra.

3. VOODOO ECONOMICS (1991)

Despite posturing by politicians of both major political parties, the U.S. federal budget deficit is growing by almost $1 billion or $3.94 per person each day. In 1992 interest on the national debt cost taxpayers more than the entire budget for the Defense Department.

4. FREEDOM OF INFORMATION SHACKLED (1991)

In theory, the twenty-five-year-old Freedom of Information Act (FOIA) is supposed to force government bureaucracies to release requested information within ten days or explain why they won't do so. In 1982, however, the Reagan administration launched a campaign to undercut the act by cutting funding to FOIA offices and by classifying documents and even reclassifying material already released. The average response time to a request to the FBI is now 300 days. The State Department often takes up to a year and the FDA two years.

5. S & L SOLUTION WORSE THAN THE CRIME (1990)

The $500 billion estimated to be needed to bail out the savings and loan industry is more than the entire cost of World War II in current dollars and including service-connected veterans' benefits. The Resolution Trust Corporation, the federal agency entrusted with solving the problem, was established without meaningful public debate. The RTC solution includes $500 million in outside legal fees, about the same amount spent annually by the federal government on problems of the homeless.

6. THE PENTAGON'S SECRET MULTIBILLION-DOLLAR BLACK BUDGET (1990)

The Pentagon has a classified "black budget," which is used to fund weapon systems and projects that the government wants to keep from public view. The money to run America's eleven intelligence agencies has always been hidden, but when Ronald Reagan came to power, the black budget exploded. By 1990 it had quadrupled in size to about $36 billion a year, or $100 million a day.

7. AFRICA AS WORLD'S DUMP SITE (1989)

Africa, in need of cash and with large unpopulated areas, has become a prime target for the world's toxic wastes. Dealers have tried to dump European and U.S. poisonous wastes on fifteen African countries — one Italian dumper rented a Nigerian's back yard to dispose of 4,000 tons of deadly cargo, including highly toxic PCBs.

8. OLIVER NORTH & CO. BANNED FROM COSTA RICA (1989)

Costa Rica's president, Oscar Arias, winner of the 1987 Nobel Peace Prize, barred Oliver North, former national security adviser John Poindexter, former U.S. ambassador Lewis Tambs, and others from entering Costa Rica after a Costa Rican congressional committee concluded that the Contra supply network in Costa Rica, which North coordinated out of the White House, doubled as a drug-smuggling operation. North's personal notebook included dozens of references to Contra-related drug trafficking.

9. ACID RAIN — ONE OF AMERICA'S BIGGEST KILLERS (1988)

Acid rain, once considered to be a threat only to crops, trees, and fish, is now reported to be a significant threat to human lives as well. In 1986 the Brookhaven National Laboratory of New York estimated that acid rain kills 50,000 Americans and 5,000 to 11,000 Canadians annually — more than die from AIDS.

10. ABUSE OF AMERICA'S INCARCERATED CHILDREN (1988)

An average of 2.5 million children between the ages of five and nineteen are incarcerated in U.S. juvenile detention facilities on any given day. Of that number, more than 1.2 million are sexually abused by their peers, while almost 150,000 more are abused by state-employed counselors and staff members.

SOURCE: Carl Jensen, Project Censored, Sonoma State University, 1801 East Cotati Avenue, Rohnert Park, CA 94928.

NOTE: For more underreported stories, see *The Book of Lists #2*, pp. 158–60, and *The Book of Lists #3*, pp. 402–5.

16 Deadliest Wars Since World War II

Location/Description	Number of Deaths		
	Civilian	Military	Total
1. Korea (1950–1953) — Korean War; China and U.S. intervene	1,500,000	1,500,000	3,000,000

Location/Description	Number of Deaths		
	Civilian	Military	Total
2. Vietnam (1965–1975) — U.S. and South Vietnam versus North Vietnam	1,000,000	1,058,000	2,058,000
3. Nigeria (1967–1970) — Biafrans versus government; massacre and famine	1,000,000	1,000,000	2,000,000
4. Afghanistan (1978–1989) — civil war; USSR intervenes	800,000	500,000	1,300,000
5. Bangladesh (1971) — India intervention; massacre and famine	500,000	500,000	1,000,000
6. Cambodia (1975–1978) — Pol Pot massacre and famine	750,000	250,000	1,000,000
7. China (1946–1950) — Communists versus Kuomintang; U.S. intervenes	500,000	500,000	1,000,000
8. China (1950–1951) — government executes landlords	1,000,000		1,000,000
9. India (1946–1948) — Muslims versus Hindus; U.K. intervenes	800,000		800,000
10. Vietnam (1945–1954) — independence from France; China and U.S. intervene	300,000	300,000	600,000

	Number of Deaths		
Location/Description	Civilian	Military	Total
11. Ethiopia (1974–1990) — Eritrean revolt and famine	500,000	70,000	570,000
12. Sudan (1984–1990) — blacks versus Islamic law	500,000	6,000	506,000
13. Iraq versus Iran (1980–1988)	50,000	450,000	500,000
14. Indonesia (1965–1966) — abortive coup; U.K. intervenes	500,000		500,000
15. Sudan (1963–1972) — blacks versus the government; U.K. and Egypt intervene	250,000	250,000	500,000
16. China (1967–1968) — Cultural Revolution	450,000	50,000	500,000

SOURCE: *World Military and Social Expenditures 1991,* by Ruth Leger Sivard. Copyright © 1991 by World Priorities, P.O. Box 25140, Washington, D.C. 20007 USA.

Country Joe McDonald's
10 Things Most People Do Not Know About the Vietnam War

A singer, songwriter, and bandleader, McDonald formed a group in 1965 called Country Joe and the Fish that produced country, folk, blues, and rock music. Forever identified with the turbulent 1960s, the group had a repertoire of protest songs, including "I Feel Like I'm Fixin' to Die Rag," which became an anthem for the Vietnam antiwar movement. When the group broke up, McDonald went solo, producing a number of albums including *Thinking of Woodie Guthrie* and *Rock and Roll Music from Planet Earth.*

McDonald Notes: The war was fought by the Democratic Republic of Vietnam (North Vietnam) with much material help and some personnel help from Communist China, the then USSR, and a tiny bit from Cuba. On the other side were what U.S. president Lyndon Baines Johnson termed the Free World Military Assistance Forces, or just Free World Forces. They were Australia, New Zealand, South Korea, Thailand, the Philippines, Taiwan, Spain, the Republic of Vietnam (South Vietnam), and the United States.

The Vietnam war era is still not clearly defined. The first military adviser from the United States was killed by hostile fire in 1959, yet the U.S. Department of Defense starts the era for purposes of military veterans' benefits in 1963. A cease-fire was agreed to in Paris in 1973 with elections to follow. There were never any elections. The end was certainly when the North Vietnamese army crossed the border into South Vietnam and in a matter of a few months captured the capital of the south, Saigon, in the spring of 1975.

1. Left Behind

When U.S. personnel left South Vietnam by order of the then U.S. president and commander in chief Gerald Ford in April of 1975, in addition to leaving behind most of their South Vietnamese military allies of the army, navy, and air force, and their families, they also left behind the following: $220 million in South Vietnamese government money in gold bars (almost all of it given over the years by the United States as aid); over $3 million in U.S. small bills stuffed into fifty-gallon drums and left at Than San Nhut airport in Saigon; over two-thirds of our intelligence personnel (spies), plus thousands of files identifying them and their history, often with photo identification; the Hmong tribesmen who guarded the U.S. embassy in Saigon; a small nuclear reactor in the city of Da Lat; over 1.5 million M-16 rifles with ammunition; plus thousands of pieces of military equipment, including planes, helicopters, tanks, and large guns.

2. The Hanoi Hilton

There were several North Vietnamese prison camps in the Hanoi area. Unknown to most was what U.S. POWs named the Hanoi Hilton. The camp held a small group of U.S. pilots who were repeatedly tortured in an effort to get them to publicly denounce the United States. It didn't work. The senior U.S. military POW in the Hanoi Hilton and North Vietnam was U.S. Navy pilot Jim "James Bond" Stockdale, Ross Perot's pick for vice-president in the 1992 U.S. elections.

3. Project 100,000

Lyndon Baines Johnson, U.S. president after the assassination of John Kennedy, established Project 100,000. He lowered the usual standards of the army in order to get more inductees. The object was to meet the demands of General Westmoreland for more troops, because many more than had been expected were being killed by the Viet Cong and the North Vietnamese army. The goal was to get 100,000 more people into the U.S. Army. Many people who lacked the physical and mental qualifications were inducted and many people in trouble with the law for minor crimes were given the choice of jail time or duty in Vietnam.

4. South Korean Troops

President Johnson cut a deal with the South Korean government in order to get their involvement in the Free World Forces. It involved the U.S. government paying death benefits for all South Korean troops killed or missing in action.

5. Thai Troops and the M-16

The Thai government agreed to fight only under condition that they got to keep all the equipment the U.S. government provided the Thai troops for the duration of the war. This was everything from uniforms to armored weapons personnel carriers. At one point, U.S. Marines were fighting with old M-1 rifles while the Thai troops were equipped with the new highly desired M-16 assault rifle. Outrage forced the military to equip the Marines with the new M-16s. Not battle-tested, the rifle repeatedly jammed in combat and many Marines were found dead beside the disassembled M-16s they had been desperately trying to un-jam. Eventually, the powder in the bullets was changed and the inside of the barrel chromed. But to the end of the war GIs refused to fill magazine clips with the full amount of recommended bullets, for fear of jamming.

6. Volunteer Army

Of the 8 million Americans serving in the U.S. military during the unpopular Vietnam War, only 2 million were drafted. The remaining 6 million were volunteers.

7. U.S. Civilian Casualties

There are approximately 58,000 names of U.S. military personnel who died fighting the war listed on the Vietnam Veterans Memorial in Washington, D.C., but those who died in civilian capacity — CIA, advisers, government employees, civilian business people, health workers, and journalists — are not listed as war dead on the memorial. Only official military personnel are listed.

8. JOURNALIST CASUALTIES

Vietnam was one of the most dangerous of wars for people in the news business. Forty-five correspondents were killed there and eighteen listed as missing. But AP correspondent and photographer Peter Arnett survived thirteen years in Vietnam.

9. CAMPUS PROTESTS

Nearly one-third of the approximately 2,500 colleges and universities in America experienced Vietnam War–related problems. The FBI reports that from 1968 to 1970 disruptive and violent protests over the war resulted in more than 11,200 arrests and over 8,200 bombings, attempted bombings, and bomb threats. By mid-1970 more than thirty states had enacted a total of nearly eighty laws dealing with campus unrest. While nearly 30 percent of U.S. campuses were involved in some degree of strike activity, only 5 percent experienced violence.

10. WOMEN IN THE WAR

Because of sloppy record-keeping by the Department of Defense, it is unclear how many women served in the Vietnam War. Because nurses are traditionally commissioned officers and hospital orderlies are enlisted, it was not possible for them to socialize together after work, because enlisted personnel are under orders not to fraternize with the officers, and vice versa. However, there was such a desire for female companionship that nurses were "ordered" after working hours to get dressed up in civilian clothes and then taken to locations to "party" with high-ranking officers (although not all the military nurses were female). In most cases there were no special considerations given to the needs of female military personnel; for example, there were few gynecologists.

10 Nations with the Largest Proven Oil Reserves

	Oil (barrels)
1. Saudia Arabia	257,842,000,000
2. Iraq	100,000,000,000
3. United Arab Emirates	98,000,000,000
4. Kuwait	94,000,000,000
5. Iran	92,860,000,000
6. Venezuela	62,650,000,000

	Oil (barrels)
7. CIS (former USSR)	57,000,000,000
8. Mexico	51,298,000,000
9. United States	24,682,000,000
10. China	24,000,000,000

Source: *Oil and Gas Journal* (December 28, 1992).

8 Foreign Officials
Flown at U.S. Taxpayers' Expense

A report released by the Subcommittee on Human Resources of the House Committee on Post Office and Civil Service revealed that during a typical twenty-seven-month period between January 1, 1989, and March 31, 1991, $4,783,783.75 was spent to fly foreign officials on U.S. military aircraft.

Although some of these trips can be justified as being geopolitically useful, others, such as those that carry dignitaries on sightseeing journeys or to Palm Springs to play golf with the president, are a waste of taxpayers' money. In addition, all of these flights could be handled with less expense by using commercial carriers or even by renting private planes.

1. PRESIDENT OCHIRBAT OF MONGOLIA

   On January 21, 1991, the White House dispatched a C-137B from Washington, D.C., to Los Angeles to pick up President Punsalmaagiyn Ochirbat of Mongolia and a party of thirty-three and fly them back to Washington. After a two-day visit, thirty of the Mongolians were flown on to New York City. Flight costs: $106,817.96.

2. GENERAL ANGELES OF GUATEMALA

   On November 6, 1989, the U.S. Air Force picked up Guatemalan air force general Angeles and four companions in Guatemala, flew to El Salvador and picked up a party of four more, and flew them all to Austin, Texas. Three days later everyone was returned to Central America. On November 15, General Angeles and companions were picked up in Miami and, over a period of six days, transported to Washington, San Antonio, and Dothan, Alabama, before being returned to Florida. Flight costs: $104,031.76.

3. AMBASSADOR NAZARKIN OF THE USSR

   In December 1989 the Soviet ambassador was flown from Washington to El Toro, California, and back, with a stop in Albuquer-

President Punsalmaagiyn Ochirbat of Mongolia (left) and a party of 33 were flown from Los Angeles to Washington, D.C., and New York City at a cost to U.S. taxpayers of over $100,000.

que, New Mexico. He was accompanied by a party of twenty-five. Flight costs: $101,074.81.

4. AIR MARSHAL KASET OF THAILAND

In February 1990 Air Marshal Kaset of the Thai air force was flown by the U.S. Air Force from Seattle to Forth Worth, Texas, and then on to San Antonio. Kaset was then picked up at Kelly Air Force Base and returned to Fort Worth. The next day he was taken to Washington, D.C. Two days after that, Kaset and a party of seven were flown from D.C. to Las Vegas before being taken to Tacoma, Washington, after another two days. Flight costs: $96,325.09.

5. GREENLAND PARLIAMENT

On May 17, 1989, the Joint Chiefs of Staff dispatched a plane from Andrews Air Force Base to Greenland to pick up eleven representatives of the Greenland Parliament. The legislators were flown to Washington, D.C. There, their party grew to fourteen and they were flown to Colorado Springs before being returned to Greenland. Flight costs: $93,003.34.

6. MINISTER OF DEFENSE COEME OF BELGIUM

During one week in September 1989, Coeme and several companions were flown by the Department of Defense from New York City to Washington, D.C.; to Norfolk, Virginia, and back to Washington; to Whiteman Air Force Base in Missouri; Carswell Air Force Base in Texas; Las Vegas; and the Grand Canyon. Flight costs: $82,190.56.

7. PRIME MINISTER KAIFU OF JAPAN

On March 1, 1990, a plane was sent from Washington, D.C., to Los Angeles. The next day, the aircraft picked up Prime Minister Kaifu and his party of thirty-four and flew forty minutes to Palm Springs, where Kaifu met with President Bush at a country club. The following day, Kaifu and a party of thirty-seven were flown back to Los Angeles, and the aircraft returned to Washington with no passengers. Flight costs: $36,202.29.

8. THE WIFE OF PRESIDENT MITTERRAND OF FRANCE

On May 20, 1989, an Air Force C-20B was sent to New York City to pick up Mrs. Mitterrand and fly her to Pease Air Force Base in New Hampshire. From there she was taken by helicopter to President Bush's home in Kennebunkport, Maine. Flight costs (not including the helicopter ride): $11,503.63.

10 AMERICA

The Real People Behind
6 Popular American Images

1. **UNCLE SAM**

   Samuel Wilson (1766–1854) was a self-made man who founded a meat-packing business in Troy, New York, in 1790. By the time of the War of 1812, Wilson had become a prominent citizen and so won a contract to supply meat to the U.S. Army. During a tour of Wilson's plant on October 2, 1812, Governor Daniel Tompkins of New York noticed the initials *EA-US* on the barrels of meat waiting to be shipped to the army. When he asked what that meant he was told that *EA* stood for Elbert Anderson, the contractor for whom Wilson worked. The *US* was an abbreviation for United States, but a workman joked that it really stood for "Uncle Sam" Wilson. The story spread, and because Wilson had a reputation for being honest and hardworking, by the end of the war Uncle Sam had become a symbol of both the national character and the federal government.

2. **THE STATUE OF LIBERTY**

   The famous statue in New York harbor was sculpted by France's Frédéric Auguste Bartholdi. Originally entitled *Liberty Enlightening the World,* it was dedicated in 1886 and became popularly known as the Statue of Liberty. At the time that Bartholdi was working on Liberty, he was in love with a young woman named Jeanne-Emilie Baheux de Puysieux, a dressmaker's assistant from Nancy. He used Baheux de Puysieux as the model for the statue's arms. However, when it came to fashioning Liberty's face, he felt that Jeanne-Emilie was too beautiful. He needed someone who looked strong, trustworthy, and long-suffering to symbolize the perseverance needed to achieve liberty. He chose his mother, Charlotte Bartholdi.

3. Indian Head/Buffalo Nickel

The buffalo nickel was minted between 1913 and 1938. On one side is the head of an American Indian. Previous designs of Indian head coins had used white models, but James Earle Fraser, the world-renowned sculptor who got the job to do the five-cent piece, chose real Native Americans. Chief John Big Tree of the Iroquois nation was the model for the nose and forehead. Two Moons, a Cheyenne, posed for the hair and headdress, and Iron Tail, one of the Sioux warriors who defeated General Custer at the Little Big Horn, modeled for the cheek and chin. For the buffalo, Fraser traveled to the wilds of Central Park Zoo in New York City and sketched an old buffalo named Black Diamond. Two years after the coin bearing his likeness was issued, Black Diamond was slaughtered and sold for $100. His body yielded 750 pounds of meat, his hide was turned into a robe, and his head became a trophy.

4. American Gothic

Grant Wood's 1930 painting portrayed a somber-faced Iowa farmer holding a pitchfork and his even more somber-faced daughter. The daughter was modeled after the artist's sister, Nan Wood Graham, who later said that the fame she gained saved her from "a very drab life as the world's worst stenographer." The model for the farmer was Byron McKeeby, a local dentist.

Nan Wood and Byron McKeeby — models for Grant Wood's *American Gothic*.

5.–6. BARBIE AND KEN

Ruth Handler watched her daughter, Barbie, play with paper dolls and thought that little girls would rather own a fashion doll with a large wardrobe and hair they could comb. In 1959 she and husband, Elliot, the founders of Mattel Inc., introduced the Barbie doll. Three years later they added a boy doll and named it after their son, Ken. By the time the dolls were marketed, the real Barbie was a teenager and too old to play with dolls. Between them, the real Barbie and Ken had three daughters, but none of them played with Barbie and Ken dolls either.

15 Best Places to Live in the United States

Each year *Money* magazine ranks three hundred U.S. metropolitan areas in nine categories: health, crime, economy, housing, education, transit, weather, leisure, and arts. Here are the overall winners for a six-year period.

	Median Placing (1987–1992)
1. San Francisco, California	5.5
2. Los Angeles, California	15.0
3. Boston, Massachusetts	16.5
3. Seattle, Washington	16.5
5. Minneapolis/St. Paul, Minnesota	21.0
6. New Orleans, Louisiana	24.5
7. Honolulu, Hawaii	27.0
8. Duluth, Minnesota	31.5
9. Fargo, North Dakota	33.0
10. Kenosha, Wisconsin	34.5
10. Oakland, California	34.5
12. Provo/Orem, Utah	35.0
13. Houston, Texas	35.5
14. Tacoma, Washington	36.5
15. San Diego, California	37.0

15 Worst Places to Live in the United States

	Median Placing (1987–1992)
1. Waterbury, Connecticut	296.0
2. Rockford, Illinois	294.0
3. Jackson, Michigan	292.0
4. Benton Harbor, Michigan	289.5
4. Fall River, Massachusetts	289.5
4. Muskegon, Michigan	289.5
7. Battle Creek, Michigan	288.0
7. New Bedford, Massachusetts	288.0
9. Mansfield, Ohio	284.5
10. Flint, Michigan	284.0
11. Poughkeepsie, New York	281.5
12. Atlantic City, New Jersey	279.5
13. Des Moines, Iowa	277.5
14. Lima, Ohio	274.0
15. Anderson, South Carolina	271.0

15 Most Segregated Cities in the United States

The index of dissimilarity represents the percentage of blacks or whites who would have to be moved to a different block to produce a completely integrated city.

	Index of Dissimilarity
1. Gary, Indiana	91
2. Detroit, Michigan	89
3. Chicago, Illinois	87
4. Cleveland, Ohio	86
5. Buffalo, New York	84
6. Flint, Michigan	84
7. Milwaukee, Wisconsin	84
8. Saginaw, Michigan	84
9. Newark, New Jersey	83
10. Philadelphia, Pennsylvania	82
11. St. Louis, Missouri	81
12. Ft. Myers, Florida	81
13. Sarasota, Florida	80
14. Indianapolis, Indiana	80
15. Cincinnati, Ohio	80

SOURCE: Reynolds Farley and William H. Frey, "Changes in the Segregation of Whites from Blacks During the 1980s: Small Steps Toward a More Racially Integrated Society" (Ann Arbor, Michigan: Population Studies Center, University of Michigan, September 1992).

15 Least Segregated Cities in the United States

This list is dominated by places whose economic base involves the armed forces; they comprise eight of the top ten.

	Index of Dissimilarity
1. Jacksonville, North Carolina	31
2. Lawton, Oklahoma	37
3. Anchorage, Alaska	38
4. Lawrence, Kansas	41
5. Fayetteville, North Carolina	41
6. Clarksville, Tennessee	42
7. Anaheim, California	43
8. Ft. Walton Beach, Florida	43
9. Cheyenne, Wyoming	43
10. Honolulu, Hawaii	44
11. Tucson, Arizona	45
12. Danville, Virginia	45
13. San Jose, California	45
14. Charlottesville, Virginia	45
15. Killeen, Texas	45

SOURCE: Reynolds Farley and William H. Frey, "Changes in the Segregation of Whites from Blacks During the 1980s: Small Steps Toward a More Racially Integrated Society" (Ann Arbor, Michigan: Population Studies Center, University of Michigan, September 1992).

10 Richest Places
in the United States

	Per Capita Income (1990)	White (%)
1. Marin Co., California	$28,381	84.6
2. New York Co., New York	27,862	48.9
3. Pitkin Co., Colorado	26,755	94.4
4. Falls Church City, Virginia	26,709	85.5
5. Fairfield Co., Connecticut	26,161	79.8
6. Arlington Co., Virginia	25,633	69.5
7. Montgomery Co., Maryland	25,591	72.4
8. Westchester Co., New York	25,584	73.3
9. Alexandria City, Virginia	25,509	64.3
10. Morris Co., New Jersey	25,177	88.4

SOURCE: 1990 Census of Population and Housing, Income Statistics Branch/HHES Division, U.S. Bureau of the Census.

10 Poorest Counties
in the United States

	Per Capita Income (1990)	Dominant Ethnic Group (%)
1. Shannon Co., South Dakota	$3,417	94.7 Sioux
2. Starr Co., Texas	4,152	97.2 Hispanic
3. Zavala Co., Texas	4,818	89.4 Hispanic
4. Todd Co., South Dakota	5,043	82.4 Sioux
5. Buffalo Co., South Dakota	5,067	77.6 Sioux
6. McCreary Co., Kentucky	5,153	98.7 White
7. Maverick Co., Texas	5,184	93.5 Hispanic
8. Sioux Co., North Dakota	5,185	75.4 Sioux
9. Jefferson Co., Mississippi	5,349	85.9 Black
10. Dimmit Co., Texas	5,386	83.3 Hispanic

SOURCE: 1990 Census of Population and Housing, Income Statistics Branch/HHES Division, U.S. Bureau of the Census.

8 Dangerous Places and
3 Safe Places
in the United States

DANGEROUS PLACES

1. HIGHEST MURDER RATE

East St. Louis, Illinois

Population:	41,346
Murders:	67
Rate:	1 of 617 murdered

2. SECOND-HIGHEST MURDER RATE

Highland Park, Michigan

Population:	20,278
Murders:	22
Rate:	1 of 922 murdered

3. HIGHEST MURDER RATE, POPULATION OVER 50,000

Compton, California

Population:	92,338
Murders:	87
Rate:	1 of 1,061 murdered

4. HIGHEST MURDER RATE, POPULATION OVER 100,000

Washington, D.C.

Population:	598,000
Murders:	482
Rate:	1 of 1,241 murdered

5. HIGHEST RAPE RATE

Benton Harbor, Michigan

Population:	12,918
Forcible Rapes:	54
Rate:	1 of 120 women raped

6. Second-Highest Rape Rate

Highland Park, Michigan	Population:	20,278
	Forcible Rapes:	76
	Rate:	1 of 134 women raped

7. Highest Rape Rate, Population over 25,000

Saginaw, Michigan	Population:	70,055
	Forcible Rapes:	198
	Rate:	1 of 177 women raped

8. Highest Rape Rate, Population over 100,000

Minneapolis, Minnesota	Population:	373,303
	Forcible Rapes:	744
	Rate:	1 of 251 women raped

Safe Places

1. Largest City Without a Murder

| Lincoln, Nebraska | Population: | 193,749 |

2. Largest City Without a Rape

| Appleton, Wisconsin | Population: | 66,543 |

3. Largest City Without a Murder or Rape

| Clay Town, New York | Population: | 54,525 |

SOURCE: *Uniform Crime Reports,* "Crime in the United States 1991"; U.S. Department of Justice, Federal Bureau of Investigation, 1992.

NOTE: Rape figures for the state of Illinois are not included because the Illinois definition of rape includes rapes of males, whereas all other states only count female victims.

13 Quotations from Foreign Observers About America and Americans

1. "The thing that impresses me most about America is the way parents obey their children." — *Edward, duke of Windsor, abdicated British king (1957)*

2. "America is a large, friendly dog in a very small room. Every time it wags its tail, it knocks over a chair." — *Arnold Toynbee, British historian (1954)*

3. "American youth attributes much more importance to arriving at driver's license age than at voting age." — *Marshall McLuhan, Canadian author (1964)*

4. "In America the young are always ready to give to those who are older than themselves the full benefits of their inexperience." — *Oscar Wilde, Irish author (1887)*

5. "America is the only nation in history which miraculously has gone directly from barbarism to degeneration without the usual interval of civilization." — *Georges Clemenceau, French statesman (1945)*

6. "What the United States does best is to understand itself. What it does worst is understand others." — *Carlos Fuentes, Mexican novelist (1986)*

After visiting the United States, Oscar Wilde said, "In America the young are always ready to give to those who are older than themselves the full benefits of their inexperience."

7. "Every time Europe looks across the Atlantic to see the American eagle, it observes only the rear end of an ostrich." — *H. G. Wells, British author (1907)*

8. "Woman governs America because America is a land of boys who refuse to grow up." — *Salvador de Madariaga, Spanish statesman*

9. "In America, through pressure of conformity, there is freedom of choice, but nothing to choose from." — *Peter Ustinov, British actor (1970)*

10. "One comes to the United States — always, no matter how often — to see the future. It's what life in one's own country will be like five, ten, twenty years from now." — *Ehud Yonay, Israeli writer (1977)*

11. "America is a country that doesn't know where it is going, but is determined to set a speed record getting there." — *Lawrence J. Peter, Canadian educator (1977)*

12. "In America you watch TV and think that's totally unreal, then you step outside and it's just the same." — *Joan Armatrading, British singer (1981)*

13. "I love America, but you don't bother to think anymore; you just want entertainment." — *Oriana Fallaci, Italian journalist (1972)*

Political Asylum Seekers
Ranked by *15* Nations of Origin

Each year the U.S. Immigration and Naturalization Service processes about 50,000 applications for political asylum. However, the disposition of these cases varies widely depending on the national origin of the applicant.

	Applications Granted (%)
1. China	89.5
2. Somalia	86.5
3. Soviet Union	82.4
4. Syria	68.4
5. Panama	67.4
6. Ethiopia	59.3
7. Romania	54.9
8. Nicaragua	16.2
9. Philippines	4.8
10. Poland	4.2
11. El Salvador	2.6

	Applications Granted (%)
12. Fiji	1.5
13. Guatemala	1.4
14. Honduras	1.1
15. Haiti	0.6

SOURCE: U.S. Immigration and Naturalization Service, *1990 Statistical Yearbook of the Immigration and Naturalization Service* (Washington, D.C.: U.S. Government Printing Office).

10 Most Common City Names in the United States

	Cities
1. Fairview	66
2. Midway	52
3. Oak Grove	44
4. Franklin	40
5. Riverside	40
6. Centerville	39
7. Mount Pleasant	38
8. Georgetown	37
9. Salem	36
0. Greenwood	34

SOURCE: Copyright 1989, *USA Today*. Reprinted with permission.

40 Curious Place Names in the United States

1. Acres of Diamonds, Florida
2. Bald Head, Maine
3. Belcher, New York
4. Ben Hur, Texas (or Ben Hur, Virginia)
5. Big Foot, Illinois
6. Boring, Maryland
7. Buddha, Indiana
8. Chocolate Bayou, Texas
9. Ding Dong, Texas
10. Disco, Tennessee
11. Dismal, Tennessee
12. Eclectic, Alabama

13. Eek, Alaska
14. Fearnot, Pennsylvania
15. Frankenstein, Missouri
16. Gun Barrel City, Texas
17. Hell, Michigan
18. King Arthur's Court, Michigan
19. Lawyersville, New York
20. Lollipop, Texas
21. Muck City, Alabama
22. Odd, West Virginia
23. Ogle, Kentucky
24. Okay, Oklahoma
25. Panic, Pennsylvania
26. Plain City, Utah
27. Porkey, Pennsylvania
28. Quiggleville, Pennsylvania
29. Rambo Riviera, Arkansas
30. River Styx, Ohio
31. Roachtown, Illinois
32. Romance, Arkansas
33. Sandwich, Illinois
34. Toad Suck, Arkansas
35. Two Egg, Florida
36. Uncle Sam, Louisiana
37. Voltaire, North Dakota
38. War, West Virginia
39. Worstville, Ohio
40. Zap, North Dakota

NOTE: For more curious place names, see *The People's Almanac #2*, pp. 1124–25.

11 Unusual Street Names

1. Road to Happiness, Vermilion, Ohio 44089
2. Sir Galahad Drive, Riverside, California 92057
3. None Such Place, New Castle, Delaware 19720
4. Almosta Road, Darby, Montana 59829
5. Ewe Turn, Kaysville, Utah 84037
6. Family Circle, Sandy, Utah 84070
7. Memory Lane, Salt Lake City, Utah 84117
8. The Living End, Austin, Texas 78746
9.–11. Damn If I Know, Damn If I Care, Damn If I Will, Boca Grande, Florida 33921

Senator Barry Goldwater's *5* Greatest Americans in History

Perhaps the best-known conservative in American politics, Barry Goldwater served as United States senator from Arizona from 1952 to 1964, and again from 1969 to 1987. He was the Republican candidate in the 1964 presidential election, and has authored the best-sellers *The Conscience of a Conservative* (1960) and *Why Not Victory?* (1962).

1. Abraham Lincoln
2. Theodore Roosevelt
3. Douglas MacArthur
4. Dwight Eisenhower
5. Geronimo

— Exclusive for *The Book of Lists*

August Meier's
12 Lesser-Known Influential
Black Americans

Meier, a historian specializing in the study of African-Americans, has taught at several black colleges, is a Guggenheim Fellow, and has been president of the Southern Historical Association. His many books include *Negro Thought in America, 1880–1915; Black Leaders of the Nineteenth Century* (with Leon Litwack); and *CORE: A Study in the Civil Rights Movement, 1942–1968* and *Black History and the Historical Profession, 1915–1980* (both with Elliott Rudwick).

1. J. MERCER LANGSTON (1829–1897)

   Abolitionist and congressman.

2. RICHARD ALLEN (1760–1831)

   Founder of the African Methodist Episcopal Church.

3. PAUL CUFFE (1759–1817)

   Turn-of-the-nineteenth-century ship owner, merchant, and nationalist (early advocate of colonization in Africa).

4. WALTER FRANCIS WHITE (1893–1955)

   Executive secretary of the National Association for the Advancement of Colored People (NAACP), 1930–1955.

5. CHARLES H. HOUSTON (1895–1950)

   Prominent lawyer and architect of the NAACP's desegregation litigation. Thurgood Marshall was his best student at Howard University Law School, and worked closely with him.

6. MARY MCLEOD BETHUNE (1875–1955)

   Important figure among both men and women. Founder, and, for many years, president of the National Council of Negro Women, and one of the leading black office holders in the New Deal period, in charge of work among blacks in the National Youth Administration. Founder of Bethune-Cookman College.

7. WILLIAM H. HASTIE (1904–1976)

   Lawyer, close to both Houston and White; governor of Virgin Islands; first black to be appointed a federal district court judge and later first circuit court judge. Important for his behind-the-scenes involvement in NAACP work.

8. MARY CHURCH TERRELL (1863–1954)

   First president of the National Association of Colored Women (1896). Active in civic work as a member of the District of Columbia Board of Education, active in the NAACP, and a noted speaker.

9. FRANCIS CARDOZO (1837–1903)

Eminent political figure during Reconstruction; especially known for serving as secretary of state of South Carolina.

0. HENRY HIGHLAND GARNET (1815–1882)

Abolitionist and nationalist (colonizationist) of the 1840s and 1850s.

1. ALEXANDER CRUMMELL (1819–1898)

Considered a leading intellectual among late-nineteenth-century blacks. Episcopal minister. Became an emigrant to Africa and advocate of colonization in mid-nineteenth century. After returning to the United States he founded the American Negro Academy.

2. JAMES FORTEN (1766–1842)

Philadelphia sailmaker in late eighteenth and early nineteenth centuries. Wealthiest black of his times. Active in abolitionist and other causes.

— Exclusive for *The Book of Lists*

Leonard Peltier's
11 Greatest Native Americans

n activist in the American Indian Movement, Leonard Peltier (a akota/Chippewa) is currently serving two consecutive life sen-ences for a 1975 incident in which two FBI agents were killed. mnesty International considers Peltier a political prisoner. The eonard Peltier Defense Committee claims the trial was unjust and s working to secure his release from prison. In 1985 Peltier re-eived the Spanish Human Rights Commission Prize.

1. CHIEF CRAZY HORSE — Oglala Lakota (Sioux)

War chief who led the Lakota nation to victory when General George A. Custer attacked their religious gathering camp on the Little Big Horn.

2. CHIEF SITTING BULL — Hunkpapa Lakota

One of the greatest leaders of the Lakota nation.

3. CHIEF GALL — Hunkpapa Lakota

Was adopted by Chief Sitting Bull as a younger brother and played a major part in the victorious battle at the Little Big Horn.

4. GERONIMO — Apache chief

5. CAPTAIN JACK — Modoc chief

Leader of the Modoc Indians in their long resistance to the outnumbering army forces. He asked for a reservation only six miles square; he got a house and six feet of ground.

6. QUANAH PARKER — Comanche chief

7. CHIEF JOSEPH — Nez Percé

Famous statement: "Hear me my chiefs, I am tired; my heart is sad and sick, from where the sun now stands I will fight no more forever."

8. CHIEF DULL KNIFE — Cheyenne

His greatest exploit was leading a homesick band of his people over hundreds of miles through troops ordered to kill them.

Quanah Parker, leader of the Kwahadi Comanches, was the son of a chief and a captured white woman.

Chief Joseph, leader of the Nez Percés.

9. DENNIS BANKS — Red Lake Chippewa
   Leader and founder of the American Indian Movement.

10. SEQUOYAH (GEORGE GUESS) — Cherokee
    Created the Cherokee alphabet, memorizing every letter in his head over a period of fourteen years.

11. CHIEF SEATTLE — Suquamish

— Exclusive for *The Book of Lists*

Victor Villaseñor's
18 Notable Chicanos of the Past

A leading Chicano writer, Villaseñor is the author of *Macho!* (1973) and *Jury: People vs. Juan Corona* (1976). His most highly acclaimed work is *Rain of Gold* (1991), which has been hailed as "the Mexican-American *Roots*." He is also the founder of Global Thanksgiving, which seeks to foster reconciliation among the races. The first celebration, held in Madrid in 1922, forgave Christopher Columbus for the atrocities committed by him and by his crews.

1. RAFAEL CHACÓN (1883–1925; New Mexico and Colorado)
   Union Army major; commander of Fort Stanton in 1864; territorial senator in New Mexico; treasurer and sheriff in Las Animas County, Colorado

2. ARCADIA BANDINI STEARNS BAKER (1827–1912; California)
   Philanthropist, socialite, investor; at time of her death, was considered wealthiest woman in southern California

3. OCTAVIANO LARRAZOLO (1859–1930; New Mexico)
   Governor and senator (first Mexican-born American elected to the U.S. Senate), attorney, district attorney for the Western District of Texas, educator

4. JOSÉ T. CANALES (1877–1976; Texas)
   Attorney, state legislator; his suit against Texas Rangers for its treatment of Mexican Americans led to its reduction in size

5. SARA ESTELA RAMÍREZ (1881–1910; Texas)
   Poet, feminist, teacher, political organizer, labor advocate, editor

6. MARIA ADELINA "NINA" OTERO WARREN (1881–1965; New Mexico)
   Businesswoman, philanthropist, author, superintendent of Santa Fe County schools, chairperson of Congressional Union (national suffragist group)

Arcadia Bandini Stearns Baker.

7. ALONZO PERALES (1899–1960; Texas)

   Attorney, diplomat, civil rights activist, one of the founders of the League of United Latin American Citizens (LULAC), author

8. DENNIS CHÁVEZ (1888–1962; New Mexico)

   U.S. congressman and senator, attorney, promoted free textbooks for children, equal rights advocate

9. ERNESTO GALARZA (1905–1984; California)

   Labor expert and organizer, author, sociologist, university professor, promoted bilingual education programs

10. CARLOS ALMARAZ (1941–1989; California)

    Prominent southern California artist, campaigned for grape workers' rights, protested materialism in the art world

11. GRACIELA OLIVÁREZ (1928–1987; New Mexico)

    First woman graduate of Notre Dame School of Law, attorney, political and civil rights advocate, director of Community Service Administration under President Jimmy Carter, TV station owner

12. MARIANO SAMANIEGO (1844–1907; Arizona)

    Elected to territorial legislature, businessman, Pima County board of supervisors, one of the founders of the Alianza Hispano-Americana

Dennis Chávez
1888–1962
United States Senator
USA 35

U.S. Senator Dennis Chávez was one of the first advocates of free textbooks for public school students.

13. CASIMIRO BARELA (1847–1920; Colorado)

Elected to Colorado house of representatives and senate, helped shape Colorado's constitution, cattle rancher

14. AMPARO RUIZ DE BURTON (1832–1895; California)

Author (among other works, *The Squatter and the Don*)

15. LEONOR VILLEGAS MAGNON (1876–1955; Texas)

Writer; teacher; set up hospital in Laredo, Texas, to nurse wounded soldiers during Mexican revolutionary period 1910–20; founder of the National White Cross (Mexico's equivalent of the Red Cross)

16. LUCÍA GONZÁLEZ PARSONS (c. 1852–1942; Texas and Illinois)

Author, labor leader, one of the founders of the Industrial Workers of the World, fought for eight-hour workday

17. GEN. JUAN NEPOMUCENO CORTINA (1824–1892; Texas)

Rancher and accused cattle rustler, Mexican provincial governor, fought with Benito Juárez against French intervention in Mexico, led resistance against Anglo injustice in Texas, perhaps best known for seizing Brownsville and proclaiming it the "Republic of the Rio Grande"

18. JUAN SEGUÍN (1806–1890; Texas)

Mayor of San Antonio and state legislator, captain in Texas cavalry and soldier for Mexico

— Exclusive for *The Book of Lists*

13 Annual Events

1. **F**ANCY **R**AT AND **M**OUSE **A**NNUAL **S**HOW (January)

   The American Fancy Rat and Mouse Association was founded in 1983 to promote the breeding and exhibition of rats and mice and to encourage their use as urban pets. The annual show features twenty exhibitors as well as competitions and trophies. Information: AFRMA (CAE), 9230 64th Street, Riverside, CA 92509. Phone: 909-685-2350.

2. **M**INNESOTA **C**HERRY **P**IT–**S**PITTING **C**ONTEST (February)

   Sponsored by the Minnesota Sit and Spit Club, whose 700 members are required to do at least one foolish thing a month. Information: Minnesota Sit & Spit Club, Omar McGuire, 45 N. Hill, Mankato, MN 56001. Phone: 507-625-4531.

Ideal markings of rats.

3. World's Shortest St. Patrick's Day Parade (March 17)

Running down Buchanan Street in Maryville, Missouri, the parade route is less than one-half block and is shortened each year. The 1993 route was 98.6 feet long. Information: Mark Allen, Chair, 422 N. Buchanan, Maryville, MO 64468. Phone: 816-562-9965.

4. International Leisure Suit Convention (March)

Although the main activity is "mingling," the convention also features a leisure suit fashion show, a white belt toss, and awards for various leisure suit categories, including Most Flammable. Information: WHO Radio, Van Harden, 1801 Grand Ave., Des Moines, IA 50309. Phone: 515-242-3671.

5. World Grits Festival (April)

A three-day celebration attended by 60,000 to 80,000 people. Events include grits-eating contests, grits grinding, music, sports, and a parade. Information: Roger Myers, Box 787, St. George, SC 29477. Phone: 803-563-2150.

6. World Championship Cow Chip–Throwing Contest (April)

Cow chips are dried cow turds. They emit no odor and when burned generate no soot. Early settlers used them for cooking and heating. The throw for distance is part of the annual Cimarron Territory Celebration. Entrants have come from all fifty states as well as six foreign countries. Information: Beaver

Richard Lee giving a disco line-dance lesson at the annual Leisure Suit Convention.

Beaver, Oklahoma, site of the Annual World Champion Cow Chip Throw.

Chamber of Commerce, Box 878, Beaver, OK 73932. Phone: 405-625-4726.

7. NATIONAL HOLLERIN' CONTEST (June)

Held the third Saturday in June to revive the lost art of hollering as a means of communication, the contest has been staged each year since 1969. Information: Spivey's Corner Volunteer Fire Dept., Ermon Godwin, Jr., P.O. Box 332, Spivey's Corner, NC 28335. Phone: 919-567-2156.

8. CHICKEN CLUCKING CONTEST (June)

Amateur chicken cluckers compete for trophies and poultry-related prizes. Live chickens are also displayed. Information: Department of Recreation and Parks, Office of Adventures in Fun, Recreation Pier, 1715 Thames Street, Baltimore, MD 21231. Phone: 301-396-9177.

9. LEFT-HANDED GOLFERS' NATIONAL AMATEUR CHAMPIONSHIP (Summer)

A seventy-two-hole tournament first held in 1937. There are separate contests for men, women, seniors, and superseniors. Information: Ken Ahrens, Exec. Secty./Treas., National Association of Left-Handed Golfers, P.O. Box 801223, Houston, TX 77280-1223. Phone: 713-464-8683.

10. UGLY TRUCK CONTEST (July)

Farm trucks and pickup trucks are eligible. Entrants are judged according to most rust, most dents, worst paint jobs, shattered or missing glass, most exhaust smoke, worst interior, and overall appearance. Information: Jeff Johnson, P.O. Box 150, Pelican Rapids, MN 56572. Phone: 218-863-6693.

11. GREAT KLONDIKE OUTHOUSE RACE (September)

Outhouses on wheels race along a 1.5-mile course through the streets of Dawson City, Yukon. Contestants who are unable to bring their own outhouses may rent them. Information: Klondike Visitors Assn., Box 389, Dawson City, Yukon, Canada Y0B 1G0. Phone: 403-993-5575.

12. RUNNING OF THE SHEEP (September)

A safe alternative to Spain's running of the bulls. Hundreds of Montana woollies charge down Main Street in Reedpoint for six blocks. Contests are held for the ugliest sheep and the prettiest ewe, and sheepherders gather to read poetry. Information: Marion Cain, Reedpoint Community Club, Reedpoint, MT 59069. Phone: 406-326-2193.

13. CALIFORNIA PRUNE FESTIVAL (September)

Staged annually in Yuba City, "the prune capital of the world," festival attendees can sample everything from prune chili to prune ice cream. Information: Ketchum Public Relations, 55 Union Street, San Francisco, CA 94111. Phone: 415-984-6353.

12 Museums of Limited Appeal

. TRAGEDY IN U.S. HISTORY MUSEUM (7 Williams St., St. Augustine, FL 32084; 904-825-2389)

Exhibits include the car in which Jayne Mansfield was decapitated, the ambulance in which Lee Harvey Oswald rode after being shot by Jack Ruby (and the stretcher he was carried in), and a 1718 Spanish jail cell complete with human skeletons.

. STRIPTEASE MUSEUM (29053 Wild Road, Helendale, CA; 619-243-5261)

Officially titled Exotic World, the Burlesque Hall of Fame and Museum, it is the domain of former exotic dancer Dixie Evans, whose specialty was imitating Marilyn Monroe. Items on display include breakaway sequined gowns, tasseled pasties, and Gypsy Rose Lee's black velvet shoulder cape.

. THE MARIE DRESSLER MUSEUM (212 King St. W., Cobourg, Ontario K9A 2N1; 416-372-5831)

Exhibits include five wax cylinders of songs by Dressler; a waxworks recreation of part of the set of *Min and Bill*, the film for which Dressler won the 1931 Academy Award; and the lace-trimmed dress she wore when she accepted the award.

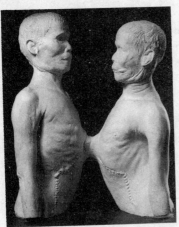

The body cast of Chang and Eng, the original Siamese twins — on display at the Mütter Museum.

Wax model of a woman's head with a six-inch, horn-like tumor — on display at the Mütter Museum.

4. AIR-CONDITIONING AND REFRIGERATION INDUSTRY MUSEUM (2220 S. Hill St., Los Angeles, CA 90007-1441; 213-747-0291)

   Open by appointment only, the museum includes a kerosene-powered fan, a leather gas mask used by workers who built ammonia-based refrigeration systems, and several displays honoring Willis Carrier who, at age twenty-five, invented air-conditioning in 1902.

5. LOCK MUSEUM OF AMERICA (130 Main St., Terryville, CT 06786; 203-589-6359)

   Terryville was the hometown of the Eagle Lock Company. On display are 22,000 locks and other lock-related items, including mail locks, iron locks, padlocks, enameled locks, and a 4,000-year-old Egyptian tumbler lock.

6. THE MÜTTER MUSEUM (College of Physicians of Philadelphia, 19 South 22nd St., Philadelphia, PA; 215-563-3737)

   This stunning collection of medical oddities and instruments includes the Chevalier Jackson collection of foreign bodies removed from the lungs and bronchi, the Sappey collection of mercury-filled lymphaticus, the B. C. Hirot pelvis collection and medical tools from Pompeii. Individual items include Florence Nightingale's sewing kit; the joined liver of Chang and Eng, the original Siamese twins; bladder stones removed

A Wire-Haired Fox Terrier modeling an adjustable repoussé dog collar made for Top and Tabinet, winners of the Great Champion all-aged (puppy) stakes for all England at Ashdown Park on December 14, 1838.

from U.S. Chief Justice John Marshall; a piece of John Wilkes Booth's thorax; a wax model of a six-inch horn projecting from a woman's forehead; a cheek retractor used in a secret operation on President Grover Cleveland, as well as the cancerous tumor that was removed from his left upper jaw.

7. THE DOG COLLAR MUSEUM (Leeds Castle, Maidstone, Kent ME17 1PL, United Kingdom; 0622-65400)

Housed in the Gate Tower of Leeds Castle, the museum features medieval and ornamental dog collars spanning four centuries. Included are numerous spiked collars designed for dogs used in hunting and bull- and bear-baiting.

8. THE OSCAR GETZ MUSEUM OF WHISKEY HISTORY (114 North Fifth Street, Bardstown, KY 40004; 502-348-2999)

Highlights of the collection are a copy of Abraham Lincoln's liquor license for the tavern he owned in New Salem, Illinois; an authentic moonshine still; and an 1854 E. G. Booz bottle from which the word *booze* was derived.

9. THE CAMPBELL MUSEUM OF SOUP TUREENS (Campbell Place, Camden, NJ 08101; 609-342-6440)

Established by the Campbell Soup Company, the museum specializes in eighteenth-century western European soup tureens. Included are tureens in the shape of swans, rabbits, vegetables, hens, ships, and even a pig head.

10. MUSEUM OF THE MOUSETRAP (Procter Bros., Ltd., Pantglas Industrial Estate, Bedwas, Newport, Gwent NP1 8XD, United Kingdom; 0222-882111)

Located at the main factory of the Procter Security Fencing Company, the museum contains approximately 150 mouse and rat traps, including a 5,000-year-old Egyptian trap and a French trap shaped like a guillotine.

11. KIM IL-SUNG GIFT MUSEUM (Mount Myohyang, North Korea)

Housed in a 120-room, six-story temple north of Pyongyang, the museum is home to 80,000 gifts that have been given to Kim Il-Sung, the fanatic dictator of Communist North Korea. Included are Nicolae Ceausescu's gift of a bear's head mounted on a blood-red cushion, a Polish machine gun, and a rubber ashtray from China's Hwabei Tire factory. Twenty rooms are devoted to gifts given to Kim's son, Kim Jong-Il, including an inlaid pearl and abalone box from the Ayatollah Khomeini and a pen set from the chairman of the journalist association of Kuwait.

12. THE VIBRATOR MUSEUM (938 Howard Street, San Francisco, CA 94103; 415-974-8985)

The Massagett, on display at the Vibrator Museum.

Between fifteen and twenty of the museum's seventy vibrators are on display at any given time. Antique models include a hand-crafted wooden vibrator that works like an egg-beater and another that advertises "Health, Vigor and Beauty" to users. The museum is housed in Good Vibrations, a sex toy emporium.

20 Unusual Items at the Smithsonian Institution

1. The seventeen-and-a-half-foot beard of Hans Langseth (1846–1927) of North Dakota
2. President Dwight Eisenhower's five-star pajamas
3. A silk purse made of a sow's ear
4. Seats and a ticket booth from Yankee Stadium circa 1920
5. General George Washington's tent (At one time the museum also had his false teeth on display, but they were stolen in 1981.)
6. Marie Antoinette's favorite earrings (confiscated from her as she tried to escape France)

7. The skeleton of a shark unearthed in Kansas
8. Archie Bunker's chair, Mister Rogers's sweater, J. R. Ewing's hat, Fonzie's leather motorcycle jacket, the scarecrow costume worn by Ray Bolger in *The Wizard of Oz*
9. The national tick collection (consisting of 120,000 ticks, representing 850 species); also 7,996 fleas, 1,272 lice, more than 14,000 neotropical mosquitoes, and 8,000 marine nematodes (threadworms)
10. Two mummified Egyptian bulls and a mummified cat and kitten
11. The gold nugget that set off the California Gold Rush of 1849
12. Owney, the Postal Dog (the mascot of the Railway Mail Service from 1888 to 1897, stuffed and on display)
13. The world's largest faceted gemstone by weight (a 22,892-carat, 12.3-pound, golden yellow topaz) and the world's largest perfect crystal ball (106 pounds)
14. Seven platypus skeletons and five wombat skins and skulls from Tasmania
15. A 1960s polka-dot bikini
16. Fourteen condom-vending machines and 108 condoms
17. Fifty parking meters
18. Soviet SS-20 nuclear missiles
19. Three-toed sloth from the island of Escudo De Veraguas near Panama
20. Detonator used by the DeAutremont brothers in a 1923 railway mail robbery

6 Esoteric Halls of Fame

1. BARBERING HALL OF FAME (Barber Museum, 2 South High Street, Canal Winchester, OH 43110)

Honors people who have made an outstanding contribution to the profession of barbering. Inductees include John Oster, inventor of the Oster motor-driven hand clipper and the Stim-U-Lax massage machine, and Robert Blacke Powell, author of *Antique Shaving Mugs of the United States* and other tonsorial works.

2. CROQUET HALL OF FAME (500 Avenue of Champions, Palm Beach Gardens, FL 33418)

Honors croquet players and enthusiasts, including ex-governor of New York Averill Harriman, playwright Moss Hart,

John Oster, inventor of the Oster motor-driven hand clipper and the Stim-U-Lax massage machine.

playwright George S. Kaufman, comic actor Harpo Marx, film producer Darryl Zanuck, and writer Alexander Woollcott.

3. FOLIAGE HALL OF FAME (57 E. Third St., Apopka, FL 32704-2507)

Recognizes people who have contributed to the foliage industry, including individuals who have developed new plants or made major contributions in foliage. Honorees include Harry Ustler, "Father of the Indoor Foliage Industry"; Dick Fuhr, who was instrumental in converting the industry from metal containers to plastic-style Lerio pots; and an abundance of growers from Apopka, Florida, which, coincidentally, is the home of the Foliage Hall of Fame.

4. PLASTICS HALL OF FAME (The Plastics Academy Inc., 280 Madison Avenue, New York, NY 10016)

Recognizes individuals whose contributions were so vital that the plastics industry would not be the same without them. Among the honorees are Ralph L. Harding, leader of the Society of Plastics Industry "during the turbulent era of 1967–80."

5. SHUFFLEBOARD HALL OF FAME (559 Mirror Lake Dr., St. Petersburg, FL 33507)

Induction is based on tournament victories, although executives of shuffleboard clubs are also allowed entry.

6. INTERNATIONAL SNOWMOBILE RACING HALL OF FAME
   (548 W34355 Rue Chantilly, Dousman, WI 53118)

   Each year three inductees are chosen, two in the driver category and one in the industry/support category. Notable honorees include Jim Aderua, who died in a snowmobile racing accident in 1975, and Audrey Decker, the only female member of the hall of fame.

Tony Wheeler's *10* Places "I Actually Like to Visit"

Tony Wheeler is an international travel writer and publisher of the Lonely Planet series of guides to out-of-the-way places. In this list he names a few locations that are better than their reputations.

1. HANOI

Despite regular visits by B-52s during the Vietnam War, Hanoi is actually a rather charming city with tree-lined streets and consistent French colonial architecture. The food and music are better in Saigon, but Hanoi can still be fun.

2. MONACO

Expensive, crowded, and snooty it may be, but once a year the principality comes alive for a week-long party to which everyone is invited: the Monaco Grand Prix. This is undoubtedly the world's most colorful and exciting auto race.

3. MEXICO CITY

You can't see through the smog, and the pickpockets are world-class, but the National Museum of Anthropology alone makes a visit worthwhile, and that's only one of the city's many attractions.

4. CALCUTTA

The very word may be synonymous with squalor and urban horrors, but Calcutta is never boring and it has an infectious zest for life. My wife and I were crossing Times Square in New York one hot August afternoon, and as we picked our way between potholes, beggars, and threatening taxis, she asked me what it reminded me of. "It's Calcutta," I replied without hesitation. I like New York, too.

A Chac Mool, a Toltec god, on display in Mexico's Museum of Anthropology.

5. RANGOON

It may not have received a lick of paint since World War II, but Rangoon is an utterly fascinating city with some of the friendliest people in the world. Now if they could just get rid of their inept, crazy government.

6. KABUL

I have not been to Kabul, Afghanistan, for many years, but I loved the place and look forward to the day I can once again wander down Chicken Street.

7. ALICE SPRINGS

Judging from its location on maps, the Alice (an area in the middle of Australia's Red Centre) looks like it should be nothing much in a lot of nothing at all. In fact it is Australia at its best — a region where you can positively feel how ancient the land is.

8. JAKARTA

Indonesia's megacity has a reputation as a boring superslum. In fact it has some colorful and intriguing corners, and the Indonesian people have an unbeatable, mischievous sense of fun.

9. NAGASAKI

The second atomic bomb to be dropped on a Japanese city actually missed the center, so many of Nagasaki's fascinating historical sites are still intact. Nagasaki also has nightlife just as active and colorful as any other Japanese city's.

10. BELFAST

As the Irish ditty goes, "She is handsome, she is pretty, she is the belle from Belfast city." I married a belle from Belfast, so how can I not like a city where *good crack* means noisy conversation and loud song over a pint of Guinness?

— Exclusive for The Book of Lists

David Stanley's
12 Worst Places to Visit

(In Alphabetical Order)

Travel writer David Stanley has visited 138 countries. His travel books include *Eastern Europe on a Shoestring* and *South Pacific Handbook*.

1. ANCHORAGE, ALASKA

   Perhaps the only exotic things in Anchorage are the table dancers who perform for oil workers flown in to let off steam. Apart from that, it's the Lower 48 at many times the price.

2. BARRANQUILLA, COLOMBIA

   If you must transit this wretched place, befriend a local resident on the bus or plane and pray that they'll accompany you to your destination. Otherwise you have a 90 percent chance of being mugged.

3. EBEYE, MARSHALL ISLANDS

   The armpit of the Pacific, Ebeye is the ghetto of the Kwajalein missile range, where native Marshallese laborers live in squalor just three miles from the country-club affluence enjoyed by the American missilemen.

4. GAO, MALI

   Here you'll have the honor of paying rip-off prices to sleep on the dirt floor of a miserable, unelectrified hotel and to eat stale food or drink warm sodas and beer. And one must give huge bribes to the police just to be allowed to leave.

5. KINGSTON, JAMAICA

   If you're white and want to feel what it's like to be on the receiving end of racial hatred, Kingston is an eye-opener. You stand a high chance of being robbed on streets where dope dealers openly ply their trades.

6. LOS ANGELES, CALIFORNIA

   If the freeways and smog don't strangle you, you may end up being liberated from your valuables at knife point if you wander into the wrong side of town. None of the area's artificial attractions are in L.A. proper, so get out while you can.

7. MANCHESTER, ENGLAND

The residents of this depressing industrial city have king-size chips on their shoulders and will treat you with the contempt you deserve for having come.

8. MURUROA ATOLL, FRENCH POLYNESIA

Unless you're French, you won't be allowed anywhere near this nuclear testing facility that Charles de Gaulle wisely placed on the opposite side of the globe from Paris. You may still get a free taste of it — nuclear contamination may already be leaking from Mururoa, though French security makes this difficult to confirm.

9. ONITSHA, NIGERIA

Unparalleled overcrowding, abject poverty, bumper-to-bumper traffic crawling along disintegrating roads, rampant disease, racial hatred, and the constant threat of violence or crime — you'll find it all in Onitsha.

10. OSLO, NORWAY

Norway is one of the most expensive countries on earth and the Norwegians seem to delight in devising new ways of extracting extra unearned income from visitors. Those who balk are treated with the utmost contempt.

11. PORT MORESBY, PAPUA NEW GUINEA

Even if you don't get robbed or raped by Port Moresby's countless "rascals," you'll face prices that are just as much of a rip-off.

12. RIJEKA, CROATIA

This Adriatic port lost its soul under a hail of wartime bombs and you don't have to drive far into the old town to sense the confusion and decay. The belching industry, automobiles, shipyards, refineries, cranes, and container ships jammed into the narrow coastal strip aren't beautiful, but if you like punishment Rijeka will give it to you.

— Exclusive for *The Book of Lists*

10 Nations Visited by the Most Tourists

	Tourist Arrivals (1992)
1. France	58,500,000
2. United States	45,500,000
3. Spain	36,054,000
4. Italy	26,974,000
5. Hungary	22,500,000
6. Austria	19,098,000
7. United Kingdom	17,855,000
8. Mexico	17,587,000
9. Canada	16,322,000
10. Germany	15,950,000

SOURCE: World Tourism Organization (WTO).

10 Countries Not Often Visited by Americans

	U.S. Visitors (1991)
1. Niue	18
2. Saõ Tomé and Principé	25[1]
3. Tuvalu	63
4. Chad	370
5. Kiribati	372
6. Gambia	381[2]
7. Iran	454
8. Bhutan	509
9. Sudan	524

Niue islanders waiting for Americans.

	U.S. Visitors (1991)
10. Nigeria	644[3]

SOURCE: World Tourism Organization (WTO).

[1] = 1987
[2] = 1990
[3] = 1989

NOTE: This list does not include nations that do not report to the World Tourism Organization, such as Albania, Cambodia, Equatorial Guinea, North Korea, and Vietnam.

10 Nations Whose Tourists Spend the Most Money Abroad

	Tourism Expenditures, U.S. Dollars (1992)
1. United States	43,648,000,000
2. Germany	37,166,000,000
3. Japan	26,982,000,000
4. United Kingdom	19,485,000,000
5. Italy	16,200,000,000
6. France	13,866,000,000
7. Canada	11,617,000,000
8. Netherlands	9,227,000,000
9. Austria	8,341,000,000
10. Belgium	6,700,000,000

SOURCE: World Tourism Organization (WTO).

6 Unusual Travel Opportunities

1. ELEPHANT POLO TOURNAMENT

Each December, the Meghauli airstrip in Nepal is shut down and transformed into a playing field for the annual world elephant-polo championships. Visitors will attend matches in the morning and view wildlife at a nearby animal sanctuary in the afternoon. (InnerAsia Expeditions, 2627 Lombard Street, San Francisco, CA 94123; 800-777-8183; 415-922-0448)

Fast action at the annual Elephant Polo Tournament.

2. SUBMARINE RIDE

For sixty-nine dollars, visitors to Grand Cayman Island can descend 150 feet in a twenty-eight-passenger, 50-foot-long submarine for a one-and-a-half-hour voyage among tropical fish and coral. (Atlantis Submarines Ltd., P.O. Box 1043, Grand Cayman Island, B.W.I.; 809-949-7700)

3. DOGSLEDDING IN GREENLAND

The highlight of a seven-day trip from Copenhagen is two days of dogsledding in the world of snow and ice surrounding Uummanaq, a town 250 miles (400 km) north of the Arctic Circle. (Borton Overseas, 5516 Lyndale Avenue South, Minneapolis, MN 55419; 800-843-0602)

4. WINTER BALLOON FESTIVAL

Sixty hot-air balloons from twenty countries converge in Switzerland in January for the annual Chateau d'Oex Winter Alpine Balloon Festival. Tour members will join in seven days of flying, including mass ascensions of the entire fleet. (The Bombard Society, 6727 Curran Street, McLean, VA 22101-3804; 800-862-8537)

5. COVERED WAGON ACROSS THE PRAIRIE

Travelers join a six-day wagon-train trek across the Nebraska prairies that recreates life along the Oregon Trail in 1850. (Oregon Trail Wagon Train, Rt. 2, P.O. Box 502, Bayard, NE 69334; 308-586-1850)

6. CAMPING IN THE SOVIET FAR EAST

Bering Air now makes regular flights between Nome, Alaska, and Provideniya, Siberia. Among the travel options of these flights is a five-night camping adventure in reindeer-hide tents in the remote Chukotka region of eastern Siberia. (Russian Desk, Bering Air, P.O. Box 1650, Nome, AK 99762; 907-443-5620)

10 Leading Sources of Visitors to the United States

	Visitors (1992)
1. Canada	18,580,620
2. Mexico	8,170,351
3. Japan	3,652,828
4. United Kingdom	2,823,983
5. Germany	1,691,663
6. France	795,444
7. Italy	589,837
8. Australia	486,851
9. Brazil	475,266
10. China	411,131

SOURCE: World Tourism Organization (WTO).

10 Leading Sources of Stowaways to the United States

	Stowaways (1986–1992)
1. Dominican Republic	720
2. Colombia	569
3. Jamaica	318
4. Haiti	56
5. Mexico	52
6. Ecuador	50
7. Honduras	44
7. Cuba	44
9. Dominica	41
10. Guatemala	36

SOURCE: U.S. Immigration and Naturalization Service, *Statistical Yearbooks of the Immigration and Naturalization Service* (Washington, D.C.: U.S. Government Printing Office).

7 Lost Treasures

According to Thomas Terry, author of the *U.S. Treasure Atlas*, there are 50,000 places where buried, sunken, or lost treasures can be found. For more information, write to Specialty Publishing Co., P.O. Box 1355, La Crosse, WI 54602.

1. MEXICAN GOLD

   In the early 1930s, a Mexican citizen smuggled almost 1 million ounces of gold bullion by plane to a remote area in the extreme northwestern corner of New Mexico. The gold, apparently still hidden in San Juan County, is now worth more than $400 million.

2. PADRE LA RUE'S CHURCH TREASURE

   Fleeing the Indian rebellion of the 1760s, Padre La Rue, a Spanish priest, took gold and silver that had been mined by the Indian laborers, as well as church vessels and ornaments. He buried the treasure in what is now part of White Sands Missile Range, New Mexico. In 1977 the government allowed a group to look for treasure buried on the base, then declared the area off-limits. Today, that cache is valued at more than $1 billion.

3. BELLAMY-WILLIAMS PIRATE LOOT

   In 1716 and 1717, pirates Charles Bellamy and Paul Williams built a fort near the mouth of the Machias River in Washington County, Maine. A vast network of underground vaults was constructed to hide their booty. Estimated value today: more than $200 million.

4. CHEROKEE CAVE OF GOLD

   In 1890 a man named William Waterhouse found a cave in Whitfield County, Georgia, in the heart of an ancient Cherokee Indian gold field. Inside, he discovered copper-coated gold bars, most of which were six feet long. He was unable to carry the treasure out and was unable to relocate the site. The cave, which was apparently used as a smelter and storehouse, holds possibly the largest remaining buried treasure in North America, valued at more than $10 billion.

5. CONFEDERATE TREASURE

   Toward the end of the U.S. Civil War, Rebel soldiers buried the treasury of the southern states, in the form of gold coins stored in 100 iron cooking pots, within 100 paces of the railroad tracks between McLeansville and Burlington, North Carolina. One kettle was recovered by a local farmer. The coins in the remaining 99 pots are now worth almost $50 million.

6. CHICAGO FIRE LOOT

   Within hours of the start of the famous Chicago fire of 1871, a band of looters plundered the homes of the wealthy, boarded a

schooner on Lake Michigan, and traveled to what is now th
Leelanau Peninsula of Michigan. There, the robbers secrete
most of the stolen goods. The spot is popular with treasur
hunters, but most of the loot, now valued at more than $6
million, remains to be found.

7. HUACHUCA CANYON GOLD

While walking with a fellow soldier near Ft. Huachuca, Ari
zona, in 1941, Robert Jones fell into a hole and discovered tw
sacks containing 100 pounds of gold bullion. Jones and hi
friend covered the hole and told no one. In 1959 Jones, with
crew and heavy machinery, was granted permission to reente
the military range and search for the hole. That search an
others since have proved futile. Value of the bullion today
more than $70 million.

9 of the World's Quietest Places

Most people have never experienced the outdoors without the in
trusion of man-made noise. Gordon Hempton, a nature recordis
tracks down the few areas where underground streams or th
wings of insects may still be heard. The result is a series of record
ings called *Earth Sounds*. Hempton lists a few of his favorite spot
here and invites reader recommendations for other quiet places
Write to The Sound Tracker, P.O. Box 9063, Seattle, WA 98109.

1. AMAZON RAIN FOREST, BRAZIL

If only one place could be heard as *the sound of life* it should b
the continuous forest north of Manaus. Layer after layer c
spectacular sounds grow upon the soundscape with only rar
intrusion by human presence; but outside the continuous for
est, where logging, mining, and subsistence farming are ev
erywhere, the noise-free interval (the period without human
caused noise) is zero. Enter this *Best Quiet Place* by specia
expedition and you will hear the memory of a lifetime.

2. KALAHARI DESERT, SOUTH AFRICA AND BOTSWANA

Very remote and desolate; however, motor-tourism is the stan
dard (for protection of tourists from wildlife attacks) an
diesel-powered generators are the rule at any settlement
therefore, the noise-free interval is often zero. Seek out th
most remote places with a guide service and the noise-fre
interval will exceed several hours. The sound of many squar

miles heard at the same time is an unforgettable experience that ranks among the world's most precious gifts.

3. SINHARAJA RAIN FOREST, SRI LANKA

Sri Lanka is a small island with 20 million people, yet, because of a cultural appreciation for wildlife and low technology (e.g., oxen instead of tractors), the opportunities for quietude are outstanding. Noise-free intervals are up to several hours at times. The most frequent noise source in most remote places is gunfire.

4. KAKADU NATIONAL PARK, AUSTRALIA

One of the world's last great quiet places, with noise-free intervals exceeding one hour. The indigenous bird population is totally intact, with a very high-spirited dawn chorus at the waterholes. Presence of numerous crocodiles contribute to long noise-free intervals.

5. FISH SPRINGS, UTAH

A very remote national wildlife refuge with a spectacular population of migratory waterfowl during early spring and fall, and some very unusual sounds of spitting fish! It's on the Pony Express route after sixty miles of unpaved road. No commercial jet traffic to speak of, probably because the air space is used for military testing. When this occurs, the quietest place suddenly becomes the noisiest place in a matter of seconds, but if you're lucky, the noise-free interval will exceed thirty minutes.

6. HAWAIIAN ISLANDS

The smallest and most remote islands in the group provide noise-free intervals which may exceed twenty minutes. Avoid tourist areas and all paved roads. Major sources of noise are commercial jet traffic and sightseeing helicopter rides. (Try Niihau.)

7. MEDICINE LODGE, KANSAS

The hills outside of this historic community offer some of the most spectacular listening in the Midwest, with noise-free intervals sometimes exceeding fifteen minutes. This is unheard of in the rest of the farming Midwest, where tractors are nearly always in the field. However, continuous noise may be present in many of the valleys outside of Medicine Lodge due to unmuffled oil wells, so watch out for these.

8. OLYMPIC NATIONAL PARK, WASHINGTON

A choice listening area for a variety of habitats that include ocean beach, mountain alpine (with glaciers), and temperate rain forests, all within a day's drive of Seattle. Noise-free intervals range from one and a half to fifteen minutes in most areas of the park that are in valleys without roads. Noise sources are usually chain saws and logging trucks operating in nearby Olympic National Forest, and from overhead commercial jet traffic.

9. SIERRA MORENA, SPAIN

Very few opportunities for quiet exist in all of Europe, but the area south of Ciudad Real is one of them. Noise-free interval is often several minutes in duration. It's never more than ten minutes, but still, this is exceptional in a region that is inundated by multiple noise sources.

10 Quotes from Astronauts About Being in Space

1. ALEKSEI LEONOV (*Voskhod 2;* March 18, 1965; first space walk)

"What struck me most was the silence. It was a great silence, unlike any I have encountered on Earth, so vast and deep that I began to hear my own body; my heart beating, my blood vessels pulsing, even the rustle of my muscles moving over each other seemed audible."

One of Leonov's tasks outside the spacecraft was to remove the lens cap from his camera and dispose of it. He considered setting it into its own orbit, "but I decided not to litter space. So I threw it with all my strength toward the Earth, looking after it until it disappeared from view."

2. JIM LOVELL (*Gemini 12;* November 11–15, 1966)

After crewmate Buzz Aldrin expressed awe at watching the blue Earth fly by, Lovell commented, "What did I tell you? Four days' vacation and see the world."

3. FRANK BORMAN (*Apollo 8;* December 21–27, 1968)

"All of us had flown airplanes many times and seen airfields and buildings getting smaller as we climbed. But now it was the whole globe receding in size, dwindling until it became a disk. We were the first humans to see the world in its majestic totality, an intensely emotional experience for each of us. We said nothing to each other, but I was sure our thoughts were

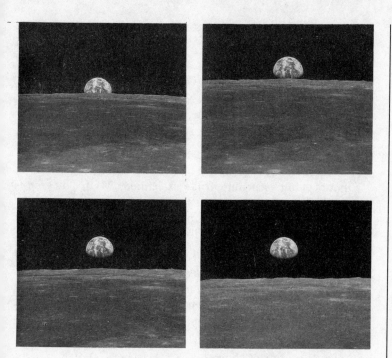

Earthrise as seen from the moon.

identical — of our families on that spinning globe. And maybe we shared another thought I had ... *This must be what God sees.*"

4. JIM LOVELL (*Apollo 8;* December 21–27, 1968)

After orbiting the moon and sending back the first televised images of its surface, Lovell, Borman, and Bill Anders successfully escaped the moon's gravitational pull and headed back to Earth on Christmas Day. Once he felt safe, Lovell contacted Mission Control in Houston, Texas, and reported, "Houston, please be informed there *is* a Santa Claus."

5. NEIL ARMSTRONG (*Apollo 11;* July 16–24, 1969; first landing on the moon)

After becoming the first human being to step onto the surface of the moon, Armstrong told the world, "That's one small step for a man, one giant leap for mankind." Because static in the transmission covered up the word *a*, Armstrong's famous quote was widely reported as "one small step for man."

6. CHARLES CONRAD (*Apollo 12;* November 14–24, 1969; second moon landing)

As he sat glued to the window, Conrad was asked to describe the moon's surface. He replied, "The moon is just sort of a very light concrete color. In fact, if I wanted to look at something that I thought was the same color as the moon, I'd go out and look at my driveway."

7. ALFRED WORDEN (*Apollo 15;* July 26–August 7, 1971)

"Now I know why I'm here. Not for a closer look at the moon, but to look back at our home, the Earth."

8. CHARLIE DUKE (*Apollo 16;* April 16–27, 1972; fifth moon landing)

As soon as the lunar module, *Orion,* landed on the moon, six hours behind schedule, Duke exclaimed, "Well, old *Orion* is finally here, Houston. Fantastic! All we have to do is jump out of the hatch and we've got plenty of rocks . . . Man, it really looks nice out there . . . I'm like a little kid on Christmas Eve."

9. HARRISON SCHMITT (*Apollo 17;* December 7–19, 1972; sixth and longest manned lunar landing)

After touching down on the moon and looking outside, Schmitt, filled with emotion, declared, "This is the most majestic moment of my life. This is something everyone's gotta do once in his life."

10. JACK LOUSMA (*Columbia STS-3;* March 22–30, 1982)

As his spaceship approached the night side of the Earth, Lousma described what he saw. "We're moving into the darkness, and the edge, the rim of the Earth, is very poorly defined. . . . It is a very poor gradation between what you see on the Earth and then the blackness of space. It's kind of, I guess, a lonely feeling of not knowing exactly where you're going because you can't define the edge of the Earth or see any stars yet."

20 Airlines Ranked by Number of Passenger Complaints

The major categories of complaints were flight problems (30.7 percent), baggage (14.5 percent), refunds (12.8 percent), and customer service (11.7 percent).

Airline	Complaints per 100,000 Passengers (1991)
1. Air Wisconsin	0.00
2. Midwest Express	0.00

3. Westair	0.14
4. Aloha	0.43
5. Horizon	0.44
6. Southwest	0.46
7. Delta	0.47
8. Alaska	0.48
9. Trump Shuttle	0.52
10. U.S. Air	0.63
11. Northwest	0.98
12. Continental	1.21
13. Markair	1.31
14. American	1.42
15. United	1.47
16. American Trans Air	1.63
17. Hawaiian	1.68
18. America West	1.76
19. Tower	4.19
20. TWA	4.46

SOURCE: *Air Travel Consumer Report,* Office of Consumer Affairs, U.S. Department of Transportation.

13 Miracle Deliveries

According to legend, several of Mark Twain's friends once wanted to send him a birthday greeting while he was traveling abroad. They had no idea where he was, so they simply addressed it "Mark Twain, God Knows Where." A few weeks later, they received this reply: "He did."

1. AN ISLAND

Actor James Cagney received a package from a foreign fan who knew only that Cagney lived on "An Island Off of Massachusetts, U.S.A." The post office delivered it to him at his Martha's Vineyard home.

2. GRANDPA AND GRANDMA

A letter addressed simply "Grandpa and Grandma, Rt. 1, Jonesboro, TX," and postmarked "Norfolk, NE," was correctly delivered in January 1990. An enterprising postmaster had telephoned the most likely recipient, whom he had seen only once or twice, and asked him whether he had a grandchild in Nebraska.

3. 30-YEAR-OLD CHRISTMAS CARD

Bert and Alberta Stocker of Blaina, Gwent, Wales, were unfortunately dead when their Christmas card finally arrived. It had taken thirty years to travel ten yards.

4. THE STONE HOUSE

A substitute carrier in Austin, Texas, successfully delivered a letter addressed to "Mr. and Mrs. Ed Ford (in the stone house with yellow trim near the end of Mansfield Drive out by the Dam)."

5. VIA QUICKEST ROUTE

A packet of mail from Shanghai, sent in 1939, took fifty years to reach England, having probably been intercepted by the Nazis. It contained among other things a request from a Methodist minister to marry. It was marked "VIA QUICKEST ROUTE." Fortunately, the Reverend Mark Earl married his bride-to-be anyway when she came out to China in 1940.

6. SOMEWHERE NEAR MILWAUKEE

A postcard mailed from Munich, Germany, traveled 4,000 miles and was properly delivered to the Harold Pipkorn family in five working days. The address was simply given as "Somewhere near Milwaukee, Freistadt, WI, USA."

7. THE NORTH POLE

The world's first nuclear-powered submarine, the *Nautilus*, traveled under the North Pole in 1958. One of the seamen, Denny Breese, wrote a lot of souvenir letters to his friends and family. One was to his brother, and it began, "Nick, this will be short, but I just found out that mail is leaving the boat in about 15 minutes." Breese needn't have hurried — the letter wasn't delivered to the family home in Chula Vista, California, for thirty-two years. Mr. Breese, Sr., who still lives there, said, "Oh my, yes, it was a big surprise. Denny didn't write that much. Maybe once a month at most."

This letter, mailed in Shanghai in 1939, was finally delivered after 50 years.

8. Grandma B

Avery Hanson, age five, of Charleston, North Carolina, had a Valentine for her great-grandmother, but didn't know how to address the envelope. In the return-address corner she wrote "Grandma B," with the apartment number, street name, and city (no state). She put an incorrect street address in the middle of the envelope and used a wildlife sticker for postage. Nevertheless, it was successfully delivered to Beatrice Folger in Greensboro.

9. Close But No Cigar

It took forty-two years for a letter from an office in the Federal Building in Eureka, California, to arrive at a post office box in the same building.

10. Behind the Water Tower

Mrs. Nancy Feldman of Spencerville, Maryland, received a letter mailed from Great Britain, even though the sender addressed it to the wrong town and could only describe Mrs. Feldman's general location: "Large old house — historic — behind the water tower — horse fence surrounding." On the envelope, the writer drew a little map to help the post office along.

11. Congratulations

A notice informing Thelma Hawkens of Tildem, Nebraska, of the birth of Beverly Hanks took fifty-one years to arrive, although it was sent from the same town. When Hawkens finally received it in 1985 (it bore a half-cent stamp), Hanks was already a fifty-one-year-old grandmother living in Illinois.

12. The World's Latest Thank-you Note

In 1922 a headmistress of a school in Somerset, England, sent a thank-you note for a Christmas calendar to a fourteen-year-old pupil, Marjorie Witts, living in Swansea, Wales. It arrived sixty-four years later, and was received by Lana Thomas, who currently lived at the address. Marjorie Witts, seventy-eight, had moved out more than fifty years earlier. Fortunately, she had stopped Mrs. Thomas in the street one day, told her she used to live in the house, and given her her new address.

13. The Slowest Delivery in History

In 1863 Union Private Horace H. Prindle lay wounded in a Tennessee hospital. He wrote a letter to Emline Marvin in Michigan, giving news of the Civil War. One hundred ten years later, it arrived at a senior citizens' home outside of Detroit, where Emline had once been a resident. No one could figure out how the postman knew this. The letter was eventually authenticated by a historical society.

9 Nations with the Most Neighbors

1. CHINA: 16

   North Korea, Russia, Mongolia, Kazakhstan, Kyrgyzstan, Tajikistan, Afghanistan, Pakistan, India, Nepal, Bhutan, Burma, Laos, Thailand, Macao, Hong Kong

2. RUSSIA: 14

   Norway, Finland, Estonia, Latvia, Lithuania, Poland, Belarus, Ukraine, Georgia, Azerbaijan, Kazakhstan, China, Mongolia, North Korea

3. BRAZIL: 10

   Guyane, Suriname, Guyana, Venezuela, Colombia, Peru, Bolivia, Paraguay, Argentina, Uruguay

4. GERMANY: 9

   Denmark, Netherlands, Belgium, Luxembourg, France, Switzerland, Austria, Czech Republic, Poland

5. SUDAN: 9

   Egypt, Libya, Chad, Central African Republic, Zaire, Uganda, Kenya, Ethiopia, Eritrea

6. ZAIRE: 9

   Central African Republic, Congo, Angola, Zambia, Tanzania, Burundi, Rwanda, Uganda, Sudan

7. FRANCE: 8

   Spain, Andorra, Monaco, Italy, Switzerland, Germany, Luxembourg, Belgium

8. TANZANIA: 8

   Kenya, Uganda, Rwanda, Burundi, Zaire, Zambia, Malawi, Mozambique

9. TURKEY: 8

   Bulgaria, Greece, Syria, Iraq, Iran, Azerbaijan, Armenia, Georgia

15 Largest
Independent Nations

	Square Miles	Square Kilometers
1. Russia	6,592,849	17,075,400
2. Canada	3,849,674	9,970,610
3. United States	3,787,425	9,809,431
4. China	3,689,631	9,556,100
5. Brazil	3,286,488	8,511,965
6. Australia	2,966,155	7,682,300
7. India	1,237,062	3,203,975
8. Argentina	1,073,400	2,780,092
9. Kazakhstan	1,049,156	2,717,300
10. Sudan	967,500	2,505,813
11. Algeria	919,595	2,381,741
12. Zaire	905,446	2,345,095
13. Saudi Arabia	830,000	2,149,690
14. Mexico	756,066	1,958,201
15. Indonesia	752,410	1,948,732

NOTE: Greenland, which is a self-governing territory under Danish protection, has an area of 840,004 square miles (2,175,600 square kilometers).

16 Smallest
Independent Nations

	Square Miles	Square Kilometers
1. Vatican City	0.2	0.4
2. Monaco	0.7	1.9
3. Nauru	8.1	21
4. Tuvalu	10	26
5. San Marino	24	61
6. Liechtenstein	62	160
7. Marshall Islands	70	181
8. St. Kitts and Nevis	104	269
9. Maldives	115	298
10. Malta	122	316
11. Grenada	133	344
12. St. Vincent and the Grenadines	150	388
13. Barbados	166	430
14. Antigua and Barbuda	171	443
15. Andorra	175	453
15. Seychelles	175	453

15 Most Populous Independent Nations

	Population (Mid-1992)
1. China	1,165,800,000
2. India	882,600,000
3. United States	255,600,000
4. Indonesia	184,500,000
5. Brazil	150,800,000
6. Russia	149,300,000
7. Japan	124,400,000
8. Pakistan	121,700,000
9. Bangladesh	111,400,000
10. Nigeria	90,100,000
11. Mexico	87,700,000
12. Germany	80,600,000
13. Vietnam	69,200,000
14. Philippines	63,700,000
15. Iran	59,700,000

SOURCE: Population Reference Bureau.

15 Least Populous Independent Nations

	Population (1993)
1. Vatican City	800
2. Nauru	9,000
2. Tuvalu	9,000
4. San Marino	23,000
5. Liechtenstein	28,000
6. Monaco	30,000
7. St. Kitts and Nevis	42,000
8. Marshall Islands	49,000
9. Andorra	54,000
10. Antigua and Barbuda	64,000
11. Seychelles	69,000
12. Kiribati	72,000
13. Dominica	87,000
14. Grenada	98,000
15. Tonga	103,000

SOURCE: Rand McNally, *World Facts and Maps* (Chicago: Rand McNally, 1993).

11 of the Oddest Items Found at London Transport's Lost Property Office

More than 100,000 items a year are lost by London Transport passengers. More than half the objects are found on London's buses, and the remainder on the Underground or the Light Railway. Unclaimed items end up in the lost property office store, which covers two-thirds of an acre.

1. A bottle of sperm from a prize bull
2. The bottom half of a theatrical coffin
3. The top bar from a Horse of the Year Show jump
4. An outboard motor
5. A stuffed bird of prey
6. Several wheelchairs
7. A box of false eyeballs (claimed by a hospital after six years)
8. A man's ashes in an urn
9. An artificial leg
10. A skeleton
11. A double bed

William Styron's
10 Favorite Novels

Born and educated in the South, Styron has a well-earned reputation for delving into controversial themes. Among his most highly acclaimed novels are *The Confessions of Nat Turner* (a first-person account of a slave revolt), which won a Pulitzer Prize, and *Sophie's Choice* (about a concentration camp survivor). His other books include *The Quiet Dust* and *Darkness Visible*.

1. *The Adventures of Huckleberry Finn,* by Mark Twain

   Still the glorious American classic.

2. *Madame Bovary,* by Gustave Flaubert

   No greater craft in a novel or keener insight into a woman's mind.

3. *Light in August,* by William Faulkner

   Among the master's most accomplished works; its tragic vision harrowing and dark.

Jennifer Jones in the title role of the 1949 film version of *Madame Bovary*.

4. *The Stranger,* by Albert Camus

Defines once and for all the stoic courage of the existential vision.

5. *Anna Karenina,* by Leo Tolstoi

One of literature's greatest creations — a woman eventually doomed but triumphantly alive.

6. *1984,* by George Orwell

An incomparably skilled satire of the totalitarian spirit.

7. *An American Tragedy,* by Theodore Dreiser

Ponderous and often crude, but a shattering chronicle of murder and puritanical guilt.

8. *Look Homeward, Angel,* by Thomas Wolfe

A lyrical and youthful celebration of small-town life in early twentieth century North Carolina. Still gorgeous.

9. *Lolita,* by Vladimir Nabokov

A great and scathing satire on America and a tragicomedy of sexual obsession.

10. *All the King's Men,* by Robert Penn Warren

About an American provincial dictator. One of the finest political novels ever written.

— Exclusive for *The Book of Lists*

James Michener's
10 Favorite Novels

American author James Michener has written some thirty-five books, the first of which, *Tales of the South Pacific* (1947), earned him a Pulitzer Prize. Other fiction works include *Hawaii* (1959) and *Centennial* (1974); his nonfiction works include *The World Is My Home: A Memoir* and *A Writer's Handbook*. During his long life (he was born in 1907), he has served in the U.S. Navy, run for Congress, taught college, and traveled to every continent, including Antarctica. *Mexico* (a project he began in 1959 but put aside and misplaced for thirty years) was finally released in 1992.

1. *Le Pére Goriot,* by Honoré de Balzac

Marvelous portrait of a city (Paris) and its minor inhabitants.

2. *Madame Bovary,* by Gustave Flaubert

As fine a portrait of a woman entangled in amorous daydreaming as has ever been composed. She leaps off the pages.

3. *The Idiot,* by Fëdor Dostoevski

I prefer this to the more famous novels of this master for its astonishing portrait of a fine young man on the edge.

4. *The Charterhouse of Parma,* by Stendhal

What a delightful depiction of a semicorrupt society as it torpedoes along in its conniving ways.

5. *Middlemarch,* by George Eliot

A softly stated, skillful depiction of the English countryside. Very shrewd observations.

6. *Anna Karenina,* by Leo Tolstoi

No young man who wants to be a writer can ever know enough about beautiful, headstrong women.

7. *The Magic Mountain,* by Thomas Mann

Masterful storytelling against a great setting and with unforgettable characters and themes.

8. *For Whom the Bell Tolls,* by Ernest Hemingway

One hell of a yarn unfolded by one hell of a writer.

9. *Oblomov,* by Ivan Goncharov

I spent most of my adult life fighting against Russia and its hideous form of government. I learned most about the Russian character from reading this book as a boy.

10. *Gone With the Wind,* by Margaret Mitchell

Sometimes you should read just for the simple pleasure it gives. What a masterfully constructed yarn on such a noble theme with such commanding characters.

Michener notes: I obviously go for the big blockbuster that gives me something to chew on for a week or more, but I also cherish the beautiful little goodies like Mann's *Death in Venice* and [Edith] Wharton's *Ethan Frome.*

— Exclusive for *The Book of Lists*

Tom Clancy's
6 Greatest War Novels

Tom Clancy's best-selling first novel, *The Hunt for Red October* (1984), was called "the perfect yarn" by President Ronald Reagan.

An insurance broker by profession, Clancy wrote *Red Storm Rising* (1986) after extensive research, including an interview of a highly placed Soviet defector. He followed that with another best-seller, *Patriot Games,* in 1987, and with *The Cardinal of the Kremlin* (1988), *Clear and Present Danger* (1989), and *The Sum of All Fears* (1991).

1. *Run Silent, Run Deep,* by Captain Edward L. Beach

   Adventures of a submarine patrol in the Pacific during World War II.

2. *The Third World War, August 1985,* by General Sir John Hackett

   Politically and technically detailed "historical" account of a future war between NATO and Warsaw Pact powers.

3. *HMS Ulysses,* by Alistair MacLean

   Men aboard British cruiser in dangerous Arctic waters during World War II are tested to limits of heroism and endurance.

4. *The Cruel Sea,* by Nicholas Monsarrat

   True story of two British ships and their crews in the North Atlantic during World War II.

5. *Fields of Fire,* by James Webb

   Marine platoon experiences horrors of jungle warfare in Vietnam.

6. *The Caine Mutiny,* by Herman Wouk

   Officers aboard U.S. Navy ship during World War II mutiny against their neurotic and exhausted captain, and are then court-martialed.

— Exclusive for *The Book of Lists*

Elmore Leonard's
10 Favorite Novels

Elmore Leonard, known for his thrillers and westerns, began his career in fiction in his spare time. In 1961 he sold *Hombre* to the movies (the film starred Paul Newman). Leonard's *Joe Kidd* (1972), starring Clint Eastwood, was followed closely by *Mr. Majestyk* (1974), with Charles Bronson. Many of Leonard's two dozen novels, including *Glitz* (1985), *Freaky Deaky* (1988), and *Killshot* (1989); his dozen screenplays; and his thirty or so short stories have won critical acclaim.

1. *All Quiet on the Western Front,* by Erich Maria Remarque

   The first book that made me want to write, when I was still in grade school.

2. *For Whom the Bell Tolls,* by Ernest Hemingway

   A book I studied almost daily when, in '51, I began to write with a purpose.

3. *A Stretch on the River,* by Richard Bissell

   The book that showed me the way I should be writing: not taking it so seriously.

4. *Sweet Thursday,* by John Steinbeck

   The book that showed the difference between honest prose and show-off writing.

5. *The Friends of Eddie Coyle,* by George V. Higgins

   Twenty years ago George showed how to get into a scene fast.

6. *Paris Trout,* by Pete Dexter

   An awfully good writer.

7. *The Heart of the Matter,* by Graham Greene

   Especially moving at the time it was written. I like everything he did, from *The Power and the Glory* to *Our Man in Havana*

8. *The Moviegoer,* by Walker Percy

   Walker, the old pro.

9. *Libra,* by Don DeLillo

   For my money, our finest current novelist.

10. Collected short stories of Hemingway, Joyce Carol Oates, Raymond Carver, and Bobbie Ann Mason

    Have studied and I hope learned from all of them.

    — Exclusive for *The Book of List*

Ken Follett's
10 Favorite Novels

Follett, one of the world's great spy-novel authors, was once a roc music columnist and later a publishing house editor. He wrote te books in his spare time, including *The Big Needle* (1974), *The Bea Raid* (1976), and *Eye of the Needle* (1978), which became his fir best-seller and allowed him to quit his day job. In 1989 he publishe a historical novel, *The Pillars of the Earth.* Now in his spare time he plays bass guitar in his son's rock band.

1. *Martin Chuzzlewit,* by Charles Dickens

   This contains my favorite character in all fiction, Sairy Gamp.

2. *Lonesome Dove,* by Larry McMurtry

   The best book of my favorite living writer.

3. *From Russia with Love,* by Ian Fleming

   I began to read James Bond stories when I was about twelve years old.

4. *Middlemarch,* by George Eliot

   The pinnacle of Victorian fiction.

5. *Summer Lightning,* by P. G. Wodehouse

   Wodehouse is the cleverest plotter in all fiction.

6. *Foundation,* by Isaac Asimov

   This and the other two books in the trilogy are among the few that I reread every ten years or so.

7. *Salem's Lot,* by Stephen King

   Still his best book, although *Needful Things* comes close.

8. *The Warden,* by Anthony Trollope

   I love Trollope and I'm so glad he wrote forty-seven novels.

9. *The Banker,* by Leslie Waller

   Uptight WASP falls in love with sexy Jewish girl and blows his cool.

10. *The Pillars of the Earth,* by Ken Follett

    Pretty darn good, though I say it myself.

— Exclusive for *The Book of Lists*

William Trevor's
10 All-Time-Favorite Novels

Irish short-story writer, novelist, and playwright, William Trevor is widely acclaimed for his genius at constructing stories about ordinary people in ordinary life. As he once said, "I'm very interested in the sadness of fate, the things that just happen to people." His novels include *The Children of Dynmouth* and *Fools of Fortune*; his short-story collections include *The Ballroom of Romance, and Other Stories* and *Angels at the Ritz, and Other Stories*. He is also the author of many television and radio plays for the British Broadcasting Corporation.

1. *Madame Bovary,* by Gustave Flaubert
2. *Great Expectations,* by Charles Dickens
3. *Middlemarch,* by George Eliot
4. *Emma,* by Jane Austen
5. *Remembrance of Things Past,* by Marcel Proust
6. *The Heart Is a Lonely Hunter,* by Carson McCullers
7. *Jude the Obscure,* by Thomas Hardy
8. *Fathers and Sons,* by Ivan Turgenev
9. *The Good Soldier,* by Ford Madox Ford
10. *Delta Wedding,* by Eudora Welty

— Exclusive for *The Book of Lists*

Sidney Sheldon's *10* All-Time-Favorite Books

Sidney Sheldon set out to become a composer but switched to screenwriting and won an Academy Award for his screenplay *The Bachelor and the Bobby-Soxer* (1947) and Screen Writers' Guild awards for *Easter Parade* (1948) and *Annie Get Your Gun* (1950). He created *The Patty Duke Show* and *I Dream of Jeannie* for television. Sheldon turned to writing novels in the 1970s and proved to be a best-selling author with such books as *The Other Side of Midnight* (1974) and *Rage of Angels* (1980). His most recent novel is *The Stars Shine Down* (1992).

1. *Rebecca,* by Daphne du Maurier

2. *Johnny Got His Gun,* by Dalton Trumbo
   A tour de force.

3. *Act One,* by Moss Hart
   One of the best autobiographies ever written about show business.

4. *Look Homeward, Angel,* by Thomas Wolfe
   Written by a man who loved language.

5. *Roosevelt and Hopkins,* by Robert Sherwood
   A spotlight on World War II.

6. Anything by James Thurber

7. *For Whom the Bell Tolls,* by Ernest Hemingway

8. *Of Human Bondage,* by W. Somerset Maugham
   Classic Maugham.

9. Anything by Booth Tarkington

10. *The Rise and Fall of the Third Reich,* by William Shirer
    Brilliant and revealing.

— Exclusive for *The Book of Lists*

The Favorite Books
of *20* Famous People

1. Jimmy Carter	*Let Us Now Praise Famous Men*, by James Agee and Walker Evans
2. Alistair Cooke	*Required Writing*, by Philip Larkin
3. Jacques-Yves Cousteau	*People*, by Peter Spier
4. Sally Field	*So Big*, by Edna Ferber
5. John Kenneth Galbraith	*Scoop*, by Evelyn Waugh
6. Whoopi Goldberg	*To Kill a Mockingbird*, by Harper Lee
7. Arsenio Hall	*Little Girl Lost*, by Drew Barrymore
8. Glenda Jackson	*Persuasion*, by Jane Austen
9. Gene Kelly	*Crock O'Gold*, by James Stephens
10. Ann Landers	*The Scarlet Letter*, by Nathaniel Hawthorne
11. Brian Mulroney	*A Thousand Days*, by Arthur Schlesinger
12. Linus Pauling	*The Origin of Species*, by Charles Darwin
13. Diane Sawyer	*Huckleberry Finn*, by Mark Twain
14. Charles Schulz	*The Silver Skates*, by Mary Mapes Dodge
15. Tom Smothers	*White Fang*, by Jack London
16. Gloria Steinem	*The Color Purple*, by Alice Walker

17. James Stewart	*Hawaii*, by James Michener
18. Jessica Tandy	*What's Bred in the Bone*, by Robertson Davies
19. Gene Tierney	*My Antonia*, by Willa Cather
20. Joanne Woodward	*Little Dorrit*, by Charles Dickens

SOURCE: "Who Reads What?," by the Gardiner Public Library, Gardiner, Maine.

11 Notable Book Dedications

1. ARTHUR ASHE, with Neil Amdue

"To that nameless slave girl off HMS *Doddington*, and her daughter Lucy, her granddaughter Peggy, her great-granddaughter Peggy, and her great-great-grandson Hammett, all of whom were born, lived and died as slaves."

— *Off the Courts*, 1982

2. BENNETT CERF

There is a young lady from Fife
Whom I never have seen in my life.
So the devil with her;
Instead I prefer
To dedicate this to my wife.

— *Out on a Limerick*, 1961

3. MAURICE CHEVALIER

"To all my American friends. Having been liked for such a long time in America is the pride of my life."

— *I Remember It Well*, 197

4. AGATHA CHRISTIE

"TO ALL THOSE WHO LEAD MONOTONOUS LIVES in the hope that they may experience at second hand the delights and dangers of adventure."

— *The Secret Adversary*, 192

5. JOHN CLARMONT

"To no one in particular."

— *Did I Do That?*, 198

6. BUCHI EMECHETA

"I dedicate this work to the memory of many relatives and friends who died in this way, especially my eight-year-old niece, Buchi Emecheta, who died of starvation, and her four-year-old sister Ndidi Emecheta, who died two days afterwards of the same Biafran disease at the CMS refugee centre in Ibuza; also my aunt Ozili Emecheta and my maternal uncle Okolie Okwuekwu, both of whom died of snake bites as they ran into the bush the night the federal forces bombed their way into Ibuza. I also dedicate *Destination Biafra* to the memory of those Ibuza women and their children who were roasted alive in the bush at Nkpotu Ukpe. May the spirit of Umejei, the Father founder of our town, guide you all in death, and may you sleep well."

— *Destination Biafra*, 1982

7. JEROME K. JEROME

"To the very dear and well beloved Friend of my prosperous and evil days. To the friend, who, though in the early stages of our acquaintanceship, he did ofttimes disagree with me, has since come to be my very warmest comrade. To the friend who, however often I may put him out, never (now) upsets me in revenge. To the friend who, treated with marked coldness by all the female members of my household, and regarded with suspicion by my very dog, nevertheless, seems day by day to be more drawn by me, and in return, to more and more impregnate me with the odour of his friendship. To the friend who never tells me of my faults, never wants to borrow money, and never talks about himself. To the companion of my idle hours, the soother of my sorrows, the confidant of my joys and hopes, my oldest and strongest Pipe, this little volume is gratefully and affectionately dedicated."

— *The Idle Thoughts of an Idle Fellow*, 1886

8. SEAN O'CASEY

"To the gay laugh of my mother at the gate of the grave."

— *The Plough and the Stars*, 1926

9. ALBERT PIERREPOINT

"To Anne, my wife, who in forty years never asked a question, I dedicate this book with grateful thanks for her loyalty and discretion."

—*Executioner: Pierrepoint*, 1974
(Pierrepoint was Britain's last hangman.)

10. STEPHEN PILE

"To Quin Xiang-Yi, who in 1846 was given the title 'distinguished failure' in recognition of his 20 years spent failing the Chinese Civil Service entrance exams. Buoyed up by this honour, he went on to fail several times more."

— *The Return of Heroic Failures*, 1988

11. JAMES RONALD

"To My Creditors, whose increasing impatience has made this book necessary."

—*This Way Out*, 1940

SOURCE: Adrian Room, *Bloomsbury Dictionary of Dedications* (London: Bloomsbury, 1990).

Maurice Sendak's *10* Favorite Children's Books

(In No Particular Order)

The prolific children's book writer and illustrator has produced 19 books, among them the classics *The Nutshell Library, Where the Wild Things Are,* and *In the Night Kitchen.* He is the recipient of the Caldecott Medal, the Hans Christian Andersen Illustration Award, and the Laura Ingalls Wilder Award for his "substantial and lasting contribution to children's literature." He is also the designer of many opera sets and costumes, and with Arthur Yorinks is the creator of The Night Kitchen, a national, not-for-profit children's theater.

1. *The Pirate Twins,* by William Nicholson
2. *Clever Bill,* by William Nicholson
3. *Little Tim and the Brave Sea Captain,* by Edward Ardizzone
4. *Tim and Charlotte,* by Edward Ardizzone
5. *Roly Poly Pudding,* by Beatrix Potter
6. *Two Bad Mice,* by Beatrix Potter
7. *Hey Diddle Diddle,* by Randolph Caldecott
8. *Baby Bunting,* by Randolph Caldecott
9. *The Story of Babar,* by Jean de Brunhoff
10. *The Tale of Peter Rabbit,* by Beatrix Potter

— Exclusive for *The Book of Lists*

15 Celebrities
Who Wrote Children's Books

1. JULIE ANDREWS (EDWARDS), actress

   Mandy (1973), the story of a little girl who lives in a city orphanage and discovers the country, and *The Last of the Really Great Whangdoodles* (1973), about two children who visit a land of wise and magical creatures.

2. ALAN ARKIN, actor

   Tony's Hard Work Day (1972), about a boy who builds his own house, and *The Lemming Condition* (1976), about a young lemming who learns to ask questions instead of blindly conforming.

3. DEBBY BOONE, singer

   Bedtime Hours for Little Ones (1987), Christian advice for children on such subjects as fear of the dark, prayer, and taking toys to bed, and *Tomorrow Is a Brand New Day* (1989), poems on diverse subjects including gratitude, spaghetti, and brushing your teeth.

4. GWENDOLYN BROOKS, poet

   Bronzeville Boys and Girls (1956) and *The Tiger Who Wore White Gloves: or What You Are You Are* (1974), poems about the experiences of children.

5. DAVID BYRNE, singer and composer

   Stay Up Late (1988), based on one of Byrne's songs about the excitement that strikes a family when a new baby is brought home.

6. CHARLES, PRINCE OF WALES

   The Old Man of Lochnagar (1980), the story of an old man who leaves his comfortable cave to explore the surrounding Scottish countryside.

7. DOM DeLUISE, comedian

   Charlie the Caterpillar (1990), about an ugly caterpillar who learns the meaning of true friendship when he transforms into a beautiful butterfly, and *Goldilocks* (1992), a retelling of the famous story, complete with recipes for porridge and other dishes.

8. SARAH FERGUSON, DUCHESS OF YORK

   Budgie, the Little Helicopter (1989), about a helicopter who rescues a little girl from kidnappers; and three other stories starring Budgie.

9. WHOOPI GOLDBERG, comedienne and actress

   Alice (1992), a retelling of *Alice in Wonderland* set in New Jersey and New York City.

10. FRED GWYNNE, actor

    Several books of puns, including *A Little Pigeon Toad* (1988), and *Pondlarker* (1990), about a frog who wants to kiss a princess.

11. KEN KESEY, novelist

    Little Fricker the Squirrel Meets Big Double the Bear (1990), about a smart squirrel who outwits a bully of a bear, and *The Sea Lion: A Story of the Sea Cliff People* (1991), about a small boy who saves his tribe from an evil spirit.

12. SALMON RUSHDIE, novelist

    Haroun and the Sea of Stories (1990), about a fanatic cult that tries to wipe out storytelling and human speech.

13. CARLY SIMON, singer and songwriter

    Amy the Dancing Bear (1989), about a bear who would rather dance than sleep, and *Fisherman's Song* (1991).

14. BOB WEIR, guitarist and singer

    Panther Dream (1991), about the African rain forest. Proceeds from the book went to support reforestation and educational projects in Africa.

15. VIRGINIA WOOLF, novelist

    Nurse Lugton's Curtain (1924), about the animals on a curtain who come alive when its seamstress falls asleep, and *The Widow and the Parrot* (1988), published posthumously, in which a parrot leads a Yorkshire widow to a hidden treasure.

13 Unusual Book Titles from the Library of *The People's Almanac*

1. *The Complete Monk*, by Dom Denys Rutledge. London: Routledge and Kegan Paul, 1966.
2. *Engineering for Potatoes*, by B. F. Cargill. St. Joseph, Michigan: American Society of Agricultural Engineers, 1986.
3. *Holiday Retreats for Cats and Dogs in England*, by Scarlett Tipping. Lewes, Sussex: Temple House, 1987.
4. *How to Be Happy Though Married*, by "A Graduate in the University of Matrimony." London: J. Fisher Unwin, 1895.

5. *How to Rob Banks Without Violence*, by Roderic Knowles. London: Michael Joseph, 1972.
6. *Learning from Salmon*, by Herman Aihara. Oroville, California: George Ohsawa Macrobiotic Foundation, 1980.
7. *Let's Be Normal*, by Fritz Künkel, M. D. New York: Ives Washburn, 1930.
8. *Maternal Behavior in the Rat*, by Berthold P. Weisner and Norah M. Sheard. Edinburgh: Oliver and Boyd, 1933.
9. *My Duodenal Ulcer and I*, by "Dr. Stuart Morton." London: Christopher Johnson, 1955.
10. *Sodomy and the Pirate Tradition*, by B. R. Burg. New York: New York University Press, 1984.
11. *The Chinese Classics of Tongue Diagnosis in Color*, by Henry C. Lu. Vancouver, British Columbia: Academy of Oriental Heritage, 1980.
12. *You Can Make a "Stradivarius Violin,"* by Joseph V. Reid. Chicago: Popular Mechanics Press, 1955.

The author of *How to Rob Banks Without Violence* preparing for a day's work.

13. *Electricity and Christianity*, by Crump J. Strickland. Charlotte, North Carolina: Elizabeth Publishing, 1938.

NOTE: For more unusual book titles, see *The Book of Lists #3*, pp. 247–50.

16 Curious Histories and Esoteric Studies from the Library of *The People's Almanac*

1. *The One-Leg Resting Position (Nilotenstellung) in Africa and Elsewhere,* by Gerhard Lindblom. Stockholm: Statens Ethnografiska Museum, 1949.
   A survey of cultures in which people commonly rest while standing by placing one foot on or near the knee of the other leg. Contains fifteen photographs from Africa, Sri Lanka, Romania, Australia, and Bolivia, as well as a fold-out locator map of Africa.

2. *Dirt: A Social History as Seen Through the Uses and Abuses of Dirt,* by Terence McLaughlin. New York: Stein and Day, 1971.
   Readers who are drawn to dirty books might also enjoy *Smut: An Anatomy of Dirt,* by Christian Engensberger (New York:

King Henry IV of France touching for scrofula.

A Mangula tribesman from northern Australia standing in the nilotenstellung, or "one-leg resting."

Seabury, 1972); *The Kingdom of Dust*, by J. Gordon Ogden (Chicago: Popular Mechanics, 1912); and *All About Mud*, by Oliver R. Selfridge (Reading, Massachusetts: Addison-Wesley, 1978).

3. *Golden Quotations of Our First Lady*, by Julio F. Silvero. Caloocan City: National Book Store, 1978.

Three hundred "golden" quotations from the speeches of Imelda Marcos, including "Reality: You can only wear one dress, one pair of shoes at a time."

4. *Birds Asleep*, by Alexander F. Skutch. Austin: University of Texas Press, 1989.

A detailed and surprisingly readable study by an ornithologist resident in Costa Rica. A twelve-page bibliography is included for serious students. Less pacific readers might prefer *Birds Fighting*, by Stuart Smith and Eric Hosking (London: Faber and Faber, 1955), which includes numerous photos of real birds attacking stuffed birds.

5. *Knight Life: Jousting in the United States*, by Robert L. Loeffelbein. Lexington Park, Maryland: Golden Owl, 1977.

A fully illustrated account of the history of jousting tournaments in the United States, with emphasis on modern contests, records, rules, and heroes.

6. *Lesbian Nuns: Breaking Silence*, by Rosemary Curb and Nancy Manahan. Tallahassee, Florida: The Naiad Press, 1985.

An oral history in which forty-nine nuns describe coming to terms with their own homosexuality.

7. *How to Conduct a Magnetic Healing Business*, by A. C. Murphy. Kansas City, Missouri: Hudson-Kimberly, 1902.

A nuts-and-bolts account including advertising tips and postal rules and regulations, as well as discussion of such difficult topics as "Should a lady healer employ a gentleman assistant?"

8. *I Dream of Woody*, by Dee Burton. New York: William Morrow, 1984.

Burton presents the cases of seventy people from New York and Los Angeles who have dreamed about Woody Allen. Fans of books on people who dream about famous people will also want to track down *Dreams About H. M. The Queen* by Brian Masters (Frogmore, St. Albans, Herts: Mayflower, 1973), a collection of dreams about Queen Elizabeth II and other members of the British royal family.

9. *Little-Known Sisters of Well-Known Men,* by Sarah G. Pomeroy. Boston: Dana Estes, 1912.

A review of the lives of eight little-known sisters, including Sarianna Browning, Sarah Disraeli, and Sophia Thoreau, as well as two known sisters of English writers, Dorothy Wordsworth and Mary Lamb.

10. *The Royal Touch: Sacred Monarchy and Scrofula in England and France,* by Marc Bloch. London: Routledge and Kegan Paul, 1973.

This book, written in 1923, examines the unusual custom of curing the disease of scrofula, a form of tuberculosis, by being touched by the king of France or the king of England. The practice died out after 1825.

11. *Lust for Fame: The Stage Career of John Wilkes Booth,* by Gordon Samples. Jefferson, North Carolina: McFarland, 1982.

A biography that ignores Booth's assassination of Abraham Lincoln and deals instead, for 234 pages, with his career as an actor, which continued until four weeks before he killed the president of the United States.

12. *Out of Our Kitchen Closets: San Francisco Gay Jewish Cooking.* San Francisco: Congregation: Sha'ar Zahav, 1987.

One hundred fifty recipes submitted by the members, families, and friends of a gay and lesbian synagogue. Seventeen of the recipes are for kugel.

13. *Lewis Carroll, Photographer of Children: Four Nude Studies,* by Morton N. Cohen. New York: Clarkson N. Potter, 1979.

A slim (thirty-two-page) treatise on a little-known aspect of the life of the author of *Alice's Adventures Underground* and

Sophia Thoreau, little-known sister of Henry David Thoreau.

Through the Looking Glass. For many years Carroll's hobby was photographing little girls under the age of ten. The four hand-colored photographs reproduced in this volume are the only nude studies he did not destroy before his death.

14. *The History and Romance of Elastic Webbing,* by Clifford A. Richmond. Easthampton, Massachusetts: Easthampton News Company, 1946.

A lively account of the birth and growth of the elastic webbing industry in the nineteenth century. In the words of the author, once a man has "got the smell of rubber in his nostrils . . . he either stays with rubber or is thereafter ever homesick to get back into the rubber industry."

15. *Canadian National Egg Laying Contests,* by F. C. Elford and A. G. Taylor. Ottawa: Department of Agriculture, 1924.

A report of the first three years of the Canadian national egg laying contests, from 1919 to 1922, as well as a preliminary contest held on Prince Edward Island in 1918–19. The work consists almost entirely of charts comparing production and costs by owner, bird, and year. In 1921–22, one of the birds belonging to Lewis N. Clark of Port Hope, Ontario, produced 294 eggs.

16. *The Rhinoceros from Dürer to Stubbs — 1515–1799,* by J. N. Clarke. London: Sotheby's, 1986.

The first rhinoceros to be brought to Europe from India arrived in Lisbon in 1515. This book details the depiction of the single-horned Indian rhinoceros in European art from the sixteenth century through the end of the eighteenth century. It also tells the story of the travels of various rhinoceroses across the continent during this period.

NOTE: For more curious histories and esoteric studies, see *The Book of Lists #3*, pp. 250–54.

Václav Havel's
4 Favorite Authors

Czech playwright, poet, and statesman Václav Havel was often arrested during the 1970s for his stand against his nation's repressive government. His works include *The Memorandum* (1965), *A Private View* (1975), and an adaptation of Tom Stoppard's *Largo*

Desolato (1987). When *The Memorandum* and others of his plays were spirited out of the country, he was arrested for that, too. In 1989 he led the Velvet Revolution, which resulted in the overthrow of Soviet-style communism in Czechoslovakia and led to the split between the Czech and Slovak republics. In January 1993 Havel became the first president of the Czech Republic.

1. Samuel Beckett
2. Eugene Ionesco
3. Tom Stoppard
4. Harold Pinter

Havel notes that his favorite play is *The Guard*, by Pinter.

— Exclusive for *The Book of Lists*

John Updike's
10 Greatest Writers

His elegant, witty, and lyrical style has made John Updike one of the nation's most widely read authors. Not only does he repeatedly write best-sellers, but he has been the recipient of almost every major American literary award. His novel *Rabbit Is Rich* (third in a series of books about Harry "Rabbit" Angstrom) won a Pulitzer Prize, the American Book Award, and the National Book Critics Circle Award. His other novels include *Couples, The Witches of Eastwick*, and *Rabbit at Rest*. He also writes poetry, short stories, essays, and plays.

1. William Shakespeare
2. Marcel Proust
3. Leo Tolstoi
4. Johann Wolfgang von Goethe
5. Euripides
6. Anton Chekhov
7. Jane Austen
8. Herman Melville
9. Dante
10. Homer

— Exclusive for *The Book of Lists*

Irving Wallace's
9 Favorite Authors

On June 29, 1990, one of the co-authors of *The Book of Lists*, Irving Wallace, died in Los Angeles at the age of seventy-four. His nearly three dozen books have sold an estimated 200 million copies and have been read by 1 billion people worldwide. He wrote eighteen novels, including *The Prize, The Man,* and *The Word.* Some time before his death, he compiled a list of his all-time-favorite authors.

1. W. Somerset Maugham — *Of Human Bondage,* because of its compelling characterization, narrative drive, crystal-clear prose; *The Summing Up,* for clarity, cynicism, philosophy; and *Moon and Sixpence.*
2. F. Scott Fitzgerald — *Tender Is the Night.*
3. Arthur Koestler — *Arrival and Departure* and *Darkness at Noon.*
4. Arthur Conan Doyle — the Sherlock Holmes books: pure pleasure, nothing more. Also, *The Lost World.*
5. James Hilton — *Lost Horizon* and *Without Armor.*
6. Raymond Chandler.
7. Graham Greene.
8. John le Carré — *The Little Drummer Girl.*
9. Nelson De Mille — *Word of Honor* and *By the Rivers of Babylon.*

W. Somerset Maugham, author of *Of Human Bondage.*

Joyce Carol Oates's
14 Favorite American Authors

A prolific storyteller, Joyce Carol Oates had her first book, *By the North Gate*, a collection of short stories, published when she was only twenty-five years old. At age thirty-one she won the American Book Award for her novel *Them*, becoming one of the youngest writers ever to receive the award. Since then she has written more than a dozen novels and numerous collections of short stories as well as poems.

1. Emily Dickinson
2. Walt Whitman
3. Herman Melville
4. Nathaniel Hawthorne
5. Edgar Allan Poe
6. Henry David Thoreau
7. Henry James
8. William Faulkner
9. Ernest Hemingway
10. William Carlos Williams
11. Mark Twain
12. Willa Cather
13. Robert Frost
14. Flannery O'Connor

OATES NOTES: This is a purely American list, suggesting, but not fully naming, the wide range and diversity of our native literature. As an American writer with a keen sense of history, I think of myself as having sprung from these nourishing sources, among others. And the list could go on and on . . .

— Exclusive for *The Book of Lists*

11 Poets and How
They Earned a Living

1. WILLIAM BLAKE (1757–1827), English poet and artist

Trained as an engraver, Blake studied art at the Royal Academy but left to earn a living engraving for booksellers. For a few years he was a partner in a print-selling and engraving business. He then worked as an illustrator, graphic designer, and drawing teacher. It became increasingly hard for Blake to earn a living. He had a patron for a few years, but lived essentially in poverty and obscurity, only occasionally receiving an art commission. Blake was later recognized as one of England's finest engravers.

2. ROBERT BURNS (1759–1796), Scottish poet

Raised on a farm in Ayrshire, Burns was a full-time laborer on the land at fifteen. He tried to become a surveyor, but ill health forced him to give up. Next he lived with relatives who ran a flax-dressing business, until their shop burned down. Farming barely paid his bills, so Burns published *Poems, Chiefly in the Scottish Dialect* in 1786 to get money for passage to Jamaica, where he had a job offer as an overseer. The book was so successful that he used the money to visit Edinburgh instead. Returning to the farm, Burns took a job as a tax inspector, trying unsuccessfully to juggle three occupations. He lost the farm, but moved to Dumfries and continued as a tax inspector and a poet.

3. JOHN KEATS (1795–1821), English poet

Keats was trained as a surgeon and apothecary in Edmonton, and later moved to London to work as a dresser in a hospital. For a year or so Keats had his own surgeon/apothecary practice, and at the same time began publishing his poetry. His first major work, *Poems*, appeared in 1817, and that year he gave up medicine for the literary life. Charles Armitage Brown became his patron, providing him with a house in Hampstead, outside London. Keats spent his last few years there, writing his best works while dying of tuberculosis.

4. WALT WHITMAN (1819–1892), American poet

Whitman had a checkered career in newspaper work, starting as a printer's assistant and eventually becoming an editor in New York throughout the 1840s. After ten years he gave up journalism for carpentry and verse. During the Civil War, Whitman moved to Washington, D.C., took a job in the paymaster's office, and spent his spare time nursing the wounded. In 1865 he became a clerk at the Department of the Interior's Bureau of Indian Affairs, but was soon fired for being the author of the scandalous *Leaves of Grass*. He then clerked in the attorney general's office until a paralytic stroke forced him to retire in 1873.

5. SIDNEY LANIER (1841–1881), American poet

After graduating from Oglethorpe University in Georgia, Lanier worked as an English tutor at the university until the Civil War broke out. A Confederate volunteer, he was taken captive, and contracted tuberculosis in a Union prison camp. He held various jobs after the war, including hotel clerk, high school principal, and law practitioner in Georgia, even though he had not been admitted to the bar. In 1873 he became a flutist for the Peabody Orchestra in Baltimore. Just a few years before his death, he was appointed lecturer in English literature at Johns Hopkins University.

6. ARTHUR RIMBAUD (1854–1891), French poet

Rimbaud's lover Paul Verlaine supported him for a while in Paris; after their separation, Rimbaud lived in London, working at various menial jobs until poverty or ill health or both caused his return to France. In 1876 he joined the Dutch colonial army and went to Indonesia, but deserted and again returned to France. From there he joined a circus en route to Scandinavia; went to Cyprus as a laborer and later as a builder's foreman; and finally gave up his wandering in Harar, Ethiopia. There he worked for a coffee exporter, and later tried (unsuccessfully) to become an independent arms dealer. In 1888 he was managing a trading post, dealing in coffee, ivory, arms, and possibly slaves.

7. CARL SANDBURG (1878–1967), American poet and biographer

The son of a blacksmith's helper, Sandburg began working at the age of eleven, sweeping floors and cleaning cuspidors in a law office. He quit school at age thirteen and took a full-time job delivering milk. Over the next few years he worked at a series of odd jobs, including harvesting ice at a frozen lake, moving scenery at a theater, shining shoes, washing dishes, and working at a racetrack. He also harvested wheat in Kansas, apprenticed to a housepainter, served in the U.S. Army in 1898, and worked as a fireman while attending college.

After leaving Lombard College without graduating, Sandburg worked as an advertising manager for a department store, a stereoscope salesman, and as secretary to Milwaukee's Socialist mayor. Late in 1912, Sandburg moved to Chicago and landed a job as a feature writer for the *Daily Socialist*. For the next sixteen years he supported himself and his family with a series of newspaper jobs, mostly as a reporter for the *Chicago Daily News*. After achieving success as a poet and biographer of Abraham Lincoln, Sandburg lectured, sang folk songs, and bred and raised goats.

8. WALLACE STEVENS (1879–1955), American poet

After leaving Harvard University without a degree, Stevens was a reporter for the *New York Herald Tribune* for a year. He then attended New York University Law School, passed the bar in 1904, and for the next twelve years practiced law in New York. In 1916 he joined the legal department of the Hartford Accident and Indemnity Company in Connecticut; by 1934 he was vice-president of the company.

9. WILLIAM CARLOS WILLIAMS (1883–1963), American poet

Williams earned a medical degree from the University of Pennsylvania in 1906, interned at hospitals in New York City, and for a year did postgraduate work in pediatrics at the University of Leipzig in Germany. He established a medical practice in his home town of Rutherford, New Jersey, in 1910, and until the mid-1950s maintained both a medical and a literary career. An appointment to the chair of poetry at the Library of Congress in 1952 was withdrawn because of Williams's radical politics. He spent his last ten years lecturing at many American universities.

10. PABLO NERUDA (1904–1973), Chilean poet and diplomat

In recognition of his poetic skills, the Chilean government awarded Neruda with a nonpaying position as Chile's consul in Burma in 1927. Eventually he graduated to a salaried office, serving in Ceylon, the Dutch East Indies, Argentina, and Spain. With the outbreak of the Spanish Civil War in 1936, Neruda, without waiting for orders, declared Chile on the side of the Spanish republic. He was recalled by the Chilean government and later reassigned to Mexico. In 1944 he was elected to the national senate as a member of the Communist Party. He later served as a member of the central committee of the Chilean Communist Party and as a member of the faculty of the University of Chile.

11. MAYA ANGELOU (1928–), American poet and memoirist

In her youth, Angelou worked as a cook and a waitress, and as the first black female fare collector with the San Francisco Streetcar Company. In the 1950s she became a nightclub performer, specializing in calypso songs and dances. She also performed in *Porgy and Bess* on a twenty-two-country tour of Europe and Africa organized by the U.S. State Department in 1954 and 1955. During the 1960s Angelou was northern coordinator of Martin Luther King's Southern Christian Leadership Council, associate editor of an English-language newspaper in Cairo, features editor of a paper in Ghana, and assistant administrator at the University of Ghana. She acted in Jean Genet's play *The Blacks*, wrote songs for B. B. King, wrote and produced educational television series, and acted on Broadway (for one night in 1973) and on television — as Kunta Kinte's grandmother in *Roots*, in 1977. In 1972 she wrote the script for *Georgia, Georgia*, the first original screenplay by a black woman to be produced. She continues to be a popular lecturer, as well as a university professor.

Maya Angelou in *Calypso Heat Wave*, 1957.

6 Curious Poetry Anthologies

1. *A Little Book of Ping-Pong Verse.* Boston: Dana Estes, 1902.

   This charming volume was published at the height of the Ping-Pong craze that began in 1900. Among the eighty-three selections included are "The Rubaiyat of Ping-Pong," "The Ping-Pong Ankle," "The Ponger and the Pingstress," and sixteen different poems entitled "Ping-Pong."

   > *How does the nimble little ball*
   > *Enjoy each "ping" and "pong!"*
   > *It also loves to take a fall*
   > *And roll the floor along;*
   > *It will lead you then a merry race,*
   > *As any maiden coy,*
   > *And should it find a hiding-place,*
   > *It hugs itself with joy.*

   > — Thomas Dykes Beasley
   > "Only a Ping-Pong Ball"

2. *The Vampire in Verse: An Anthology,* edited by Steven Moore. New York: Dracula Press, 1985.

A publication of the Count Dracula Fan Club, this anthology includes works by Byron, Keats, Kipling, Baudelaire, Yeats, and F. Scott Fitzgerald.

> *From my grave betimes I have been driven,*
> *I seek the good I lost, none shall me thwart,*
> *I seek his love to whom my teeth was given,*
> *And I have sucked the lifeblood from his heart.*
> *If he dies, I will*
> *Find me others, still*
> *With my fury tear young folk apart.*

> — Johann Wolfgang von Goethe,
> "The Bride of Corinth"

3. *The Poetry of Chess,* edited by Andrew Waterman. London: Anvil Press Poetry, 1981.

Sixty-nine chess poems divided into six sections, including "The Game," "Players," and "Personal Relations."

> *Men tend to think in a prosaic way,*
> *Identify the ends and find the means,*
> *And chess to them is somewhat like a play*
> *With all the plotting done behind the scenes,*
> *But chess to women is like everyday*
> *Only even more so, and Kings and Queens*
> *Are you and me, in an odd sort of way.*
> *(They think of knights as horses though, it seems.)*

> — Simon Lowy,
> "On Her Taking my Queen at Chess"

4. *The Poetry of Geology,* edited by Robert M. Nagen. London: George Allen & Unwin, 1982.

All selections are from eighteenth- and nineteenth-century English and American literature. Titles include "A Meditation on Rhode-Island Coal," "The Nautilus and the Ammonite," and "To A Fossil Fern." Especially noteworthy is the work of John Scafe, who in 1820 published *A Geological Primer in Verse,* as well as "King Coal's Levee," a 1145-line poem about the succession of stratification in England and Wales.

> *Of Feldspar and Quartz a large quantity take,*
> *Then pepper with Mica, and mix up and bake.*
> *This Granite for common occasions is good;*

But on Saint-days and Sundays, be it understood,
If with bishops and lords in the state room you dine,
Then sprinkle with Topaz, or else Tourmaline.

— John Scafe,
"To Make Granite"

5. *Mary Queen of Scots: An Anthology of Poetry,* chosen by Antonio
   Fraser. London: Eyre Methuen/Greville Press, 1981.

   Poems both by and about Mary Queen of Scots, the sixteenth-
   century queen of Scotland who was executed by her cousin,
   Queen Elizabeth I of England. Featured poets include Lope de
   Vega, Algernon Swinburne, William Wordsworth, Edith Sitwell,
   and Boris Pasternak.

   O! soon, to me, may summer-suns
   Nae mair light up the morn!
   Nae Mair, to me, the autumn winds
   Wave o'er the yellow corn!
   And in the narrow house o'death
   Let winter round me rave;
   And the next flowers, that deck the spring,
   Bloom on my peaceful grave.

   — Robert Burns,
   "Lament of Mary Queen of Scots on the Approach of Spring"

6. *Gems from an Old Drummer's Grip,* compiled by N. R. Streeter.
   New York: Groton, 1889.

   A collection of poems by and about traveling salesmen, or
   "drummers," as well as a few verses that, although not about
   traveling salesmen, have been enjoyed by traveling salesmen.

   It was two rival drummers,
   The merits they did blow
   Of safes were in St. Louis made
   And safes from Chicago.

   They chanced upon a merchant
   Who fain a safe would buy,
   And in the praise of their houses' wares
   The drummers twain did ire,
   Each striving to see which could construct
   The most colossal lie.

   — N. R. Streeter,
   "The Rival Drummers"

10 Recent Cases of Book Censorship

1. *Father Christmas,* by Raymond Briggs (1979)

   Removed from all elementary classrooms in Holland, Michigan, when several parents complained that it portrayed Santa Claus as having a negative attitude toward Christmas.

2. *The Living Bible,* by William C. Bower (1981)

   Burned in Gastonia, North Carolina, because it was allegedly "a perverted commentary of the King James Version."

3. *Doris Day: Her Own Story,* by Doris Day (1982)

   Removed from two high school libraries in Anniston, Alabama, due to its "shocking" contents, particularly "in light of Miss Day's All-American image." It was later reinstated on a restricted basis.

4. *Working,* by Studs Terkel (1983)

   This oral history of Americans and their jobs was removed from an optional reading list at the South Kitsap, Washington, high school because the chapter about a prostitute "demeaned marital status and degraded the sexual act." It was also deleted from the seventh- and eighth-grade curriculum by the Washington, Arizona, school district with the following explanation: "When we require idealistic and sensitive youth to be burdened with despair, ugliness and hopelessness, we shall be held accountable by the Almighty God."

5. *American Foreign Policy,* vol. II, by Thomas Paterson (1984)

   Banned by the school board of the Racine, Wisconsin, unified school district for containing "judgmental writing" and, in the words of one board member, "a lot more funny pictures of Republicans and nicer pictures of Democrats." It was returned to the curriculum one week later.

6. *The Adventures of Tom Sawyer,* by Mark Twain (1985)

   Removed from school libraries in London by education officials who accused it of being "racist" and "sexist."

7. *Encyclopaedia Britannica* (1986)

   Banned and pulped in Turkey for spreading "separatist propaganda."

8. *The Satanic Verses,* by Salman Rushdie (1988)

   Banned in India, Pakistan, Saudi Arabia, Egypt, Somalia, Sudan, Malaysia, Qatar, Indonesia, and South Africa for allegedly blaspheming Islam and the Koran. In Iran, Ayatollah Khomeini sentenced to death Rushdie and anyone else in-

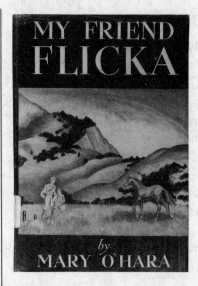

My Friend Flicka — **banned in Florida.**

volved in the publication of the book. Khomeini also offered a substantial cash reward to whoever assassinated Rushdie.

9. *Cerberus,* by Bernard Evslin (1990)

Removed from elementary school library shelves in the Francis Howell school district in St. Peters, Missouri, for being graphic and gruesome and because its illustrations were "pornographic." The illustrations were drawings by Michelangelo and other masters. The book was also said to "encourage Satanism."

10. *My Friend Flicka,* by Mary O'Hara (1990)

Pulled from optional reading lists for fifth- and sixth-graders in Clay County, Florida, because the book uses the word *bitch* to refer to a female dog.

PRIMARY SOURCE: Robert P. Doyle, *Banned Books Week '92 Celebrating the Freedom to Read* (Chicago: American Library Association, 1992).

NOTE: For more cases of book censorship, see *The Book of Lists #3*, pp. 226–29.

8 Writers and
1 Artist Watched by the FBI

The FBI, famous for investigating anyone suspected of "un-American" activities, has zealously kept files on many of America's greatest writers and artists. Author Herbert Mitgang obtained portions of those records under the Freedom of Information Act, and made them public in his book *Dangerous Dossiers: Exposing the*

Secret War Against America's Greatest Authors (New York: Ballantine, 1989).

1. SINCLAIR LEWIS

Lewis, the Nobel Prize–winning author of such classics as *Babbitt* and *Elmer Gantry*, was the subject of a 150-page FBI file. His "un-American" activities included not living with his wife, being a member of the American Birth Control League, holding anti-Nazi sentiments, and writing a novel, *Kingsblood Royal*, which the FBI called "propaganda for the white man's acceptance of the Negro as a social equal."

2. PEARL S. BUCK

The year Buck won the Nobel Prize (1938), the FBI began its 280-page file on her subversive activities. The surveillance included watching her mail. The author of *The Good Earth* was considered suspect because she opposed racism, adopted a half-black, half-Japanese child, and belonged to the American Civil Liberties Union, a group the FBI called a "Communist-front organization."

3. ERNEST HEMINGWAY

J. Edgar Hoover was obsessed with proving Hemingway a Communist. His 122-page file, complete with a table of contents, cites Hemingway's support of the Loyalist cause in the Spanish Civil War, his opposition to Spanish dictator Franco, his authorship of an article against war for *Esquire* magazine, and even his arguments with his wife.

4. DOROTHY PARKER

Parker, as well known for her wit as for her writing, was a major affront to the FBI. Her file runs to a voluminous 1,000 pages. She was carefully watched, and while she was never proved to be a member of the Communist Party, her record shows that she did belong to the Consumers Union, the Friends of the Abraham Lincoln Brigade, and the League of Women Shoppers.

5. LILLIAN HELLMAN

Like Dorothy Parker, Hellman belonged to the League of Women Shoppers. According to her 307-page file, the playwright also attended a testimonial dinner for Theodore Dreiser and traveled with a copy of *The Little Oxford Dictionary*. Because of her liberal views, Hoover took a particular interest in her, and arranged for her bank accounts to be checked, her mail to be watched, and her handwriting to be analyzed.

6. TENNESSEE WILLIAMS

The fact that a Communist newspaper praised Williams's play *A Streetcar Named Desire* drew the attention of the FBI. Additionally, "the bureau ascertained that Thomas Lanier Williams has the reputation of being a homosexual."

7. ARCHIBALD MACLEISH

A three-time Pulitzer Prize winner, poet MacLeish held several important government posts, including Librarian of Congress. Nevertheless, Hoover found him "prematurely anti-Fascist" and "a liberal of the New Deal type." The most sordid information the bureau could dig up was that he had once been arrested for illegally fishing on private property and was fined ten dollars.

8. ALLEN GINSBERG

Poet Allen Ginsberg has a stack of documents three feet high reflecting the FBI's interest in him. Though he was ejected from Cuba and Prague for his anti-Communist remarks, the FBI considers him "potentially dangerous," "subversive," and possessed of "emotional instability (including unstable residence and employment record.)" A photo of him in "an indecent pose" has been placed in a sealed envelope and locked in an FBI vault for "safekeeping."

9. PABLO PICASSO

Although the Spanish-born artist never visited the United States, the FBI considered him subversive, and a threat to the welfare of America. His 187-page file was kept for twenty-five years and continues to be maintained today, despite Picasso's death in 1973.

15 Politically Incorrect Terms and Their Alternatives

1. BORING — Differently interesting; charm-free.
2. CLUMSY — Uniquely coordinated.
3. DEAD — Terminally inconvenienced.
4. DISHONEST — Morally different; ethically disoriented.
5. DRUNK — Sobriety deprived.
6. HERPES — His 'n' herpes.
7. MAFIOSO — Member of a career-offender cartel.
8. MEAT — Processed animal carcasses; scorched corpses of animals.
9. OLD JOKE — Previously recounted humorous narrative.
10. PANHANDLER — Unaffiliated applicant for private-sector funding.
11. SERIAL KILLER — Person with difficult-to-meet needs.
12. SHOPLIFTER — Nontraditional shopper.
13. SNOWMAN — Person of snow.
14. VAGRANT — Directionally impoverished person.
15. WHITE (person) — Melanin impoverished.

SOURCE: *The Official Politically Correct Dictionary and Handbook* by Henry Beard and Christopher Cerf. Copyright © 1992 by Henry Beard and Christopher Cerf. Reprinted by permission of Villard Books, a division of Random House, Inc.

A gathering of the terminally inconvenienced.

Willard R. Espy's
10 Ugliest Words in the English Language That Are Not Indecent

Willard R. Espy has had a multifaceted career as a reporter, editor, publisher, radio interviewer, public relations manager for *Reader's Digest*, and as a panelist on the *Harper Dictionary of Contemporary Usage*. His books include *The Game of Words* (1972), *O Thou Improper, Thou Uncommon Noun* (1978), *The Garden of Eloquence* (1983), and *Words Gotten Out* (1989).

Mr. Espy notes: A while back, A. Ross Eckler, editor of the journal of linguistics *Word Ways*, asked his readers to send me what they considered to be the ten ugliest words in English. Dozens obliged. I made a list of their choices and forwarded them — more than 200 reeking specimens — to knowledgeable friends for additions and a vote. The vote was lopsided — and every one of the ten winning candidates was a word that until recently was taboo in polite conversation.

This is not the way I had planned things. I turned to the ten runners-up, only to find almost all of them equally indecent. I determined then to confine my quest to words that were innocuous in meaning, however they sounded. These ranked far down the list — but here they are.

I think there is a lesson to be drawn. Clearly, meaning eclipses sound (gutturals, clashing consonants, and the like) in the measurement of a word's ugliness. "Gonorrhea" and "diarrhea" would ring like church chimes in our ears if we did not know what they signified. A single suggestive syllable — the "fruc" in "fructify," for instance, or the "pus" in "crepuscular" — can turn an otherwise charming sound into an insult to the eardrums. "Yearn," "kiss," and "shrine" are worshipful; the nearly indistinguishable "urine," "piss," and "slime" are loathsome.

Mind you, the ten words listed below are quite ugly enough for most of us. If, however, you insist on extremes, just mail me a stamped, self-addressed envelope — Willard R. Espy, 529 W. 42nd Street, New York, NY 10036 — and I shall be happy to send you the real McCoy. No need to take the trouble, though; you know every one of those words already.

1. FRUCTIFY — to make fruitful
2. KUMQUAT — a kind of small yellow to orange citrus fruit
3. QUAHOG — a thick-shelled American clam
4. CREPUSCULAR — relating to or like twilight

5. KAKKAK — a small bittern of Guam
6. GARGOYLE — a gutter spout shaped like a grotesque figure
7. CACOPHONOUS — harsh-sounding
8. AASVOGEL — an African vulture
9. BROBDINGNAGIAN — marked by tremendous size
0. JUKEBOX — a cabinet player and records, activated by inserting a coin

— Exclusive for *The Book of Lists*

19 Obscure and Obsolete Words

he average adult recognizes 30,000 to 50,000 words, but only uses 0,000 to 15,000. However, there are actually about 1 million words 1 the English language, some of which — although obscure, forotten, or rarely used — are worth reviving.

1. BOANTHROPY — A type of insanity in which a man thinks he is an ox.
2. DIBBLE — To drink like a duck, lifting up the head after each sip.
3. EOSOPHOBIA — Fear of dawn.
4. EUGERIA — Normal and happy old age.
5. EUNEIROPHRENIA — Peace of mind after a pleasant dream.
6. EYESERVICE — Work done only when the boss is watching.
7. GROAK — To watch people silently while they are eating, hoping they will ask you to join them.
8. GYNOTIKOLOBOMASSOPHILE — One who likes to nibble on a woman's earlobes.
9. HEBEPHRENIC — A condition of adolescent silliness.
0. IATROGENIC — Illness or disease caused by doctors or by prescribed treatment.
1. LAPLING — Someone who enjoys resting in women's laps.
2. MEUPAREUNIA — A sexual act gratifying to only one participant.
3. NEANIMORPHIC — Looking younger than one's years.
4. ONIOCHALASIA — Buying as a means of mental relaxation.
5. PARNEL — A priest's mistress.
6. PILGARLIC — A bald head that looks like a peeled garlic.
7. PREANTEPENULTIMATE — Fourth from last.
8. RESISTENTIALISM — Seemingly spiteful behavior manifested by inanimate objects.
9. SUPPEDANEUM — A foot support for crucifix victims.

13 Names of Things
You Didn't Know Had Names

1. ARMSAYE — The armhole in clothing.
2. CHAD — The tiny bits of paper left over from punching data cards.
3. CHANKING — Spat-out food, such as rinds or pits.
4. FEAT — A dangling curl of hair.
5. MINIMUS — The little finger or toe.
6. OBDORMITION — The numbness caused by pressure on a nerve; when a limb is "asleep."
7. OPHRYON — The space between the eyebrows on a line with the top of the eye sockets.
8. PEEN — The end of a hammer head opposite the striking face.
9. PURLICUE — The space between the thumb and extended forefinger.
10. RASCETA — Creases on the inside of the wrist.
11. SCROOP — The rustle of silk.

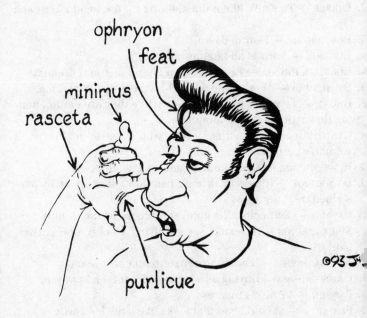

12. SPRAINTS — Otter dung.
13. WAMBLE — Stomach rumbling.

NOTE: For more names of things you didn't know had names, see *The Book of Lists #1*, pp. 162–63, and *The Book of Lists #3*, pp. 395–96.

10 Untranslatable Words

Here are ten words and phrases that have no equivalent in English.

1. CAVOLI RISCALDATI (Italian)

   The attempt to revive a dead love affair. Literally, "reheated cabbage," usually unworkable and messy.

2. DOHADA (Sanskrit)

   Unorthodox cravings of pregnant women.

3. DRACHENFUTTER (German)

   A gift brought home from a husband to his wife after he has stayed out late. Literally, "dragon fodder."

4. ESPRIT DE L'ESCALIER (French)

   The brilliantly witty response to a public insult that comes into your mind only after you have left the party. Literally, "the spirit of the staircase."

5. KYOIKUMAMA (Japanese)

   A mother who pushes her children into academic achievement. A derogatory term that literally means "education mama."

6. NAKHES (Yiddish)

   A mixture of pleasure and pride, particularly the kind that a parent gets from a child.

7. ONDINNONK (Iroquoian)

   The soul's innermost benevolent desires; the angelic parts of human nature.

8. RAZBLIUTO (Russian)

   The feeling a man has for someone he once loved but now does not.

9. SCHADDENFREUDE (German)

   The joy that one feels as a result of someone else's misfortune, like seeing a rival slip on a banana peel.

10. TARTLE (Scottish)

    To hesitate in recognizing a person or thing, as happens when you are introduced to someone whose name you cannot recall.

SOURCE: Reprinted by permission of The Putnam Publishing Group from *They Have a Word for It* by Howard Rheingold. Copyright © 1988 by Howard Rheingold.

13 Winning Words in the National Spelling Bee

The National Spelling Bee is sponsored by daily, Sunday, and weekly newspapers throughout the United States, Mexico, Guam, Puerto Rico, and the Virgin Islands. State Department and Department of Defense schools in Europe and North Africa are also represented. About 9 million children — under sixteen years old and not past the eighth grade — participate annually in the bee at the local level. All but approximately 230 children are eliminated before the two-day national contest in late May. Each finalist is given one word at a time to spell orally. If a child misses a word, he or she is out of the competition. This process of elimination continues until there is a champion. First prize is $5,000.

Year	Winning Word	Winning Contestant
1. 1981	*Sarcophagus:* Limestone used for coffins	Paige Pipkin, El Paso, Texas
2. 1982	*Psoriasis:* Chronic skin disease characterized by circumscribed red patches covered with white scales.	Molly Dieveney, Leesburg, Virginia
3. 1983	*Purim:* A Jewish holiday celebrated on the 14th of Adar in commemoration of the deliverance of the Jews from the massacre plotted by Haman.	Blake Giddens, Alamagordo, New Mexico
4. 1984	*Luge:* A small sled that is ridden in a supine position and used in competition.	Daniel Greenblatt, Sterling, Virginia
5. 1985	*Milieu:* Midst, middle.	Balu Natarajan, Bolingbrook, Illinois
6. 1986	*Odontalgia:* A pain in the tooth, toothache.	Jon Pennington, Mechanicsburg, Pennsylvania
7. 1987	*Staphylococci:* A bunch of germs.	Stephanie Petit, Pittsburgh, Pennsylvania

Year	Winning Word	Winning Contestant
8. 1988	*Elegiacal:* Of, relating to, or consisting of two dactylic hexameter lines the second of which lacks the arses in the third and sixth feet.	Rageshree Ramachandran, Sacramento, California
9. 1989	*Spoliator:* The act of plundering.	Scott Isaacs, Denver Colorado
10. 1990	*Fibranne:* A fabric made of spun-rayon yarn.	Amy Marie Dimak, Seattle, Washington
11. 1991	*Antipyretic:* An agent that reduces fever.	Joanne Lagatta, Clintonville, Wisconsin
12. 1992	*Lyceum:* Gymnasium near Athens where Aristotle taught.	Amanda C. Goad, Richmond, Virginia
13. 1993	*Kamikaze:* A member of a Japanese air attack corps in World War II assigned to make a suicidal crash on a target.	Geoff Hooper, Arlington, Tennessee

NOTE: For more wining words in the National Spelling Bee, see *The Book of Lists #2*, pp. 150–51.

Leo Rosten's
13 Favorite Yiddish
Words or Phrases

Leo Rosten has been a novelist, a journalist, a humorist, a social scientist, an essayist, and a social commentator. He has served as a professor and lecturer at various universities and has authored numerous screenplays. His love of language, especially verbal humor, is evident in many of his books: *The Education of Hyman Kaplan, The Mischief of Language, Leo Rosten's Treasury of Jewish Quotations, The Joys of Yiddish,* and the more recent *The Joys of Yinglish.*

ROSTEN NOTES: Many of my favorite Yiddish words are already part of demotic English — due to television, movies, talk shows, etc. For example: *bagel, chutzpa, noodge, blintz, shtik, yenta,* and *lox* are found in many recent English dictionaries, and in the trade argot of Broadway, the badinage of nightclub routines, and (most important) television. Yiddish words continue to infiltrate English (and/or American-English) simply because they convey a flavor,

Leo Rosten — mensch.

an irony, a nuance or colorful, sarcastic tone not found in their nearest English equivalent. Examples:

1. SHMOOZ (or *shmooze*, or *shmues*). Formally, unimportant gossip; but briskly used as a wholly unstructured, lingering, heart-to-heart exchange of intimate news, confidences, complaints, etc. "We had a good long *shmooze* about the children and Harry and Celia — and — *did* you notice the way she decorated her new living room!"

2. TUMMLER. An energetic, ever-active, stirrer-up of things. A go-getter, often out for his own *gelt*. One who stirs things up. A *makher* or *macher* (maker of things happening). A live wire. A noisemaker. A clown.

3. FONFER. Originally, one who talks through his (or her) nose. More common these days, a blabbermouth, a promiser who does not come through, an exaggerator, a constant gossip and tale-spreader; usually, an unsuccessful optimist.

4. SACHEL (or *tsachel*). Sense, common sense, good judgment. "Jack has the imagination, but for real *sachel*, listen to what Sam suggests." *Sachel* is an exceptionally rare attribute — especially in a complicated world.

5. KLUTZ. From German meaning "a leg." A heavy-handed, clumsy, oaflike character, lacking in sensitivity, charm, wit, or ingenuity. Never take a *klutz* to a ballet.

6. PASKUDNYAK. I have searched for decades for a word remotely like *paskudnyak* (or its adjectival derivative *paskudne*) with woeful results. This word describes a thoroughly unpleasant, uncouth, unreliable perpetrator of the tactless or the tasteless. He can ruin any dinner party, or offend even the most gracious hostess. He is often a guiltless liar, a cheat — in any case, a thoroughly undesirable, offensive no-goodnick.

7. NARR. A simple-enough word with oh such a panoply of meaning! A *narr* is a fool. In our circles he was more likely to be a fool's fool. Unlike the gallery of characters above, *narr* may convey sympathy, or regret — but not any of the tactless, foolish, gormless (walk down Piccadilly) traits that flourish in a community where *naronim* (plural) are simply simpleminded souls. A Talmudic gloss tells me "against a *narr*, even the Lord Himself is helpless."

8. CHAUCHEM. A wise man; a real expert, authority, man of judgment (Hebrew).

9. KOCHLEFFEL. A stirrer-up of things (German); a hot potato; mischief maker.

10. K'NOCKER. A big shot who acts like one, shows off, puts on an egotistical show of importance that turns out to be mostly braggadocio.

11. KVETCH. Literally, to squeeze. As used, a chronic complainer, alibi-ist; a perpetual wet blanket; this is a marvelously mimetic word for anyone who frets, gripes, derides, and sour-pusses — for no reason other than psychological necessity. His function in life seems to be to darken the mood, or decrease the pleasure, of everyone else.

12. FARTOOST. (A pip from German.) Mixed-up, confused, befuddled. An excellent synonym for *farchadat, farmisht, tsedoodelt*.

13. KOSHER (or not kosher). According to dietary laws; strictly ethical; honest, honorable, reliable; right on the mark. "Not kosher" means something is awry — not strictly legal, cutting corners, tricky, deceptive.

— Exclusive for *The Book of Lists*

18 Sayings of Oscar Wilde

Born in Dublin and educated at Oxford, Wilde (1856–1900) wrote one novel, *The Picture of Dorian Gray*, and a number of successful plays, including *Lady Windermere's Fan* and *The Importance of Being Earnest*. Considered the master of social comedy, Wilde was an expert craftsman of witty sayings and paradoxes. Even on his deathbed, as he sipped champagne, he quipped, "I am dying beyond my means."

1. Murder is always a mistake. One should never do anything that one cannot talk about after dinner.
2. I don't recognize you — I've changed a lot.
3. Always forgive your enemies — nothing annoys them so much.
4. The idea that is not dangerous is unworthy of being called an idea at all.
5. To love oneself is the beginning of a lifelong romance.
6. Anybody can sympathize with the sufferings of a friend, but it requires a very fine nature to sympathize with a friend's success.
7. When one is in love, one always begins by deceiving oneself; and one always ends by deceiving others. That is what the world calls a romance.
8. To get back my youth I would do anything in the world, except take exercise, get up early, or be respectable.
9. I can resist everything except temptation.
10. What is a cynic? a man who knows the price of everything and the value of nothing.
11. Experience is the name everyone gives to their mistakes.
12. We are all in the gutter, but some of us are looking at the stars.
13. There is a luxury in self-reproach. When we blame ourselves we feel that no one else has a right to blame us.
14. Only dull people are brilliant at breakfast.
15. A cigarette is the perfect type of a perfect pleasure. It is exquisite, and it leaves one unsatisfied. What more can one want?
16. Nothing succeeds like excess.
17. In this world there are only two tragedies. One is not getting what one wants, and the other is getting it.
18. Education is an admirable thing, but it is well to remember from time to time that nothing that is worth knowing can be taught.

The Truth Behind
10 Popularly Held Beliefs

We all take a lot of sayings for granted. Are they fact, or are they old wives' tales? Author Alfie Kohn, in his book *You Know What They Say . . .* (HarperPerennial, 1990), examines the truth behind popular beliefs. Here are ten of our favorites:

1. READING IN THE DARK WILL RUIN YOUR EYES

   Not so, says the American Academy of Ophthalmology — "Reading in dim light can no more harm your eyes than taking a photograph in dim light can harm the camera."

2. AN ELEPHANT NEVER FORGETS

Well, maybe once in a while, but on the whole, elephants have excellent memories. A Cornell University researcher, Bill Langbauer, observed that elephants often travel more than thirty miles in search of water. "The most likely explanation for their being able to find these sources of water is that they remember where they are," he says.

3. DON'T HAVE SEX BEFORE THE BIG GAME

While there is little hard data on this subject, there was a modest study conducted in 1968 indicating that pregame sex *is* safe for athletes. A 1988 survey of baseball and basketball coaches indicates that only 9 percent advised against it, though 41 percent were not sure. Perhaps the real strain is in the mating dance: as Casey Stengel reportedly said, "It's not the catchin' that causes problems — it's the chasin'."

4. FEMALE PRAYING MANTISES EAT THEIR MATES

Only in captivity do the ladies eat the heads of their partners. The August 1984 issue of *Animal Behavior* ran an article debunking this myth: the authors videotaped thirty pairs of praying mantises in the act, and not a single one lost its head.

5. CARROTS ARE GOOD FOR YOUR EYES

Carrots contain carotene, which your body converts to vitamin A, and a shortage of this vitamin would indeed cause night blindness. However, most people in the developed world store plenty of vitamin A in their livers. The extra vitamin A in carrots doesn't really do your eyes any good.

6. CATHERINE THE GREAT DIED HORSING AROUND

Popular as this story is — that the empress Catherine was killed by sexual congress with a horse — it just isn't true. It was merely a scurrilous rumor circulated by her contemporaries. She may have been lusty, but only with *Homo sapiens*, and she died of a stroke at the age of sixty-seven.

7. DON'T SWIM FOR AN HOUR AFTER EATING

This bit of folk wisdom is entirely false. Fifty years ago, the Red Cross published a booklet stating that stomach cramps that could lead to death resulted from eating before swimming. While it may not be comfortable to eat before going in the water, it is not dangerous, according to the YMCA, the Boy Scouts, and the current Red Cross brochure.

8. SPICY FOOD IS BAD FOR THE STOMACH

Apparently not. Gastroenterologist David Graham researched this subject, and found that a steady diet of Mexican meals with

Catherine the Great: no horsing around.

jalapeño peppers did no harm to his test subjects, though taking aspirin with bland meals damaged their stomachs. In another study, even ulcer sufferers fared well with hot chili powder sprinkled on their food.

9. **THE FULL MOON MAKES PEOPLE CRAZY**

This has never been proven, despite constant rumors to the contrary. In a review of thirty-seven studies on the subject, researchers James Rotton and Ivan Kelly found no evidence that the full moon affects murder rates, suicide rates, crime rates, or numbers of admissions at hospital emergency rooms.

10. **MORE PEOPLE COMMIT SUICIDE DURING THE HOLIDAYS**

Contrary to rumor, December is not a popular month for ending it all. In fact, there are significantly *fewer* suicides on most holidays than on other days. According to statistics, suicides peak in the spring, and April is, indeed, the cruelest month.

8 Winning Tall Tales

Since 1929 the Burlington Liar's Club has been giving an annual award to "The World's Greatest Liar." Entries may be sent to Don Reed, vice-president, 149 N. Oakland Avenue, Burlington, WI 53105. For copies of *"I Never Lie" and Other Lies from the Burlington Liar's Club*, send $12.95 to Shepherd, Inc., Evergreen Park, 10340 Military Road, Dubuque, IA 52003. Here are some sample winners:

1. FALLING TEMPERATURE (1935)

During an extra-cold winter, a rat took refuge in my home. I exercised all my wiles, but was unable to trap it. Finally, I hit upon an idea.

"The cold chased you in here," I said, "and the cold will catch you." So I took one of those big thermometers and hung it in the kitchen with the bottom about three feet from the floor. Under it I placed a chunk of cheese. In the morning, sure enough, I had Mr. Rat. The rat had gone for the cheese, and the mercury in the thermometer fell so fast that it pinned the rat to the floor!

— Jim Jordan
Chicago, Illinois

2. LAZY WIFE (1937)

My wife is so lazy that she feeds the chickens popcorn so that the eggs will turn themselves when she fries them.

— John P. Zelenak, Jr.
Tacoma, Washington

3. DOG FISH (1938)

My big adventure came when I was working on a fishing boat out of New Orleans. Having good luck one day and getting in early, we decided to make another trip out into the Gulf. Our luck held, and we had no trouble in filling the hold with fish, but on the trip back to port we ran out of coal.

I saved the situation by having the crew sort out all the dog fish. When we had a lot of them, I tickled each fish until it barked. The crew gathered up the bark, threw it into the fire-pot under the boilers, and it was only a matter of time until the engineer had steam up, and we were merrily on our way back to New Orleans.

— Gilbert Boettcher
Milwaukee, Wisconsin

4. BIG FARM (1957)

We had one farmer out here who has a field so long that he started out last spring with a tractor, a plow, and a drill. He was gone so long that his wife drew three widow pension checks; she thought he had got plowed under. But he got back the other day. When he got to the other end of the field he had traded his plow and drill for a combine and harvested on the way home.

— Harry Berogan
Mission, South Dakota

5. BAD FISHING (1963)

Fishing around here was so bad this summer that even the biggest liars didn't catch any.

— Richard K. Boutin
Chathaw, Massachusetts

6. TOO POOR (1974)

We were so poor in our youth that our parents couldn't afford window shopping.

— Robert E. Regent
Milwaukee, Wisconsin

7. TOO COLD (1979)

It was so cold in Missouri last winter that I saw a politician standing on a street corner with his hands in his own pockets.

— C. A. Laurie
Eckland, Missouri

8. STRONG WINDS (1985)

Here in Oklahoma, we have very high winds, but two years ago they were higher than usual, and the tomatoes in my garden couldn't get ripe because the wind kept blowing the sun off them.

— Mary Marie Weatherly
Oklahoma City, Oklahoma

16 Recent Examples of Doublespeak

Each year, the committee on doublespeak of the National Council of Teachers of English announces its Doublespeak Awards, given to public figures or agencies using deceptive, evasive, or confusing language.

1.–3. PRESIDENT GEORGE BUSH

During the 1989 invasion of Panama, Bush tried desperately to avoid using the word *invasion*. Rather, he "sent troops down to Panama," "deployed forces," and "directed United States forces to execute . . . preplanned missions in Panama."

When he campaigned for president in 1988, Bush promised "no net loss of wetlands." After his inauguration, he clarified his pledge to mean no net loss of wetlands except "where there is a high proportion of land which is wetlands"; in other words, those areas most in need of protection, such as the Alaskan tundra and the Florida Everglades.

Following the Persian Gulf War, Bush proposed a Middle East arms control initiative designed to halt "the proliferation of conventional and unconventional weapons in the Middle East." Immediately afterward, the Bush administration announced plans to sell over $5 billion in new weapons to Saudi Arabia, Egypt, Israel, Turkey, Oman, Bahrain, and the United Arab Emirates.

4. BRIGADIER GENERAL ROBERT DROLET

During the Persian Gulf War, the U.S. Army claimed that the Patriot missile "intercepted" 45 of 47 Scud missiles, and President Bush claimed 41 out of 42. When it was later revealed that most of the Patriots had actually missed their targets, Drolet maintained that President Bush had not lied because the army definition of *intercept* was not "destroyed." Instead it meant that "a Patriot and Scud passed in the sky."

5. DENNIS KLOSKE, UNDERSECRETARY OF COMMERCE FOR EXPORT ADMINISTRATION

After the Bush administration suddenly discovered that Saddam Hussein was an enemy of the United States, senior officials became worried about records citing the Reagan administration's sale of military trucks to Iraq. So, before the records of the sales were released to Congress, Kloske authorized the changing of the phrase *military trucks* to *commercial utility cargo vehicles.*

6. MICHAEL STONE, DARRYL MOUNGER, PAUL DEPASQUALE, AND JOHN BARNETT

These four lawyers persuaded a Simi Valley, California, jury that Rodney King was in full control of the Los Angeles police officers who were beating him. One juror was convinced that "Mr. King was controlling the whole show with his actions," despite his taking fifty-six blows and two taser darts from the police.

7.–8. THE U.S. SUPREME COURT

The eighth amendment to the Constitution of the United States prohibits cruel and unusual punishments. In 1991 the Supreme Court ruled that a sentence of life in prison without the possibility of parole for the possession of 672 grams of cocaine might be cruel, but it was not unusual. In other words, as long as a punishment is imposed often enough, it is not unconstitutional.

The Refugee Act of 1980 authorizes asylum to a person with "a well-grounded fear of persecution on account of race, religion, membership in a particular group, or political opinion." In 1987 masked, machine gun–toting Guatemalan guerrillas came to the door of nineteen-year-old Jario Elias-Zacarias and demanded that he join their fight against the government. Instead, Elias-Zacarias fled to the United States, where he was denied asylum. Justice Antonio Scalia ruled that the young man had failed to show that the guerrillas would persecute him for his political views "rather than because of his refusal to fight with them."

9. U.S. Representative Newt Gingrich and GOPAC

GOPAC, a conservative Republican group headed by Gingrich, published a booklet entitled "Language: A Key Mechanism of Control," designed to be used by Republican candidates for office. The booklet includes sixty-nine positive words to be used to "help define your campaign and your vision," and sixty-four negative words to "define our opponents." The positive list included "environment, peace, freedom, fair, flag, we/us/our, moral, family, children, truth, hard-working, reformer, and candid." The negative list included "traitors, betray, sick, lie, liberal, radical, corruption, permissive attitude, they/them, anti-flag, anti-family, anti-job, unionized, bureaucracy, and impose."

10. Deputy Assistant Secretary of State David Mack

During the conflict with Iraq, the Bush administration was caught between wanting to convince the American people that U.S. soldiers were fighting for democracy and not wanting to offend the governments of Kuwait, Saudi Arabia, Syria, and Egypt, which were not democratic. So, instead of using the dreaded D-word, Mack called on Kuwait to "maximize internal political participation in accordance with all traditional institutions."

11. U.S. Senator Ted Stevens

When the U.S. Senate voted itself a $23,000 pay raise, Senator Stevens of Alaska declared that it was not a pay raise, but rather "a pay equalization concept."

12. The U.S. Air Force

After a Midgetman missile blew up seventy seconds after launch, Air Force spokesman Captain Ron Joy said the flight was successful because "a major part" of the mission was getting the missile off the ground.

13. EXXON CORPORATION

   After the *Exxon Valdez* oil spill, Exxon pronounced thirty-five miles of beaches in Alaska "environmentally clean" and "environmentally stabilized." When it was pointed out that the beaches were still covered with oil, Otto Harrison, general manager of Exxon's cleanup operations, explained that clean "doesn't mean every oil stain is off every rock. . . . It means that the natural inhabitants can live there without harm."

14. CHUCK JOHNSON, MARYLAND STATE POLICE SPOKESMAN

   When seven Maryland state police officers were disciplined for failing to make a minimum number of drunk-driving arrests, Johnson defended the actions. "These are not quotas," he said. "They are minimum expectations."

15. PAT ROBERTSON

   Robertson accused Tom Brokaw of NBC of displaying religious bigotry because Brokaw referred to him as a "television evangelist" instead of a "religious broadcaster."

16. U.S. SENATOR ORRIN HATCH

   Hatch said that "capital punishment is our society's recognition of the sanctity of human life." In saying this, he followed in the footsteps of Yasir Arafat, the leader of the Palestine Liberation Organization, who once declared, "It is precisely because we have been advocating coexistence that we have shed so much blood."

NOTE: For more examples of doublespeak, see *The Book of Lists #3*, pp. 162–67.

10 Examples of Doublespeak from the Persian Gulf War

In 1991 the Doublespeak Award given by the National Council of Teachers of English to public figures or agencies using the most deceptive, evasive, or confusing language was awarded to the Defense Department for the euphemisms it used during the Persian Gulf War. See how many you can match.

1. ARMED SITUATION	A. Bombing human beings and buildings
2. FORCE PACKAGES	B. Censorship
3. EFFORT	C. Killing the enemy

4. VISITING A SITE D. Shooting down enemy planes
5. SERVICING THE TARGET E War
6. COLLATERAL DAMAGE F. Bombing mission
7. SECURITY REVIEW G. Bombs
8. AIRBORNE SANITATION H. Warplanes
9. WEAPONS SYSTEMS I. Killing innocent victims
10. SUPPRESSION OF ASSETS J. Bombing attack

ANSWERS: 1 (E); 2 (H); 3 (J); 4 (F); 5 (C); 6 (I); 7 (B); 8 (D); 9 (G); 10 (A).

16 Memorable Responses to Critics

"I had another dream the other day about music critics. They were small and rodent-like with padlocked ears." — Igor Stravinsky

1. WINSTON CHURCHILL, British statesman

At a dinner party one evening, there was a heated exchange between Churchill and a female MP. At the end of the argument, the lady said scornfully, "Mr. Churchill, you are drunk."

"And you, madam," replied Churchill, "are ugly. But I shall be sober tomorrow."

2. LIBERACE, U.S. entertainer

Liberace's 1954 concert in Madison Square Garden was a huge success with his fans, but the critics lambasted him. He responded with the immortal lines, "What you said hurt me very much. I cried all the way to the bank."

3. ELIZABETH TAYLOR, U.S. actress

Taylor attended a wedding wearing the 33.19-carat diamond given to her by Richard Burton. Princess Margaret looked at it and said, "That's the most vulgar thing I've ever seen."

"Want to try it on?" asked Taylor.

"Oh, yes, please," said the princess, putting it on and holding it up to the light to admire it.

"See, there," replied Taylor, "it's not so vulgar now, is it?"

4. ERNEST HEMINGWAY, U.S. author

In 1937 author-critic Max Eastman panned Hemingway's novels in an article titled "Bull in the Afternoon." Shortly after the piece had been published, the two men happened to meet in the

Elizabeth Taylor with her "not so vulgar" Krupp diamond ring.

office of Maxwell Perkins, Hemingway's editor. The results of that meeting were not revealed until years later, when a copy of Eastman's *Art and the Life of Action* was put up for auction. It was autographed not by Eastman but by Hemingway and Perkins. According to the catalogue, on page 95 of the book there was spot where it had hit "Mr. Eastman's nose when Mr. Hemingway struck him with it in a gesture of disapproval."

5. MAX REGER, German composer

Dr. Louis, music critic for Munich's *Presse*, never wrote one favorable word about Reger's compositions. His review of Reger's *Sinfonietta* (1906) was particularly hostile. The composer sent Dr. Louis this famous reply: "I am sitting in the smallest room in the house, and your review is before me. Soon, it will be behind me."

6. JODY POWELL, press secretary to then governor Jimmy Carter

A lady wrote Carter and called him "a gutless peanut brain" because he had not protested against the busing of schoolchildren to achieve racial integration. Powell wrote back to her:

"Among the many burdens that fall upon a governor, one of the most exasperating is having to read barely legible letters from morons like you.

"I am very happy that I can at least spare the governor from having to respond. I respectfully suggest that you take two running jumps and go straight to hell."

7. JOHN RUSKIN'S FRIEND

Ruskin, the nineteenth-century art critic, viciously attacked a friend's painting, but added that his views should not, of course, be allowed to interfere with their friendship. The man responded, "Ruskin — next time I meet you I shall knock you down, but I hope it will make no difference in our friendship."

8. RAPHAEL, Italian Artist

While Raphael worked on his Vatican frescoes, two cardinals stood by criticizing his painting.

Said one, "The face of the Apostle Paul is too red."

Replied the painter, "He blushes to see into whose hands the church has fallen."

9. ERMA BOMBECK, U.S. newspaper columnist

Bombeck received the following letter of complaint: "You gripe about everything. Aspirin bottles that only a two-year-old can open, grocery carts with wheels that go in four different directions, carrying on when the plants in your doctor's office are dead, and your stupid ironing board that hasn't been down in years. You hate dogs, children, and urologists who offer you a drink. You're sick!

"P.S. I never read you!

"I was married to a shrew like you once for three days."

Bombeck replied to this note with the question "How did you last so long?"

Her correspondent wrote back, "I drank."

10. JEAN COCTEAU, French author, artist

Cocteau's 1951 play, *Bacchus*, was about a cardinal and a heretical lunatic. The pious writer François Mauriac was so outraged by it that he stormed out of the premiere, and described the play in a review as "spittle." Cocteau replied, "I would prefer not going to heaven since that would apparently entail running into Mauriac."

11. SAMUEL JOHNSON, English author

When Johnson was completing his dictionary, a London journal published two anonymous "previews" of the book. The articles were favorable but superficial. When Johnson learned that they had been written by the wealthy Earl of Chesterfield, he was outraged. Johnson had applied to him repeatedly for patronage while writing the dictionary, but the earl had been cheap, giving the poverty-stricken writer no more than ten pounds (about $250). Now, Johnson felt, he was trying to take credit as a patron. In the dictionary, he defined *patron* as "commonly a wretch who supports with insolence, and is paid with flattery."

12. JOHN SINGER SARGENT, U.S. portrait painter

A woman who was paying $5,000 for her portrait by Sargent said that there was something wrong with the nose. Singer handed her the canvas and said, "Oh, you can easily put a little thing like that right when you get home."

On another occasion, a woman objected to his treatment of her mouth in a painting. He told her, "Perhaps, madam, we'd better leave it out altogether." (Sargent suggested that "A little something wrong with the mouth" should be written on his tombstone.)

13. CURRAN, a dinner guest of King George IV

The following anecdote appeared in the journal of the English clergyman, Augustus Hare. It had been told to him by his old friend, the Honorable Augusta Barrington.

"George IV, as Prince Regent, was very charming when he was not drunk, but he generally *was*. Do you remember how he asked Curran to dinner to amuse him — only for that? Curran was up to it, and sat silent all through dinner. This irritated the Prince, and at last, after dinner, when he had had a good deal too much, he filled a glass with wine and threw it in Curran's face, with 'Say something funny, can't you!' Curran, without moving a muscle, threw his own glass of wine in his neighbor's face, saying, 'Pass His Royal Highness's joke.'"

14. GEORGE BERNARD SHAW, Irish author

After the premiere of *Arms and the Man* (1898), Shaw took the stage to make a curtain speech. When the applause subsided, there was a solitary boo from London critic Reginald Golding Bright. Shaw looked directly at Bright and said, "My dear fellow, I quite agree with you, but what are we two against so many?"

15. JEAN SIBELIUS, Finnish composer

English critic Ralph Wood called Sibelius's *Seventh Symphony* (1924) "a failure." The composer replied, "A statue has never yet been erected to a critic."

16. HARRY TRUMAN, U.S. president

In 1950 Truman's daughter, Margaret, gave a public singing recital in Washington. Her performance was attacked by the *Washington Post*'s music critic, Paul Hume.

Truman wrote him the following letter: "I have just read your lousy review buried in the back pages. You sound like a frustrated old man who never made a success, an eight-ulcer man on a four-ulcer job, and all four ulcers working. I have never met you, but if I do you'll need a new nose and plenty of beefsteak and perhaps a supporter below."

Hume published the note, and the incident caused an uproar, but most Americans approved of Truman's fatherly behavior. Years later Margaret wrote, "Dad never felt the slightest remorse about sending it. He always insisted that he had a right to be two persons — the President of the United States and Harry S. Truman, father of Margaret, husband of Bess Wallace. 'It was Harry S. Truman, the human being, who wrote that note,' he said."

10 Commandments

1. Thou shalt have no other gods before Me.
2. Thou shalt not make unto thee any graven image, or any like-ness of any thing that is in heaven above, or that is in the earth beneath, or that is in the water under the earth.
3. Thou shalt not take the name of the LORD thy God in vain.
4. Remember the sabbath day to keep it holy. Six days shalt thou labour, and do all thy work: But the seventh day is the sabbath of the LORD thy God.
5. Honor thy father and thy mother.
6. Thou shalt not kill.
7. Thou shalt not commit adultery.
8. Thou shalt not steal.
9. Thou shalt not bear false witness against thy neighbor.
10. Thou shalt not covet thy neighbor's house, thou shalt not covet thy neighbor's wife, nor his manservant, nor his maidservant, nor his ox, nor his ass, nor any thing that is thy neighbor's.

SOURCE: The Holy Bible in the King James Version.

Polonius's *10* Pieces of Advice to Laertes

1. Give thy thoughts no tongue,
   Nor any unproportion'd thought his act.
2. Be thou familiar, but by no means vulgar.
3. Those friends thou hast, and their adoption tried,
   Grapple them unto thy soul with hoops of steel;
4. But do not dull thy palm with entertainment
   Of each new-hatch'd, unfledg'd comrade.
5. Beware of entrance to a quarrel, but, being in,
   Bear't that th' opposed may beware of thee.

6. Give every man thy ear, but few thy voice;
7. Take each man's censure, but reserve thy judgment.
8. Costly thy habit as thy purse can buy,
   But not express'd in fancy; rich, not gaudy;
   For the apparel oft proclaims the man . . .
9. Neither a borrower nor a lender be;
   For loan oft loses both itself and friend,
   And borrowing dulls the edge of husbandry.
10. This above all: to thine own self be true,
    And it must follow, as the night the day,
    Thou canst not then be false to any man.

SOURCE: William Shakespeare, *Hamlet*, I, iii, 59–79.

General Colin Powell's
13 Rules to Live By

Born in Harlem and raised in the South Bronx, Colin Powell worked
in the administrations of Richard Nixon and Jimmy Carter before
being appointed Ronald Reagan's national security adviser following the Iran-Contra scandal. Despite his extensive civilian service,
Powell has remained at heart a military man. Commissioned a second lieutenant in the army in 1958, he rose to become chairman of
the Joint Chiefs of Staff in 1989.

1. It ain't as bad as you think; it will look better in the morning.
2. Get mad, then get over it.

3. Avoid having your ego so close to your position that when your position falls, your ego goes with it.
4. It can be done!
5. Be careful what you choose. You may get it.
6. Don't let adverse facts stand in the way of a good decision.
7. Check small things.
8. Share credit.
9. You can't make someone else's choices. You shouldn't let someone else make yours.
10. Remain calm. Be kind.
11. Have a vision. Be demanding.
12. Don't take counsel of your fears or naysayers.
13. Perpetual optimism is a force multiplier. (In the military, one is always looking for methods of increasing or multiplying one's forces.)

SOURCE: David Wallechinsky, "Have a Vision," *Parade* magazine (August 13, 1989).

Erma Bombeck's *10* Rules to Live By

Bombeck's syndicated humor column appears in 800 newspapers. She is the author of several best-selling books, including *The Grass Is Always Greener over the Septic Tank* and *When You Look Like Your Passport Photo, It's Time to Go Home*. Bombeck draws most of her material from the trials and tribulations of daily life.

1. Never have more children than you have car windows.
2. Gravity always wins. Accept that. Science is trying to reverse the aging process. The kicker is you look young on the outside, but inside you're still aging. There is no advantage to looking like Arnold Schwarzenegger on the beach if you can't travel two feet away from a restroom.
3. Never loan your car to someone to whom you have given birth.
4. Pick your friends carefully. A friend never goes on a diet when you are fat or tells you how lucky you are to have a husband who remembers Mother's Day — with a smoke alarm.
5. Seize the moment. Remember all those women on the *Titanic* who waved off the dessert cart.
6. Given a choice between the man of your dreams and a plumber, choose the latter. Men who can fix your toilet on Sundays are hard to come by.
7. Know the difference between success and fame. Success is Mother Teresa. Fame is Madonna.
8. Never be in a hurry to terminate a marriage. Remember, you may need this man/woman someday to finish a sentence.

9. There are no guarantees in marriage. If that's what you're looking for, go live with a Sears battery.
10. Never go to a class reunion pregnant. They will think that's all you have been doing since you graduated.

— Exclusive for *The Book of Lists*

Coach John Wooden's *10* Rules to Live By

John Wooden, head basketball coach at UCLA from 1948 to 1975, once defined success as the peace of mind "that comes from knowing you did your best to become the best that you are capable of becoming."

1. 1 Corinthians 13. (This Bible chapter addresses the importance of charity — love — and ends with the verse, "And now abideth faith, hope, charity, these three; but the greatest of these is charity.")
2. Make each day your masterpiece.
3. Drink deeply from good books.
4. Freedom from desire leads to inner peace (Lao-Tzu).
5. Failure to prepare is preparing to fail. I will get ready and then, perhaps, my chance will come.
6. Ability may get you to the top, but it takes character to keep you there (Abraham Lincoln).
7. Help others.
8. It is better to trust and be disappointed occasionally than to distrust and be miserable all the time.
9. Almost anyone can stand adversity, but to test a person's character, give them power (Abraham Lincoln).
10. Be more interested in your character, which is what you really are, than in your reputation, which is what others perceive you to be.

— Exclusive for *The Book of Lists*

I. King Jordan's *10* Rules to Live By

When he was twenty-one years old, I. King Jordan was hit by a car while riding a motorcycle. The accident resulted in profound deafness. After earning a doctorate in psychology at the University of Tennessee, Jordan became a faculty member at Gallaudet University in Washington, D.C., the world's only university with programs and services designed specifically for students who are deaf and hard of hearing. In 1988, following student protests, Jordan was appointed president of Gallaudet, the first deaf president since the university was established in 1864.

1. Recognize that my family is my most valuable asset.
2. Run every morning. This is the focus of a daily routine and a source of energy.
3. Value diversity. Cherish and learn from the differences among people.
4. Have a "cause" and know that I can make a difference. Use my political and economic power for the "cause."
5. Always be decent, honest, and fair.
6. Take risks; don't be afraid of failing. It's how we learn.
7. Recognize that learning is a life-long process.
8. Strive for excellence. Never be satisfied with "good enough."
9. Live in the present. Don't use the past as an excuse for how to act or think.
10. Never take life too seriously.

— Exclusive for *The Book of Lists*

Walter Anderson's 7 Rules to Live By

Since 1980 Anderson has been the editor of *Parade* magazine, the largest-circulation periodical in the world. He is also a champion of the cause of literacy and the author of three books, *Courage Is a Three-Letter Word, The Greatest Risk of All,* and *Read with Me.* In addition to earning numerous humanitarian awards, in 1992 Anderson was named to the list "10 Best-Mannered Americans."

. *Know who is responsible.* "I am responsible." When you begin with these three words, you can build a new life, even a new world.

. *Believe in something big.* Be assured, it's not possible for human beings to be empty vessels. No person who has ever lived has been an unbeliever, despite what they may argue. Everyone believes in something. It might be God or no God, manifest greed for money or power, a career or a friend, science, a principle — *something.* Remember, whatever it is we place before ourselves is what we run toward. When we commit to high ideals, we succeed before the outcome is known. Your life is worth a noble motive.

Practice tolerance. You'll like yourself a lot more and so will others.

4. *Be brave.* Remember, courage is acting with fear, not without it. If the challenge is important to you, you're supposed to be nervous; we only worry about things we care about.
5. *Love someone.* Because you should know joy.
6. *Be ambitious.* No single effort will solve all of your problems, achieve all of your dreams, or even be enough — and that's okay. To want to be more than we are is real and normal and healthy.
7. *Smile.* Because no one else can do this for you.

— Exclusive for *The Book of Lists*

Satchel Paige's
7 Rules to Live By

Born in Mobile, Alabama, in 1906, Leroy "Satchel" Paige was one of the greatest pitchers in baseball history. Because he came of age in an era when only white players could play in the major leagues, Paige became a star in the Negro leagues, eventually pitching in seven different countries. In 1948 he was signed by the Cleveland Indians and helped them win the American League pennant. In 1965 he pitched three shutout innings for Kansas City and became the oldest person to appear in a major-league game. He was fifty-nine years old. Once, when asked why he didn't run before a game in order to warm up, he replied, "Where I come from we throw the ball across the plate; we don't carry it across." Paige died in 1982.

1. Avoid fried meats which angry up the blood.

Satchel Paige — "Avoid running at all times."

2. If your stomach disputes you, lie down and pacify it with cool thoughts.
3. Keep the juices flowing by jangling around gently as you move.
4. Go very lightly on the vices, such as carrying on in society. The social ramble ain't restful.
5. Avoid running at all times.
6. Age is a question of mind over matter. If you don't mind, it doesn't matter.
7. Don't look back. Something might be gaining on you.

Miss Manners' *10* Worst Faux Pas

According to the ever-correct Miss Manners (Judith Martin), she was "born a perfect lady in an imperfect society" and "considers it her duty and privilege to lead the way to a more civilized — and cheerful — society." Since 1978 Martin has been giving etiquette (and relationship) advice in her Miss Manners column, syndicated by United Feature Syndicate. Her most recent book is *Miss Manners' Guide for the Turn of the Millennium.*

1. HONESTY

   When what this means is insulting other people to their faces, and then, when they are hurt, insulting them again by inquiring whether they don't believe in honesty.

2. HELPFULNESS

   When this consists of minding other people's business by volunteering, unasked, your opinion of how they should lead their lives.

3. HEALTH-CONSCIOUSNESS

   When this is an excuse for spoiling other people's dinners by telling them that what they are eating, or serving their guests, is poison.

4. IDEALISM

   When this leads to humiliating other people for unexceptionable activities — pointing at strangers who are using two sheets of paper towels to dry their hands, for example — that violate your own resolutions.

5. BEING TRUE TO YOUR OWN FEELINGS

   When this is cited as a reason for your neglecting duties toward others, such as writing thank-you letters or attending funerals, that you happen to find distasteful.

6. **SELF-ASSERTIVENESS**

When this means elbowing others out of the way so you can get what you want.

7. **FRIENDLINESS**

When this is held to be the motivation for taking unauthorized liberties with others, such as addressing strangers by their first names or making personal remarks to acquaintances.

8. **SPONTANEITY**

When this translates into not being willing to answer invitations or honor acceptances because you feel like doing something else on the night of the party.

9. **HOSPITALITY**

When this consists of inviting your own guests to someone else's wedding or party, or telling your guests that they are expected to supply the meal or pay for what they ate.

10. **CREATIVITY**

When fostering this is cited as an excuse for allowing your children to destroy other people's property or peace of mind.

— Exclusive for *The Book of Lists*

Don't Get Conned: 9 Rules Con Men Follow

Victor "The Count" Lustig (1890–1947) devoted his life to scamming and cheating people. His most famous con came in 1922 when he sold the Eiffel Tower to a greedy scrap-metal dealer for $50,000. Here are the rules that Lustig followed when dealing with a potential victim.

1. Be a good listener.
2. Never give political opinions until the mark has expressed his, and then agree.
3. Wait for the mark to reveal his religion, and then become a member of the same church.
4. Hint at sex, but don't pursue it unless the mark is eager to explore the subject.
5. Never discuss personal ailments unless the mark shows an interest in the subject.
6. Never be untidy or drunk, yet always be ready for a party.

7. Never appear bored.
8. Never pry; let the mark volunteer information.
9. Never brag; let the mark sense your success.

SOURCE: James F. Johnson as told to Floyd Miller, *The Man Who Sold the Eiffel Tower* (London: W. H. Allen, 1962). Copyright A. M. Heath & Co., Ltd., London.

Muhammad Ali's
8 Tips for Young Heavyweight Fighters

One of the greatest boxers in history, Muhammad Ali is a three-time heavyweight champion — the first heavyweight boxer to regain the title twice. His awesome power and grace combined with his unbridled showmanship ("I am the Greatest") and ring antics (rope-a-dope; the Ali shuffle) have made him one of the most widely recognized people in the world. His advice was originally intended for boxer Leon Spinks.

1. Drive that big car until it don't run no more. The worst thing is to keep buying cars. You can't get your money back. They get old every year they make a new one.

2. Get a good hunk of money, put up $20,000 for each child now, while you're making it, in case you die or get hurt or something, so their education will be paid for. Leave something for your wife. After that your mother. Make her burdens a little lighter.

3. Establish a nice home for your wife and your children. Don't invest in nothing, no real estate, no restaurants, no nightclubs. Put your money in government tax-free bonds, because when you retire, you still have to live; your children need money to go to school.

4. Get yourself one lawyer and have him on standby. Don't keep him year-round. Get a good lawyer and keep him; don't go from lawyer to lawyer and don't listen to lawyers who have one-shot deals, because those one-shot deals will kill you. There are no good deals. I'm talking from experience.

5. When you put up money, direct the bank to use it for your children's education. Buy fifty acres of land outside some major city, someplace for your family to retreat to.

6. Don't carry a lot of cash with you because you'll give it all away to your friends. If your family or friends ask for money, give it to them, don't loan it to them. If you loan it to them, they end up your enemies. People hate you for helping them.

7. Don't forget your wife in the midst of all the parties and the young

girls hanging around you. Remember, she was with you whe you weren't nothing.

8. You're not like me. When you lose, it's all over. When I lose, I ge invited to more countries. What did the man say? Loser and sti champion.

SOURCE: Phil Pepe and Zander Hollander, *The Book of Sports Lists* (Los Angeles: Pi nacle Books, 1979).

The 2,000-Year-Old Man's **4** Secrets of Longevity

1. Don't run for a bus — there'll always be another.
2. Never, ever touch fried food.
3. Stay out of a Ferrari or any other small Italian car.
4. Eat fruit — a nectarine — even a rotten plum is good.

SOURCE: Mel Brooks, as quoted in Jon Winokur, *Friendly Advice*, copyright 1990 by Jo Winokur. Reprinted by permission of the author.

Steve Allen in- terviewing the 2,000-year-old man.

21 Pieces of Good Advice

1. "Never eat at a place called Mom's. Never play cards with man named Doc. And never lie down with a woman who's g more trouble than you do." — *Nelson Algren*
2. "Beware of all enterprises that require new clothes." — *Henr David Thoreau*
3. "It is better to keep your mouth shut and appear stupid than t open it and remove all doubt." — *Mark Twain*

4. "Never get involved with anyone who wants to change you." — *Quentin Crisp.*

5. "Throw high risers at the chin; throw peas at the knees; throw it here when they're lookin' there; throw it there when they're lookin' here." — *Satchel Paige*

6. "Never say anything on the phone that you wouldn't want your mother to hear at your trial." — *Sydney Biddle Barrows*

7. "You put your left index finger on your eye and your right index finger on the [camembert]. . . . If they sort of feel the same, the cheese is ready." — *M. Taittinger*

8. "Whenever you find that you are on the side of the majority, it is time to reform (or pause and reflect)." — *Mark Twain*

9. "When you're wearing a short skirt and walking past a crew of construction workers, always pick your nose. It acts as a deterrent to catcalls." — *Amy Wallace*

10. "The idea is to die young as late as possible." — *Ashley Montagu*

11. "To fall in love with yourself is the first secret of happiness. I did so at the age of four and a half. Then if you're not a good mixer you can always fall back on your own company." — *Robert Morley*

12. "There are only two ways to live your life. One is as though nothing is a miracle. The other is as though everything were a miracle." — *Albert Einstein*

13. "Sometimes you have to play a long time to be able to play like yourself." — *Miles Davis*

14. "The denunciation of the young is a necessary part of the hygiene of older people, and greatly assists the circulation of the blood." — *Logan Pearsall Smith*

15. "Whenever you're sitting across from some important person, always picture him sitting there in a suit of long underwear. That's the way I always operated in business." — *Joseph P. Kennedy*

16. "There are two things that one must get used to or one will find life unendurable: the damages of time and injustices of men." — *Nicolas Chamfort*

17. "The hymn 'Onward, Christian Soldiers,' sung to the right tune and in a not-too-brisk tempo, makes a very good egg timer. If you put the egg into boiling water and sing all five verses and chorus, the egg will be just right when you come to Amen." — *Letter in the London Daily Telegraph*

18. "Never eat in a restaurant where there's a photo of the chef with Sammy Davis, Jr." — *Alf*

19. "Believe nothing, no matter where you read it, or who said it — even if I have said it — unless it agrees with your own reason and your own common sense." — *Guatama Buddha*

20. "I always advise people never to give advice." — *P. G. Wodehouse*
21. "Pay no attention to whatever advice you receive." — *Edward Gorey*

SOURCE: *Friendly Advice*, compiled and edited by Jon Winokur, copyright 1990 by Jon Winokur. Reprinted by permission of the author.

5 Pieces of Advice on How to Survive an Encounter with a Bear

The following situations may occur anywhere in bear country. This recommended behavior is generally advised, but is no guarantee of averting a mishap. Above all, remain calm and give the bear the opportunity to learn that your intentions are not hostile.

1. NEVER RUN

   Do not run. Bears can run faster than 30 miles per hour (50 kilometers per hour) — even faster than Olympic sprinters. Running can elicit a chase response from otherwise nonaggressive bears.

2. AN UNAWARE BEAR

   If the bear is unaware of you, detour quickly and quietly away from it. Give the bear plenty of room, allowing it to continue its own activities undisturbed.

3. AN AWARE BEAR

   If the bear is aware of you but has not acted aggressively, back away slowly, talking in a calm, firm voice while slowly waving

Remain calm and give the bear the opportunity to learn that your intentions are not hostile.

your arms. Bears that stand up on their hind legs are usually just trying to identify you, and are not threatening.

4. An Approaching Bear

Do not run; do not drop your pack. A pack can help protect your body in case of an attack. To drop a pack may encourage the bear to approach people for food. Bears occasionally make "bluff charges," sometimes coming to within ten feet of a person before stopping or veering off. Stand still until the bear stops and has moved away, then slowly back off. Climbing trees will not protect you from black bears, and may not provide protection from grizzlies.

5. If A Bear Touches You

If a grizzly bear does actually make contact with you, curl up in a ball, protecting your stomach and neck, and play dead. If the attack is prolonged, however, change tactics and fight back vigorously. If it is a black bear, do not play dead; fight back.

Source: Denali National Park and Preserve, Denali Park, Alaska.

11 Olympic Medalists
Who Acted in Movies

1. JOHNNY WEISSMULLER (4 golds; 1924 and 1928 swimming

   One of Weissmuller's posters advertising swimsuits for the BV[
   underwear company caught the eye of Hollywood talent scout
   In 1932 he made his film debut in *Tarzan, the Ape Man*. He ever
   tually starred in eleven more Tarzan films.

2. BUSTER CRABBE (gold; 1932 400-meter freestyle)

   Crabbe won his gold medal by one-tenth of a second. He late
   recalled that that tenth of a second led Hollywood producers t
   discover "latent histrionic abilities in me." In 1933 Crabbe mad
   his film debut as Karpa the Lion Man, in *King of the Jungle*. H
   eventually appeared in fifty-three movies, but is best known fo
   his roles as Flash Gordon and Buck Rogers.

3. HELENE MADISON (gold; 1932 100-meter freestyle)

   Madison, who once set sixteen world records in sixteen and
   half months, was invariably described by sportswriters a
   "shapely." After her Olympic triumph, she played an Amazo
   captain of the guards in the 1933 satire *The Warrior's Husban*
   Unfortunately, her performance was undistinguished and sh
   never acted again.

4. SONJA HENIE (3 golds; 1928, 1932, and 1936 figure skating

   Henie's first film, *One in a Million* (1937), was a box-office wir
   ner, and nine more followed. Although her acting was never a
   smooth as her skating, her Hollywood career brought her gre
   financial success.

5.–6. GLENN MORRIS (gold; 1936 decathlon) and ELEANOR HOL
   (gold; 1932 100-meter backstroke)

   Tarzan's Revenge (1938) starred two Olympic champions a
   Tarzan and Jane. Unfortunately, Holm was described as lookir
   "bored" throughout the film, and reviewers found Morris's pe
   formance "disappointing" and "listless." Holm never acte

again, while Morris made one more film: *Hold That Co-Ed* (1938).

7. CAROL HEISS (gold; 1960 figure skating)

Heiss, described by *Variety* as "a fetching lass," made her film debut in the title role in *Snow White and the Three Stooges* (1961). The film was panned but she received praise for her acting, singing, and, of course, her skating. However, she never appeared in another movie.

8. HAROLD SAKATA (silver; 1948 light-heavyweight weight-lifting)

After the Olympics, Sakata pursued a successful career as a professional wrestler and then moved on to acting. He appeared in eight films, but it was his first role that gained him international stardom — the evil Oddjob in *Goldfinger* (1964).

9. JEAN-CLAUDE KILLY (3 golds; 1968 Alpine skiing)

Killy co-starred as a con-man ski instructor in the mediocre 1972 film *Snow Job*.

10. BRUCE JENNER (gold; 1976 decathlon)

Jenner's one and only film appearance was in the loud and awful 1980 film *Can't Stop the Music*. He played a staid lawyer who is drawn into the irresistibly fun New York disco scene.

11. MARK BRELAND (gold; 1984 welterweight boxing)

Breland is one of the few athletes to appear in a movie *before* he appeared in the Olympics. In 1983 he received good re-

Despite good reviews, Carol Heiss abandoned her film career after starring with Larry, Curly, and Moe in *Snow White and the Three Stooges.*

views for his role in *The Lords of Discipline*. He played the first black cadet in a southern military academy.

NOTE: Among the more than forty other Olympic athletes who have appeared in movies are 1924 pole-vault champion Lee Barnes, who served as a stand-in stuntman for Buster Keaton in *College* (1927); 1948 and 1952 decathlon champion Bob Mathias, who appeared in three films including *It Happened in Athens* (1962) with Jayne Mansfield; Ken Richmond, who won a bronze medal as a wrestler in 1952 but was better known as the muscleman who struck the gong at the beginning of J. Arthur Rank films; and Herman Brix, who placed second in the 1928 shot put, changed his name to Bruce Bennett, and pursued a successful career that included performances in *Mildred Pierce* (1945) and *The Treasure of Sierra Madre* (1948). He also acted in such clunkers as *The Alligator People* (1959) and *The Fiend of Dope Island* (1961).

10 Athletes
Who Dominated Their Sport

1. The most famous ancient Olympian was Milo of Croton, who won the boys' wrestling event in 540 B.C., six successive senior Olympiads, and more than two dozen crowns in other Panhellenic festivals.
2. In 1889 Boston Braves pitcher John Clarkson led the National League in wins, ERA, strikeouts, shutouts, complete games, innings pitched, games, and winning percentage.
3. In the 1910s, Fanny Durack of Australia once held every world record in women's swimming from fifty yards to one mile.
4. In women's figure skating, no one was greater than Sonja Henie. She won the Norwegian figure skating championships at age ten, first competed in the Olympics at eleven, captured ten consecutive world championships from 1927 to 1936, and the Olympic gold medals in 1928, 1932, and 1936. Her reported earnings at the time of her death were $45 million.
5. Chiquito de Cambo was rated as the world's best jai alai player from the beginning of the century through 1938.
6. Oscar Robertson averaged a triple double with the Cincinnati Royals in the 1961–1962 basketball season. (A triple double is ten or more points, rebounds, and assists per game.)
7. Kelso was named Horse of the Year five times, from 1960 through 1964.
8. Squash player Heather McKay lost only two games, and no matches, from 1961 to 1980.
9. Between 1972 and 1980, Soviet Vassily Alekseyev broke eighty

official world weightlifting records. He won two Olympic golds, eight world titles, and nine European championships.

10. In 1988 West German tennis star Steffi Graf pulled off an unprecedented Golden Slam by winning the Grand Slam and the Olympic tennis gold medal.

SOURCE: Andrew Postman and Larry Stone, *The Ultimate Book of Sports Lists* (New York: Bantam Books, 1990).

6 Bizarre Sports Events

1. CHARIOT RACING

The world chariot racing championship has been held annually since 1965, usually in Pocatello, Idaho. These chariots are less warlike than those used by Ben-Hur and the ancient Romans, but the principle is basically the same. The race is 440 yards without a curve. Each chariot has one rider and one horse. For information, write to Vic Adams, Secretary/Manager, World Champion Cutter & Chariot Racing Association, 957 East 2000 North, Layton, UT 84040.

2. ONE-HOLE GOLF TOURNAMENT

The annual Elfego Baca golf tournament consists of only one hold — but it's not your typical hole. The tee is placed on top of Socorro Peak, 7,243 feet above sea level. The hole, which is actually a patch of dirt 60 feet in diameter, is two and a half miles away and 2,500 feet below. The course record, eleven, is held by Mike Stanley, who has won the tournament ten times since 1981. The first competition was held in 1969. For information, write to Elfego Baca Shoot, Jean A. Stanley, P.O. Box Z, Socorro, NM 87801.

3. LAWN-MOWER RACING

The first national lawn-mower racing championship was held in Grayslake, Illinois, during the Labor Day weekend of 1992. The event was surprisingly controversial. The Outdoor Power Equipment Institute, a trade association that represents lawn-mower manufacturers, formally opposed the concept of lawn-mower racing because it does not promote "the effective and safe use of outdoor power equipment." Nonetheless, 3,000 spectators had a good time and the proceeds from admissions went to fight Lou Gehrig's disease. For information, write to the U.S. Lawn Mower Racing Association, 1812 Glenview Rd., Glenview, IL 60025.

Hot competition at the U.S. National Lawn Mower Racing Championship.

4. ROBOT SUMO

The all-Japan robot sumo tournament, first held in 1989, has two categories: radio-controlled models and stand-alone models. Robots may be any height, but they may not exceed twenty centimeters in width or depth. They may not throw things, but they are allowed to have bodies that stretch. First prize in each division is 1 million yen. For information, write to the All-Japan Robot Sumo Tournament Office, Operations Dept., Fuji Software, 13-18, 2 cho-me, Okamoto, Kamakura-shi, Kanagawa-ken, Japan 247.

5. STONE THROW

The Unspunnen Festival celebrating Swiss costume and folklore has been held irregularly since 1805. One of the highlights of the festival is the throwing of the 185-pound (83.5 kilograms) Unspunnen Stone. The record throw is 3.61 meters (11 feet 2

Robot sumo wrestler "Brutal Tank" charges "Satoru" to drive it out of the ring during the 2nd All-Japan Robot Sumo Tournament.

inches) set by Josef Küttel of Vitznau at the 1981 festival, the last before the September 1993 gathering. For information, write to the Tourist Office Bernese Oberland, 3800 Interlaken, Switzerland.

6. NONVIOLENT HUNTING TOURNAMENT

Archers who don't like to kill animals can enter the National Field Archery Association's 3-D tournament held annually in the United States. Competitors take aim at life-size dummies of deer, bears, mountain lions, wild pigs, and wild turkeys. There are six divisions for men and women of all ages, using equipment ranging from *traditional,* with no sights or mechanical assistance, to *compound bow,* which allows sights, stabilizers, wheels, and cams. For information write to: National Field Archery Association, 31407 Outer I-10, Redlands, CA 92373.

20 Prominent Bespectacled Sports Figures

1. Richie Allen, baseball player
2. Livio Berruti, 1960 Olympic 200-meter champion
3. Clint Courtney, first bespectacled catcher (1951)
4. Dom DiMaggio, baseball player
5. Jaroslav Drobny, tennis player
6. Ryne Duren, pitcher
7. Laurent Fignon, two-time Tour de France winner
8. Bob Griese, Miami Dolphin quarterback
9. Chick Hafey, the first bespectacled player to make it to the Baseball Hall of Fame
10. Hale Irwin, three-time U.S. Open–winning golfer
11. Reggie Jackson, baseball player
12. Matti Järvinen, 1932 Olympics javelin gold medalist
13. Billie Jean King, tennis player
14. Ingrid Kristiansen, Norway's world-champion distance runner
15. George Mikan, Minneapolis Laker center
16. Chuck Muncie, running back
17. Martina Navratilova, tennis player
18. Kurt "Clark Kent" Rambis, basketball forward
19. Eddie Rommel, first bespectacled umpire (1956)
20. Kent Tekulve, relief pitcher

SOURCE: Andrew Postman and Larry Stone, *The Ultimate Book of Sports Lists* (New York: Bantam Books, 1990).

12 Athletes Who Were Asthma Sufferers

1. Rick DeMont, Olympic swimmer
2. Virginia Gilder, Olympic rower
3. Nancy Hogshead, Olympic swimmer
4. Jackie Joyner-Kersee, Olympic track-and-field athlete
5. Bill Koch, Olympic cross-country skier
6. Greg Louganis, Olympic diver
7. George Murray, wheelchair athlete and Boston Marathon winner
8. Rob Muzzio, Olympic decathlete
9. Sam Perkins, basketball player
10. Donovan "Razor" Rudduck, heavyweight boxer
11. Jim Ryun, runner, former record holder in the mile and 1500 meters
12. Michael Secrest, long-distance cyclist

Despite suffering from asthma, Jackie Joyner-Kersee has won three Olympic gold medals.

13 Athletes Who Died as a Result of Competing

(Not Including Boxers and Race Car Drivers)

1.–2. BERTRAM BOARDLEY AND KENNETH HILL (soccer)

The 1948 British Army Cup final pitted the Royal Armoured Corps (Bovington) against the No. 121 Training Regiment of the Royal Artillery (Oswestry). Their first meeting ended in a tie. The replay took place at the Command Central Ground in Aldershot. Oswestry scored twice in the first twenty minutes as storm clouds gathered in the distance. They held their lead in the second half. Both teams were taking their positions for a throw-in when there was a sudden roar of thunder and a flash of lightning. Eight players and the referees were knocked to the ground. Two of the players, Boardley of Oswestry and Hill of Bovington, died instantly.

3. SERGEI CHALIBASHVILI (diving)

At the 1983 World University Games in Edmonton, twenty-one-year-old Sergei Chalibashvili from Tbilisi, Georgia, attempted the most difficult dive on the platform program: a three-and-a-half reverse somersault in tuck position. But on the way down he smashed his head on the board and was knocked unconscious. He remained in a coma for a week before dying on July 16.

4. RAY CHAPMAN (baseball)

Chapman, a catcher for the Cleveland Indians, was at bat in a 1920 away game against the New York Yankees. Yankee pitcher Carl Mays threw wild and hit Chapman in the head. Chapman started toward first base, collapsed, and never regained consciousness.

5. HANK GATHERS (basketball)

Loyola Marymount University's twenty-three-year-old star center had just made a spectacular slam dunk in the first half of a March 4, 1990, Western Coast Conference game against Portland State. As the crowd stood and cheered, Gathers raced upcourt and suddenly collapsed at midcourt. He was taken to a nearby hospital, but one hour and forty minutes later he was declared dead. The exact cause of death remains a subject of

Hank Gathers in his final game.

controversy, but it is known that Gathers, who had collapsed and fainted during a game three months earlier, was taking medication for an irregular heartbeat.

6. FRANK HAYES (horse racing)

In July 1923, jockey Frank Hayes rode to victory the horse Sweet Kiss, a 20-1 long shot in a steeplechase race at Belmont Park. When friends rushed up to congratulate him, they found Hayes slumped forward, dead. He is believed to be the only deceased jockey to win a race.

7. CHUCK HUGHES (football)

Hughes, a wide receiver for the Detroit Lions, was injured during an October 24, 1971, game against the Chicago Bears. Hughes continued to play, but the injury caused a blood clot, which then caused a heart attack. He collapsed and died on the field.

8. FLO HYMAN (volleyball)

Hyman, a star of the U.S. Olympic silver medal–winning volleyball team in 1984, collapsed and died during a match in Japan in January 1986. The thirty-one-year-old Hyman was a victim of Marfan's syndrome, a rare connective-tissue disorder found in tall people.

9. KNUT JENSEN (cycling)

The 1960 road race at the Rome Olympics was held in ninety-three-degree heat on August 30. Danish cyclist Jensen collapsed from sunstroke and suffered a fractured skull. It was later determined that before the race Jensen had taken Ronicide, a blood-circulation stimulant. He was one of only two athletes to die as a result of Olympic competition.

10. FRANCISCO LAZARO (running)

Toward the end of the marathon race at the 1912 Olympics in Stockholm, Portuguese runner Lazaro collapsed from sunstroke and heart trouble. He died the following day, July 15.

11. BILL MASTERSON (ice hockey)

Masterson, a rookie for the Minnesota North Stars, fell over backward after being checked during a January 15, 1968, game against the Oakland Seals. He hit his head on the ice and died two days later. His is the only pro-hockey death in the modern era.

12. RUSSELL MOCKRIDGE (cycling)

Mockridge, who won two gold medals at the 1952 Olympics, was competing in the 1958 Tour of Gippsland in Melbourne when he was struck by a bus and killed instantly. He was thirty years old.

13. VLADIMIR SMIRNOV (fencing)

Two years after winning a gold medal in the individual foil at the 1980 Moscow Olympics, Smirnov was defending his world championship in Rome against Matthias Behr of West Germany. In a freak accident, Behr's foil snapped, pierced Smirnov's mask, penetrated his eyeball, and entered his brain. Smirnov, twenty-eight, died nine days later.

Joe Montana's
11 Greatest Passers

Joe Montana, star quarterback for the San Francisco 49ers, was voted Most Valuable Player for Super Bowls XVI and XIX. He holds NFL records for highest pass-completion percentage in a career and the most consecutive 300-yard games in a season.

1. Bart Starr (Green Bay Packers; 1956–1971). NFL Most Valuable Player in 1966. Most Valuable Player, Super Bowls I and II.
2. Joe Namath (New York Jets, Los Angeles Rams; 1965–1977). First quarterback to pass for more than 4,000 yards in one season. Most Valuable Player, Super Bowl III.
3. Y. A. Tittle (Baltimore Colts, San Francisco 49ers, New York Giants; 1948–1964). NFL's Most Valuable Player in 1961 and 1963.
4. Fran Tarkenton (Minnesota Vikings, New York Giants; 1961–1978). Pro Bowl selection nine times. Holds NFL records for touchdown passes, complete passes, and passing yardage.
5. Dan Fouts (San Diego Chargers; 1973–1987). Holds records for most 300-yard games and most 3,000-yard seasons.

Bart Starr, of the Green Bay Packers, was voted Most Valuable Player of Super Bowl I, in 1967.

6. Terry Bradshaw (Pittsburgh Steelers; 1970–1983). Voted Most Valuable Player, Super Bowls XIII and XIV.
7. Dan Marino (Miami Dolphins; 1983–present). Holds NFL records for touchdown passes in a season and most 400-yard games.
8. John Elway (Denver Broncos; 1983–present). Associated Press's Most Valuable Player, 1987.
9. Bob Griese (Miami Dolphins; 1967–1980). Held AFL record for highest pass-completion percentage.
10. Johnny Unitas (Baltimore Colts, San Diego Chargers; 1956–1973). Holds NFL record for throwing touchdowns in forty-seven consecutive games.
11. Len Dawson (Pittsburgh Steelers, Cleveland Browns, Dallas Texans [AFL], Kansas City Chiefs; 1957–1975). Most Valuable Player of Super Bowl IV.

— Exclusive for *The Book of Lists*

Arthur Ashe's
10 Greatest Male Tennis Players of All Time

Arthur Ashe was the first African-American male to win a major tennis singles championship. He won the U.S. hard-court singles title in 1963, led the U.S. team to Davis Cup championships in 1968, 1969, and 1970, and turned professional in 1970. He became the top-ranked tennis player in the world when he won the Wimbledon singles championship in 1975. His criticism of apartheid led to the exclusion of South Africa from Davis Cup competition in 1970. Ashe was also an author; among his credits is a three-volume history of black sports figures since 1619: *A Hard Road to Glory: The History of the African-American Athlete.*

1. Rod Laver
2. Bjorn Borg
3. Bill Tilden
4. Don Budge
5. Jack Kramer
6. Pancho Gonzales
7. John McEnroe
8. Fred Perry
9. Ken Rosewall
10. Jimmy Connors

— Exclusive for *The Book of Lists*

Martina Navratilova's
8 Best Women Tennis Players of All Time

Tennis superstar Martina Navratilova has been walking off with top tennis honors for two decades. Czech-born, she won her first national title at the age of fourteen and is one of a select group of players who has won a Grand Slam, winning consecutive victories at the 1983 Australian, 1984 French and U.S. Opens, and at Wimbledon. In 1992 she surpassed Chris Evert's record of 157 tournament victories. She is noted for her mighty topspin forehand, cannonball service, and punishing volleys.

1. Billie Jean King
2. Chris Evert
3. Margaret Court
4. Suzanne Lenglen
5. Helen Wills Moody
6. Steffi Graf
7. Maureen Connolly
8. Alice Marble

— Exclusive for *The Book of Lists*

Red Auerbach's
10 All-Time-Greatest Basketball Players

(*Excluding Current Players*)

Red Auerbach coached the Boston Celtics basketball team from 1950 to 1966 and is now its president and general manager. He was Coach of the Year in 1965 and was named to the National Basketball Hall of Fame in 1968. His list of the all-time greats of basketball includes only retired players, and is in no particular ranking order.

1. Bill Russell
2. Bob Pettit
3. Elgin Baylor
4. Kareem Abdul-Jabbar
5. Oscar Robertson
6. Jerry West

7. Bob Cousy
8. Larry Bird
9. Julius Erving
10. Dolph Schayes

— Exclusive for *The Book of Lists*

Sir Stanley Matthews's
11 Greatest Soccer Players

British footballer Sir Stanley Matthews is perhaps the greatest dribbler in soccer history. In his thirty-three-year professional career he played for the Stoke City and Blackpool teams, competing in 886 matches, including 88 international matches. He was the first British soccer player to receive a knighthood.

1. Johan Cruyff, Netherlands
2. Diego Maradona, Argentina
3. Alfredo Di Stéfano, Spain
4. Garrincha, Brazil
5. Ferenc Puskas, Hungary
6. George Best, Ireland
7. Pelé, Brazil
8. Eusébio, Portugal
9. Peter Doherty, Ireland
10. Tom Finney, England
11. Frank Swift, England

— Exclusive for *The Book of Lists*

Bill Shoemaker's
10 Greatest Racehorses
of All Time

The winningest jockey in racing history, Bill Shoemaker also holds the record for most stakes wins, and wins in races of more than $100,000, including three Kentucky Derbies. Twenty-four percent of his mounts finished first — the best record among name jockeys. "The Shoe" raced for more than forty years. He rode his first winner in 1949 and retired in 1990 with 8,833 wins.

1. Swaps
2. Spectacular Bid
3. Citation
4. Ribot
5. Forego
6. Secretariat
7. Sea Bird
8. Alleged
9. Exceller
10. Gallant Man

— Exclusive for *The Book of Lists*

Malcolm Baldrige's
5 Greatest Rodeo Performers
in History

Malcolm Baldrige, U.S. secretary of commerce under President Ronald Reagan from 1981 to 1987, learned roping as a teenager on cattle ranches in Nebraska, and participated on the professional rodeo circuit. (His sister, Letitia, took quite another career path — she instructs the nation on how to mind its manners and was Jacqueline Kennedy's White House social secretary.) In 1984 Baldrige was inducted into the Hall of Fame of Great Westerners at the National Cowboy Hall of Fame in Oklahoma City. He was killed on July 25, 1987, when his horse reared and fell on him during a practice session for a rodeo competition.

1. Jim Shoulders: Winner of a record sixteen world championships in twenty years. Six-time all-around champion.
2. Casey Tibbs: Nine-time world champion cowboy. Five saddle-bronc titles. All-around champion in 1951 and 1955. Rodeo legend — was the most popular rodeo cowboy in his day.
3. Dean Oliver: Eight-time world champion calf roper. Three all-around titles.
4. Larry Mahan: Qualified twenty-six times for National Finals Rodeo. Six-time all-around champion. World champion bull rider in 1965 and 1967.
5. Tom Ferguson: Recognized as one of rodeo's greatest competitors. Rodeo's first "Million Dollar" winner. Six-time all-around champion from 1974 to 1979.

— Exclusive for *The Book of Lists*

10 Babe Ruths

Babe Ruth was probably the greatest baseball player of all time. H
led the league in home runs 12 times, slugging percentage 13 time
runs scored 11 times, and runs batted in 6 times. When Ruth hit 5
home runs in 1920, he *doubled* the number hit by anyone else i
one year prior to that time. Before his slugging exploits earned hi
the nickname the Sultan of Swat, Ruth was known as a great pitche
In 1916 he led the American League with an earned-run average
1.75 and in 1917 he led the league in complete games pitched (35
For an athlete to be called the Babe Ruth of anything means that th
athlete is not only the best, but the best by far.

1. THE BABE RUTH OF BASKETBALL

   John Beckman, captain of the original Celtics and his sport
   first great gate attraction.

2. THE BABE RUTH OF SOCCER

   Billy Gonsalves, member of the United States World Cup team
   in 1930 and 1934.

3. THE JEWISH BABE RUTH

   Moses Solomon, a slugger who played at the end of the 192
   season for the New York Giants. Before being called up to th
   majors, he hit 49 home runs for Hutchinson of the Southwester
   (Class C) League. He was also called the Rabbi of Swat.

4. HOCKEY'S ANSWER TO BABE RUTH

   Howie Morenz, the swift and great scorer for the Montreal Ca
   nadians in the 1920s and 1930s.

The *real* Babe Ruth trying h
hand at football.

5. THE BABE RUTH OF THE MINORS

Joe Bauman, who hit 72 home runs for the 1954 Roswell (New Mexico) Rockets in the Class C Longhorn League, a professional baseball record for one season. He later became manager of a beer distributorship in Albuquerque, where he was known as the Sultan of Schlitz.

6. THE BLACK BABE RUTH

Josh Gibson, who hit 89 home runs in one Negro League season and 75 in another.

7. THE BABE RUTH OF JAPAN

Sadaharu Oh, the great Japanese player who launched 868 home runs in twenty-two years.

8. THE BABE RUTH OF JUGGLING

Enrico Rastelli.

9. THE BABE RUTH OF HARNESS RACING

Billy Haughton, winner of 4,910 races in his career.

10. THE COLLEGE BABE RUTH

Ruth's future New York Yankees teammate, Lou Gehrig, earned this sobriquet while he was a student at Columbia University.

SOURCE: Andrew Postman and Larry Stone, *The Ultimate Book of Sports Lists* (New York: Bantam Books, 1990).

11 Commonly Flouted Baseball Rules

1. From Rule 3.09: "Players of opposing teams shall not fraternize at any time while in uniform."
2. Rule 3.02: "No player shall intentionally discolor or damage the ball by rubbing it with soil, rosin, paraffin, licorice, sand-paper, emery-paper or other foreign substance."
3. From Rule 8.04: "When the bases are unoccupied, the pitcher shall deliver the ball to the batter within 20 seconds after he receives the ball. Each time the pitcher delays the game by violating this rule, the umpire shall call 'Ball.'"
4. From Rule 3.01.e: "After a home run is hit out of the playing grounds, the umpire shall not deliver a new ball to the pitcher or the catcher until the batter hitting the home run has crossed the plate."

5. From Rule 3.17: "Players on the disabled list are permitted to participate in pre-game activity and sit on the bench during a game but may not take part in any activity during the game such as . . . bench-jockeying."

6. From Rule 1.10.a: "The bat shall be one piece of solid wood."

7. From Rule 6.02.b: "Umpires may grant a hitter's request for 'Time' once he is in the batter's box, but the umpire should eliminate hitters walking out of the batter's box without reason. If umpires are not lenient, batters will understand that they are in the batter's box and they must remain there until the ball is pitched."

8. From Rule 9.05 (General Instructions to Umpires): "Umpires, on the field, should not indulge in conversation with players. Keep out of the coaching box and do not talk to the coach on duty."

9. From Rule 5.09.e: "When . . . a foul ball is not caught . . . the umpire shall not put [a new] ball in play until all runners have retouched their bases."

10. From Rule 9.05 (General Instructions to Umpires): "You no doubt are going to make mistakes, but never attempt to 'even up' after having made one."

11. From Rule 8.02.d: "To pitch at a batter's head is unsportsman-like and highly dangerous. It should be and is condemned by everybody. Umpires should act without hesitation in enforcement of this rule."

SOURCE: *Official Baseball Rules, 1992 Edition* (Sporting News, 1992), courtesy of Andrew Postman and Larry Stone.

The **12** Gentlest College Team Names

1. New York University Violets
2. Whittier (California) Poets
3. Centenary (Louisiana) Gentlemen
4. St. Joseph's (Maine) Monks
5. Heidelberg (Ohio) Student Princes
6. St. Mary of the Woods (Indiana) Woodsies
7. University of Pennsylvania Quakers
8. St. Bonaventure (New York) Bonnies
9. Whitman (Washington) Missionaries
10. University of New England (Maine) Pilgrims
11. Thomas Jefferson (Pennsylvania) Medics
12. Boston University Terriers

SOURCE: Andrew Postman and Larry Stone, *The Ultimate Book of Sports Lists* (New York: Bantam Books, 1990).

18 Celebrities
Who Were Cheerleaders

1. Paula Abdul (singer, dancer, choreographer). Van Nuys High School, Van Nuys, California.
2. Ann-Margret (actress). New Trier High School, Winnetka, Illinois.
3. Sally Field (actress). Birmingham High School, Van Nuys, California.
4. Eydie Gorme (singer). William Taft High School, Bronx, New York.
5. Patty Hearst Shaw (newspaper heiress). Sacred Heart School, Menlo Park, California.
6. Ben Hecht (author, screenwriter). Racine High School, Racine, Washington.
7. Jerry Lewis (comedian). Irvington High School, Irvington, New Jersey.
8. Susan Lucci (soap-opera actress). Garden City High School, Long Island, New York.
9. Madonna (singer, actress). Adams High School, Rochester, Michigan.
10. Steve Martin (comic actor). Garden Grove High School, Garden Grove, California.
11. Michael Milken (junk-bond peddler). Birmingham High School, Van Nuys, California.
12. Dinah Shore (singer). Hume-Fogg High School, Nashville, Tennessee.

Madonna (upper right) was a star cheerleader at Rochester Adams High in 1973. She liked to shock the crowd by wearing flesh-colored panties.

13. Carly Simon (singer, songwriter). Riverdale Girls' School, Bronx, New York.
14. Pamela South (opera singer). Salmon High School, Salmon, Idaho.
15. Meryl Streep (actress). Bernardsville High School, Bernardsville, New Jersey.
16. Lily Tomlin (comedienne). Cass Technical High School, Detroit, Michigan.
17. Raquel Welch (actress). La Jolla High School, La Jolla, California.
18. Vanna White (game-show hostess). North Myrtle Beach High School, North Myrtle Beach, South Carolina.

13 Odd Odds

The corporation of bookkeeper William Hill of London will offer odds to gamblers on "virtually anything providing it is legal, decent, honest and truthful." Here are some of the more unusual events for which they gave odds in 1993.

1. 6 to 1   Prince Charles to renounce his right to the throne.
2. 16 to 1   Snow to fall in London/Glasgow on Christmas Day.
3. 40 to 1   NASA to confirm the existence of intelligent extraterrestrial life before the year 2000.
4. 50 to 1   Queen to abdicate.
5. 100 to 1   Boris Becker to wed Steffi Graf.
6. 250 to 1   Britain to switch to driving on the right before the year 2005.
7. 250 to 1   Natural history museum to confirm existence of Loch Ness Monster.

Michael and Elvis — together at last.

8. 500 to 1   Elvis Presley to be proved still alive.
9. 500 to 1   Michael Jackson and his sister La Toya to be proved one and the same person.
10. 1000 to 1   Archbishop of Canterbury to confirm Second Coming.
11. 1000 to 1   Female pope to be appointed.
12. 1000 to 1   British person to win Wimbledon singles.
13. 1,000,000 to 1   Screaming Lord Sutch [British 1960s cult rock star] to become prime minister.

Charles Hamilton's
10 Most Unusual Collectibles

Charles Hamilton began his seventy-year career as a manuscript collector and dealer in 1924 when he salvaged some old documents from a trash can in Flint, Michigan. Among his eighteen published books are fourteen on autographs, the latest of which is *The Hitler Diaries: Fakes That Fooled the World.*

1. CELEBRITY HAIR

Locks, even single strands, of celebrity hair fascinate collectors. Among those whose hair is available: Washington, Lincoln, Andrew Jackson, Franz Schubert, U. S. Grant, Baron von Richthofen, Robert E. Lee, and even hair from the tail of Lee's horse Traveller. A few strands of Lincoln's hair fetch $1,000 or so, but a lock of Keats's hair would set you back several thousands. British poet Leigh Hunt boasted a collection that included the hair of Keats, Shelley, Byron, Milton, Lamb, Coleridge, and Browning. I own a gold ring into which is set a locket containing three strands of Napoleon's hair. I wear it whenever I attempt any task that requires special courage.

2. BARBED WIRE

There are nearly 2,000 varieties known, each with its own special wire barb, or rowel. An avid collector will shell out hundreds of dollars for a rare eighteen-inch (approved length) specimen of this cruel fencing that restrained cattle or marked the boundaries of early American ranches. Armed with wire cutters and metal detectors, even wealthy buffs enjoy a ramble through an old dump.

3. OLD SHOES

A single silk slipper of Pavlova, frayed at the toe, sold at auction for $625. This does not compare to the $165,000 fetched by the ruby slippers worn by Judy Garland in *The Wizard of Oz*. Chinese collectors specialize in the old shoes of judges known to be honest. Psychiatrists say that shoes are sex symbols. Perhaps this is why Imelda Marcos hoards thousands of shoes in her closets.

4. DRIED FLOWERS FROM GRAVES

They are dark brown and not beautiful, but when carefully labeled and pressed between leaves of a book they make a provocative and inexpensive collection. Queen Victoria started her collection with flowers that grew on the grave of her husband, Prince Albert, but did not cease until she had scores of similar mementos, all from royal graves. Flowers that sprang from the graves of Shelley and Keats are often encountered.

5. UNEXPECTED ART

Paintings and sketches by celebrities, most of whom never took a course in art, are one of the most alluring of collectibles. Some amateurs show astonishing talent. Take Eisenhower, Churchill, and Hitler. All three turned out handsome landscapes. Churchill's paintings fetch about $50,000, five times as much as Hitler's. More versatile are the movie stars. John and Lionel Barrymore turned out professional-caliber work. Olivia de Havilland creates beautiful flower paintings; Frank Sinatra's views of New York City (worth $7,000 each) are masterfully executed; Noel Coward indulged in quaint seaside views; James Cagney painted with emotion and some skill; but Irving Berlin! I hate to say it, but you should have stuck to the songwriting, Irving! Even criminals join the collector's gallery. Jack Ruby's intricate geometric designs are intriguing, and serial killer John Gacy will paint a pretty clown to order for a fee of about $100. Three letters of Theodore Roosevelt to his children, each containing sketches by the president, recently fetched $45,000, whereas an ordinary letter of Teddy's can be had for less than $500.

6. INTIMATE PROPERTY OF CELEBRITIES

There are collectors who will snap up almost any personal relic of a celebrity. Among items that were recently sold privately or at auction are Greta Garbo's vanity case; Hitler's jacket and medals (valued at $25,000); Dickens's traveling desk; Willa Cather's beaded evening bag; John Lennon's flashy coat; Lincoln's personal seal; Mussolini's violin; Washington's brocaded waistcoat; Einstein's calabash pipe, personally authenticated by him; a bit of silvery fabric from Lindbergh's plane *The Spirit* *of* *St. Louis* ($450); a swatch of Queen Victoria's gown; and a sni*p*pet of black cloth from Lincoln's catafalque ($75). Grisly reli*cs* add piquancy to a collection. I once sold at auction, for a su*b*stantial sum, a piece of wire from the electric chair in whic*h* Leon Czolgosz, assassin of President William McKinley, was e*x*ecuted. But beware of bogus relics. The day after the notoriou*s* outlaw John Dillinger was gunned down by the FBI, I spotted *in* a large hardware store a cardboard sign under which wer*e* pasted three black buttons with the hand-lettered messa*ge* "These buttons are off John Dillinger's coat." I coveted the bu*t*tons and asked the proprietor to put a price on them. He laughe*d* and said: "I have had seven sets of buttons stolen already th*is* morning." When he saw my shocked look at his deception, h*e* explained: "The buttons are really *off* Dillinger's coat. In fac*t* they were never *on* it."

7. Body Parts of Noted Persons

Call it gruesome, if you wish, but this bizarre hobby has ma*ny* devotees. Just consider that in the past fifty years or so collecto*rs* have bartered for the apocryphal corpses of Jesse James a*nd* John Wilkes Booth. Two skulls of Oliver Cromwell were on di*s*play in London at the same time, a fact that prompted a Briti*sh* wag to offer the explanation that the smaller skull was Cro*m*well's when he was a youth. I once sold the mossy skull of fam*ed* American artist James Peale, who painted Washington from lif*e.* It came to me with a provenance that traced it into the grave a*nd* out of it. The skull of Charles XII, slain by an enemy bullet *in* 1718, is a Swedish national treasure, on display in Stockhol*m* where the visitor may view the huge bullet hole near his rig*ht* eye. Toenails of St. Peter, enough to fill a large sack, were mo*re* available a few centuries ago than now, but these sacred co*l*lectibles may still be viewed in some of the more ancie*nt* churches in Europe. I was once offered — and declined — N*a*poleon's penis. It was then put up for sale by Christie's and d*e*scribed in their catalog as "a bit of withered tendon." Later *it* found a buyer in Paris and is now the property of a famous uro*l*ogist. I was asked by *People* magazine whether it was genuin*e,* and I replied, "Only Josephine could tell for sure." Russia st*ill* retains the teeth of Adolf Hitler. If you were able to purchase *an* incisor, or preferably a canine, for your private collection, *it* would take a very large bite out of your purse. The more gru*e*some the relic, the more sought-after. Hence, greatly prized a*re* the lampshades, book bindings, and gloves made from the sk*in* of tattooed inmates in Buchenwald concentration camp for Ils*e* Koch, known as the Bitch of Buchenwald. It is said that Ilse ha*d* new arrivals at camp stripped naked so she could inspect the*ir* for desirable tattoos. If a tattoo pleased her, she ordered that the possessor be shot and skinned so she could improve her collection. (Ilse committed suicide in 1967.)

8. COMIC NAMES

Here's a collectible that doesn't cost a counterfeit copper, yet will bring hours of pleasure. I have half a dozen friends who search avidly for quaint names. In former days, authors relied upon their imagination to devise alliterative names, like Smollett's *Peregrine Pickle,* whose modern counterpart was a Sotheby's official, Peregrine Pollen. Charles Dickens was a master at digging up unusual names. Don't for a moment suppose that Dickens invented names like *Pecksniff.* Not a bit of it! He roamed the streets of London by night, jotting down odd cognomens from trade signs. He then created characters to fit the names.

9. FORGERIES OF CELEBRITY WRITINGS

Believe it or not, there are collectors who prefer fake autographs to originals. Their hobby is gathering bogus documents. In my own collection of forgeries I have letters by Lincoln, Washington, Edgar Allan Poe, Theodore Roosevelt, Mark Twain, Thomas Jefferson, and many others, all of them spurious writings that once, or maybe twice, fooled the experts. These forgeries capture with great skill every curlicue and swirl of the script they mimic. Still, it is well to remember that it is the forgers who add piquancy and excitement to the gathering of collectibles. Almost any hobby would become dull without pitfalls.

0. BLOOD

Yes, human blood! Vampires aren't the only ones who seek it. Nearly 2,000 years ago drops of blood from Jesus dying on the cross were collected by his devoted followers. In the French national library (*La Bibliothèque*) is preserved the very document Robespierre was signing when he was shot. Splattered

Abraham Lincoln's *real* signature (top) and six forgeries.

with his blood, it is one of the most dramatic — and tre
sured — documents in all history. When Lincoln was mu
dered, relic seekers followed his bloody trail as he was carri
from Ford's Theater across the street to the house where l
died. They soaked up his blood in their handkerchiefs. Tl
blood-soaked towels the doctor used to stem the bleeding fro
the bullet hole in his head were later cut into tiny pieces a
sold as souvenirs. Similar relics exist of many whose hea
were lopped off, such as Charles I, Louis XVI, and Marie A
toinette. I once was shown the typed speech Malcolm X w
holding when the assassin's bullet struck him down. It w
blotched with blood. I know a few collectors who would bart
a gallon of their own blood to get their hands on this precio
relic.

18 Unusual Objects
Sold at Auction

1. Dorothy's ruby slippers from *The Wizard of Oz* (193!
   $165,000.
2. The baseball that rolled through Bill Buckner's legs in game s
   of the 1986 World Series (bought by actor Charlie Shee
   $93,500.
3. The bullwhip used by Harrison Ford as Indiana Jones: $24,3(
4. A flowered headband worn by Jimi Hendrix in 1969 (bought
   comedian Eddie Murphy): $19,500.
5. Marilyn Monroe and Arthur Miller's marriage certifica
   $13,700.
6. The Blues Brothers's (John Belushi and Dan Aykroyd) sui
   with sunglasses: $12,000.
7. Elvis Presley's driver's license, issued to him at age sevente
   $7,400.
8. James Dean's toy monkey (held by him in *Rebel Without*
   Cause, 1955): $6,800.
9. A body tag from Lee Harvey Oswald's corpse: $6,600.
10. An early nineteenth-century French condom: $6,300.
11. The peace pipe used in Kevin Costner's *Dances with Woli*
    (1990): $6,000.
12. Two of Sammy Davis, Jr.'s hats: $5,000.
13. Prince Charles's plaster cast from his broken arm: $3,230.
14. The spandex outfit Arnold Schwarzenegger wore in *The Ru*
    ning Man (1987): $2,400.
15. Dan Aykroyd's conehead from *Saturday Night Live:* $2,200.

The Conehead family with Elliott Gould on *Saturday Night Live*—Dan Aykroyd's conehead (*right*) sold at auction for $2,200.

16. A slice of toast served to George Harrison at breakfast in August 1963, and a twig from John Lennon's hedge, along with an unusual assortment of rock-and-roll memorabilia: $2,000.
17. Joan Crawford's membership and credit cards: $1,400.
18. Liberace's paper napkins (imprinted with his logo): $182.

NOTE: For more unusual objects sold at auction, see *The Book of Lists #2*, pp. 276–77.

5 Lives Norman Cousins Would Like to Have Lived

Norman Cousins was perhaps best known for having served more than thirty years as editor of the *Saturday Review*. His books included *Modern Man Is Obsolete* (1945), *In Place of Folly* (1961), *Anatomy of an Illness* (1979), and *The Pathology of Power* (1987).

1. Aristotle, who had a prodigious effect not only on the education of Athenians but on ways of thought that persist to this day.
2. Francis Bacon, whose tightly disciplined mind made it possible for scholars to understand that what was most important about science was the scientific method.
3. Benjamin Franklin, whose involvement in the major issues and events of his time was exceeded only by his enjoyment of living and his appreciation of intelligent and beautiful women.
4. Thomas Jefferson, probably the most versatile and intellectually gifted man to occupy the White House. Equally important, perhaps: He was a master of the art of friendship.
5. Franklin D. Roosevelt, for my money the greatest American of the twentieth century.

— Exclusive for *The Book of Lists*

Alice Miller's
5 Most Admired Thinkers
in History

Dr. Alice Miller worked and taught for twenty years as a psychoanalyst before she discovered the devastating effects of child mistreatment and neglect, both to the individual concerned and to society as a whole. She then also discovered that the effects remained unidentified in all the theories then known to her. At that time, 1980, she gave up her psychoanalytical practice in order to write. Her books have been translated into nineteen languages. Among the books are *The Drama of the Gifted Child, For Your Own Good, Hidden Cruelty in Child-Rearing and the Roots of Violence, Banished Knowledge, Breaking Down the Wall of Silence,* and *The Liberating Experience of Painful Truth*. All these books deal with the issue of repression, its causes and effects, which can have far-reaching political consequences, as in the cases of Hitler and Stalin.

Ms. Miller decided to choose names of people who have made a great contribution to the self-awareness of humanity by radically questioning established opinions. People in power (in government and religion) have always felt threatened by the discovery of the truth and have often persecuted, even to death, those responsible.

1. SOCRATES (C. 469–399 B.C.), Athenian philosopher. His resolute stance against tyranny brought about his trial on charges of corrupting the youth, and he was condemned to die by drinking poison.

2. GIORDANO BRUNO (1548–1600), Italian philosopher. Tried by the inquisition, refused to recant his pantheistic ideas, and was burned.

3. GALILEO GALILEI (1564–1642), Italian scientist. After he had publicly expressed his agreement with the Copernican system, silence was imposed on him by the Inquisition. He was forced to recant under threat of torture and was condemned to house arrest until his death. It was not before 1992, 350 years after his death, that Galileo Galilei's work was finally fully accepted by the Church. The fear of truth is almost indestructible. But so is courage.

4. JANUSZ KORCZAK (1887–1942), Polish pedagogue who founded an orphanage based on self-administration of children. He wrote books on "how to love children," which have been translated into English, that are deeply understanding, full of respect for the child, and totally different from anything else revealed in pedagogical literature. Korczak died in the gas chambers of a

concentration camp together with 200 Jewish children. He protected and accompanied them in the face of death.

J. Konrad Stettbacher (1930–), Swiss psychotherapist. He developed a revolutionary, groundbreaking therapy based on natural laws that makes it possible to resolve repression step by step, to face the old wounds, and to heal. He published the description of this method in 1991 under the title *Making Sense of Suffering: The Healing Confrontation with Your Own Past.* It enables people to discover their true histories, if they so wish. Although his method is very different from all traditional therapeutic schools, and very much a challenge to them, Stettbacher has not been persecuted. Switzerland is an old democracy and people are free to say and write what they think.

— Exclusive for *The Book of Lists*

Stephen Spender's
10 People He'd Like to Invite to Lunch

...ender, who was born in London and educated at Oxford, was one ...a handful of young writers who revolutionized English poetry in ...e 1930s by including images of everyday life in their work. *Poems ...r Spain* (1937), *Trial of a Judge* (1938), and *European Witness* ...946) describe his early observations and experiences in Spain ...d Germany. Later works include *The Generous Days* (1971), *Let-...s to Christopher: Stephen Spender's Letters to Christopher Isher-...ood 1929–1939* (1980), *Collected Poems 1928–1985* (1986), and ...e Temple* (1988). During the 1950s and 1960s, Spender taught at ...veral U.S. universities, and he spent one year as poetry consul-...nt to the U.S. Library of Congress. He now divides his time be-...een homes in England and the south of France.

. Alcibiades without Socrates
. Francis Beaumont without John Fletcher
. James Boswell without Samuel Johnson
. George Gordon, Lord Byron, without his "last attachment"
. Oscar Wilde without "Bosie" [Lord Alfred Douglas]
. Gustave Flaubert without George Sand
. Algernon Charles Swinburne without Theodore Watts-Dunton
. Gertrude Stein without Alice B. Toklas
. Alice B. Toklas without Gertrude Stein
. Jesus Christ without Andrew Lloyd Webber

— Exclusive for *The Book of Lists*

Paul Bowles's
10 Favorite Dinner Guests in History

First published at the age of sixteen, Bowles has written novels, short stories, and poetry. His fiction is characterized by exotic locales (oftentimes Morocco) and existential concerns. His best-known novel, *The Sheltering Sky*, was made into a movie in 1990. Also a composer, he has written music for plays, operas, films, and ballets.

1. Gautama Buddha
2. Isabelle Eberhardt
3. Judas Iscariot
4. Dr. Carl Jung
5. Petronius Arbiter
6. Joseph Conrad
7. Isidore Ducasse (Comte de Lautréamont)
8. Erik Satie
9. Jeanne d'Arc
10. Anton Chekhov

MR. BOWLES ADDS: It will be noted that the guest list flouts the rules of etiquette, there being included only two women, as against eight men, but since both of the females habitually dressed as men, the occasion could have been referred to as a "stag dinner" without causing unfavorable comment.

— Exclusive for *The Book of List*

Ned Rorem's
19 Favorite Dinner Guests in History

Ned Rorem is a Pulitzer Prize–winning composer who has produced works in every medium. He has written operas, symphonies, chamber music, hundreds of songs and choral pieces, ballets, and concertos. He is also the author of twelve books, including *The Par Diary* (1966) and *Settling the Score* (1988).

1.–2. Jesus Christ and Mary Magdalene
3.–4. Faye Dunaway and Henry James
5.–6. John Simon and Jane Bowles
7. Queen Elizabeth I

Faye Dunaway and Henry James engrossed in serious conversation at Ned Rorem's dinner party.

8.–9. Colette and Janet Flanner
0.–11. Yukio Mishima and Lady Murasaki
2.–13. Marie Laure de Noailles and Francis Poulenc
4.–15. Billie Holiday and Malcolm X
6.–17. Jean Cocteau and Sergei Diaghilev
8.–19. Mr. and Mrs. Isaac B. Singer

— Exclusive for *The Book of Lists*

Arrigo Cipriani's
10 People in History
to Whom He Would Like to Have
Served Dinner

rrigo Cipriani is the proprietor of Venice, Italy's, renowned arry's Bar, which was founded by his father Giuseppe in 1931 and as one of Ernest Hemingway's favorite watering holes. Cipriani lso opened two New York restaurants — Bellini by Cipriani and arry Cipriani — and is the author of *The Harry Cipriani Cookbook* nd a novel, *Heloise and Bellinis*.

1. Madonna
2. The Virgin Mary
3. Margaret Thatcher

4. Diana Ross
5. Agatha Christie
6. Jane Birkin
7. Jan Morris
8. Robert De Niro
9. Woody Allen
10. General H. Norman Schwarzkopf

— Exclusive for *The Book of Lists*

Agatha Christie's
15 Likes and *14* Dislikes

British mystery writer Agatha Christie (1890–1976) published more than a hundred titles (novels, short-story collections, plays) in a career that spanned more than fifty years. Her most memorable characters were Hercule Poirot (an eccentric Belgian detective) and Miss Jane Marple (a cunning spinster). It's estimated that Christie's works, which have been translated into more than a hundred languages, have sold 2 billion copies. Her most popular books include *The Murder of Roger Ackroyd, Death on the Nile, And Then There Were None (Ten Little Indians), Witness for the Prosecution,* and *Murder on the Orient Express.* Her play *The Mousetrap* is the longest-running off-Broadway play in history.

I DON'T LIKE

1. Crowds
2. Being jammed up against people
3. Loud voices
4. Noise
5. Protracted talking
6. Parties, and especially cocktail parties
7. Cigarette smoke and smoking generally
8. Any kind of drink except in cooking
9. Marmalade
10. Oysters
11. Lukewarm food
12. Gray skies
13. The feet of birds, or indeed the feel of a bird altogether
14. Final and fiercest dislike: the taste and smell of hot milk

I LIKE

1. Sunshine
2. Apples
3. Almost any kind of music

4. Railway trains
5. Numerical puzzles and anything to do with numbers
6. Going to the sea
7. Bathing and swimming
8. Silence
9. Sleeping
0. Dreaming
1. Eating
2. The smell of coffee
3. Lilies of the valley
4. Most dogs
5. Going to the theater

SOURCE: Agatha Christie, *An Autobiography* (New York: Dodd, Mead & Company, Inc., 1977).

9 Simple Ways to Help the Environment

FAUCET AERATORS

A normal faucet lets out as much as 3 to 5 gallons of water a minute. By attaching a simple device called a "low-flow faucet aerator" to home faucets, you can reduce the flow by 50 percent. Incredibly, though the flow is reduced, it will seem stronger because air is mixed into water leaving the tap. Installing low-flow aerators on kitchen and bathroom sink faucets will save hot water and cut water use by as much as 280 gallons a month for a typical family of four — over 3,300 gallons a year for one family. So if only 10,000 families installed low-flow aerators, we could save over 33 million gallons a year. Note: Don't confuse low-flow aerators with standard screen aerators (which don't reduce the flow); portable dishwashers won't work with low-flow aerators.

DRIVING

The more gasoline your car uses, the more it contributes directly to problems like acid rain, smog, and the greenhouse effect. A few simple steps for reducing gas consumption:

- Keep your car tuned up. A well-tuned car uses up to 9 percent less gasoline.
- Use radial tires. They can improve gas mileage by up to 10 percent. And keep tires properly inflated; it can save as much as 5 percent of the gas.
- Use air-conditioning sparingly. Driving with the air conditioner on cuts gas mileage by about 2.5 miles per gallon.

- Drive smoothly. Experts say that accelerating and slowing down gently can increase gas mileage by about 5 percent.

    For more information: *Car Tips for Clean Air,* by Robe[rt] Sikorsky ($9.95), Perigee Books.

3. BUY RECYCLED

Recycling saves resources and cuts down pollution. For exam[]ple: Making aluminum from recycled (instead of virgin) mat[e]rials cuts related air pollution by 95 percent and saves 95 perce[nt] of the energy, recycling a ton of glass saves more than a ton [of] resources; making new paper from recycled writing pap[er] saves 33 percent of the energy needed to make it from tree[s.] But as the Worldwatch Institute says, "There's no cycle in r[e]cycle until a throwaway is reused." Turning in bottles, can[s] and paper every week or two won't save any resources unle[ss] the recycled materials are used to make new products a[nd] consumers buy them.

- Buy recycled products for your home. See what's available [at] the stores where you normally shop. Look for recycled writi[ng] paper, envelopes, motor oil, greeting cards, toilet pap[er,] Kleenex, etc. Read the labels — be sure to recognize the d[if]ference between a recycled product and one that just has r[e]cycled packaging.
- Get your business to buy recycled products. If you own yo[ur] own business or order supplies for your company, make [a] commitment to buying recycled products like stationery, toi[let] paper, and towels. Also look for pens, rulers, scissors, a[nd] other office products made partly or entirely of recycled pl[as]tic; garbage bags made of recycled material; recycled mot[or] oil; etc. As an employee, you can encourage your employer [to] buy recycled products by locating the merchandise yourse[lf.]

    For a copy of the *Shopper's Guide to Consumer Produc[ts]* send $3 to Californians Against Waste Foundation, 926 J S[t.,] Suite 606, Sacramento, CA 95814. They also have a guide [to] recycled writing and printing paper.

4. CARPOOL

Each year, commuters waste an estimated 3 billion gallons [of] gasoline — 5 percent of America's annual gas consum[p]tion — in bumper-to-bumper traffic. That's enough gas to dri[ve] a car to the sun and back more than 300 times. The avera[ge] commuter car carries only 1.3 passengers, so there's plenty [of] room for carpooling. One-third of all private auto mileage [is] racked up commuting to and from work.

- To help co-workers form carpools: Place a large map of t[he] surrounding area on a bulletin board. Ask interested empl[oy]ees to write their names and phone numbers on a small pie[ce] of paper and pin it on the map to show where they live. Make a list of the names and phone numbers of people who live near each other and distribute it to co-workers.

- Employers can give employees an incentive by providing free or reduced-rate parking and prime parking spaces for ride shares.

- If your company has too few employees to organize pools, contact your local government or public library for the names of ride-sharing networks in your area. Post and distribute that information.

5. PRECYCLE

Each American uses an average of about 190 pounds of plastics a year — and about 60 pounds of it is packaging we discard as soon as the package is opened. In fact, packaging waste accounts for approximately one-third of all the garbage we send to landfills annually. By precycling — reducing waste before you buy — you can help keep "excessive and unbound" materials out of our waste stream.

- The key to precycling is "think ahead." Figure out how you are going to dispose of a product and its packaging before you buy it.

- Look for containers that can be reused or recycled, like aluminum and glass.

- Buy in bulk whenever you can — everything from beans to hardware is available without packaging.

- Avoid items that are made to be thrown away after only a few uses, like some razors and flashlights. Look for products that can be used over and over again — Thermos jars, sponges, rechargeable batteries, and so on.

- Avoid buying products that contain hazardous materials, which are difficult to dispose of safely.

6. LIGHT BULBS

Newly developed compact fluorescent light bulbs use one-fourth the energy of standard incandescent bulbs and last ten times longer. Substituting a compact fluorescent for a traditional bulb will keep half a ton of carbon dioxide out of the atmosphere over the life of the bulb. If every household in America replaced just one incandescent bulb with a compact fluorescent, the energy saved would be equivalent to all the energy generated by one nuclear power plant running full-time for a year. If compact fluorescents aren't available in your area, you can get them by mail order from Real Goods Trading Co., 966 Mazzoni Rd., Ukiah, CA 93443.

Tips for saving energy with standard incandescents:
- Use fewer bulbs in multibulb fixtures. One large incandescent bulb is more efficient than two small ones. A 100-watt bulb, for

example, puts out as much light as two 60 watt bulbs . . . and saves energy.

- "Long-life" incandescents are more inefficient than the regular ones. They can easily cost more in extra energy than they save on replacement bulbs.
- Believe it or not, dust on a light bulb or dirt on a glass fixture can reduce the light it gives off by 10 percent and make it seem that you need a brighter, higher wattage light.

7. LOW-FLOW SHOWER HEADS

Showers account for about 32 percent of home water use. A standard shower head uses about 5 to 7 gallons of water a minute, so even a 5-minute shower can use 35 gallons. "Low-flow" shower heads reduce water use by 50 percent. They typically cut the flow rate to just 3 gallons per minute or less. So installing one is the single most effective water conservation step you can take inside your home. You also save energy. According to the Department of Energy, heating water is "the second-largest residential energy user." With a low-flow shower head, energy use (and costs) for heating hot water for showers may drop as much as 50 percent.

- There are two types of low-flow shower heads. "Aerated" heads mix air in with the water to maintain a steady spray as pressure equal to or higher than a standard shower head. This is by far the most popular type.
- A "nonaerated" head mixes no air into the flow. Its spray "pulses," so if you are partial to massage shower heads, you may prefer this.
- Note: Don't buy "flow restrictors" (disks that insert into your existing shower head) or cheap, plastic shower heads. Both deliver far less satisfying showers than a well-designed, low-flow model.
- If you can't find a good low-flow shower head locally, write to Real Goods (address listed on the previous page.)

8. PHOTOCOPY MACHINES

Americans alone make almost 400 billion photocopies a year — about 750,000 every minute of every day. If each copier in the United States used five fewer copies every business day, by utilizing two-sided copying or by cutting back on unnecessary copies, we would save up to 17.5 million reams of paper annually — the estimated equivalent of 1.4 million trees. It could also keep about 26 million cubic feet of paper out of landfills. Some copiers have a power-saver feature, which reduces energy use. I just 10 percent of office copiers had power-saving features — o were turned off when not in use — it could save as much as billion kilowatt hours of electricity, the energy equivalent of million barrels of oil.

9. Fax Machines

If everyone who owns a fax machine switched from full-page to half-page cover sheets, it would save an estimated 2 million miles of unrecyclable fax paper a year.

SOURCE: *50 Simple Things You Can Do to Save the Earth* ($4.95) and *50 Simple Things Your Business Can Do to Save the Earth* ($6.95) by the EarthWorks Group. To obtain copies of these books, send a check plus $1.00 for postage and handling to EarthWorks Press, 1400 Shattuck Ave., #25, Berkeley, CA 94709.

9 Prodigious Savants

Savant syndrome is a rare condition in which people suffering from mental retardation, autism, or schizophrenia nonetheless possess an unusual ability in a single field, most often relating to music, art, or numbers.

1. THOMAS "BLIND TOM" BETHUNE (1849–1908)

Although his vocabulary was limited to less than a hundred words, Blind Tom could play more than 5,000 pieces on the piano, an instrument he had mastered as a four-year-old slave on a Georgia plantation. At age eleven, he performed at the White House for President James Buchanan. He learned each piece after hearing it only once; his repertoire included Mozart, Beethoven, Bach, and Verdi.

2. ELLEN BOUDREAUX (1957–)

A California resident, Boudreaux, also blind, shares with Blind Tom Bethune the ability to learn a musical piece after hearing it once. Despite an IQ of only 50, she can play rock-and-roll songs in minuet form and vice versa. She performs on both piano and guitar.

3. ALONZO CLEMONS (1958–)

Clemons, who has an IQ of 40, lives in a home for the developmentally disabled in Boulder, Colorado. An exceptionally talented sculptor, he has sold hundreds of pieces, including one for $45,000. Many buyers have purchased his work unaware that it was created by a mentally handicapped artist.

4. THOMAS FULLER (1710–1790)

Born in Africa, Fuller was brought to Virginia as a slave in 1724. He was a calculating wonder who could easily multiply nine-digit numbers. At the age of seventy-eight, Fuller, who was never able to learn to read or write, was asked, "How many seconds has a man lived who is seventy years, seventeen days, and twelve hours old?" Ninety seconds later he gave the answer — 2,210,500,800. Informed that he was wrong, Fuller corrected his interrogator by pointing out that the man had forgotten to include leap years.

5. LESLIE LEMKE (1952–)

Like many prodigious savants, Leslie is blind, was born prematurely, and possesses an extraordinary memory. He sings and plays the piano and has appeared on numerous television shows, including *60 Minutes* and *Donahue.* He has also been the subject of two films, *An Island of Genius* and the Emmy-winning *The Woman Who Willed a Miracle.*

6. STEPHEN WILTSHIRE (1974–)

Although Wiltshire, who lives in London, has the IQ of someone half his age, he is able to glance briefly at a building and then draw it in exquisite detail. Wiltshire has produced three books of drawings, one of which, *Floating Cities,* was a number-one best-seller in Great Britain.

7.–8. GEORGE AND CHARLES (1939–)

Known as the Bronx Calendar Twins, they first attracted national attention when they were featured in a 1966 *Life* magazine article. The retarded brothers can give the day of the week for any date over a period of 80,000 years. They can also recall, in detail, the weather for any day of their lives.

9. KIM (1951–)

A mathematical savant, Kim, who lives in Salt Lake City, Utah, was the inspiration for the character played by Dustin Hoffman in the 1988 Academy Award–winning film *Rain Man.*

NOTE: The best book on savant syndrome is *Extraordinary People,* by Darold Treffert, M.D. It is also worth noting that there exists a school — Hope University, in Anaheim, California — devoted solely to educating gifted mentally retarded persons.

First Names of 13 Fictional Sleuths Better Known by Their Last Names

1. Tony: Baretta
2. Frank: Cannon
3. Frank: Captain Furillo
4. Ken: Hutch (Hutchinson)

Dave and Ken

5. Theo: Lieutenant Kojak
6. Thomas Sullivan: Magnum
7. Jules: Commissaire Maigret
8. Joe: Mannix
9. Jane: Miss Marple
10. Benjamin: Matlock
11. André: Navarro
12. Frank: Serpico
13. Dave: Starsky

15 Good Questions (and Their Answers)

Every minute of every workday, the New York Public Library's telephone reference service handles a half-dozen queries from people around the world. In *The Book of Answers*, the libraries have compiled the most often asked, the trickiest, and the most entertaining of the more than 6 million questions they have fielded. Here are just a few.

1. *Did Betsy Ross design the American flag?*
   No, it was designed by Francis Hopkinson, a naval flag designer, who was never reimbursed by the U.S. government for his services.
2. *What is the most despised household task?*
   According to a 1991 Gallup poll, washing the dishes far outweighs its closest competitors, cleaning the bathroom and ironing.

3. *Do different species have different colors of blood?*
   Yes. The blood of mammals is red, the blood of insects is yellow
   and the blood of lobsters is blue.

4. *What is the most unlikely mating on record between dogs?*
   In 1972 in South Wales, a male dachshund is said to have crept
   up on a sleeping female Great Dane. The union produced thirteen "Great Dachshunds," with short legs, large heads, and
   raised ears.

5. *Where did the part of the throat known as the Adam's apple get
   its name?*
   The Adam's apple refers to a legend which claims that a piece
   of the forbidden fruit from the Garden of Eden stuck in Adam's
   throat. It is actually a projection of the thyroid cartilage of the
   larynx.

6. *Who wrote "Candy is dandy / But liquor is quicker"?*
   Ogden Nash wrote the ditty in 1931. In 1968 he updated it:

   > Candy is dandy
   > But liquor is quicker.
   > Pot is not.

7. *How did the kingdom of Oz get its name?*
   Author L. Frank Baum claimed he was inspired by a file cabinet
   drawer marked "O–Z."

8. *What does saltpeter do?*
   Contrary to dormitory fears, it does not inhibit sexual desire.
   Instead, saltpeter, or potassium nitrate (KNO_3), is a diuretic.

9. *How long was the Berlin Wall?*
   The wall that divided Berlin from 1961 to 1989 was 26.5 miles
   long.

10. *How many Africans were brought to the United States as slaves.*
    Approximately 15 million.

11. *Can any creatures besides humans get a sunburn?*
    Yes — pigs.

12. *Where did the term* best man *originate?*
    It has its origins in Scotland, and refers to the era when men
    kidnapped their would-be brides. The best man was consid-
    ered the toughest of the bridegroom's friends who helped in the
    abduction.

13. *How many muscles does it take to smile? To frown?*
    Seventeen to smile, forty-three to frown.

14. *What does the Lone Ranger's title* Kemo Sabe *really mean?*
    As used by Tonto on the show *The Lone Ranger,* it was supposed
    to mean "faithful friend." In Apache, it really means "white
    shirt"; in Navajo, it means "soggy shrub."

15. *How many females have appeared on U.S. currency?*
    Aside from the representations of Justice and Liberty, only
    three: Martha Washington, Pocahontas, and Susan B. Anthony.

13 Groups That Are Not for Everyone

1. ANNETTE FUNICELLO FAN CLUB (Box 134, Nestleton, ON, Canada L0B 1L0; 416-986-0196)

   Funicello was a popular Mouseketeer on the *Mickey Mouse Club* television series (1955–1959). She also appeared in several beach films and peanut butter commercials. Her fan club publishes the *Annette Featurette* journal. Members: 200.

Annette Funicello

2. ACADEMY OF ACCOUNTING HISTORIANS (James Madison University, School of Accounting, Harrisonburg, VA 22807; 703-568-6607)

Encourages research about the history of accounting and its importance to general business and economic history. Publishes the *Accounting Historians Journal,* a page-turning periodical that comes out twice a year. Members: 850.

3. ASSOCIATION OF SPACE EXPLORERS — U.S.A. (35 White St., San Francisco, CA 94109; 415-931-0585)

An exclusive club made up of space travelers from eighteen countries who have made at least one orbit around the Earth. Their beautiful book, *The Home Planet,* is a compilation of photographs and quotations about the Earth as seen from space. Members: 150.

4. DIGNITY AFTER DEATH (613 Cedar Circle, Spencerport, NY 14559; 716-352-1105)

Dedicated to boycotting and protesting the commercialization and marketing of John Lennon since his death. Urges supporters to complain to store owners who carry "tasteless Lennon items."

5. DIVING DENTISTS SOCIETY (1101 N. Calvert St., Baltimore, MD 21202; 410-837-5852)

Membership is made up of North American dentists who like to go scuba diving. Members: 100. Not to be confused with the Flying Dentists Association (4700 Chamblee-Dunwoody Road, Dunwoody, GA 30338; 404-457-1351), whose 500 members belong to the American Dental Association *and* have active aircraft-pilot licenses.

6. GIRTH AND MIRTH (P.O. Box 14384, Chicago, IL 60614; 312-776-9223)

A social club for gay adult males who are overweight and live in the Midwest. Publishes the monthly *Girth Shaking News/Midwest.* Members: 200.

7. HUBCAPPERS (Box 54, Buckley, MI 49620; 616-269-3555)

Also known as the Hubcap Collector's Society. Brings together people who collect threaded hubcaps manufactured before 1930. Members: 63.

8. INSTITUTE OF TOTALLY USELESS SKILLS (Box 181, Temple, NH 03084; 603-654-5875)

Dedicated to the promotion of nonproductive skills such as juggling, yodeling, feather balancing, paper-airplane making, napkin stunts, pen bouncing, creative beer-can crushing, odd finger snapping, and creating symptoms of false physical self-abuse. Members: 354.

9. INTERNATIONAL BRICK COLLECTORS' ASSOCIATION (8357 Somerset Dr., Shawnee Mission, KS 66207-1843)

Brings together people who are interested in the history and manufacture of bricks. Organizes semiannual brick exchanges and publishes a quarterly journal. Members: 420.

0. INTERNATIONAL SOCIETY OF COPIER ARTISTS (800 West End Ave., Suite 13B, New York, NY 10025; 212-662-5533)

Promotes the use of photocopy machines as an instrument for creating artwork. Members: 160.

1. JIM SMITH SOCIETY (2016 Milltown Road, Camp Hill, PA 17011; 717-737-7406)

A social club for men *and* women named Jim Smith. Organizes a golf tournament in which all entrants are named Jim Smith. Members: 1,538. Of related interest are the 15,000-member Mikes of America (P.O. Box 676, Minneapolis, MN 55440; 612-827-4868) and Bobs International (Route 1, Box 120, St. Peter, MN 56082; 507-931-6667), which is made up of 500 people who are named Bob or who would like to be named Bob.

2. SOCIETY OF AMERICAN FIGHT DIRECTORS (1834 Camp Ave., Rockford, IL 61103; 815-962-6579)

Membership is mostly actors and stage-fight choreographers. Provides instruction in fight choreography and promotes historical accuracy in staged fights. Members: 300.

The world's most coveted brick.

13. Witches Anti-Discrimination Lobby (Nero Press, 153 W. 80th St., Suite 1B, New York, NY 10024; 212-362-1231)

Fights discrimination against witches, and lobbies to obtain paid legal holidays (such as Halloween) for its members. Members: 5,000.

Source: From *Organized Obsessions*, Deborah M. Burek, Martin Connors, Christa Brelin, editors. Copyright © 1992 by Visible Ink Press, a division of Gale Research Inc. Reprinted by permission of the publisher.

17 Household Items and When They Were Introduced

1. Pressure cooker — 1690 (called a steam digester by its inventor, physicist Denis Papin).
2. Tin can — 1810 (The first patented tin cans were expensive because they were made by hand).
3. Adhesive postage stamp — 1840 (first used in England).
4. Mechanical dishwasher — 1879 (invented by Illinois housewife Josephine Cochrane, who was upset by the number of dishes her kitchen help broke).
5. Contact lenses — 1887 (designed by a German glassblower; plastic lenses available about fifty years later).
6. Electric oven — 1889 (first installed in a Swiss hotel).
7. Lipstick — 1915 (marketed in a metal cartridge-type case).
8. Radio — c. 1920 (became available for use in the home).
9. Kleenex — 1924 (The first disposable handkerchiefs were originally called Celluwipes).
10. Electric blender — 1936 (Inventor Stephen Poplawski's blender was successfully marketed by bandleader Fred Waring).
11. Nylon-bristle toothbrush — 1938 (The toothbrush was originally developed in China around 1500).
12. Microwave oven — 1946 (discovered when microwaves melted candy in scientist Percy Spencer's pocket).
13. Transistor radio — 1955 (first inexpensive transistor offered)
14. Aluminum can — 1960 (Tab tops came three years later).
15. Felt-tip pen — 1960 (first marketed by a Japanese stationery firm).
16. Electric toothbrush — 1961 (first manufactured by Squibb).
17. Sony Walkman — 1979 (portable personal tape player).

Source: *The New York Public Library Book of Chronologies*, by Bruce Wetterau. Copyright 1990 by Bruce Wetterau, Stonesong Press, and the New York Public Library. Used by permission of the publisher, Prentice Hall Press / a division of Simon & Schuster, New York.

Marcello Truzzi's
10 Best-Documented Scientific Anomalies

Dr. Truzzi is a professor of sociology at Eastern Michigan University (Ypsilanti) and director of the Center for Scientific Anomalies Research (Ann Arbor). The CSAR works to promote cooperation between critics of and believers in the paranormal. Truzzi is the editor and author of ten books, including *Sociology: The Classic Statements* and *The Blue Sense: Psychic Detectives & Crime* (with Arthur Lyons). His list is in order of importance, not degree of evidence.

1. Psi (especially telepathy via automated "ganzfeld" [sensory deprivation] experiments)
2. Cold fusion (table-top anomalous nuclear reactions, especially the Japanese and now U.S. replications)
3. Unidentified aerial phenomena (not to be confused with purportedly *identified* phenomena such as alleged extraterrestrials)
4. False Memories Syndrome (which might account for many stories of abductions and abuse by extraterrestrials and Satanists)
5. Therapeutic touch and extraordinary mind-body healing processes
6. Psychokinetic effects (on the atomic level as in the randomly generated targets in the Princeton Engineering Anomalies Research lab studies)
7. Physiological change effects found in patients with multiple personality disorder
8. Transmutation of elements at a cost-effective rate (in recent physics experiments)
9. The Mars Effect (a neo-astrological correlation phenomenon [i.e., that the position of the planets at the time of a person's birth is related to the profession he or she chooses] discovered by Michel Gauqueline, and since replicated even by skeptics)
10. Persons with next-to-no-brain (hydrocephalic cases) who function at normal or about-average levels

— Exclusive for *The Book of Lists*

The 15 Strangest Stories, Selected by Paul Sieveking, Coeditor of the *Fortean Times*

The *Fortean Times,* "The Journal of Strange Phenomena," is a bimonthly magazine of news, reviews, and research on all types of unusual phenomena and experiences. It was named after philosopher Charles Fort (1874–1932), who thought that data that didn't fit the scientific norm should not be excluded or ignored by the scientific community. (To subscribe, write care of John Brown Publishing Ltd., 20 Paul Street, Frome, Somerset BA11 1DX, United Kingdom.)

1. FISH IN TREE

   Farmer Heino Seppi was collecting cut timber from the woods of Yrjo Kanto in the Palloneva region of Finland in October 1969. Splitting an aspen log, he found its middle rotten, forming a hollow that contained a dried fish about forty centimeters long, resembling a perch. There was no clue as to how the fish got there.

2. X-RAY VISION

   Crane driver Yuliya Vorobyeva, thirty-seven, received a 398-volt shock in a mine near Donetsk, Ukraine, in 1978, and was pronounced dead. She regained consciousness two days later during an autopsy. She didn't sleep for six months, then slept for a long time and awoke to find she could see right through people — literally. She was employed at Donetsk hospital to diagnose rare illnesses, such as diseases of the pancreas. She impressed a reporter from *Izvestia* by telling him what he had for breakfast.

3. MR. ROBINSON COMES TO HIS SENSES

   Edwin Robinson suffered a severe head injury in a 1971 road accident and gradually lost his sight and hearing. On June 4, 1980, he was struck down by lightning outside his house in a suburb of Portland, Maine, and remained unconscious for twenty minutes. He survived because of his rubber-soled shoes. Afterward, he found his central vision was back and he could hear perfectly.

4. A MODERN NOAH

   Police raided the house of John Roeleveld, seventy-two, in Eerbeeck Holland, in April 1982 and discovered a warren of concrete bomb shelters containing an estimated 250,000 preserved and stuffed animals and birds, many of them protected species. Most had been stuffed by Roeleveld himself. Forty years earlier, God had instructed him to collect and mount two of every species in preparation for the end of the world, which was imminent.

5. THE SKY CHILDREN

On December 22, 1980, an explosion tore a hole in a Saudi Arabian aircraft flying 29,000 feet above the Persian Gulf. Sudden decompression sucked out Samina Khatoon, ten, and her brother Ahmed, ten. An immediate search after an emergency landing was fruitless. Three years later, a Pakistani visiting a small port in Abu Dhabi met the children. The girl said they had been found in the sea by an Arab fisherman. Thinking they had been dropped from heaven, he took them home and raised them as his own.

6. GOOD SHOT!

George, a nineteen-year-old Canadian, suffered from a compulsion to wash his hands fifty times a day, take four-hour showers, and check whether all windows and doors were locked. In 1983, taunted by his mother, he attempted suicide by shooting himself in the mouth. By chance, he performed a precise left-frontal lobotomy and his ritualistic behavior was much reduced. Most of the .22-caliber slug was removed and the man's IQ was unimpaired. The case was written up in various professional psychiatric journals.

7. WORLD WAR II SHELL FALLS IN BACKYARD

At about 4:00 P.M. on New Year's Day 1984, a rusty nine-inch, twenty-two-pound shell of World War II vintage crashed from a sunny sky into the backyard of Fred Simons, seventy-nine, in Lakewood, twenty-miles southeast of Los Angeles. It left an oblong crater four feet deep in Fred's patio. Neighbors heard a whistling sound before the shell hit, but no one reported seeing or hearing a plane. A bomb squad from the sheriff's department found that the shell contained no explosives.

8. TOO RICH TO EAT

George Veriopoulos, a Greek Orthodox priest, was preparing a meal of boiled sheep's head in 1984 when he noticed the glint of gold on the roots of its teeth. Scraping away some flesh, he saw gold all along the jawbone. It proved to be fourteen karat, with an estimated value of $6,000. The eight-month-old sheep had been provided by the priest's brother-in-law from his herd in Patission, near Athens. The Greek ministry of agriculture investigated and found the story true, unique, and inexplicable.

9. STRANGE LAND

In 1985 the Chinese press announced a discovery on a strip of land 1,000 meters by 15 meters, running down from a hill to a river, in Huanre County, Liaoning province. In winter when the surrounding temperature drops to $-30°$ C, the strip remains at $17°$ C. In summer the reverse occurs, and the strip freezes to a depth of 1 meter. The local people use the strip for growing vegetables in winter and as a refrigerator in summer.

10. MUSHROOM MEMORIAL

A nun called Sister Stanislaus tried in vain for many years to grow mushrooms at the House of the Mother of God in Hawarden, Clwyd, Wales. In 1986 she died, at the age of seventy-nine, and every autumn since then a healthy crop of mushrooms has appeared on her grave and nowhere else in the convent grounds. The nuns regularly tuck in. "They are very tasty," said the mother abbess, Mother Francesca.

11. FISHFALL FOR CASTAWAYS

In 1986 Take Taka, Tatiete Kannangaki, and Bakatarawa Labo, three fishermen from a Pacific island in the Kiribati group, survived 119 days adrift in a sixteen-foot open boat by catching twenty-five sharks with their bare hands and eating them raw. One night they prayed for a different kind of fish, and something fell into the boat. It was a rare blackish fish that was never caught by trawling, as it lives about 620 feet down.

12. HOUSE SWEATS BLOOD

Minnie Clyde Winston, seventy-seven, stepped out of the bath at 1114 Fountain Drive, in southwest Atlanta, Georgia, on September 8, 1987, to find the floor oozing blood "like a sprinkler." There was also blood in most of the rooms of the house. She and her husband, William, had lived in the six-room brick house for twenty-two years. They had no pets and the house was free from rats, mice, and cockroaches. The state crime lab revealed the blood was human, type O. Both Mr. and Mrs. Winston had blood type A.

13. VIRGIN BIRTH IN LESOTHO

In October 1988 the *British Journal of Obstetrics and Gynaecology* reported that a fifteen-year-old girl from Lesotho in southern Africa, born without a vagina, had given birth to a son, presumably by cesarean section. Immediately after she had performed fellatio on her boyfriend, an ex-boyfriend burst in and stabbed her repeatedly. One of the blows pierced her stomach, allowing ingested sperm to seep into her fallopian tubes.

14. Betty Louty Calling

As a child, Elizabeth Atkins from New York had an imaginary playmate, with whom she had tea every afternoon. She told her parents that her friend was Betty Louty, and she lived far away. Several years later, the family went on holiday to Jamaica and visited the straw market in Kingston. Elizabeth took great care in choosing a handmade doll from among hundreds. Sometime later, Elizabeth's mother, Jo, found that the doll was signed by the maker on the inside of her apron: "Betty Louty."

15. Woman Gives Birth to Fish

Mrs. Felina de la Cruz, forty-five, a laundrywoman from Cabanatuan in the Philippines, claimed to have given birth to an eighteen-centimeter mudfish on October 13, 1990. She called it Angelique Jezebel and tried to bottle-feed it before skeptical journalists. Her husband, Romeo, said he heard the fish say "ik-ik" shortly after his wife delivered it, but admitted there were no outside witnesses. They planned to give it a Catholic baptism. Alas, Angelique Jezebel died the following January.

10 Strange Events

ach year, the editors of *Strange Magazine,* a periodical devoted to ne study of unusual phenomena, choose the ten strangest events of ne past twelve months. Herewith, ten of the more noteworthy winers of recent years. Editor-publisher Mark Chorvinsky stresses nat inclusion on the list does not constitute endorsement of the eality of the events. Each event, however, was covered in the inernational press. (To subscribe, write to: *Strange Magazine,* P.O. ox 2246, Rockville, MD 20852.)

Lizard Man

In June and July 1988, several sightings were recorded of a large upright scaly creature in the vicinity of Scape Ore Swamp near Bishopville, South Carolina. Liz-a-Rid spray repellents were marketed in local stores and must have proved effective because reports of the Lizard Man died out by August.

Jesus in Japan

A transcript of an ancient scroll discovered in 1988 near Shingo village in northeastern Japan states that Jesus Christ married a woman named Yumiko, fathered three daughters, and died at the age of 106.

3. GIANT GREEK FOG MAN

On June 29, 1989, eleven-year-old Evvi Sottiropoulou was playing with her brother in their grandmother's yard in Chrysopetra, Greece. The grandmother heard a loud noise and rushed outside to find the children in a panic. Evvi had seen a twenty-five-foot-tall deformed manlike entity shrouded in a cloud which disappeared with a bang. When police arrived, they found two three-foot-long humanlike footprints in front of the house.

4. CHESS WITH THE DEAD

Between 1984 and 1989, chess star Viktor Korchnoi played a chess match with Hungarian master Geza Maroczy, who died in 1951. Korchnoi contacted Maroczy through a Hungarian medium, Robert Roland. Korchnoi had originally wanted to play the deceased Raoul Capablanca, but Capablanca could not be reached.

5. SNAKE SHOOTS MAN

Pulling the trigger with its tail, a snake fatally shot Iranian hunter Ali-Asghar Ahani in the head on April 23, 1990, as the hunter pressed the shotgun's butt behind the snake's head in an attempt to capture it. Another hunter tried to grab the shotgun, but the snake coiled around it and triggered the other barrel.

6. SAVED BY A STINGRAY

Lottie Stevens, an eighteen-year-old fisherman from the Pacific island nation of Vanuatu, fell into the water when his boat capsized on January 15, 1990. When he washed up in New Caledonia twenty-three days later, he claimed that a stingray had carried him on its back for almost two weeks, keeping him safe from menacing sharks.

7. LEGALLY HAUNTED HOUSE

Because Jeffrey and Patrice Stambovsky had not been told by Helen Ackley in 1989 that the house on the Hudson River they bought from her was haunted, they sued for the return of their $32,500 deposit. Ackley had previously described to the media the apparitions, which she found "comforting." The Stambovskys felt otherwise. In the majority opinion, Justice Israel Rubin of the New York state supreme court's appellate division wrote that the usual "as is" requirement of the sale contract did not extend to ghosts and that the Nyack, New York, house had not been delivered vacant, as promised.

8. RAIN MAN

On February 18, 1986, U.S. district court judge Samuel King, unhappy at the absence of some jurors due to heavy rains, de-

In 1986, U.S. District Court Judge Samuel King ordered rain to stop falling in California. After five years of drought, King rescinded his order — and the rain returned.

creed, "I hereby order that it cease raining by Tuesday." California then suffered five years of drought. In February 1991 King rescinded his order and ordered instead that "rain shall fall in California beginning February 27, 1991." Later that day, California was deluged with four inches of rain, the heaviest in a decade. Judge King proclaimed that the events of the day constituted "proof positive that we are a nation governed by laws."

9. WEREWOLVES IN WISCONSIN

On October 31, 1991 — Halloween — Doristine Gipson twice encountered a strange wolflike entity at an intersection near Delavan, Wisconsin. Two years earlier, Lorianne Endrizzi had encountered a lupine, hunched, humanlike figure half a mile away on the same road.

0. "HARD TO BELIEVE" AWARD: IMELDA MARCOS CLAIMS LATE HUSBAND'S SPIRIT CAUSED HURRICANE ANDREW

According to Ferdinand Marcos's widow, Imelda, Marcos's spirit has unleashed numerous natural disasters, including Hurricane Andrew in 1992. "For the sake of the republic of the Philippines," pleaded the former dictator's widow, "for the Filipino people, [we must] put the remains of the president to rest so that these negative vibrations will leave us." Philippines president Fidel Ramos had agreed to allow the deceased a simple military burial in his hometown, but Imelda Marcos continues to hold out for a Manila funeral with full honors.

9 Extraordinary Coincidences

1. ### THE MISSING THUMB

   In July 1991 Robert Lindsey was boating at a reservoir in Green River, Wyoming. A friend's daughter fell into the water and he dived after her. The boat ran over him, cutting off three of his fingers, two of which were found and reattached. Nearly seven months later a fisherman hooked a lake trout that contained a severed thumb. The county coroner was contacted. Said Lindsey, "As soon as I saw it, I was pretty sure it was mine." He added, "I'll probably just put it on a shelf to show people."

2. ### REUNITED

   Twenty-one-year-old Tammy Harris had spent nearly a year searching for her biological mother, while Joyce Shultz had spent twenty years trying to find her daughter. The women lived two blocks from each other and worked together at a convenience store. One day, Shultz overheard Harris talking about her quest, and said she "might know somebody who can help." Harris lent her a baby picture, which Schultz compared with photos of her daughter. After keeping quiet for three days, Shultz confided the truth to the store manager, and mother and daughter were ecstatically reunited.

3. ### *SAILFISH* VS. *SCULPIN*

   On May 23, 1939, the newly built submarine USS *Squalus* sank off the eastern seaboard. A sister ship, the USS *Sculpin,* sped to the rescue, and saved more than half of the fifty-six-man crew. The *Squalus* was salvaged and renamed the *Sailfish.* In 1943 the *Sculpin* was sunk by the Japanese, who took forty-two crew members prisoner, and placed half of them on board the aircraft carrier *Cuyo.* As it approached Japan, the *Cuyo* was torpedoed by the *Sailfish* and went down with all hands. The crew of the *Sailfish* rejoiced at their victory — unaware that they had just killed half the survivors of the sub that had come to their rescue four years earlier.

4. ### WRITER'S INTUITION?

   When author Norman Mailer began his novel *Barbary Shore,* there was no Russian spy in it. Over time, he added such a character in a minor role. As the novel progressed, the spy became the main character. After the book was completed, the immigration service arrested a man living one flight below Mailer. He was Colonel Rudolf Abel, the top Russian spy in the United States.

5. DESTINED TO DINE

As a child in school, French poet Emile Deschamps shared a table with a M. de Fortgibu. The man offered Emile his first taste of a novel dessert, plum pudding, which M. Fortgibu had acquired a taste for in England. Ten years later Deschamps passed a restaurant and saw a plum pudding being prepared inside. He entered and asked for a slice, but the pudding was being saved for someone — who turned out to be M. de Fortgibu. Many years later, at a dinner party where plum pudding was being served, Deschamps, about to have this dessert for the third time, told his amusing story. And lo and behold, Fortgibu arrived at the door! He too had been invited to dinner, to another apartment in the same building, and had lost his way. Said Deschamps, "My hair stood up on my head."

6. JAILED BY JAWS

In 1799, an American privateer, the *Nancy*, sailing in Caribbean waters, was being pursued by a British warship. Before he was captured, the Yankee skipper, Thomas Briggs, managed to throw the ship's American papers overboard and to replace them with forged Dutch papers. He was taken to Jamaica, where he was placed on trial for running a British blockade during wartime. But it appeared he would go free — the court was faced with having to dismiss the case for lack of evidence. During the trial, another British ship, the HMS *Ferret*, arrived in port and produced the damning papers. The *Ferret* had captured a large shark off the coast of Haiti which, when opened, revealed the evidence. These documents were used to convict Briggs and his entire crew, and are on display today in the Institute of Jamaica, Kingston.

7. MYSTERY TWINS

On February 20, 1947, two pregnant women were examined by their interns in a hospital in Ogden, Utah. Each doctor thought he heard double heartbeats — an indication of twins — and was surprised when each woman had a single birth, within five minutes of each other. The mothers remained strangers until three years later, when the Hendersons built a home next door to the Ritters. Within a few days, a comedy of errors was occurring — both sets of parents confused little Joyce with her identical three-year-old neighbor, Jean. The girls became friends, and found they liked the same foods, the same sports, and the same music. Their voices sound alike, and when they were five, they lost their baby teeth one by one within hours of each other. Their teachers had trouble telling them apart, but, said one, "It doesn't matter. They always get the same marks anyway."

8. A TRIO OF TRAGEDIES

Abraham Lincoln's eldest son, Robert Todd Lincoln, had the singular misfortune to be at the scene of three presidential assassinations. On April 14, 1865, he rushed to Ford's Theater, where his father lay fatally wounded. In 1881 he was at President Garfield's side just seconds after the president was shot. Twenty years later, he was about to join President McKinley at the Pan American Exhibit when he learned that McKinley was the victim of an assassin's bullet. Lincoln might never have witnessed these tragedies if he himself had not had a narrow escape in his youth. While standing on a crowded railroad platform, he tripped and nearly fell onto the tracks. He was pulled to safety in the nick of time by Edwin Booth — brother of John Wilkes Booth.

9. REUNION #2

In 1975 John Starr left his wife and three-year-old son in Illinois and headed for the East Coast. After seventeen years of drifting, using the name John McDaniel, he wandered into the Wayside Cross Rescue Mission in Aurora, Illinois. Meanwhile, his son, John Earl, had grown up and led a life similar to that of his father. Down on his luck, with a wife and child back in Texas, he wound up in the Wayside Cross Rescue Mission. One day, Mr. Starr stepped outside for a smoke and struck up a conversation with John Earl. Soon they were chatting about local acquaintances, and John Earl asked Starr if he knew a man named John McDaniel. Starr answered, "I sure do. That's me." To which John Earl replied, "I think you're my father." The younger man's first reaction was anger, but over time father and son have begun to mend fences.

NOTE: For more extraordinary coincidences, see *The Book of Lists #2*, pp. 426–27.

John Earl (left) befriended John Starr at a homeless mission and then discovered that Starr was his father.

8 Onlies

1. ### THE ONLY PRESIDENT TO GET STUCK IN THE WHITE HOUSE BATHTUB

   William Howard Taft, U.S. president from 1909 until 1913, weighed more than 300 pounds. Once, after getting stuck in the White House bathtub, he ordered a new one installed, large enough for four men. At a dinner in the Panama Canal Zone, engineers built him a dining room chair reinforced with steel. Jokes about Taft's size were common and he took them with good humor. According to Paul L. Boller, Jr., in *Presidential Anecdotes,* Taft was swimming off Cape Ann, Massachusetts, when two neighbors walked by and said, "We'd better wait. The president is using the ocean."

2. ### THE ONLY PRESIDENT TO WEIGH UNDER 100 POUNDS

   James Madison, the fourth president of the United States (1809–1817), stood five feet four inches and weighed ninety-eight pounds. Had he lived in the twentieth century he probably could not have gotten elected — although the average American male is 5 feet 9 inches tall, the last twenty-two presidential elections have been won by a candidate who was taller than the average.

3. ### THE ONLY FOOT DEODORANT ELECTED TO PUBLIC OFFICE

   In the early 1970s, during an election campaign in Ecuador, a foot deodorant manufacturer used the advertising slogan "Vote for any candidate, but if you want well-being and hygiene, vote for Pulvapies." The day before the election, the manufacturer distributed a leaflet reading "For Mayor: The Honorable Pulvapies." Voters in the coastal village of Picoaza (pop. 4,100), unimpressed with the alternatives, elected Pulvapies by a clear majority.

4. ### THE ONLY ENGLISH MONARCH NEVER TO SET FOOT IN ENGLAND

   Berengaria, the daughter of King Sancho VI of Navarre, married King Richard the Lion-Hearted and was crowned queen — in Cyprus — in 1191. She never visited England and spent most of her eight-year reign in Italy and France.

5. ### THE ONLY BONE IN THE HUMAN BODY NOT CONNECTED TO ANOTHER

   The hyoid is a V-shaped bone located at the base of the tongue between the mandible and the voice box. Its function is to support the tongue and its muscles.

6. THE ONLY 7-LETTER WORD THAT CONTAINS ALL 5 VOWELS

The word is *sequoia*, referring to the giant trees of California. The sequoia is named after the Cherokee Indian scholar who created a written alphabet for the Cherokee language.

7. THE ONLY BASEBALL PLAYER TO GET A HIT FOR 2 DIFFERENT TEAMS IN 2 CITIES ON THE SAME DAY

Joel Youngblood began August 4, 1982, as the starting right fielder for the New York Mets in their game against the Chicago Cubs. He singled in the third inning, but was immediately pulled from the game and told that he had been traded to the Montreal Expos. Youngblood flew to Philadelphia, took a taxi to Veteran's Stadium, put on a Montreal uniform, and entered the game in the sixth inning. In his only at-bat, he singled again.

8. THE ONLY NONHUMAN LAND ANIMAL THAT COMMONLY MATES FACE TO FACE

Two-toed sloths typically mate vertically while hanging by their arms from a tree branch.

SOURCE: Bruce Felton, *One of a Kind* (New York: William Morrow, 1992).

16 Cases of People Killed by God

1. ENTIRE WORLD POPULATION EXCEPT NOAH AND 7 RELATIVES (Genesis 6, 7)

Transgression: Violence, corruption and generalized wickedness.
Method of execution: Flood.

2. ENTIRE POPULATIONS OF SODOM AND GOMORRAH EXCEPT LOT, HIS WIFE, AND THEIR 2 DAUGHTERS (Genesis 19)

Transgression: Widespread wickedness and lack of respect for the deity.
Method of execution: Rain of fire and brimstone.

3. LOT'S WIFE (Genesis 19)

Transgression: Looked back.
Method of execution: Turned into a pillar of salt.

4. ER (Genesis 38)

Transgression: Wickedness.
Method of execution: Unknown.

Lot's wife —
don't look back

5. ONAN (Genesis 38)

Transgression: Refused to make love to his brother Er's widow.
Method of execution: Unknown.

6. ALL THE FIRSTBORN OF EGYPT (Exodus 12)

Transgression: Egypt was cruel to the Jews.
Method of execution: Unknown.

7. PHAROAH AND THE EGYPTIAN ARMY (Exodus 14)

Transgression: Pursued the Jews.
Method of execution: Drowned.

8. NADAB AND ABIHU (Leviticus 10)

Transgression: Offered strange fire.
Method of execution: Fire.

9. KORAH, DATHAN, ABIRAM, AND THEIR FAMILIES (Numbers 16)

Transgression: Rejected authority of Moses and started own congregation.
Method of execution: Swallowed by earth.

10. 250 FOLLOWERS OF KORAH (Numbers 16)

Transgression: Supported Korah.
Method of execution: Fire.

11. 14,700 ISRAELITES (Numbers 16)

Transgression: Murmured against Moses and his brother Aaron following execution of Korah and his supporters.
Method of execution: Plague.

12. UNKNOWN NUMBER OF RETREATING AMORITE SOLDIERS (Joshua 10)

Transgression: Fought the Israelites.
Method of execution: Hailstones.

13. Uzzah (2 Samuel 6)

Transgression: Touched the ark of God after oxen shook it while pulling it on a cart.
Method of execution: Unknown.

14. 70,000 People (2 Samuel 24)

Transgression: King David ordered a census of the population.
Method of execution: Plague.

15. 102 Soldiers of King Ahaziah (2 Kings 1)

Transgression: Tried to capture Elijah the Tishbite.
Method of execution: Fire.

16. Ananias and Sapphira (Acts 5)

Transgression: Land fraud.
Method of execution: Unknown.

12 Strange Deaths

1. Among the Many Dangers of the Material World

A Brink's armored-car guard, Hrand Arakelian, thirty-four, of Santee, California, was crushed to death by $50,000 worth of quarters. Arakelian was guarding a load of twenty-five-pound coin boxes in the back of a truck traveling down the San Diego Freeway on February 3, 1986, when the driver braked suddenly to avoid a car that had swerved in front of him. When he pulled over to check on his partner, he found Arakelian completely covered by boxes of coins.

2. Drowned at a Lifeguards' Party

On August 1, 1985, lifeguards of the New Orleans recreation department threw a party to celebrate their first drowning-free season in memory. Although four lifeguards were on duty at the party and more than half the 200 party-goers were lifeguards when the party ended, one of the guests, Jerome Moody, thirty-one, was found dead on the bottom of the recreation department pool.

3. Strangled by a Garden Hose

Thirty-five-year-old Richard Fresquez of Austin, Texas, became drunk on the night of May 7, 1983. He tripped on a garden hose, became tangled in it, and strangled to death while trying to break free.

4. Fatal Cure for Hemorrhoids

Norik Hakpisan, a twenty-four-year-old music student of Sloane Terrace, Chelsea, in London, was found dead on October 5, 1982, after being caught in a flash fire while trying to relieve a bad case of hemorrhoids with gasoline. The fumes from an open bottle of petrol had been ignited by a hot plate. Hakpisan's brother, Hiak, said that relieving hemorrhoids with paraffin was an old family remedy, but that Norik had apparently used petrol instead.

5. Killed by a Waterbed

Donald King, twenty-eight, of Stockton, California, was smothered to death by a waterbed mattress on the night of August 20, 1983. King fell asleep next to the bed while waiting for it to fill with water. The mattress overfilled, burst its wood frame, and rolled on top of him.

6. Perfect Re-creation

On April 27, 1991, Yooket Paen, fifty-seven, of Angthong, Thailand, slipped in some mud, grabbed a live wire, and was electrocuted. Later that day, her fifty-two-year-old sister, Yooket Pan, was showing some neighbors how the accident happened when *she* slipped, grabbed the same live wire, and was also electrocuted.

7. Killed by Art

In 1991 Bulgarian environmental artist Christo erected 1,760 yellow umbrellas along southern California's Tejon Pass and another 1,340 blue umbrellas in Ibaraki Prefecture north of Tokyo. Each of the umbrellas weighed 488 pounds. On October 26, Lori Jean Keevil-Mathews, a thirty-three-year-old insurance agent, drove out to Interstate 5 to view the California umbrellas. Shortly after Keevil-Mathews and her husband got out of their car, a huge gust of wind tore one of the umbrellas loose from its steel screw anchors and blew it straight at Keevil-Mathews, crushing her against a boulder. Christo immediately ordered the dismantling of all the umbrellas in both countries. However, on October 30, another umbrella-related death occurred when fifty-seven-year-old crane operator Wasaaki Nakamura was electrocuted by a power line in Japan as he prepared to take down one of the umbrellas.

8. Self-Induced Capital Punishment

Michael Anderson Godwin was convicted of murder and sentenced to the electric chair, but in 1983 his sentence was changed to life in prison. On March 5, 1989, Godwin, twenty-eight years old, was trying to fix a pair of earphones connected to the television set in his cell at the Central Correctional Institution in Columbia, South Carolina. While sitting on a steel toilet, he bit into a wire and was electrocuted.

9. THE BOWLING BALL FROM NOWHERE

Thomas Hart, thirty, and his wife, Linda, were driving home in suburban Detroit in the early morning of December 4, 1982, when out of the darkness a fourteen-pound burgundy bowling ball bounced on the hood of their car, crashed through the windshield, and struck Hart in the head. He was pronounced dead the following day.

10. AMONG THE MANY DANGERS OF THE SPIRITUAL WORLD

John Edward Blue, thirty-eight, of Dorchester, Massachusetts, was being baptized in Natick's Lake Cochituate on August 13, 1984, when he and the minister performing the baptism slipped and fell backward into deep water. The minister survived, but Blue drowned.

11. THE PERILS OF POLITICS

Nitaro Ito, forty-one, a pancake-shop operator in Higashiosaka City, Japan, concluded that he needed an extra edge in his 1979 campaign for the House of Representatives. He decided to stage an attack on himself and then draw sympathy by campaigning from a hospital bed. Ito's scheme was to have an employee, Kazuhiko Matsumo, punch him in the face on the night of September 17, after which Ito would stab himself in the leg. After Matsumo had carried out his part of the plan, Ito stabbed his right thigh. Unfortunately, he cut an artery and bled to death before he could reach his home, fifty meters away.

12. KILLED BY A ROBOT

Ford Motor Company's casting plant in Flat Rock, Michigan, employed a one-ton robot to fetch parts from a storage rack. When the robot malfunctioned on January 25, 1979, twenty-five-year-old Robert Williams was asked to climb up on the rack and get the parts. While he was performing the task, the robot suddenly reactivated and hit Williams in the head with its arm. Williams died instantly. Four years later a jury ordered Unit Handling Systems, the manufacturer of the robot, to pay Williams's family $10 million. Williams is believed to have been the first person killed by a robot.

NOTE: For more strange deaths, see *The Book of Lists #1*, pp. 445–57, *The Book of Lists #2*, pp. 454–56, and *The Book of Lists #3*, pp. 407–10.

15 People Buried 2 or More Times

1. **JOHN WILKES BOOTH (1838–1865), U.S. actor**

   Twelve days after he assassinated Abraham Lincoln, Booth himself was shot to death. His body was transported to Washington, D.C., and secretly buried under a flagstone floor in the Washington Arsenal Prison. Two years later it was exhumed and stored in a pine box in a warehouse. In 1869 President Andrew Johnson ordered the box moved to a funeral home, where it was claimed by Booth's brother, the famous actor Edwin Booth. Finally, on June 26, 1869, it was reburied in an unmarked family plot in Greenmount Cemetery in Baltimore, Maryland.

2. **PABLO CASALS (1876–1973), Spanish cellist**

   When he left Spain in 1939, as the Fascist dictator Francisco Franco took power, Casals swore he would return only when democracy was restored. He died before that happened and was buried in Memorial Cemetery in Carolina, Puerto Rico. His will contained the request that his body be buried in Spain whenever it would be possible. That time came with the change of government in 1979. Casal's coffin was put on display in Barcelona and then reburied in the church cemetery of Vendrell, the village where he was born and raised.

3. **CHARLIE CHAPLIN (1889–1977), British actor**

   Chaplin was buried in the village cemetery of Corsier, Switzerland. On March 1, 1978, Galtcho Ganav of Bulgaria and Roman Wardas of Poland dug up his grave, stole the body, and hid it in a field ten miles away. After the grave robbers were arrested, Chaplin's body was recovered and reburied — this time in a vault surrounded by cement.

. **CHRISTOPHER COLUMBUS (1451–1506), Spanish explorer**

   Originally, Columbus was buried in the Franciscan monastery of Valladolid, Spain. A few years later his body was transferred to the Carthusian monastery in Las Cuevas. In 1541 his remains were put on a ship and sent across the ocean to be buried in a cathedral in the Dominican Republic. However, in 1795 Spain ceded the island of Hispaniola to France, so Columbus was moved to Havana, Cuba. Then, in 1898, Spain lost the Spanish-American War and had to give up its West Indian colonies. So Columbus's remains were shipped back across the Atlantic Ocean and once again enshrined, this time in a cathedral in Seville, where they rest today. It is worth noting, however, that in 1877 a vault in the Cathedral of Santo Domingo was opened and a casket was discovered that many scholars believe to contain the real bones of Columbus.

5. **ARTHUR CONAN DOYLE (1854–1930), British author**

The creator of Sherlock Holmes died sitting up in an armchair and was buried in the garden of his estate in Windlesham, Sussex. In 1955 the family sold Windlesham (which was turned into a hotel), and the bodies of Conan Doyle and his wife, Jean, were moved to a grave at Minstead Churchyard, Hampshire. To avoid publicity, the press was decoyed and the coffins were transported in a laundry van to their new resting place.

6. **F. SCOTT FITZGERALD (1896–1940), U.S. author**

Fitzgerald had hoped to be buried in his family's plot in the graveyard of St. Mary's Roman Catholic church in Rockville, Maryland. But when he died he was refused a Catholic burial because, in the words of a Baltimore diocesan aide, he "had not performed his Easter duty and his writings were undesirable." It was discovered that a single plot remained in the nondenominational Rockville Union Cemetery, and he was interred there instead. By 1975 Fitzgerald had regained his lost fame, and the authorities at St. Mary's had a change of heart. On November 7, Fitzgerald and his wife, Zelda, were reburied in the Catholic cemetery.

7. **FREDERICK II, KING OF PRUSSIA (1712–1786), German military leader**

In his will, Frederick the Great asked to be buried beside his greyhounds on the grounds of the palace of Sans Souci in Potsdam. He got his wish, but it took 205 years and six stops along the way. When he died, his successor, Frederick William II, thought it too undignified to bury Frederick with his dogs, so he had the great leader entombed instead with his father, Frederick Wilhelm I (who had once imprisoned Frederick and whom Frederick hated), in the Garrison church of Potsdam. In February 1945, as Allied bombs edged closer to Potsdam, Adolf Hitler had the two bodies moved to the Luftwaffe bunker of Hermann Göring. A few weeks later they were surreptitiously transferred to a salt mine in Thuringia. Six weeks after that, American troops found the sarcophagi and seized them. Frederick and his father were buried again, this time at a church in the town of Marburg. In 1952 Prince Louis Ferdinand had his ancestor moved to the crypt at the Hohenzollern castle in Hechingen and vowed that someday he would return them to Sans Souci, which was then in Communist East Germany. After the fall of the Berlin Wall, Louis Ferdinand saw his chance. On August 7, 199 with great pomp and ceremony, not to mention antimilitari protests, Frederick the Great was finally laid to rest alongsid his greyhounds and separated at last from his father, who was interred elsewhere on the palace grounds.

8. JOSEPH HAYDN (1732–1809), Austrian composer

Haydn was originally buried in the Hundsthuron Cemetery in Vienna. When his body was exhumed in 1820 for reburial in the Bergkirche on Prince Nicolaus Esterhazy's Eisenstadt estate, it was discovered that the head was missing. It was soon determined that two friends of Haydn's, Carl Rosenbaum and Johann Peter, had bribed the grave digger to let them steal Haydn's head "to protect it from desecration." Rosenbaum produced a bogus skull, which was buried with Haydn's body. From 1895 to 1954, the real skull was kept in the museum of the Vienna Academy of Music, after which it was reunited with Haydn's skeleton and reburied in the Bergkirche.

9. JOHN PAUL JONES (1747–1792), Scottish-born U.S. naval officer

One of the heroes of the American Revolution, Jones died a lonely death in Paris and was buried in a cemetery for foreign Protestants. In 1899 the U.S. ambassador to France, General Horace Porter, initiated a search for Jones's grave. It was finally located and his body was exhumed in 1905 and carried back to the United States. Because of bureaucratic red tape, it was not until January 26, 1913, that John Paul Jones's body was laid to rest in a tomb on the grounds of the U.S. Naval Academy in Annapolis, Maryland.

0. IMRE NAGY (1896–1958), Hungarian political leader

As Hungary's premier, Nagy led the revolt against Stalin that prompted the Soviet Union to invade Hungary in 1956. Nagy was hanged as a traitor on June 16, 1958. Thirty-one years later to the day, Nagy and four aides were exhumed from their unmarked graves and reburied after an emotional memorial service attended by 100,000 people and televised live for nine hours. Also buried was a sixth empty coffin, which symbolized the hundreds of other Hungarians who were executed for their part in the 1956 uprising.

1. ZINTKALA NUNI (MARGUERITE COLBY) (1890–1919), Lakota Indian

When soldiers of the U.S. 7th Cavalry massacred hundreds of unarmed Lakota Sioux Indians at Wounded Knee Creek in South Dakota on December 29, 1902, a four-month-old baby girl was found alive, lying underneath the body of her dead mother. She was adopted by Brigadier General Leonard Colby and raised by Colby's suffragette wife, Clara. For a time Marguerite worked in Buffalo Bill Cody's Wild West Show. She died at the age of twenty-nine and was buried in Hanford, Califor-

nia. French-Canadian author Renée Sanson-Flood traced th
story of Marguerite Colby, located her grave, and arrange
with leaders of the Lakota community to have her reburie
The Lakota renamed her Zintkala Nuni — Lost Bird — and o
July 12, 1991, following a symbolic freeing-of-the-spirit cer
mony, she was laid to rest near the mass grave at Wounde
Knee that included the body of her mother.

12. IGNACE JAN PADEREWSKI (1860–1941), Polish pianist an
political leader

Paderewski died in New York City during World War II. U.
president Franklin Roosevelt directed that his body be temp
rarily interred at Arlington National Cemetery, where it wa
placed in a zinc casket at the base of the mast of the USS *Mair*
memorial. The intention was to return Paderewski to h
homeland after the war, but when Poland fell to communism
it was decided to keep his body in the United States. On July
1992, following the fall of communism in Poland, Paderewski
body was buried at St. John's Cathedral in Warsaw.

13. EVA PERON (1919–1952), Argentine First Lady

When she died, the popular second wife of President Jua
Peron was embalmed, but not buried. After Peron was ove
thrown in 1955, Eva's body was kidnapped and smuggled o
of the country. She was buried in the Musocco Cemetery i
Milan under the name of Maria Maggi to discourage potenti
grave robbers. In 1971 her body was transferred to Madri
where Juan Peron was living in exile. Two years later, Per
briefly returned to power. Upon his death, his third wife, Mar
Estela, became president. In an attempt to link herself wi
Eva Peron's popularity, she brought Eva's body back to Arge
tina on November 17, 1974. It didn't help. Maria Estela wa
deposed by a coup in March 1976. In October of that year, Ev
was buried in an armored vault in the Recoleta Cemetery
Buenos Aires.

14. HAILE SELASSIE (1892–1975), Ethiopian dictator and mil
tary leader

Emperor Haile Selassie died mysteriously a year after bein
overthrown by Mengistu Haile Mariam, who had him burie
deep in the ground under a latrine in Mengistu's office at th
grand palace. According to Ethiopian state radio, the new di
tator "chose this site to see that the body did not rise from th
dead." When Mengistu himself was overthrown in May 199
the new government approved plans to exhume Haile Selas
ie's body. It took workers three days of digging to reach th
body. On July 23, 1992, the one hundredth anniversary of th
emperor's birth, he received a formal burial in Trinity Chur
in the presence of family members and former supporter

15. JAMES SMITHSON (1765–1829), British founder of the Smithsonian Institution

Smithson died in Italy and was buried in Genoa's English cemetery. By 1900 it became clear that nearby quarrying would require the transfer of all graves to a new location. British authorities, aware of American interest in Smithson, wrote to officials of the Smithsonian Institution in Washington, D.C., asking if they would like to take charge of his body. In December 1903, a mission headed by the inventor Alexander Graham Bell arrived in Genoa and oversaw the disinterment of Smithson's body and its transfer by ship to the United States. It now rests in a tomb in the institution that bears his name.

7 Last Facts

1. BABE RUTH'S LAST HOME RUN

Ruth hit his 714th and last major-league home run, a towering out-of-the-park drive off of Pittsburgh Pirates' pitcher Guy Bush, on May 25, 1935. However, eleven years later the owner of the Veracruz Blues of the Mexican League hired the famous slugger for $10,000 to come and bat once in a game against the Mexico City Reds. The pitcher, Ramon Brazana, threw three balls and was removed from the game. A reliever was brought in and threw his first pitch straight down the middle. The fifty-one-year-old Ruth hit it deep into the right-field bleachers, much to the delight of 10,000 Mexican fans.

2. THE LAST AMERICAN KILLED IN THE VIETNAM WAR

Kelton Rena Turner, an eighteen-year-old Marine from Los Angeles, was killed in action on May 15, 1975, two weeks after the evacuation of Saigon, in what became known as the Mayaguez incident. His body was never recovered.

3. THE LAST VICTIM OF SMALLPOX

On October 26, 1977, Ali Maow Maalin, a hospital cook in Somalia, became the last person to contract smallpox through natural transmission when he chose to tend an infected child. The child died but Maalin survived. In September 1978, Janet Parker, an English medical photographer, was exposed to smallpox as the result of a laboratory accident. She subsequently died. The virologist in charge of the lab felt so guilty that he committed suicide. On May 8, 1980, the World Health Organization declared smallpox eradicated. However, some samples remained in laboratories in Atlanta and Moscow. If scientists go ahead with a plan to destroy the samples, the smallpox virus would become the first life form intentionally eliminated from the earth.

Nicole Dunsdon, the last Miss Canada.

4. The Last Playboy Club in America

The final day of business for the Lansing, Michigan, Playboy Club was July 30, 1988. Four clubs remained in Japan and one in Manila.

5. The Last Crank Phone in the United States

On July 12, 1990, America's last hand-cranked, party-line telephone system was replaced by private-line, touch-tone technology. The system had serviced the eighteen year-round residents of Salmon River Canyon, near North Fork, Idaho.

6. The Last Miss Canada

In 1991 women's groups successfully lobbied to have the Miss Canada contest canceled, claiming that it was degrading to women. The last Miss Canada, Nicole Dunsdon, completed her reign in October 1992.

7. The Last Message from the Authors to the Readers

We hope you have enjoyed *The Book of Lists: The '90s Edition.* If you have any comments or suggestions, please write to:

> *The Book of Lists*
> *P.O. Box 49699*
> *Los Angeles, CA 90049*

We are sorry that we cannot provide you with copies of earlier editions of *The Book of Lists.* You will have better luck contacting your local bookstore, new or used, or your local library. Because of the volume of mail, we cannot respond to all letters, but we do read every letter that comes our way.

Note: For more last facts, see *The People's Almanac #2,* pp. 25–31.

3 (left and right), John Seabury; 6, WBRZ, Baton Rouge, Louisiana; 10 (left), Reuters/Bettmann; 10 (right), Reuters/Bettmann Newsphotos; 12 (left), Reuters/Bettmann; 12 (right), AP/Wide World Photos; 18, Courtesy of Debbie Reynolds; 24 (left), Courtesy of the Academy of Motion Pictures Arts and Sciences; 26, Courtesy of the Academy of Motion Picture Arts and Sciences/Tri-Star Pictures, Inc.; 31, AP/Wide World Photos; 34, Andy Schwartz/Twentieth Century Fox Film Corp.; 36, AP/Wide World Photos; 43, Kerry Hayes/Tri-Star Pictures, Inc.; 45, Universal City Studios, Inc.; 47, Courtesy of the Academy of Motion Picture Arts and Sciences/Warner Bros.-Seven Arts; 49, Courtesy of the Academy of Motion Picture Arts and Sciences/United Artists; 51 (top), Universal Pictures Company, Inc.; 51 (bottom), Twentieth Century Fox Film Corp; 54, Courtesy of the Academy of Motion Picture Arts and Sciences/Universal Pictures; 55, Courtesy of the Academy of Motion Picture Arts and Sciences/Universal City Studios, Inc.; 56, Courtesy of the Academy of Motion Picture Arts and Sciences/Universal Pictures; 58, Courtesy of the Academy of Motion Picture Arts and Sciences/MGM; 61, Warner Bros.; 62, Courtesy of the Academy of Motion Picture Arts and Sciences/MGM; 5, United Artists Company; 66, Courtesy of the Academy of Motion Picture Arts and Sciences/Warner Bros.; 73, Viacom; 76, Courtesy of the Academy of Motion Picture Arts and Sciences; 79, Capitol Records; 83, The Bettmann Archive; 89, AP/Wide World Photos; 96 (top), Ricky Jay; 96 (bottom), Ricky Jay; 01, Courtesy of Leslie Hindman Auctioneers, Chicago; 106, The Wellcome Institute Library, London; 107, Alinari/Art Resource, New York; 110, Courtesy

of Sid Caesar; 119, Amateur Athletic Foundation, Los Angeles; 127, Courtesy of the Academy of Motion Picture Arts and Sciences; 128, Courtesy of the Academy of Motion Picture Arts and Sciences/Paramount Pictures Corp.; 142, *Dana* Expeditions, Carlsberg Foundation, Copenhagen, Denmark; 148, *Fortean Times*; 153, Quaker Oats; 173, White River Economic Development Office, White River, Ontario, Canada; 178, Norwegian School of Management; 179–181, U.S. Patent Office/Courtesy of Longacre & White, Arlington, Virginia; 185, The Mansell Collection, London; 189, Courtesy of Randy Skretvedt/Past Times; 195, The Robert Wolders Collection; 196, AP/Wide World Photos; 197, AP/Wide World Photos; 201 (top), Courtesy of the Academy of Motion Picture Arts and Sciences; 201 (bottom), Photo News; 207, UPI; 209, Courtesy of the Academy of Motion Picture Arts and Sciences; 217, AP/Wide World Photos; 219, Time-Life Films, Inc.; 222, UPI/Bettmann Newsphotos; 228, Courtesy of Michael and Judy Ann Newton, from *The FBI Most Wanted: An Encyclopedia*, New York: Garland Publishing, Inc., 1989; 230, Scala/Art Resource, N.Y.; 233, Universal City Studios, Inc.; 234, Universal City Studios, Inc.; 236, Jim Wilson/NYT Pictures; 240, Amanda and David Cronin; 245, AP/Wide World Photos; 247 (left), AP/Wide World Photos; 247 (right), AP/Wide World Photos; 255, Archive Photos, New York; 260, Warner Bros.; 262, AP/Wide World Photos; 271, Amnesty International, USA; 274, UPI/Bettmann; 275, AP/Wide World Photos; 287, Reuters/Bettmann; 290, Courtesy ARTnews; 297, George Eastman House, Rochester, New York; 300, *The People's Almanac* Archives; 301, Sandra Bitar; 304 (left), National Archives, photo no.

111-SC-87722; 304 (right), William H. Jackson/Courtesy of the National Anthropological Archives; 306, The Huntington Library, San Marino, California; 307, United States Post Office; 308, American Fancy Rat & Mouse Association, Riverside, California; 309, Photo courtesy of 1040 WHO Radio, Des Moines, Iowa; 310, Beaver County Chamber of Commerce, Beaver, Oklahoma; 312 (left), Courtesy, Mütter Museum, College of Physicians of Philadelphia; 312 (right), Courtesy, Mütter Museum, College of Physicians of Philadelphia; 313, Reproduced by permission of Leeds Castle Foundation. Collars on view during normal opening hours; 314, jill posener photographs; 316, Barber Museum-Library-Barbering Hall of Fame, Canal Winchester, Ohio; 318, Mexican National Tourist Council; 321, Flora Chavez; 323, Alf Leif Erickson/InnerAsia Expeditions; 329, NASA; 332, *Fortean Times;* 338, Courtesy of the Academy of Motion Picture Arts and Sciences/MGM; 351, Roderic Knowles/Michael Joseph, Ltd., 1972; 352 (left), Routledge & Kegan Paul, Ltd. and McGill-Queen's University Press, Great Britain, 1973; 352 (right), The Ethnographical Museum of Sweden, Stockholm, 1949; 354, Dana Estes & Company, Boston, 1912; 357, Syndication International; 362, Van Pelt/Columbia Pictures Corp.; 366, J. B. Lippincott & Co., 1941; 369, Cheryl Mick; 372, John Seabury; 380, Library of Congress; 387, Courtesy of the Academy of Motion Picture Arts and Sciences; 392, Warner Bros./Icon Distribution; 396, Amateur Athletic Foundation, Los Angeles; 400, NBC/Workman Publishing Company, 1977; 402, Museum of the City of New York; 405, Twentieth Century Fox; 408 (top), U.S. Lawn Mower Racing Association, Glenview, Illinois; 408 (bottom), AP/Wide World Photos; 410, AP/Wide World Photos; 411, AP/Wide World Photos; 413, UPI/Bettmann; 418, Amateur Athletic Foundation, Los Angeles; 421, From *Madonna Unauthorized* by Christopher Anderson; 423 (right), Photo Trends; 427, Charles Hamilton collection; 429, NBC; 433 (left), Courtesy of the Academy of Motion Picture Arts and Sciences/Cannon Releasing; 433 (right), Archive Photos, New York; 441, ABC; 445, Ken Jones/International Brick Collectors Association; 453, U.S. District Court Judge Samuel King; 456, Barry Jarvinen/NYT Pictures; 459, Harper and Row, 1954; 468, Canapress/John Felstead.

INDEX